THE
PERFECT
LAW OF
LIBERTY

Plate 1. Elias Smith (1769–1846): evangelical Republican, preacher, journalist, and herbal physician. Courtesy American Antiquarian Society; reprinted from Elias Smith, *The Life, Conversion, Preaching, Travels, and Sufferings of Elias Smith* (Portsmouth, N.H.: Beck & Foster, 1816).

THE PERFECT LAW OF LIBERTY

Elias Smith and
the Providential
History of America

Michael G. Kenny

SMITHSONIAN INSTITUTION PRESS
WASHINGTON AND LONDON

Copy Editor: Craig Noll
Production Editor: Duke Johns
Designer: Linda McKnight

Library of Congress Cataloging-in-Publication Data
Kenny, Michael G., 1942–
    The perfect law of liberty : Elias Smith and the
providential history of America / Michael G. Kenny.
        p.   cm.
    Includes bibliographical references and index.
    ISBN 1-56098-321-3 (alk. paper)
    1. Smith, Elias, 1769–1846. 2. Christian Connection—
Clergy—Biography. 3. Restoration movement
(Christianity)—New England—Biography. 4. Universalist
churches—New England—Clergy—Biography.
5. Herbalists—New England—Biography. 6. United
States—History—Religious aspects—Christianity. I. Title.
BX6793.S6K46   1994
286'.63—dc20
[B]   93-29969

British Library Cataloguing-in-Publication Data is available

Manufactured in the United States of America
01 00 99 98 97 96 95 94   5 4 3 2 1

⊗ The paper used in this publication meets the minimum
requirements of the American National Standard for
Permanence of Paper for Printed Library Materials Z39.48-
1984. For permission to reproduce illustrations appearing in
this book, please correspond directly with the owners of the
works, as listed in the individual captions. The Smithsonian
Institution Press does not retain reproduction rights for these
illustrations individually, or maintain a file of addresses for
photo sources.

Whoso looketh into the perfect law of liberty, and continueth therein . . .
this man shall be blessed in his deed.

JAMES 1:25

❧

One God—one Mediator—one lawgiver—one perfect law of Liberty—
one name for the children of God, to the exclusion of all sectarian
names—A Republican government, free from religious establishments
and state clergy—free enquiry—life and immortality brought
to light through the gospel—the reign of Christ on earth one thousand
years—the new heavens and earth at last—the utter destruction of all
who at the last day are found enemies to Christ—the eternal state of the
righteous in the new earth.

ELIAS SMITH,
"HERALD OF GOSPEL LIBERTY"

CONTENTS

Contents

3

FREE RADICALS
Federalists, Republicans, and the Second Awakening
100

4

A THIEF IN THE NIGHT
Prophecy and Politics
130

5

PREPARE YE THE WAY
Smith as Christian Communicator
162

6

PHYSICIANS OF VALUE
Medicine for the People
194

7

AGE OF MIRACLES
Smith and the Universalist Movement
221

EPILOGUE
257

NOTES
263

REFERENCES
305

INDEX
325

ILLUSTRATIONS

PREFACE

THIS BOOK CAME INTO EXISTENCE indirectly, as a by-product of my investigation into the history of the concept of multiple personality in American psychiatry—a study that resulted in *The Passion of Ansel Bourne: Multiple Personality in American Culture* (Smithsonian, 1986). That work attempted to situate the origin of a modern psychiatric construct relative to the culture that helped produce it and to which it somehow seemed uniquely suited: nineteenth-century America. I began with William James and his personal research into the strange case of the Reverend Ansel Bourne, a carpenter and sometime itinerant preacher who disappeared from his home in Rhode Island in 1887 and reappeared in Pennsylvania months later, having in the interim assumed an alternate identity—Albert John Brown—of which he, as Bourne, had no memory. James published his observations on this case, and others culled from the literature, in his 1890 *Principles of Psychology*.

With respect to the task at hand, the most interesting feature of the Bourne case is the fact that he had not just one but two episodes of multiplicity, the former occurring during a general religious revival in 1857. At that time he abruptly lost his sight and hearing (though not on that occasion his memory), which—as with the apostle Paul—were just as suddenly restored after public repentance of his sins and acknowledgment of Jesus as Savior. An earlier instance also cited by James, that of Mary Reynolds, has similar features. Reynolds was the daughter of

British Calvinist Baptists of republican sentiment who had emigrated to western Pennsylvania in the 1790s following persecutions they endured in England at the height of the anti-Jacobin hysteria sparked by the French Revolution. She was transformed in the heady air of republican America from a rigidly pietistic girl whose greatest pleasure was the Bible into a vivacious and hedonistic young woman whose only thought was of "liberty." After a period of alternation between these personae, during which she came to the attention of the medical profession and through this to wider public view (her physician had been a student of Jefferson's friend Benjamin Rush), she finally stabilized into a mature and competent adult.

William James and others reflected deeply on what Bourne, Mary Reynolds, and their like imply about a human capacity to assume radically incommensurate alternate identities; since these cases and others of more recent fame ("Eve," "Sybil") contain a religious element, I speculated on the role of evangelical Christianity in providing the moral antinomies that make these alternate identities incommensurate in the first place and so lead to the creation of a "mental disorder" with definite, culturally specific features. It came as a surprise to learn that one of Elias Smith's sons suffered from a "dissociative disorder" himself, one similar to that experienced by Ansel Bourne in 1887; Matthew Hale Smith, conservative son of a radical father, experienced the tension between liberty and order in an acutely personal form.

In my previous book I also explored the connection between multiple personality and the evangelical belief that one must, as a condition of salvation, be converted and born again as a new person in this life. Tracking Ansel Bourne's career backward from his encounter with James, it emerged that the setting in which he was reborn in 1857 was that of the Christian Chapel in Westerly, Rhode Island, and that Bourne had previously been attached to a Free-Will Baptist church near Providence. "Christians" and "Free-Will Baptists": what were these? In pursuit of that question, I found that the pastor of the Christian Chapel in Westerly, Elder John Taylor, had himself been converted to Jesus by someone named Elias Smith.

And that is how all this began. Feeling a need to understand the religious tradition from which Bourne and Reynolds came, I developed an interest in this tradition itself, in the sometimes extraordinary characters that it produced, and in the society from which they emerged in America of the late eighteenth and early nineteenth centuries. Multiple personality is an affair of contradictions. A central proposition of my first book was that the early cases of so-called multiple personality expressed through their lives some of the essential tensions of the times in which they lived, tensions that became manifest in the symptoms of their presumptive "disorders." I was then concerned with the intersection of biography and the history of an idea. That idea was multiple personality itself, and the biographical component was supplied via the lives of the persons seen as suffering from it. The present study follows the same method. Here the idea is republicanism, and the process at issue the way in which this notion manifested itself through the life of Elias Smith.

I had the good fortune of being in Cambridge, Massachusetts, when first made aware of Smith's significance; the Harvard Union Catalog directed me to a series of lectures given in 1917 by Dean William Fenn of the Divinity School on the general subject of the religious history of New England. One of these lectures was entitled "The Revolt against the Standing Order," in which Fenn pointed out the family resemblance between the Free-Will Baptists and Smith's "Christians." In suggesting that the biographical material pertaining to the founders of these movements is an invaluable resource with respect to the period in question, Fenn alerted me to the potential significance of Smith's autobiography; once I began reading that extraordinary document, the present endeavor was under way. As I read on, a connection emerged between Smith's evangelical background and his Democratic-Republican political sympathies. The nature of that linkage is the subject of the present book.

Smith bequeathed his autobiography to posterity explicitly in the hope that both the present and following generations would find it interesting. I indeed found it interesting for reasons he would never have suspected. Beginning with anthropological fieldwork on oral tradition in East Africa, I have been concerned with the way in which historical consciousness is socially constituted. What is accomplished by construing contemporary situations in historical terms? What is the ideological motivation in thinking historically? Reconstruction of the past is always a selective process that utilizes theories, metaphors, and myths to

impose meaning and moral relevance on what is supposed to have occurred before us. Historical consciousness therefore provides an implicit rule for future action insofar as one places oneself in history (however construed). As Bernard Bailyn, an eminent historian of the early
republic, has noted: "The sense we make of the history of our national
origins helps to define for us, as it has for generations before us, the
values, purposes and acceptable characteristics of our political institutions and cultural life" (1973, 3).

Elias Smith and his fellows construed the events of their time as
an apocalyptic unveiling of what prophecy had foretold, while other of
his contemporaries, among them the authors of *The Federalist*, looked
back at what they took to be the course of secular history in order to
situate the prospects of their newly created nation. My study of Smith
is therefore not only an example of the broadly based democratization
of sentiment and social practice in the post-Revolutionary years
(though it is certainly this as well); it is also a study of how theology,
historical consciousness, and social experience fed into one another to
produce the ideological amalgam of which Elias Smith represents a
particular but not unique case. Through him one may grasp the nature
of the process at large: the permutation and transformation of elements
of a common Anglo-Protestant culture in a time of rapid change.

The writing of these two books has had the unexpected effect of
allowing me to articulate my own life and the history of my family
with respect to the history of the country at large. On my father's side,
a set of connections emerged of which I had only been dimly aware.
My great-grandfather Moses Kenny was a Free-Will Baptist preacher
in Ohio, as such, a member of a sect closely related in its beginnings to
Smith's Christians. He was the grandson of another Moses Kenny,
who had emigrated from Northborough, Massachusetts, to Newfane,
Vermont, in the 1780s as part of the process that, as with Elias Smith's
father, drew so many New Englanders from the longer-settled areas
into the agricultural hinterland. The first Moses became deacon of the
local Congregational church and probably voted Federalist, like many
of the residents of his town, who imported their conservative electoral
preferences from Massachusetts.

The second Moses Kenny came into the world in 1816. He was
apprenticed to a master in Lower Canada to learn woolens manufac-

ture and, in the winter of 1837, having completed his term of service, set out by sleigh to try his fortunes in Ohio, where a brother had gone. In 1842 Moses was ordained a minister of the Free-Will Baptist Church and then served a number of pastoral charges in Ohio; strong in the causes of temperance and abolition, he lost a son at the Battle of Perryville in Kentucky during the Civil War. Moses finally settled in Michigan and lived there to the end of his long life in 1905; he had three wives, two of whom predeceased him. His third—Caroline Gage Kenny of Topeka—was the mother of my paternal grandfather, who studied pharmacy at Hillsdale College, founded by the Free-Willers in the 1840s, and cared for Moses in his last years, accompanied by his wife and two young sons, who were destined to become my father and uncle.

I have said that the motivation for much of my work has been to track the intersection of history and biography; upon completion of *The Passion* and *The Perfect Law*, it seems that, as much as anything else, I have been tracking my own. In recognition of this fact, I wish to dedicate this book to the memory of my parents.

Since this book has had rather a long gestation (I began research on it in 1979–80), there are a number of people and organizations to be thanked who were helpful at different times. I should begin with the most important. In 1986–87 I received a Rockefeller Fellowship in Atlantic History, Culture and Society at Johns Hopkins University; this period was essentially devoted to the Elias Smith problem, and I am especially grateful to David Cohen and Gillian Feeley-Harnik for making it possible, secondarily to the Departments of Anthropology and History for being such good hosts. ·

A number of individuals were also a very great help, most particularly Enos Dowling of Lincoln (Ill.) Christian College, who made available reproductions of most of Elias Smith's journalistic output and other of his writings; Lisa Compton, director of the Old Colony Historical Society in Taunton, Massachusetts, for her assistance with research into the history of the Congregational Church in Berkley (Mass.) and the Christian Church in Dartmouth; Kevin Shupe, archivist of the Portsmouth Athenaeum, for his researches into the history of Elias Smith's Portsmouth church; finally, Edward Little, a genealogist resident in Old Saybrook, Connecticut, for his very considerable aid with Smith's family history.

Other individuals and organizations to be mentioned are Dana Parks, director of the Salisbury, New Hampshire, Historical Society; Harold Worthley of the Congregational-Christian Historical Society in Boston; the Woodstock Historical Society; Richard Candee, of the American Studies Program at Boston University; the Houghton Library at Harvard; the Vermont State Library; the New Hampshire State Historical Society; the New England Historical Genealogical Society; the Countway Library of the Harvard Medical School; Anne Rose of Carnegie Mellon University; Jim Eckert of the College of Physicians of Philadelphia; Gene Bridwell and Ed Weinstein of the Simon Fraser University Library; the family history section at the Church of Jesus Christ of Latter Day Saints in Burnaby, British Columbia; Doug Schwartz, Duane Anderson, Cecile Stein, and Jane Gillentine of the School of American Research in Santa Fe, for their hospitality to unanticipated sojourners; Mark Hirsch of the Smithsonian Institution Press for his help and encouragement; the anonymous reviewers for the Smithsonian; my copy editor, Craig Noll, for his valuable suggestions and meticulous attention to the manuscript; and lastly, Rebecca Bateman, who provided useful comments of her own.

INTRODUCTION
The Republican Idea

Stand fast therefore in the liberty
wherewith Christ hath made us free.
GALATIANS 5:1

IN 1792 THE AMERICAN CONSTITUTION was five years old, George Washington president of the United States, the king of France the prisoner of the Legislative Assembly, and the District of Columbia newly acquired as the future federal capital as part of a deal to balance southern and northern interests. In the same year a youthful Elias Smith, fresh from Vermont and never having given politics a thought, arrived in Boston, the first city he had ever seen. "I came in sight of Boston for the first time towards night, on the day of the commencement in Cambridge. When in Charlestown, near the bridge, I saw a constant stream of carriages, passing and repassing, from Cambridge. It looked to me like confusion, and thinking all Boston must be in an uproar, having never before been in so large a place, nor seen how people conducted where they made ministers; I thought it unsafe to go in that night" (196–97).[1]

Smith was daunted by the proceedings, much taken aback by what he well knew to be his own rustic awkwardness: "I felt very uneasy that night, and wished for morning, that I might find a country preacher, in finding my brother Thomas Baldwin, whom I loved above all men on earth. I then thought, through ignorance, that Boston folks knew more than country people" (197).

Commencement Day at Harvard was the year's major social occasion, the day on which the already venerable college sent its own young men out into the world to become lawyers, doctors, merchants, and parsons. Commencement was "not only a holiday through the Province, but also the scene of considerable disorder, gambling, and dissipation in Cambridge" (Warren 1931, 22). Smith already shared the Baptist antipathy for such worldliness, as well as for the college-educated orthodox clergy who depended for their support not on divine inspiration but on formal learning and state-supported religious taxes; later he would turn on his Baptist brother for betrayal of these very principles.

As Smith passed through Cambridge, another young man, John Snelling Popkin, was delivering the commencement address. In the rhetorical figures of the eighteenth-century Enlightenment, Popkin (1792) spoke of the liberalizing and civilizing tendencies of higher education, of the establishment of truth through the free exchange of ideas: "The mind, which glows with the love of knowledge, will not be satisfied with the result of investigations made by others. It will aspire to take the draught of science pure and transparent from the fountain. In this way only shall we be enabled to distinguish the true from the false, the specious from the solid; the dreams of visionaries, and the chance-born dogmas of empirics, from conclusions, drawn from pure and simple truths, or from rational and repeated experiments. Let the sons of Harvard remember this. We stand trembling on the shore of life's stormy ocean, ready to launch with a timid hope, with an ambition half dismayed."[2]

Both of them trembling on this shore, Elias Smith and John Popkin went on from that July day to radically different ends expressive of their classes, their respective personalities and faiths. Soon the former's immediate fate would be decided by the Baptist clergy, while the latter would find for a time a career within the established church of the Commonwealth of Massachusetts. Whereas Popkin represents the values of the American Enlightenment—of reason, decorum, social order, and a classic republican sensibility—Elias Smith exemplifies the powerful force of radical Jeffersonian Republicanism: antielitist, raucous, and full of faith in the ability of common people to decide for themselves in all things whatever.

Popkin was all that Elias Smith came to despise: a scholar who, relying on logic rather than inspiration, became a "hireling" Congregationalist pastor, a doctor of divinity, and eventually professor of Greek at Harvard. Smith's opponents saw him as an empiric visionary, an anti-intellectual church-wrecker, a subverter of Christian doctrine, and threat to the public order. Smith and Popkin would never meet, yet these two men brought by chance so close together, and so far apart in other respects, exemplify the greatest social divide in America's formative years—that which took party form in the opposition between Federalism and Jeffersonian Republicanism. Historians have accorded Popkin a status as a representative Federalist, while Smith emerges as his antithesis—a radical evangelical democrat, a new kind of republican, a harbinger of nineteenth-century America.

Born in 1769 in the already overcrowded coastal town of Lyme, Connecticut, Elias Smith grew up in the 1780s on a hardscrabble farm in the recently opened upcountry settlement of Woodstock, Vermont. Even as a youth, thinking it "better to die than be confined in such a place," he endeavored to escape the backwoods, with its isolation, hardships, and boredom. He succeeded, leading a busy life of preaching, agitation, and doctoring in such places as Portsmouth (N.H.), Portland (Maine), Philadelphia, and Boston.

Brought into life a Calvinist Baptist, as such convinced of the righteousness of predestination, Smith left this world convinced that it is God's intent to condemn no one, to redeem all humanity rather than just a predestined elite. Brought up in what was only recently the frontier, he became a frontier democrat. Though frightened as a boy by rumors of revolutionary war, who for long gave no thought to politics, yet he became an ardent Jeffersonian Republican who found in this persuasion the political equivalent of universal salvation. Along with others independently arriving at similar conclusions, Smith attempted to fuse religion and politics, and eventually medicine, into a mutually consistent democratic scheme.

John Popkin was born in 1771. Though the son of a Boston custom inspector and failed businessman of no great wealth, his family nevertheless found a place for him at Harvard, where he distinguished himself in classical studies and divinity. Spending a short time as pastor of a Boston church, Popkin—remembered as "a man of great talent and of great self-distrust; eccentric, unmarried & a very devout and conscientious Christian"—found himself uncomfortable with such a sophisticated congregation and undertook care of the church in rural Newbury, near the thriving merchant town of Newburyport on the Merrimack (Sibley n.d., 28). He stayed in Newbury until 1815, when he was called back to Harvard. During his term in active ministerial life, he exhibited precisely the attitudes that distinguished the Federalist clergy from Elias Smith and the evangelicals.

Smith habitually derided "unspiritual" preachers who found themselves unable to deliver their sermons without written notes, and he judged the success of his own performances by the degree to which the Spirit gave him liberty to speak. Popkin encountered a kindred attitude from a local boatman hauling firewood—"a preacher in some separatical school"—who asked the pastor how long it took him to prepare a sermon. Popkin replied, "'A week perhaps, sometimes a fortnight or even several months.' 'Three months!' said the astonished Cicero; 'why I can prepare a sermon at any time in ten minutes.' 'Very likely,' said Dr. Popkin, 'but remember, I preach to people of sense'" (Felton 1852).

Popkin, like the Congregational ministry at large, had definite ideas about a pastor's place in the social order. He saw it as his duty to instruct and guide those with less formal education, less comprehensiveness of vision—and not just in matters of religion, but also in what he took to be the inseparably related questions of politics and social ethics. The exalted opinion that the clergy had of its mission emerges in the numerous ordination sermons that have come down to us, delivered to mark the entry of a new pastor into his charge, and in the countless sermons and discourses marking important national or local occasions, such as elections and Independence Day. In this collective vision, the clergy defined itself as a rock of stability in times in which even the ignorant and unlettered claimed a natural right to pronounce on matters far beyond their capacity.

Elias Smith had a different vision. In an increasingly fractious and divisive period of sectarian conflict, in which the great promise of the Revolution seemed to be coming unhinged, Smith sought to unify the warring denominations under the name that the Acts of the Apostles assured him had first been applied to the followers of Jesus: simply "Christians." In categories reminiscent of the radical wing of Cromwell's Commonwealth, Smith took aim at those he held to be subverters of the American Revolution, and throughout his life railed at "anti-Christian" elites of whatever description—first the college-educated Congregational clergy, then the Baptists themselves, the Federalists, practitioners of orthodox medicine, and all those who branded Smith and his kind as a dangerously ignorant and incendiary Jacobin rabble. His revivalist and democratic creed equated primitive Christianity with republican virtue and sought its ends through a rich partisan rhetoric that assimilated Monarchist to Tory to Federalist to Antichrist, an association that was extended to subsume the more mundane local elites of town squire, lawyer, doctor, and pastor.

The difference between Smith and Popkin—more broadly between Jeffersonian and Federalist—was no less marked when it came to overtly political issues. By 1810 some old Federalists were willing to consider dissolution of the Union in order to defend the regional interests of New England. Smith would therefore conclude that the Federalists had misappropriated and perverted their own party name: "Federalists, though this is the name you are called by, yet I do not think you deserve it; for you appear opposed to real *federalism,* which means a firm union among the States of America. Your proper name is *antifederal federalists*" (1805e, 81).

Calling upon prophecy as his guide, Smith foretold an already partially fulfilled New World Millennium and, in the title of an 1809 discourse preached of "The Loving Kindness of God Displayed in the Triumph of Republicanism in America." His literalist approach to Scripture arose from the same democratic roots as the rest of his thought. Since God does not dissimulate or speak in riddles, his word should be self-evident to all who attend closely to it; those, like Popkin and his fellows, making claims to specialist knowledge of the Bible's meaning, deceive the people with human words. In answer to doubt, Smith's prescription was always simply to search the Scriptures. Because of failure to find them in literal form in the Bible, he dismissed such established Calvinist doctrines as the Trinity, election, original sin, the immortality of the soul, the divinity of Christ, the covenant of grace, and eternal damnation as human inventions, as mere fables. Through a radical critique of language itself, he attempted to free the people from the shackles of an antiquated and un-American predestinarian theology and to overcome thereby the linguistic basis of party distinction. True to his democratic principles, Smith supported the religious and political rights of blacks and quarreled with his former Baptist associates because of it. To the dismay and wrath of the opposition, he and the early Christian movement at large found a considerable place in their scheme of things for female evangelists.

Again, the contrast between Smith and Popkin could not be clearer. With the onset of the War of 1812, Popkin found ample occasion to expand on the distinction between Federalism and its Republican opposition. Popkin, "a thorough Federalist," believed with most of his Congregationalist ministerial colleagues that the then Virginia-dominated national government was leading the country into ruin through its war with England and its policies more generally. There is considerable irony in this attitude, in that Popkin accused the Republicans of the same centralizing and militarist tendencies that Jefferson himself had once perceived to be at the heart of Alexander Hamilton's nationalist program. Equating the earlier Antifederalist opposers of the American constitutional settlement with the French Jacobins and contemporary Republicans, Popkin declared of the latter that the name *republican* was one "to which they are least of all entitled; for they are the supporters of arbitrary power, whether it be in France or in America. The Federalists, the friends of the Constitution and of Washington, are the true republicans. The other side boast of Jefferson, and follow him as the first head and leader of the party. . . . With the Jefferson side are associated [and] identified, war and violence, and taxation, and the destruction of commerce and of the commercial States, and of essential rights and liberty, violence in our land, wasting and destruction on our borders" (Felton 1852, li, lv).[3]

In company with an early developed suspicion of "empiric visionaries" went an even more profound suspicion of the kind of thinking these New England Federalists attributed to Jefferson and his followers—an opinion that, since the French Revolution, they had reiterated from pulpit after pulpit in paroxysms of woe over the immanent prospect of republican leveling, anarchy, infidelity, and terror. This extremist paranoia was to pass with the end of the war and Britain's defeat of France, but it nonetheless reflects a wider confrontation already deeply rooted in American home soil and taking practical expression in class antagonisms, opposition between centralists and localists, and very different notions of what the Christian message entails for the constitution of political society.

With age, Popkin withdrew into himself along the pathways of his own obsessions; though once evangelically inclined, in his later years he found the liturgy and sedate order of the Episcopal Church more congenial than that of the Congregationalists and Unitarians, and concerns over the nature of liberal education more engaging than political matters. He left this world in 1852 at age eighty-one as (it might be supposed) an almost congenitally predisposed eccentric old bachelor don. Elias Smith—a man with many eccentricities of his own—went to his reward in 1846 at age seventy-seven in the burgeoning shoe-making town of Lynn, Massachusetts, a center of the early labor movement. Smith's life spanned the formative years of the republic, times well suited to his nature.

Some of the causes that Smith espoused went awry; others worked their way through to completion or were transformed in the course of the nineteenth century into forms, such as fundamentalism and populism, recognizable today. But rather than establishing the ecumenical creed of a democratic nation, the body that Elias Smith helped found—the Christian Church, or "Christian Connection"—in the end became another sect, then a denomination, and in this respect followed the developmental course of many another body like it. As Smith pursued his erratic theological course toward the doctrine of universal salvation and away from it again, his erstwhile colleagues were obliged to close ranks and establish a new orthodoxy in order to limit the divisive consequences of his apostasy. Thus a movement became a church.

Smith himself would oscillate between the Christians and the Universalists, only as an elderly man equivocally to go back where he started. His original defection was accompanied by a substantial change in his circumstances, necessitated by a need to secure a more regular income for his family. Having been personally exposed to the virtues of the system of herbal medicine developed by Dr. Samuel Thomson, another product of backcountry New England (and another Universalist), Smith became a herbalist himself, settled in Boston, and established a private hospital. In his personal demonology, orthodox physicians came to occupy a place analogous to that of the orthodox clergy: just as Calvinists are poisoners of souls, these quacks are deceivers who hide their ignorance with Latin terminology, poison the bodies of their unwitting victims with alien chemical substances, and attempt to prosecute or legally exclude from practice the watchmen who call attention to their crimes. Thomsonians, in contrast, were to treat American bodies democratically using the natural products of the American earth.

A historian of the Christian movement remarked of Smith that "the career of the man was very remarkable and very romantic and checkered" (Morrill 1911, 44). Nathan Hatch finds him one of the most "inherently interesting" characters in Jeffersonian America (1989, 69). But in Smith's time all were agreed, whatever their opinions otherwise, that he was a changeable fellow; a eulogist wrote, "His instability was the great obstacle to his excellence. Had he carried out the principles he adopted, as a minister of Christ; and pursued an undeviating course to the day of his death, I doubt not he would have been truly one of the first men of his age" (Hazen 1846). A Christian colleague, shocked at Smith's Universalist deviation, noted, "You seem not so averse to frequent changes as some might be" (Rand 1818, 2). A Universalist friend concluded in an obituary that, "with too many, the memory of his good works is lost in the recollection of his eccentricities. Those eccentricities belonged to the man; they were a part of his essential being; without them he would have lost his identity; and if he must be said to have had a fickle intellect, it must also be admitted that he had a sound heart" (Bacon 1847, 76). Smith once himself wrote, with uncharacteristic self-awareness, of "my old trouble, discontent" (238).

If excuse were needed to write of Smith, his intriguing life and character would be more than enough justification. But he was also a party to fundamental debates that still retain their salience. Did the equivocal revolution on which the United States was founded entail an elitist republicanism designed to limit democracy for the sake of political stability, or did it imply practical popular sovereignty without the constraints and the natural social deference that conservatives believed necessary for the maintenance of order? Could the people assume for themselves the powers of specialist functionaries such as lawyers and doctors? And what would be the role of the churches in all this: shrines of a reborn primitive Christian spiritual fellowship, or political theaters of oligarchic dominance? Throughout his life Smith argued the democratic option against conservatives like Popkin, and since his vision was in large measure adopted by the nation he so passionately addressed, Elias must be counted the victor.

Except for a small band of professional historians and the lineal descendants of his religious tradition, few have heard of Smith. He was of humble origins, self-educated, and perennially in financial difficulty. When he came to the attention of his betters, it was as a gadfly who confirmed just what they thought to be wrong with the anarchistic and leveling tendencies of the new democracy. Whatever his obscurity in our times, Smith was a significant man in his own. He was, in any event, not one of the *silent* masses. Smith had an obsession with the printed word, and in sermons, discourses, books, and his newspaper the *Herald of Gospel Liberty (HGL)* used the press to spread his vision of America. In forcefully doing so, he helped to articulate an enduring aspect of American thought and political life, to crystallize poorly defined tendencies into an ideology and a program—a process that is the background theme of this book.

The pattern of Smith's life should be seen in relation to an evolving democratic ethos among the kind of people from which he came. Those who became the early New England Christians and members of kindred sects were—like Smith—of agricultural, urban working-class or artisanal background. Their fellow travelers to the south and west were similar and, more than their northeastern compatriots, would give permanent denominational shape to the movement. Given this, the question is that of how the American Revolution and its consequences were apprehended and ideologically transmuted into a distinctive view of the world and an important aspect of national culture by those for whom Smith shall stand as representative and catalyst.

What, then, does Elias Smith represent? Certainly not the product of definitive causal links between class and ideology, or region and culture, or religious persuasion and political affiliation. The historical and economic circumstances to which Smith was subject were not unlike those experienced by a very considerable proportion of the American population, but his personal career abounded in idiosyncrasy. Others exposed to similar conditions took different paths. Yet linkages there were, though it is possible to define them in only a crude and approximate way. The attitudes of Elias Smith and his kind grew not just out of popularized republican theories working their way down through the media but also out of the experiences of everyday life in the social milieus of the villages, towns, and port cities of that day—experiences that it remains a major historical task to define and interpret. The essential social feature of this period is just how undefined everything was.

Rural Vermont, like much of hill country New England, was characterized by a generally democratic tone and hostility to religious establishments. Joseph Smith was a western Vermonter, as was the Adventist prophet William Miller. The Berkshire region of western Massachusetts proved hospitable to early Universalism. The coastal Maine agricultural frontier was Democratic-Republican in politics, antipathetic to monied Federalist interests and absentee landlords, Calvinistic or Free-Will Baptist in religious persuasion, and a fertile field for Christian evangelists. In consequence of such facts, historians have referred to "the cultural fragmentation of the hill country," to how Smith's Christians are an example of "rural pietism," and to how the dispersal of settlement into interior New England and beyond set in train the developments that transformed the region "from Puritan to Yankee"—from corporatism to individualism, from Federalist oligarchy to Jeffersonian popular democracy. Elias Smith himself believed that the free air of outer New England had bred a commitment to freedom in all things.[4]

All this may be so; the theme of the democratic frontier is an enduring one, as is the notion that social disorganization in newly settled and socially peripheral areas provided particularly fertile ground for populist revivalism. But when Smith's career is considered as a whole and situated in its wider context, it can be seen that—whatever else he may have been—Elias was no mere by-product of an inherently antiestablishment rural society. The Christian Connection, which he helped found, was not essentially a religion of the oppressed and dislocated, nor was it inevitably rural (see Chapter 5 below). Most of the work of Smith's adult life was based in Portsmouth, Portland, Philadelphia, and Boston. There were churches of the Christian Connection in each of these towns, and Smith reached out from them to a national audience in national terms via his newspaper the *Herald of Gospel Liberty*. In its later days the *Herald* could be purchased by pedestrians from bookshops in Boston and by recent settlers in Illinois and Missouri territories with any degree of proximity to a U.S. post office. People in both town and city bought Elias Smith's paper as, in fact and fancy, America expanded beyond what anyone considered even remotely possible when he was a child.

Smith's career therefore must be considered both in relation to a rapidly evolving national political society and the local situations in which his preaching took fire. If internal migration, demographic expansion, and economic change set up the general conditions for a democratization of sentiment and the emergence of an individualistic ethos, it still remains necessary to examine the specific forms these processes took. The relationship between ideology and culture should be construed dynamically as one between cultural preconception and social experience (a point that in no way undercuts the possibility of an analysis stressing class, social mobility, and power). Elias Smith, who was himself enchanted by a class-conscious rhetoric, deployed concepts that were widely abroad in the republican political culture of his time and had a long history before he heard of them. He comprehended his situation through a culturally embedded political idiom of considerable antiquity. But in this revolutionary time, old concepts could, under press of circumstances, take on new connotations.[5]

That is just the process that Elias Smith was involved in, and at the heart of it was the protean ecclesiastical and political concept of *liberty,* which in the period at issue was to expand far beyond either its traditional Christian meaning or its use in conventional republican discourse. When politicians addressed "the people" through the established canons of Anglo-American political rhetoric, Elias Smith and his friends were certain just who and what this meant. Like "liberty," the concept of "the people" has proven susceptible to progressive redefinition and expansion, a process that is another aspect of Smith's ideological endeavor. As Edmund Morgan has said, "the sovereignty of the people has been filled with surprises for those who invoked it" (1988, 306). This is what those of conservative sentiment discovered when the concept of the people originally used against the British as a justification for revolution was appropriated by the social orders beneath them and employed against themselves.[6]

In the early years of the nineteenth century Elias Smith and his fellows disrupted community after community with their preaching of a new democratic gospel through which gospel liberty and political liberty became inseparably linked; it is one of my primary aims to show how this came about, thus helping to unravel the cultural process underlying it—through which, as Gordon Wood puts it, America "emerged as the most egalitarian, most materialistic—and most evangelical Christian—society in Western history" (1992, 230).

Wood adds that "in many respects this new democratic society was the very opposite of the one the revolutionary leaders had envisaged." This is precisely what led to such passionate debate between Federalists and Democratic-Republicans over the course the new nation should follow. Conservatives, looking over their shoulders at the fates of past republics, asked themselves about what it would take to uphold the stability and legitimacy of a state organized on such uncertain principles. One answer took constitutional form: the famous division of powers, not by social estate (sovereign, lords, and commons), but by function (executive, legislative, and judicial)—a system of checks and balances deliberately instituted in order to prevent one element of the body politic from gaining despotic ascendancy over the others.

Another answer lay in the virtue of the citizenry, a collective willingness to put society above self and an independence of mind and means to make this a viable proposition (hence property criteria for the suffrage and also the Jeffersonian emphasis on the yeoman freeholder). If only such economic and intellectual independence guarantees virtue, however, then the organization of society, however republican in principle, must be oligarchic and hierarchical in practice unless relative equality of property is absolutely guaranteed. If virtue is an essential moral quality of the republican citizen, it is a commodity in notoriously short supply among the people at large. If the vitality of the republic depends on deference to those who wield the legitimate powers of government and on the virtue of both ruler and ruled, history seems to show that democratic masses are little prone to deference, and that ultimately only force can control them. Thus, down to the American constitutional debates, there were persistent questions about whether a democratic as opposed to an oligarchic republic can be a stable social form able to withstand the entropic forces of time without giving way to anarchy and despotism.

Federalist senator William Plumer of New Hampshire, writing in 1804 at the end of Jefferson's first term and observing the decline of the Federalist party, concluded that "Democracy must overrun us. Must we travel, as other states have done before us, through Democracy to despotism?" (1857, 319). Elias Smith—with whom Plumer would later be allied over the issue of religious disestablishment—addressed this issue by a sweeping claim that a democratic republic is the only polity compatible with *gospel* liberty, and that a true republic *must* endure because it is concordant with divine purpose. Through this hopeful claim Smith evaded the pessimism characteristic of classic republican thought as manifest in the doubts of his Federalist opponents about whether a democratic citizenry can possibly have enough virtue to maintain a viable republic. God, through his providence, has brought into being the conditions for the restoration of New Testament religion in this New World as an example for the rest of humanity to follow in preparation for Christ's second coming: the institution of a New Heaven and a New Earth, which transcends time and change.

> In hope of seeing Jesus, when all my conflict ceases,
>
> My love to him increases his name to adore;
>
> O then, my blessed Saviour, vouchsafe to me the favour,
>
> To reign with thee forever when time shall be no more.
>
> (JONES 1804, 70)

Smith and his friends were redefining the meaning of liberty in a manner whereby the traditional Christian concept of liberty—liberty from sin gained through faith in Christ as Savior—began to elide with conceptions of political and personal liberty derived from the Revolution and enshrined in the Declaration of Independence and the federal Constitution. Elias Smith's central contribution lay in the translation of this evolving and increasingly widely shared perception into an ideology and a program.

Bernard Bailyn, a leading historian of the early republic and much attracted to a cultural interpretation of political ideology, has written:

> Discourse becomes politically powerful when it becomes ideology: when it articulates and fuses into effective formulations opinions and attitudes that are otherwise too scattered and vague to be acted upon; when it mobilizes a general mood . . . , when it crystallizes otherwise inchoate social and political discontent and thereby shapes what is otherwise instinctive and directs it to attainable goals; when it clarifies, symbolizes, and elevates to structured consciousness the mingled urges that stir within us. But its power is not autonomous. It can only formulate, reshape, and direct forward moods, attitudes, ideas, and aspirations that in some form, however crude and incomplete, already exist. (1973, 11)[7]

This formulation pertains directly to what, in retrospect, Elias Smith and the Christians thought it was they had been up to.[8] Writing in a presociological age, an in-house Christian historian gave an account of his movement strikingly parallel in specifics to Bailyn's more general rendering of the process by which sentiment may be transformed into ideology.

> Like seeds borne far away and widely scattered by the wind, germinating and springing up in most out-of-the-way places, the seeds of this new movement for religious liberty were quickly and widely disseminated, and appeared most unexpectedly. It was a truly sporadic growth. Because it was a movement among the common people it was tremendously popular. Many ministers came from among the people, and lacked scholastic training. Often they prejudiced their hearers against an educated ministry, and against orderly proceedings. Coming from the common walks of life, educated to mediocrity or little above it, and yet possessed of unquestioned ability, they appealed powerfully to their fellows because they spoke the language of the average heart and voiced a common feeling. (Morrill 1911, 103)

The truth of this perception is echoed by the early Christians themselves—for instance, in the pages of the *Herald of Gospel Liberty,* edited fortnightly with only slight interruption by Elias Smith from September 1808 to October 1817. Even as early as the first number of the first volume (then produced in Portsmouth, N.H.), Smith was publishing letters from those who were discovering for the first time that their opinions on religious and political liberty were shared by groups in other parts of the country. In the first issue there is a report—under the banner "Last Will and Testament of the Springfield Presbytery"—of how some Kentucky Presbyterians dissolved their own church organization in favor of primitive Christian equality.⁹ In the sixth number came word of believers in Virginia who had separated out of the Methodists, Baptists, and Presbyterians, "and discarding all party names, acknowledged no other than that of *Christian.*" And so it went in successive issues of the *Herald* as one group after another reported in from the South and West to what was fast becoming the intellectual clearinghouse of the movement—one through which they were learning to talk to one another across national regions. Elias Smith expressed how it struck him personally in a letter to a Virginia brother in 1809:

> There is nothing to hinder a general union among the brethren from north to south, that I can see: but there is something to be done; that is, to let all our brethren through the whole know that we are striving for the same thing. It is wonderful to me, that while I was labouring to convince men that Christ is all; not knowing there was another person on earth striving for the same thing, that others in the South should be doing the same. Had I known it before now, I might have leaned on them; but we have done like those in the days of Nehemiah; each built the wall over against his own house till they joined all in one, and set up the gates; while their enemies were saying, "What do these feeble Jews?"
>
> My Br., have we not built enough to join the wall? I think we have. With pleasure I look forward to a day, I hope, not far off; which I shall meet some of my brethren from the south, to join in *Christian Union,* endeavouring to promote harmony and love among thousands of our brethren widely spread throughout the United States of America! (*HGL* 1, no. 12 [Feb. 2, 1809]: 47)

Elias Smith gave voice and coherence to sentiments already abroad in the land. Of course he gave these sentiments a definite slant of his own. One could be a fervent democrat without being a millenarian or even a conventional Christian (witness Thomas Paine or Jefferson himself); Smith, however, was democrat and Christian millenarian rolled into one. It was possible to participate actively in the Christian movement and yet abstain, as Smith could not, from secular politics altogether (Smith's one-time associate Mark Fernald boasted that he had never participated in a civil election). One could be a good evangelical and still see more need for formal churchly order than Smith did.

Yet when one concentrates on the main themes rather than the nuances, it can be seen that Smith had much in common with his contemporaries. In his writings and preaching Elias Smith deployed the theoretical capital of the heritage he shared with the other contestants in the debates about the structure and historical potential of the new republic. He differed from the more secular in his tendency to interpret historical events in prophetic terms. Elias took elements of republican thought and permuted them—most commonly through his assaults on elements of Calvinist theology and ecclesiology —according to his understanding of what the New Testament was saying about liberty. Accordingly, four interrelated clusters of ideas continually reappear in Elias Smith's reflections on politics and society—republicanism, repudiation of deferential politics, emphasis on individual autonomy, and millennial expectation. I briefly outline them in historiographic context as a prelude to their frequent reemergence in the chapters below.

Republicanism. The themes of republicanism as ideology, and ideology as culture, are of ongoing debate and contention among historians; at the center of it all is the role of culture in the shaping of political action, behind which lies the more traditional theme of the degree to which sociological determinants of one or another kind shape cultural perception. The general drift of writings on this subject has been to progressively refine perception of the so-called republican elements in late eighteenth-century American political thought. Whereas it once became possible to speak of a monolithic "Republican Mind," now it is perceived that there were in fact republican "minds"—different ways of interpreting and applying the heritage of Anglo-American political thought, dependent, among other things, on social stratum and class.[10] As one historian has written: "Republicanism may be used as a theme that helps us to understand not only particular political arrangements, but the complexity of a culture" (Kerber 1985, 482).

Elias Smith called himself a republican and, when addressing his brethren, called for them to aim for consistency in the matter. He said, "Let us be republicans indeed. Many are republicans as to government, and yet are but half republicans, being in matters of religion still bound to a Catechism, creed, covenant, or a superstitious priest. Venture to be as independent in things of religion, as in that which respects the government in which you live" (1809b, 32). This was not the republicanism of Madison and Adams, certainly not that of Hamilton, or even in a direct way that of Jefferson—not a theory of balanced government nor the fruit of proto-liberal economic reasoning about the nation-building capacities of free individuals.[11] Though Elias Smith did at times address matters originating in elite republican theory—criticisms of the national debt, of standing armies, the excise tax, and the like—what he mainly concerned himself with personally was in the first instance freedom of religion and religious inquiry.

Deference. The Christians and their sympathizers aimed at pulling down the cultural hegemony of the privileged. But what exactly was the point? Smith's own efforts were at first aimed at the pretensions of the clergy and their demand for deference on the basis of superior education—just the attitude that Popkin displayed in his encounter with the boatman. Smith denied such claims: "It is thought by many that none can teach the scriptures, unless they have been through college, and that any man who has, is fit for a preacher. Those teachers kept the people in fear of them; so it is now, people in general are afraid of a college minister, honoring him as a kind of god" (1805b, 29). But he extended this critique from the clergy to the class alignments of the communities in which they worked and thus attacked all forms of deference based on awe of wealth and station. Speaking in the name of "the people," he aimed his barbs at those who claimed the privilege to govern as an inherent right: "To govern us, to be sure! A pretty kind of governing, truly! We have the toil, and you the enjoyment; we produce and you spend; wealth flows from the sweat of our brows, and you engross it to yourselves. Go, ye dignified and privileged, who are not of the people, go and form a nation apart, and govern yourselves!" (1810, 27).

Smith was acutely conscious of class, though to put it in these terms again runs the risk of anachronism—if by "class consciousness" we assume a structural analysis of social ills and an attack on wealth-based power differentials as such; in fact he was not so much against privilege as against preferment. Smith was neither leveler nor socialist; in commenting on the fourth chapter of Acts, where it is said the apostles had all things in common, he wrote, "I do not find that Christ or the Apostles ever laid this down for a standing rule for the Gentiles to observe" (1804c, 4).[12] Neither, therefore, would the Christians. The problem for Smith was not wealth but antidemocratic and hence anti-Christian claims to deference made on its basis; to this extent, what he aimed at was a reformation of social manners. But Smith's program went deeper than this, insofar as it also aimed at empowerment—the seizing by "the people" of functions that had been the prerogative of specialist elites, in the areas of religion, law, politics, and medicine. Here the economic and political consequences of his views were real and direct; he was a Jeffersonian who looked forward to a nation of equals and worked toward that end. Opposition to the Federalist worldview was based on this attitude.

Federalist opposition to the Democratic-Republicans and evangelicals like Smith evinces a reciprocal concern for the maintenance of social order in unsettled times agitated by antielitist democratic sentiments. As one Congregationalist clergyman (who had good reason to worry) put it: "In the present state of man . . . some must be clothed with power and authority to administer government: and others are bound to be subject to its regular administration" (Buckminster 1796a, 11). Battle was joined in 1802 when Smith arrived on the concerned clergyman's own doorstep with an apocalyptic vision of a nation committed, not to order, hierarchy, and deference, but to a new world of "Liberty; Equality; Unity, and Peace."[13]

Individualism. Smith never talked about the community, the church, or the state as an organic unity. Rather, he spoke of liberty and of the absolute personal right of the individual to make autonomous decisions in all things religious and political. He absolutely rejected hierarchy as having any necessary basis in the nature of things. The idea of the Great Chain of Being would have been adamantly rejected, had Smith ever heard of it. To be sure, there must be leaders, but only if freely chosen by those who see some advantage in being led. He saw a republic as a polity in which the people are fully capable of governing themselves, rather than as being seen as their own worst enemies. He asked, If people cannot be entrusted with the care of their own soul, then what can they be entrusted with? (Smith 1810). The operations of the human mind, he said, are no more susceptible to human control than the weather. Likewise, everyone has the *inalienable right* to search the Scriptures for oneself and to follow them wherever they might lead.

Such ideas have been associated with an evolving liberalism in American society in the late eighteenth and early nineteenth centuries, according to which individual rights are of paramount importance, and those of the community a secondary derivation. As one historian puts it, this was the time in which "the individual was taking shape as the conceptual building block of society," a time in which political society was coming to be seen, not as an entity of which one is but a member, but rather as "the arena for sorting and settling the interests of self-controlled individuals" (Watts 1987, 113, 251). Following this logic, the result would not be chaos, as conservatives feared, but rather the creation of a greater harmony derived from the balance of competing interests (Ellis 1979, 26).

The period from 1790 through 1820 has come to be perceived as a transitional phase between the corporatist ideas of classic republican thought that dominated the perceptions of the Revolutionary generation and the liberal ideology of nineteenth-century America with its exaltation of the individual in a free, competitive, aggressively entrepreneurial society. The opposition between Federalism and Jeffersonian Republicanism is taken to be reflective of these competing visions (McCoy 1980). Elias Smith was most certainly an individualist of some kind, but he did not root his conceptions in eighteenth-century political science but rather in a very literal reading of the Declaration of Independence coupled with a libertarian exegesis of the New Testament. But like the proto-liberal Jeffersonians, he believed that exercise of near absolute individual rights would not destroy the republic; rather, it would confirm its promise, which he believed to be guaranteed in apocalyptic prophecy.

Millenarianism. Elias Smith was what has been called a premillennialist—one who believes, following Revelation 20, that Christ will return bodily to earth before the onset of his thousand-year reign. This view is contrasted to postmillennialism, in which it is believed there will be a spiritual rule of Christ, marked by progressive signs of the work of his Spirit, before the actual return and the final battle with the forces of Antichrist. By Smith's time these were self-consciously alternative ways of interpreting scriptural prophecies concerning the Millennium.[14] In 1808 Smith published his *Sermons, Containing an Illustration of the Prophecies,* in which he describes his point of view and what he takes prophecy to have foretold about the pattern of the world to be. Smith wrote of how he had once held postmillennial views and of why he no longer did. The drift of his argument was that all "spiritual" (i.e., metaphoric) interpretations of Scripture should be rejected. His reasons for adopting such a position are entirely consistent with his thought in general. In the first instance, it is dishonoring God to do otherwise; the Bible represents his plain word, not a hidden truth embedded in metaphor: "There cannot be a greater dishonor done to a superior than to say that he does not mean as he says; for it makes him a deceiver" (Smith 1808a, 288). But his main practical target was the earthly opposition—the educated pastorate cleaving to postmillennialism and figurative interpretation.

Smith wrote, "When we leave the plain words of scripture, and undertake to spiritualize plain positive declarations, there is no telling what lengths imagination will carry us. . . . Laying aside all human covenants, let us now attend to the sure word of prophecy" (1808a, 38; see also 55). Returning to the literal word of the Bible was, as always, his primary means of attacking the divisive consequences of religious partisanship, elite pretension, and, not incidentally, his enemies of the day. Speaking of those men who called themselves "Reverend," Smith contemptuously said of these "learned men" that, "as soon as the light of the scriptures come, they are afraid, lest their works will be discovered. The light is to them as the terrors of death. By laying aside the true meaning of the scriptures, they have turned another side to the people from what is meant. The consequence of all this is people are become so expert, that each one can prove from the scriptures what he wishes to believe. The scriptures, (a sealed book to them) is laid aside, and the fear, or our duty to God is taught by the precepts of men, because men's precepts can be understood" (ibid., 284–85).

This literalism was one mode of Smith's general assault on deference. But there were also more directly political implications to his attitude. The preaching of the patriotic clergy of the Revolutionary generation has been described as an "amalgam of traditional Puritan apocalyptic rhetoric and eighteenth-century political discourse" (Hatch 1977, 22–23).[15] But this ideological capital was available to anyone and therefore could be deployed depending on where one stood along the political spectrum of post-Revolutionary America; Elias Smith and his opponents were part of the same universe of discourse and engaged so strenuously in verbal combat precisely because they were (Pocock 1975, 449). Nathan Hatch points out that "the most crucial aspect of this Christian republicanism is its function as an idiom through which intense Christian beliefs and symbols came to focus on the preservation of republican principle. The cause of liberty thus became a sacred one" (1977, 157). Certainly that is how Elias Smith saw it. But times had changed, and Scripture now applied to different ends than when Satan's kingdom was represented by Lord North's government; in Smith's hands "preservation of republican principle" was equated with opposition to the Federalist party. Elias's own worldview might be characterized as "millenarian republicanism." It combined an evangelical, born-again spiritual perfectionism with the dream of a Christian commonwealth hinted at in the prophetically foretold victory of Jefferson, a victory that many of the formerly patriotic and now deeply anxious conservative clergy saw as a prophetically foretold transitory victory for Antichrist.

This amorphous though widespread democratic millennialism utilized symbolism as old as Christianity itself, yet applied it in novel circumstances. The spiritual fellowship of the early Christian church, as described in the Gospels and the Acts of the Apostles, was employed to interpret and judge a democratic experiment of a thus far unique kind, to point out in the light of prophecy its implications and shortcomings with respect to a perceived divine plan.

The passage in Acts from which Elias Smith and his friends derived the term *Christians* as the only scripturally legitimate name for true followers of Christ is itself a case in point. Acts relates that ordinary believers went out from Jerusalem to Antioch in Syria, there "preaching the word to none but unto the Jews only." But other evangelists from Cyprus and Cyrene (hence most probably Jews of the Diaspora) also descended on Antioch and "spake unto the Grecians, preaching the Lord Jesus." Hearing of successes among the latter, the Jerusalem church dispatched Barnabas to Antioch, where he witnessed the good work and then went to fetch Paul from Tarsus. "And when he had found him, he brought him unto Antioch. And it came to pass, that a whole year they assembled themselves with the church, and taught much people. And the disciples were called Christians first in Antioch" (11:26).

This passage in itself is sufficient charter for the name of a church, but its significance grows when seen in its wider scriptural context, which is the extraordinary episode in Acts 10 known as Peter's Dream. In this sequence the apostle Peter was in Joppa, in prayer before his noon meal. "And he became very hungry, and would have eaten: but while they made ready, he fell into a trance, and saw heaven opened, and a certain vessel descending unto him, as it had been a great sheet knit at the four corners, and let down to the earth: wherein were all manner of fourfooted beasts of the earth, and wild beasts, and creeping things, and fowls of the air. And there came a voice to him, Rise, Peter; kill, and eat. But Peter said, Not so, Lord; for I have never eaten any thing that is common or unclean. And the voice spake unto him again the second time, What God hath cleansed, that call not thou common" (10:10-15).

Until this point Peter, unlike Paul later, had attempted to maintain his commensal exclusivity as a Jew, but in the light of this vision—which symbolically abrogated the Levitical dietary taboos through which the Jews defined themselves as a pure and exclusive nation—Peter was open to go visit the Gentile Cornelius, a centurion in the local Roman capital of Caesarea. There he told Cornelius that things had fundamentally changed: "Ye know how that it is an unlawful thing for a man that is a Jew to keep company, or come unto one of another nation; but God hath shewed me that I should not call any man common or unclean. . . . Of a truth I perceive that God is no respecter of persons: but in every nation he that feareth him, and worketh righteousness, is accepted with him. . . . While Peter yet spake these words, the Holy Ghost fell on all them which heard the word" (10:28, 34, 44).

In Acts 11 Peter related to the church in Jerusalem what had happened in Caesarea, and "when they heard these things, they held their peace, and glorified God, saying, Then hath God also to the Gentiles granted repentance unto life" (v. 18). This striking revelation through Peter of the universality of the Christian message then leads on to Barnabas's trip to Antioch and ultimately the evangelistic travels of Paul as far as Rome itself.[16]

What Elias Smith—this latter-day Paul—made of the scriptural message may be seen in the *Articles of Faith and Church Building*, which he composed on behalf of like-minded brethren as the result of a Christian Conference in Sandbornton, New Hampshire, in July 1802: "Having considered the various denominations of People who profess to be the desciples [*sic*] of Christ, and being convinced that those denominations are not only unscriptural, but also serve to divide the desciples of Christ into parties, we think it dishonoring Christ to uphold any of the party names by which the saints are called in the present day. Believing it our duty to resume the name given at Antioch, which was CHRISTIANS" (Smith et al. 1802, 3).

These people conceived of the American social order in denominational terms. The churchly order was a mirror of society; what politics one espoused, what class of people one was in, could be directly gauged by what church one attended and what kind of theology one subscribed to: Federalists (Monarchists and Tories) were Congregationalist, Presbyterian, or Episcopal; theologically, they were Calvinists, supporters of ecclesiastical hierarchy, or both. Democratic-Republicans (The People) were Free-Will Baptists, Christians, and their fellow travelers in other sects; theologically, they were Arminian revivalistic Free-Willers who found the doctrine of predestination incompatible with God's justice, the work of the Spirit more important than form of worship, and ecclesiastical hierarchy utter anathema as a work of Antichrist. As Perry Miller put it, the general effect of their activities, coupled with a general process of democratic liberalization, was "to transform Calvinism . . . into an operational Arminianism." The Methodists, though evangelical and Arminian, were suspect because they based their church organizations on the same anti-Christian hierarchical and aristocratic principles as those held by the Anglican Church, which spawned them (and not least because of John Wesley's antipathy to the Revolution).

Therefore, if antidemocratic hierarchies and the political divisions that accompanied them were to be effaced through the results of the recent triumph of the Sovereign People in war, this had to be accompanied by the foundation of a universal Christian church that transcended sectarian divisions. As Elias Smith constantly maintained, there is a great deal of significance in what things are called; he wrote his *New Testament Dictionary* in proof of the point. There, under the heading *Name,* may be found the following: "Christians . . . is the only name in which all the disciples of Christ can agree to be called; this is that worthy name by which the saints of old were called. This is calculated to bury all party names and party distinctions now in the world among such as profess to belong to Christ. Every name which professors of religion wear, not mentioned in the New Testament, is the name of the beast . . . and no doubt there are at least 666 of them" (1812, 278–80).

The fundamental message comprising the scripturally derived "Christian" program therefore had two parts. First, in accord with Peter's dream, no one is to be regarded as common or unclean. Those who think otherwise—Federalists, the Congregational clergy, Monarchists, and so forth—are a part of the nation described in one of Smith's favorite scriptural passages as "MYSTERY, BABYLON THE GREAT, THE MOTHER OF HARLOTS AND ABOMINATIONS OF THE EARTH" (Rev. 17:5). Second, in accord with the above strictures on human antiscriptural names, all those who would renounce Babylon must renounce their old sectarian appellations and join in the new fellowship offered by the "Christians," and also in Thomas Jefferson's correlative new democratic order.

Jefferson's rise to power was as foretold by Revelation 16:12: "And the sixth angel poured out his vial upon the great river Euphrates; and the water thereof was dried up, that the ways of the kings of the east might be prepared." Elias Smith, well knowing that he "may be called enthusiastic" for saying so, was convinced that Jefferson himself was the sixth angel of the apocalypse (1805e, 77). To follow will be the seventh angel, who brings all things to completion and Babylon herself to ruin: "And the seventh angel poured out his vial into the air; and there came a great voice out of the temple of heaven, from the throne, saying, It is done. . . . And great Babylon came in remembrance before God, to give unto her the cup of the wine of the fierceness of his wrath" (16:17–19). To the discerning it was possible to see the wine of the fierceness of God's wrath in the electoral misfortunes of the Federalists and the progressive collapse of established religion, while the temporal rule of Thomas Jefferson and the Democratic-Republicans could equally well be seen as standing in very close proximity to the second coming of Christ.

By virtue of his editorial role in the *Herald,* Smith was obliged to deal with events on a national scale, and in so doing, he drew on themes that had originated in elite classic republican theory and in the developing liberal tendencies of Jeffersonian thought, as well as on elements from his own evangelical background. As a result of these varied influences, his own political and ecclesiastical attitudes changed considerably from what they had been when he composed the *Articles* for his brethren in 1802. In short, he became a more radical and consistent democratic individualist.

In 1802 Smith and his fellow Christians closely resembled in point of principle those who had become Separate Baptists in the wake of the Great Awakening. Both groups advocated a closed-communion church organization established by mutual covenant—partaking of the Lord's Supper only with those who had undergone the experience of saving grace, testified to its effectual power, and been baptized as adults in virtue of the fact. There were, to be sure, theological differences with other sects. The Christians de-emphasized the Old Testament and were anti-Calvinist unitarians. In sum, however, the similarities with other spiritual descendants of the New Lights of the 1740s outweighed the differences; all favored withdrawal from a sinful world and from congregations containing the unregenerate, knowing "as the disciples of Christ . . . that the people shall dwell alone, and shall not be reckoned among the nations" (Smith et al. 1802, 3).[17]

That Smith and his friends favored the elimination of religious parties and party names, while at the same time being closed-communion separate Baptists, was an inconsistency not lost on the opposition. In the end, Smith himself came to believe that the American situation demanded an open-communion ecumenicalism for all those who could be reasonably counted as reborn in Christ. He put it in summary form in a diagram he constructed while going through another "Christian" phase in the late 1820s after a bout of Universalism. (See Fig. 1.)

Smith had by then occupied about every quadrant of the diagram himself, and even at this late date (when he was fifty-nine years old), he was attempting to overcome the warring sects and theologies by turning as always—with mutually inconsistent results at different periods—to the New Testament as his one and only guide. Now once more (though noting a sinister tendency toward denominational elitism) he maintained that "the people who are called *Christians,* without any sectarian name, holding Christ their lawgiver only, naming his name, may be found in the centre of all others" (352). In 1840, in one of the few amendments made to his autobiography of 1816, Elias Smith, now seventy-one, continued to insist that, "every *Christian* is under an indispensable obligation to *search the Scriptures for himself,* and make the best use of it he can for information in the *will of God,* and the nature of *'Pure Religion';* that he hath an *unalienable* right, impartially to judge of the sense and meaning of it, and to follow the Scriptures wherever it leads him." Properly done, it should lead to only one conclusion: "There is but one head, *name* and *rule* under which men can remain united to glorify God, and be useful to each other. That head is *Christ,* that name is the *name* of Christ, and that *rule* is the perfect law of Liberty, to which all believers in Christ, may submit and be at peace in themselves and with each other" (352, 365).

It could also be said that the only way in which such a reconciliation was practically feasible was the mutual disavowal of *any* formal theology, and in its place an emphasis on the work of the Spirit as the essence of the Christian message. Such would in fact prove to be the general drift of American religion in these years, though it took some hard-fought controversies to get from perfectionistic exclusivism to the broad-based, relatively nondoctrinal revivalistic evangelicalism characteristic of the middle years of the nineteenth century. Elias Smith's meandering course from Calvinist Baptist, to Christian, to Universalist

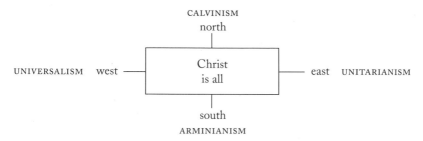

Fig. 1. Smith's theological phases

illustrates one of the more radical forms the process could take.

   Though his course was erratic, he strove for ideological consistency and to a degree achieved it. The corporatism of Smith's earlier thinking, based as it was on the traditional idea of the church covenant, gave way to an attack on this old Puritan idea itself and in that regard was at one with the emerging individualism of the country at large. Yet, to the end, Elias Smith's thought was in his own eyes based on nothing else than the plain word of Scripture. Since the Bible provided for him a total map of the world, he enunciated his evolving political perceptions in its terms; therefore he was faced with the task of harmonizing theology with social experience. Smith's politics and his perception of the movement of history provided a sense of what the Bible, if properly interpreted, was saying to him and to his nation; since Scripture can be all things to all men, he was able to find there what he sought—confirmation of his own interpretation of God's plan for America. Nowhere is this most apparent than in the relief he so obviously felt upon his conversion to Universalism in 1817, when he wrote of the consonance of American democracy with universal salvation.

Elias Smith's career spanned a historically formative period that should be seen in its entirety; this is one of the attractions of studying those times through his life. However, even though Smith lived until 1846, well past the Republican-Federalist controversies into the age of

Jackson and beyond, his political attitudes were formed in the crucible of events and opinions surrounding the election of 1800; his earlier career will therefore be the primary focus of this book so far as the genesis of his distinctive mode of thought is concerned.

What Smith represents for the purpose at hand is the process whereby a rapidly evolving *national* political culture impinged on specific individuals, and in turn was affected by them, as they began to interpret their experience in its terms—a compass shift in political attitudes from periphery to center, from locality to nation. This was not a simple business. I will show below the complexity of the Christian movement, the variety of circumstances that generated it and allowed it to take root. I also explore the contexts in which new political conceptions were evolved and deployed via theological disputation, so bringing about the fateful elision mentioned above.

Elias Smith's life was punctuated by doctrinal controversies in which seemingly abstruse dogmas were fought out in terms of their moral and political consequences. Is Christ part of the Godhead, or is he a derivative being created in order to reconcile humanity to God through him? So far as Smith was concerned, to claim the former is mere mystery mongering, while the latter is consistent with the tenor of Scripture and no less than common sense, since everyone knows what a mediator is, but no one can give a sensible account of the Trinity. To demystify Christianity in this way was to reclaim a once-pristine faith from elite theological pretension. To deny the validity of the Calvinist interpretation of predestination and election was to reassert the primacy of Scripture, to focus on human free agency in accepting or rejecting the truths of the gospel, and to undercut the notion that anyone at all has a prima facie claim to "elect" status by virtue of worldly appearances. To suppose that all humanity has been granted an ultimate universal right to sit at the feet of the Lamb is a consummately political notion.

And so back again to the primacy of the concept of liberty, around which all these controversies revolved. *Liberty* was the crux of the matter, and Smith its self-appointed herald. The task now is to trace the workings of the four central interrelated themes—republicanism, individualism, millenarianism, and the attack on deference—as manifest in the extraordinary life and times of Elias Smith. Elias exemplifies and incarnates many of the trends and preoccupations abroad in his time: he was born before the Revolution, lived into the administration of President James Polk, and saw many changes. Even when not a major actor in the events of his time, Smith serves from our perspective as bellwether of them.

❦

As to sources, the chronological base for this study is primarily derived from Smith's autobiography, *The Life, Conversion, Preaching, Travels, and Sufferings of Elias Smith* (1816 and 1840), supplemented by other sources to cover his later life. That pithy and opinionated book is extraordinarily rich in detail and a delight to read. It is also an apologia—stereotypical, self-serving, and inevitably a retrospective account of what Smith took to be the meaning and pattern of his life from the perspective of the year 1816, when he was forty-seven years old. It belongs to the well-known genre of spiritual autobiography and therefore reiterates the standard theme of how God's grace manifested itself in the course of a particular life. Smith's biases are not a disadvantage as long as due caution is exercised; the account of his own life exemplifies fundamental attitudes about the kind of sense a life was supposed to make among the people from whom he came.

Smith's *Life* therefore remains of great importance to the present effort; it is far richer than the memoirs published by or about Smith's immediate associates—which are sometimes only edited versions of daybook diaries recounting births, deaths, marriages, sermons preached, heretics put down. It seems that Smith's very inconstancy made him more creative than his fellows. Though the book was first published in 1816, with a slightly modified second edition issued in 1840, its substantive content effectively terminates in 1810, the year Smith moved to Portland, Maine; what Elias includes pertaining to subsequent years, even in the 1840 edition, is very sketchy indeed—as though, with the changes in his life, he had lost heart for the task, or did not care to remember what he would have to include in order to bring things up to date. Fortunately there is much more than his autobiography to go on: Smith's voluminous journalistic output, numerous published sermons, discourses and polemics, medical tracts, and hymnbooks. Together, the works of Elias Smith, supplemented by what others had to say about him, are the basis for the story recounted below. Other sources—probate records, church archives, land deeds, genealogies, and wills—help to establish the framework of Smith's life, the social milieu in which he moved.

Little was published on the group that called themselves the Christians, except by the Christians themselves, until William Mc-Loughlin's *New England Dissent, 1630–1833* (1971), which concentrates on the Baptists and their role in bringing about religious disestablishment in New England; McLoughlin accords Elias Smith's Christians a minor role as a Baptist fringe movement. Likewise Stephen Marini, in his *Radical Sects of Revolutionary New England* (1981), has examined the sociological origins and worldviews of the Shakers, the Free-Will Baptists, and the Universalists, each of which was related in one way or another to the Christians, though once more the latter get only passing mention. Along with theology and ecclesiology, Marini, with a keen interest in early American church music, also considered hymnody, the use of song by these movements to inspire and instruct their followings. In the same spirit I occasionally illustrate the argument below through inclusion of didactic hymns and verses composed by the Christians as an essential part of their evangelical project.

More recently Richard Hughes and C. Leonard Allen's *Illusions of Innocence: Protestant Primitivism in America, 1630–1875* (1988) documents the Restorationist theme in American Protestantism—the belief that it is a distinctive American mission to re-create the purity, coherence, and organizational forms of the primitive Christian church. They identify the paradox inherent in this stance, namely, that attempts to efface sectarian distinctions through recourse to the pristine gospel have repeatedly and inevitably led to the formation of new sects, which turn inward to defend the purity of their own message and so become yet another example of what they had rebelled against.

Hughes and Allen, who dealt in part with the Christian movement sparked in western Virginia and Kentucky by former Presbyterians Barton Stone and Alexander Campbell, have been powerfully supplemented by Paul Conkin's *Cane Ridge: America's Pentecost* (1990); Conkin examines the great revival of 1801 initiated by Stone at Cane Ridge, Kentucky, tracing the phenomenon back to its roots in Ulster and southwest Scotland, and then to the expansion of the Scots-Irish population in America and the network of like-minded revivalistic evangelicals to which it gave rise. It was Campbell's great accomplishment to articulate the broadly based but organizationally scattered western Christians into a powerful new denomination, the Disciples of Christ. Smith was well aware of Stone's work, while Campbell looked back to Smith as one of the founders of their transregional ecumenical movement, and to the New England Christians as being particularly effective in spreading the word to Ohio.

While Elias Smith has been accorded casual mention in the works above, and most recently in Gordon Wood's *Radicalism of the American Revolution* (where Smith is labeled "a renegade Baptist"), Nathan Hatch is the only historian to have treated systematically the New England Christian movement that Smith helped found. His book *The Democratization of American Christianity* (1989) asks what produced the rise of a variety of regionally separate but ideologically similar populist religious movements in post-Revolutionary America. In addition to the Christians and Elias Smith, Hatch examines a number of black preachers, the antielitist content of the Book of Mormon (Hughes and Allen also touch on this), and the preaching of the Primitive Methodist Lorenzo Dow, a figure well known to the early Christians as they were to him; Hatch, as did Marini, also considered the importance of hymnody as an emotive vehicle for evangelical propaganda. For Hatch, these revivalistic populists represent a fusion of evangelical religion with the rapidly evolving democratic ethos of the new nation, an incendiary combination that resulted in a restructuring of American Protestantism and the emergence of the religious landscape known to us today.

Hatch has documented the widespread nature of evangelical populism in the early years of the nineteenth century. I am concerned with one life only and therefore can be more attentive to detail. I am also more concerned than Hatch with the formal content of the theological wranglings that were so much a part of the general process at issue, and with the social composition of the Christian movement and the local political contexts in which it developed. Hatch chose instead to concentrate on the leadership of these populist movements rather than on their followings. In his first major work, *The Sacred Cause of Liberty*

(1977), Hatch examined the way in which the patriotic clergy of the Revolutionary generation assimilated the events of their time to God's redemptive plan. *The Perfect Law of Liberty* examines how, once won, that cause was generalized by Elias Smith and his associates into a scripturally justified attempt to create a popular democracy centered on the Jeffersonian ideals of liberty and equality.[18]

The argument proceeds as follows. Chapter 1 ("When I Was a Child") considers the formative influences on what would become Smith's populist republicanism. I deal with his New Light Congregationalist and Baptist family background and with the influence of his family on him, also with the external intellectual influences that impinged on Elias's early career: Protestant stress on the right of the individual to read and interpret the Bible for oneself; the origins of Smith's fascination with the English language; his encounter with Calvinism and with providential interpretations of history.

Chapter 2 ("The Fire Next Time") introduces Portsmouth, New Hampshire, where Smith spent his most creative years, and also evokes the incendiary political scene of the 1790s, when the first American party system took form. It then drops backward in time to pick up Smith's conversion and call to the ministry, his early experiences as a Calvinist Baptist preacher and increasing doubts about whether he was following the right theological course, and finally his determination that he must leave human works behind him and take Scripture as his only guide. This is followed by an account of the origins and program of the Christian Connection and the departure this marked from the Calvinism of Smith's youth. The chapter concludes with Smith's conversion to Democratic-Republicanism, the fusion of his religious beliefs with his new political opinions, and his move to Portsmouth as a self-styled *free man.*

Chapter 3 ("Free Radicals") begins in Portsmouth and describes the events that followed upon Smith's move there once he had renounced the Calvinist Baptists and determined upon a course of direct confrontation with the forces of Antichrist. I therefore give an account of the origins of Smith's own church, how the community reacted to it, and what effect Smith's radical preaching had upon the community at large and the local ecclesiastical establishment in particular. Seemingly parochial disputes were in fact an aspect of far-ranging disagreements over the role of the citizen and the proper constitution of political society. Smith is contrasted to opponents among the orthodox Congregational clergy who rightly saw Elias's seditious church-wrecking activities as intimately connected to his Democratic-Republican political sympathies.

The title of Chapter 4 ("A Thief in the Night") alludes to the scriptural promise that Christ will return when least expected. The initial focus of this chapter is the apocalyptic component of Elias Smith's thought and his application of prophecy to interpreting the political scene. Having discussed the Christian message in this and the previous chapter, I turn to those who heard it; using rolls from three churches of the Christian Connection, including Smith's own church in Portsmouth, the members of these congregations are examined by trade, gender, financial status, presence of kinsfolk within the church, and whatever else is known about them from probate records and other documents. This is a type of analysis not so far attempted for the Christian movement, and the exercise reveals considerable social heterogeneity in and between the churches. I conclude with a discussion of how these people might have heard Smith's libertarian message and why they were susceptible to it.

"Prepare Ye the Way" (Chapter 5) refers to the mission of John the Baptist. Through his interpretation of prophecy, Elias Smith believed Christ's return to be very near and undertook to broadcast that good news to his fellow citizens, along with word of the progress of the Christian Connection in undermining what he took to be religious sectarianism. Focusing on Smith's approach to language, this chapter deals with the practical effect of the Christian message on the churches that it undertook to reform, with the vicissitudes of Smith's family life, and above all with the foundation and nature of his newspaper the *Herald of Gospel Liberty,* through which Elias acquired a national audience for his blend of religious libertarianism and republican political opinion.

Chapter 6 ("Physicians of Value") is concerned with the way in which Elias Smith amalgamated his opinions concerning spiritual, political, and bodily health. Evangelical itinerants were often traveling doctors, and these practitioners had the advantage over weakly organized "regular" professional doctors by virtue of their availability, affordability, and antielitist appeal. The beginnings of Smith's association with Samuel Thomson marked a decisive change in his personal life. Elias's adoption of a Thomsonian herbal medical practice made it possible for him to settle down in Boston with a more or less stable source of income. However, sectarianism was as much the rule in medical circles as in religious, and Elias soon quarreled with Thomson and branched off into a practice of his own. This period marks the effective end of Smith's evangelical career.

The first sections of Chapter 7 ("Age of Miracles") are occupied with Smith's conversion to Universalism and his (albeit temporary) renunciation of the Christian Connection. It then follows the events of his life through to his death in 1846. The remainder of the chapter traces the fate of the connection as it shifted west along with the movement of population into New York, Ohio, and beyond, while simultaneously going through a phase of organizational consolidation. Elias had continued to keep a close though skeptical eye on these developments and did not like what he saw: a general decline of zeal, pressures toward formal education of preachers, and increasing respectability of the church. Yet these were natural processes, not unlike what happened to early Christianity itself. When Smith died in 1846, the world was very different from that in which he had been born; it was agitated by the Prohibition and Abolitionist movements, by transcendentalists and Swedenborgians, by Christian socialists and other utopians, by American imperial expansion, and renewed millennial hopes. His movement had become a church that endures to this day.

The Epilogue relates the present book to my former one on the social history of the multiple personality concept, summarizes Smith's significance, and calls for further research on a number of questions.

1 WHEN I WAS A CHILD
From Lyme, Connecticut, to Woodstock, Vermont

Woe is me, my mother, that thou hast borne me a man of strife!

JEREMIAH 15:10

IN 1769 THE CONNECTICUT SONS of Liberty, galvanized by the Stamp Act controversy of 1765, were ready to defend the rights of Connecticut and of the other British colonies. Connecticut New Light Congregationalists opposed the conservative Old Light establishment, which in their opinion had been too submissive with respect to imperial encroachments on the traditional prerogatives of the quasi-autonomous Puritan colony. The Townshend Acts of 1767, which imposed duties on a number of imported commodities—notably tea—had inflamed local sentiments still more, and by 1769 local merchants were willing to go along with nonimportation agreements akin to those arrived at in Boston. In the same year westward-moving Connecticut settlers who believed themselves, by virtue of their sea-to-sea colonial charter, to have rights to lands in the Wyoming Valley around the town of Wilkes Barre, engaged in open hostilities with Pennsylvanians who laid claim to the same territory. Meanwhile Vermont was emerging as a distinct political entity out of the turmoil created by conflicting claims of New Hampshire and New York to the northern lands west of the Connecticut River.

When Revolution came, Elias Smith was five years old. He had little recollection of the events of those years, though he did remember his terror when the British burned New London on the Connecticut coast, not far from where he grew up. Smith later thought that what he then heard about "Redcoats, Tories, and Regulars" formed the basis of the antipathy he felt for beings of that stripe ever after. Otherwise, Smith had nothing to say about the war with Britain or about the role of his family in it. It appears that the Smiths—like many Americans who had farms to tend and concerns of their own—did not give the Revolution much thought unless it directly affected them. Smith's political education would have to wait for the turbulent decade of the 1790s, when, with the emergence of overt partisan conflict in the new Republic, he began to apply his antipathy for Tories to the scene around him. Smith's adult life was shaped by the emergence of a national political culture, and in turn he did what he could to shape it.

Elias Smith was born in Lyme, Connecticut, on June 17, 1769. He was named after an uncle killed in the French and Indian War. However, "This name never pleased me; and I often wished my name had been some other" (15). Why the name *Elias* did not please, Smith fails to say, nor what he would have preferred in its place. In any event, the practice of naming offspring after relatives dying without issue was common at the time.[1] In the same spirit Elias's brother Richard Ransom Smith would name a son Elias in honor of his sibling, thus producing (to the confusion of future genealogists) yet another Elias Smith, a name now perpetuated over three generations.

However extraordinary Elias's life may have been in some respects, in others it was quite typical, shaped by processes that had an impact across broad sectors of the American population, such as the stratum into which he was born—economically marginal farmers and craftsmen in areas that had been longer settled. To discern the hidden workings of such processes is to go much of the way toward understanding the world of Smith and his fellows and the nature of their response to it. But we also must consider their common Anglo-American Protestant culture—the understandings that they together brought to bear on their changeable situation. Smith retrospectively saw his erratic life as an instrumentality of God's will, and his account of it as an example to his readers: "Could I now write upon myself as a creature of

God; as one, in his hand, the instrument of good to others; the subject would to me be pleasing, and to others profitable. In this way, the history of my life would be to others an account of the glory and grace of God to an individual, and an instructive lesson to all who shall come after who may doubt, or be ignorant of the grace of him who is 'good to all; and whose tender mercies are over all his works'" (13).

Smith lived in a world imbued with meaning, in which every event and every life contained a parable or an admonition to the unwary. This necessity to comprehend reality in theocentric terms weighed heavily upon him and New Englanders in general. Nothing was outside God's scheme for the redemption of individual sinners or, by extension, of the national collectively to which they belonged. Adapting the traditions of Puritan exemplary biography, Elias Smith interwove an account of his individual life with that of America as a whole, believing that both he and his country had been called to a unique and related mission. An understanding of the cultural idiom through which he did so is an essential part of the present task: hence attention will be given to Smith's religious tradition, to what he read and how he read it, to how he managed to fuse autobiography, political history, and his understanding of God's redemptive plan into a comprehensive understanding of the world and a framework for action within it.

The social and cultural milieu in which Elias Smith was reared is accordingly the subject of this chapter, beginning in 1769 with the small world of his childhood: Lyme, Connecticut. We then consider his later life as an adolescent and young adult in Woodstock, Vermont, after the move of his family north to the agricultural frontier in 1782.

Elias was the eldest son of Stephen Smith and Irene Ransom Smith (called Raney by her family). Stephen was a Baptist, and most of Irene's family were New Light Congregationalists, reborn in the awakenings of the 1740s and separated from conservative Old Lights because of it (24). Elias's father had been married before, to Lydia Alger, who died in 1766 without issue; he married Irene in 1768, who was then

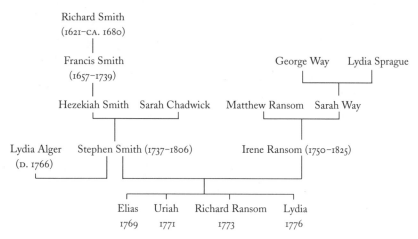

Fig. 2. The Smiths

seventeen years old and thirteen years Stephen's junior. As Figure 2 shows, Elias was followed in rapid order by three younger siblings (Jacobus 1949).

It is important to determine the factors that eventually led Stephen to move with his family to Woodstock, since much else of consequence for Elias Smith's life follows from that choice. In the process it will be possible to locate the Smiths relative to the evolving society of late eighteenth-century America.

First to be considered is the social setting of the town of Lyme, where by 1769 the Smiths had lived for three generations. Lyme is on the east side of the mouth of the Connecticut River across from the town of Saybrook, from which Lyme amicably split off in 1667 because of problems caused by maintaining a common political and religious society divided by the river. In 1769 Lyme already had one hundred years of independent existence, being part of the second wave of town foundation along the Connecticut coast after the creation of the new Puritan colony by settlers from Massachusetts and England (Daniels 1979, 35, 16).[2]

The first recorded Smith of Elias's line, Richard Smith, was born in England and came to Lyme about 1660 from Lancaster, Massachu-

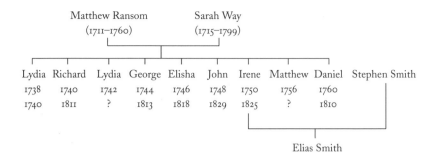

Fig. 3. The Ransoms

setts, with his family—including his son Francis, Hezekiah's father. Hezekiah Smith, Elias's grandfather, was the first ascendant to have been born in Lyme; in turn he had nine children, five boys and four girls, of whom Stephen Smith was the third son (Jacobus 1949). There is no sign that Hezekiah, though solvent, was of any great wealth. Instead of land, his inheritance from Francis Smith in 1746 took the form of £150 cash; whatever family farmland there was went to one or both of his other brothers.[3] Together these facts imply that in the next generation Hezekiah faced a standard predicament of colonial life: how to provide for such a large family out of limited and diminishing resources? What is known of Lyme in the period shows that this was a problem faced by many in the town, presumably including the large family of Elias Smith's mother, Irene.

The Ransom family had no less than six sons and two daughters (see Fig. 3), all of whom left Lyme—five of them for the vicinity of Woodstock—in the migration conjoining their fates with that of their brother-in-law, Stephen Smith.[4] This affinal connection must have been important in Stephen's own decision to move, because no other Smiths except his wife and children went to Vermont with him.

Lyme had become crowded through natural increase, a fact established by Jackson Turner Main, who shows that in eighteenth-century Lyme there was a diminishing emphasis on farming as primary means of subsistence and a progressive emphasis instead on craftwork or other form of paid employment.[5] Debt increased, income decreased. Tax lists reveal a decline in the population of the town, presumably brought about by the same causes that led to the exodus of the Smiths and Ransoms. By the 1780s, "although most of the poor were young, a much larger proportion of the middle-aged, probably twenty-five percent, had failed to acquire enough property to support their families. A century earlier such a situation was almost unknown" (Main 1977, 42). In turn, however, families were interrelated so as to produce complex social networks exploitable as human capital through mutual aid; the Smiths and Ransoms were to draw on this fund in frontier Woodstock, in a world where ties of consanguinity, affinity, and faith provided the only social security there was outside of poor relief.[6] (See Fig. 4.)

In 1782 Stephen Smith was forty-five years old with a wife, three sons, a daughter, and limited prospects. He seems to have been making do out of a mixture of farming and shoemaking; the receipt for the land Smith purchased in Woodstock lists his occupation as cordwinder (i.e., cordwainer), or shoemaker—a trade for which he seems to have been destined ever since youth when he had served as an apprentice to one Capt. Abner Lee, "an humble, happy disciple of Jesus" (226–27). Though he had property sufficient upon its sale to acquire land in Vermont, Stephen does not appear to have had an estate sufficient by itself to supply the needs of his family in Lyme, and still less the future needs of a new generation. It is not clear, in fact, that Stephen Smith owned any land at all. We learn from Elias that in 1772 Stephen "moved into a new house which he had built" and that "the spring before I was nine years old [1778], my father went to the east part of the town, within ten miles of New-London with his family, to live on a farm belonging to a widow [a sharecropping arrangement perhaps]. In this place he lived two years." The final move was in 1780, "when, in my eleventh year, my father hired a Farm of Capt. *John Robinson* in

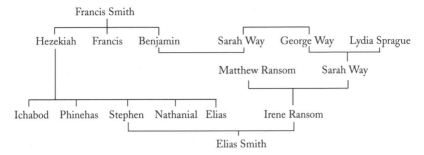

Fig. 4. The Smith-Ransom connection

Hebron, thirty miles from Lyme; he carried his family there in April, and lived there over two years" (15, 27, 29). Unlike their well-remembered, desperately poor situation in Woodstock during the early years, the condition of Elias's family in Connecticut elicited no direct comment; the relevant passages in his autobiography describe mainly childhood reminiscences of local life, rumors of war, and the prophetic early religious experiences that are so much a part of the standard spiritual autobiography. However, the circumstantial accounts that he does give suggest dependence on others for land and (in confirmation of Main's findings) supplementary or perhaps even primary dependence on craft work for wages.

Elias Smith tells us that in 1782 Stephen was able to sell his property in Lyme for £80, which appears to be nearly the total value of his estate. Stephen was therefore considerably worse off than his father, Hezekiah, had been, who in 1746 had inherited £150. If Stephen Smith was worth only £80, then, as shown by Main's analysis, he fell in the lower middle range of Lyme's citizens during the relevant period. (The median probated estate in the years 1775–89 was £55.) Lyme, however, was itself a comparatively poor town with respect to its agricultural land-base and per capita income, so the size of Stephen's estate indicates only that he was not quite as poor as some (Main 1977, 43).[7] When his age at this time (forty-five years) is taken into account, it appears once again that he was anything but wealthy and that the only way in which he could reasonably expect to better his condition, and to leave anything worth having to his children, was to depart Lyme in search of a more independent situation.

The Ransoms were no better off. The family genealogist records that when Richard Ransom, "was married in 1759, it is said he was so poor that his intended made him a suit of clothes to be married in," and that, "at the death of his father in 1760 [during service with Colonial forces in Upper New York against the French] the family were in low pecuniary circumstances, and Richard being the oldest, he and his mother provided for the family." Richard, who was a carpenter, twenty years later led the move to Woodstock, where in the course of time he and Stephen Smith were to better their condition considerably; as a sign of the connection between them, Stephen named his third son Richard Ransom Smith ("Ransom Genealogy"). The first federal census (1790) shows that the Ransoms had by then five independent households in Woodstock, headed by Elisha, George, John, Richard, and Lynde (one of Richard's sons)—a clan consisting in total of twelve "free white males" over sixteen, ten males under sixteen, and sixteen free white females. Stephen Smith's household consisted of himself, two of his three sons, and three females. Elias was the missing son. By 1789, loathing farm life and finding himself physically unsuited for it, he had begun to work as a largely self-taught schoolteacher and, with the counsel of his uncle Elisha Ransom, a staunch partisan of Baptist religious liberty, was heavily engaged in the spiritual travail that later led him to the ministry.

The Connecticut River Valley was the great road north, with settlers progressively moving up along it into what became Vermont and fanning out on either side of the river to occupy cultivable land in more peripheral areas (Roth 1987, 15–20). Woodstock, which lies some ten miles west of the Connecticut, was deeded out to speculative town-builders in the 1760s, who then proceeded to sell off the better part of their holdings to those who became the actual settlers. Stephen Smith was to benefit from the fate of one of the speculators, Charles Ward Apthorp of New York City, who had the misfortune to take the wrong side during the Revolution and have his holdings confiscated as a result (Dana 1980, 1–7).[8] Apparently in payment of delinquent taxes on behalf of some third party, some of Apthorp's holding was assumed by Phinehas Hemingway of Windsor, Vermont, who then sold part of it to Stephen Smith for £100.[9]

In the spring of 1782 Stephen Smith, in company with Elias's brother Uriah, trekked north to Vermont. In Elias's words, he there "purchased one hundred acres of land in the south part of Woodstock, made what preparation he could for the convenience of his family, and leaving my brother, returned home in June, to make ready to carry his family there before winter." The family traveled the 180 miles from Connecticut in thirteen days and finally "arrived at the town we set out for, which was represented to me as resembling the land of Canaan; a land of hills and vallies, flowing with milk and honey. The first part I found true, for the country appeared to be hills and vallies, and this was not an imaginary appearance, for so it remains in that part of the country, to this day." Elias Smith's heart sank, however, upon discovering that this was no Canaan.

> After many sweats and hard pulls, my father pointed us to the house, about forty rods ahead, the sight of which struck a damp on my spirits, as it appeared to me only an abode of wretchedness. After going to it and taking a general view of the house and land around, before the team came up, I determined within myself to return to Connecticut. . . . I went down to the team, and passed by the team down the steep and dismal hill as fast as possible. My father observing my rapid course, called after me, asking me where I was going; and commanded me to return to him. I feared to disobey him and returned. He asked me where I was going; my reply, was to *Connecticut*. He ordered me to return. This order I obeyed, though with great reluctance, as it appeared to me better to die than be confined in such a place. (32)

Since Stephen Smith had received only eighty pounds for his property in Lyme, he was twenty pounds in debt to Phinehas Hemingway for the land in Vermont. He reduced this debt by selling Hemingway the oxen, horse, and cart that had brought them to Vermont, thus depriving his family of draft animals for their first winter. With a poor first harvest on top of this, it was at first doubtful that Stephen and his family could survive at all. In December he walked all the way back to Lyme, obtained what was still owed him on his property there, bought a yoke of oxen, and retraced his steps in January.

> We rejoiced to see him and the oxen, hoping we should be able to clear our land of the heavy timber which stood or lay upon it, that in a future day we might be delivered from that want we then felt, and the greater we feared. It was with great difficulty we wintered our oxen and cows; we were obliged to fall elm and maple trees, and cut off the limbs for the cattle the small ends of which they ate with a little hay we gave them. In this way they lived through the winter. The first snow that fell that year, was on the sixteenth day of October; it fell about twelve inches deep. This greatly alarmed us, as we had never before lived where there was much snow. This soon went off, and we had pleasant weather till the first of December. After that we never saw the ground again till some time the next April. (36)

That first winter the Smiths made great quantities of maple syrup to help them get by, and Elias well remembered what drudgery it all was and how, with an empty belly, he would take to his bed "that I might forget my poverty, and remember my wants no more till morning" (38). Things slowly got better; the second year in Woodstock Smith's father carried on a tanning and currying business and made shoes in the winter. Elias learned the cordwainer's craft from him but found the business intolerably confining. It did, however, allow them finally to pay for their land.

Yet, trials remained. In the spring of 1785, in the wake of an exceptionally severe winter, Stephen Smith concluded that since they could not plant, they would have to engage in monthly hired labor. On this occasion Elias worked for a neighboring farmer. His autobiography indicates a general pattern of part-time wage work to supplement the family income, or at first simply to obtain the wherewithal to sustain himself when his family could not provide for him. Income from these sources, for example plowing for his carpenter uncle, Richard Ransom, enabled them to do such things as frame a new house (87).

This picture is reinforced by the reminiscences of one of Elias's cousins, Daniel Ransom, about the tactics of his grandfather, Richard. Like Stephen Smith, Richard Ransom obtained land in Woodstock, then, leaving some of his children behind to take care of things for the first winter (1781–82), returned to Lyme to fetch the rest of his family. In these early days Richard Ransom's family produced most of what it consumed; for what they had to buy they exchanged the potash derived from burning the slash on their land. "But their necessities were very limited for each family relied upon their own hands and lands to produce and manufacture whatever was needed, and they practiced the closest economy."[10] Through such accounts as Elias Smith's and Daniel Ransom's, it becomes clear just how interdependent local society was. In large measure this was a barter economy based on the exchange of goods and services; cash was in short supply.[11]

Though he had been a house joiner and cabinetmaker by trade, Richard Ransom in time accumulated a modest fortune in Woodstock through farming and shopkeeping, thus fulfilling the dream that had led him to depart Lyme, where dependent wage-work would appear to have been his fate had he stayed. Stephen Smith, when he came to make his will, showed that he too had prospered to a degree. First he settled matters with his Maker:

> In the name of God Amen—I Stephen Smith of the town of Woodstock Windsor County and State of Vermont—Tho' infirm in body yet firm and sound in mind and memory . . . do make and ordain this my Last Will and Testament—that is to say principally and first of all I give and recommend my soul into the hand of Almighty God that gave it and my body I recommend to the earth to be buried in a decent Christian burial . . . nothing doubting but—at the general resurrection—I shall receive the same again by the mighty power of God.

Stephen then bequeathed his dwelling house, shed, one half of the barn, ten acres of land around them, and a three-acre woodlot to his wife, Irene; thirty acres of land to Uriah Smith; thirty acres to Elias; and twenty-seven acres to Richard Ransom Smith. In 1806, when Stephen died, the assessors of his estate determined that his one hundred acres of land and buildings were worth $1,000 and his chattels $323.26.[12] This was a respectable though not large estate that he had preserved and enhanced from the time he and his family came to Woodstock; its distribution, however, into economically nonviable thirty-acre parcels among his sons once more reveals the demographic pressures that would drive many Vermonters and other New Englanders to the growing industrial towns or the fertile lands of the Midwest. For example, Elias's uncle, Elisha Ransom, following the classic pattern of the Yankee diaspora, went to Indiana in 1818 and settled in a spot "so near like the old home in Vermont that they were content and made it their home, clearing the forest as he had done in Vermont."[13]

Smith remembered that in the spring of 1783, "as soon as the snow was gone so that we could work upon the land, we began to clear off the timber, and make ready for planting and sowing. The first piece we cleared, my father fixed upon as a burying place. This he told us of in his last sickness, and when he died he was buried in the same ground he and I cleared first on his farm" (38). As for Elias Smith, in 1811 he sold for $270 his portion of the land they had worked so hard to clear, and in which Stephen now rested,[14] thus ending his economic connection to the agricultural world of the New England hinterland in favor of the urban port towns where he would henceforth live to the end of his days as editor, preacher, and herbal physician. His brothers, Uriah and Richard, made similar choices, the former becoming active in the Christian Church, then a Universalist minister in Woodstock; the latter first became a Baptist minister in New Hampshire, then a goldsmith in Woodstock, and finally a physician in Boston dispensing a cancer cure that he had acquired from a Canadian (Dana 1980, 385–86, 404, 132).

In a general way the careers of these Smiths and Ransoms resemble those of others who came to be affiliated with the Christian Connection and kindred sects such as the Free-Will Baptists and Universalists. They all belonged to a common stratum of the population, sharing a common culture, political attitudes, and life experiences; they had frequent personal contact via revivals, associational meetings, and itinerancy, which bound them into overlapping social networks of like-minded evangelicals through which information and opinion were circulated and discussed and for which Elias Smith's *Herald of Gospel Liberty* would come to serve as literary vehicle. The careers of several other men who will appear again in this story will illustrate the social type that Smith represents.

Abner Jones was Elias Smith's closest colleague in the early days of the Christian movement. He was born in 1772 of Baptist parentage in Royalston, Massachusetts; his father, "wishing to enlarge his borders," removed from there in 1790 to Bridgewater, Vermont, near Woodstock, and in consequence exposed the family to the same frontier hardships described by Elias Smith and Daniel Ransom.[15] Like Elias, the young Abner Jones fell under the powerful influence of Elisha Ransom, who baptized him in 1793 and thus set Jones on his own path toward the ministry (Jones 1842, 23). Like many of Smith's other friends, Abner parted company with him over the doctrine of universal salvation. Later Jones enhanced the income derived from his religious activities by dispensing a mysterious cancer cure, and he also became involved with the Masons, which he left when that organization came under suspicion of being an elitist conspiracy.

Much the same pattern was true of Smith's erstwhile spiritual brother, Thomas Baldwin, who was influential in Elias's early career, only to be rejected in a sharp conflict when Smith left the Baptists to help found the Christian movement. Baldwin was born in 1753 in Bozrah, Connecticut (by one account, out of wedlock). In 1769 his family emigrated to Canaan, New Hampshire, due east of the Connecticut River from Woodstock—a place that "was rapidly peopled by emigrants from Connecticut and Massachusetts." He too was a creature of the New England hinterland and of the diaspora from older areas that settled it. Baldwin lost a son and, not having thought much about religion until then, was soon exposed to the preaching of itinerant Baptists, who drew his thoughts toward Christ. He was reborn in the Holy Spirit and baptized in Canaan by the ubiquitous Elisha Ransom.[16] In 1783 he was described by a local resident as "a Baptist Elder . . . who Caries Conviction in all that Hear him that he is a [Saint] of God and hath a Great Gift in Doctrine Hardly his Eaquil To be found" (McLoughlin 1971, 2:859). After a period of preaching in New Hampshire, Baldwin was settled in the Second Baptist Church of Boston and there spent the rest of his days; more than any other man, he was responsible for drawing Elias Smith into the Baptist ministry (Chessman 1826; see Goen 1962, 252). In 1785 Baldwin came from Boston to Woodstock, where Elias heard his preaching. "I was exceedingly charmed with the man," Smith remembered. "He was then about thirty years old; was a well built man, plainly dressed; and I believe felt the glory of God's grace in his heart. The last named now lives in Boston, and is styled Rev. Thomas Baldwin, D.D. and wears a dress something like that worn by the ancient *pagan priests,* called a surplice. He was then called Elder Baldwin" (1816, 84).[17]

Mark Fernald, an influential early Christian evangelist and preacher, had a similar background, though not one rooted in the agricultural frontier. Fernald was born in 1784 in Kittery, Maine, across the Piscataqua River from Portsmouth, New Hampshire; his father was a carpenter and joiner from whom Mark learned this craft, which he practiced when he was not a sailor in the coastal trade. His early religion had been a lukewarm Congregationalism; however, grim events at sea and a life-threatening illness, abetted by evangelical Free-Will Baptist preaching, turned Fernald toward Christ. In 1807 he was "baptized in the Atlantic Ocean. Thanks to God that ocean was my baptismal fount instead of my grave, as it had often threatened." Shortly thereafter he was exposed to the Christian message of Elias Smith in Portsmouth, with whom he traveled on itinerant labors, just as a younger Smith had earlier traveled with the Baptists in Vermont. In 1809 Fernald was ordained a Christian preacher and worked out of Kittery in that capacity thereafter (Fernald 1852).

Dr. Samuel Thomson, from whom Elias Smith acquired his herbal medical practice, is a final case in point. Thomson, whose antielitist populism equaled Smith's own, was born in the same year, 1769, in Alstead, New Hampshire, east of the Connecticut near Bellows Falls, Vermont. His family history matches that of Smith, Jones, and Baldwin. Thomson's father was a recent immigrant from Massachusetts in search of opportunity; as Thomson recalled, "the country was a wilderness when I was born. My parents were poor, having nothing to begin the world with; but had to depend upon labor for support. My father had bought a piece of land on credit, and had to pay for it by his labor . . . which caused us great hardships and deprivations for a long time." Thomson's parents were Baptists, and Samuel remembered

48

Plate 2. Samuel Thomson (1769–1843): Universalist and creator of popular system of herbal medical practice adopted by Elias Smith in later life. Courtesy American Antiquarian Society; reprinted from Samuel Thomson, *A Narrative of the Life and Medical Discoveries of Samuel Thomson* (Boston: E. G. House, 1822).

his father as having been brutally strict until humanized by the doctrine of universal salvation. Meanwhile, the son developed an understandable distaste for farming and, through the influence of local "root doctors," an interest in herbal remedies that would lead him and his followers to a practice that, in the name of the people, would for a time successfully challenge the orthodox medical profession and its claim to superior knowledge and legal authority (Thomson 1835).

Moving beyond these specific individuals, we can see a general social and cultural portrait of the society from which such men came. One obvious association is with newly settled rural areas of the New England hinterland and with the artisans and laborers of the port towns. For example, Windsor County, Vermont (of which Woodstock is the shire town), consistently voted Republican after the emergence

of that party and was also "the heartland of the New Lights, of popular
non-Calvinist dissent, and of Vermont's revolution"; likewise, Elias
Smith's preaching in Portsmouth, New Hampshire, attracted an urban
clientele involved, like Mark Fernald, in a variety of maritime trades
(Roth 1987, 76). Many early Christians, Free-Will Baptists, and Universalists either were country people themselves or of back-country origins, with a Baptist or New Light Congregationalist heritage. They often came from areas in which religious establishment was weak and
institutions in general fluid, and in which class hierarchy, as compared
with the older areas of New England, was as yet poorly developed and
social relations more egalitarian. What emerges from historical schol-
arship on the region is a modified Turnerite frontier thesis about the
democratic and ultimately individualistic nature of local society, one in
part substantiated by what the early Christian Church was about and
who its founders were.

Historians have posited a correlation between radical sectarianism
and the hill country of New England, brought about by "a fragmentation of binding social and intellectual habits and the emergence of
hybrid forms of culture congruent with the new realities of the hill
country. The result might be termed Antifederalist culture, reflecting
the localist, egalitarian, and tribal world view of the settlers and their
institutions" (Marini 1982, 31, 39).[18] The presumed result was a "gospel
of the backcountry" that "challenged the right of a natural elite to
speak for the people and empowered those who could claim no real
stake in the promise of America" (Hatch 1989, 34). The upper Connecticut Valley was socially and religiously pluralistic, out of which
emerged a complex unstable syncretism out of revolutionary ideology,
evangelical religion, and a social experience shaped by familial values,
relative openness of opportunity, and absence of formal institutions.[19]

There are, to be sure, rough correlations between class, circumstance, religion, and political opinion, but they are not in any strict
sense predictive. It is easier to say who the Christians and other evangelical sectarians were not than who they were. (They were *not* Federalists, former Anglicans, Old Light Congregationalists, merchant oligarchs, or small-town gentry.) Given the relative paucity of the data,
one must largely generalize by inference and exclusion—by judging the

Christians according to what they supported and who they opposed, and conversely by who opposed them and why.

It is clear enough that the world in which Elias Smith grew up was not one in which hierarchy and deference could take root or acquire any significant degree of cultural legitimacy. Elias Smith was no doubt a typical Baptist Vermonter in his attitudes toward the down-country ecclesiastical elite and, by extension, their gentrified employers. He once commented that such a clergyman "was almost as great an abomination to a baptist minister, as a shepherd was to the Egyptians in the days of Jacob." While traveling in New Hampshire during his early flirtations with the ministry, Smith encountered a couple of clergymen. Smith "concluded that they must be very plenty in that part of the country, if they were not useful. Living in Vermont, a climate not suited to their *constitution,* I had never seen but a few of them" (66). In 1787 Elias stopped to witness a Congregational service in Springfield, Massachusetts, on his way back to Lyme for a visit. He remembered how the meetinghouse "was adorned beyond what I had ever seen in the log meeting-houses in Vermont," and of how sharply the "costly array" of the other young men in the congregation contrasted with his own. He also remarked on the preacher's extravagant wig and of how, being of a serious and inquiring cast of mind, he supposed "much divinity and good matter was contained in the head the wig contained." But, Elias continued, "when he read his psalm, it was in a cold, dull, lifeless manner. When he prayed, his prayer was as long as a Pharisee's prayer. . . . As I understood him, a good citizen was as good a christian as he knew" (92–93).[20]

Yet, underneath Elias's hostility toward the college-educated settled ministry was a good deal of ambivalent respect for higher learning itself. Though Smith was by some lights anti-intellectual, he was not at all against education (reading was the great joy of his youth) but rather against claims to deference made on its basis. These antiestablishment attitudes were not peculiar to the hinterland; they had roots in a general evangelical opposition to conservative orthodoxy wherever the two confronted one another, and perhaps went deeper still into the class structures and social relations of the older seaboard communities and perhaps into old England itself. So far as the hinterland is concerned, it appears that the sectarians were in fact quite typical members of the local population in general, thus ruling out any clear-cut sociological explanation of what differentiated them from their less radical brethren.[21] Other explanations are called for, such as ties of family, places of origin, personal history, influential preachers, and wider cultural trends. Elias Smith's own trajectory points back to the religious history of Lyme.

Edwin Gaustad's *Great Awakening in New England* (1965, 42–60) points out that the awakening of the 1740s transcended regional and class boundaries and had profound impact in the towns as well as the rural areas. Undoubtedly its meaning differed according to social stratum, but in one way or another the great revival interpenetrated them all. Lyme, which by the 1740s already had a long history, was deeply affected by the awakening.

By 1769 dissent was already well established in Lyme. A Baptist church is reported as having been formed there in 1743, while in 1744 Baptists in neighboring Saybrook were persecuted for holding meetings independently of the legally established Congregational Church (Denison 1900, 8). There were Baptist sympathies in Lyme as early as 1726, when Valentine Wightman, since 1705 the pastor of the Groton Baptist Church—the first in Connecticut—debated a local Congregationalist on the question of whether the ministry should be supported by compulsory taxation (McLoughlin 1971, 1:266).[22] Lyme experienced the throes of the Great Awakening in the early 1740s under the impact of extravagant preachers such as James Davenport of Long Island, who produced ecclesiastical chaos throughout the coastal region by exhorting his listeners to withdraw from unregenerate churches and unspiritual pastors. Jonathan Parsons, a student of Jonathan Edwards and prominent New Light, fell prey to the "enthusiasm" of the awakening and in consequence was dismissed from his Lyme church in 1745 "for zealous itinerant preaching" (Goen 1962, 78; McLoughlin 1971, 1:364). Isaac Backus, recently reborn as a New Light Separate and later to become a Baptist, participated in a Lyme revival in 1747 (McLoughlin 1967, 32).[23]

In the wake of these events the churches of Lyme, like those of many other towns, underwent schisms that gave rise to a partition of believers between Old Lights, New Lights, and Baptists. Radical New Light separatists refused to commune with those of their former colleagues who found the revival emotionally repugnant, spiritually pretentious, and politically seditious. Some of these radicals, among them Ebenezer Mack of East Lyme, formed Separate churches of their own that in due course became Baptist (i.e., reserving the baptismal sacrament for adults who had experienced and demonstrated spiritual rebirth). Mack himself fell out with other members of his church over the issue of whether they should have open communion with those who had not been properly baptized (Backus 1871; Graves 1952, 4).[24] Others did not go so far, among these Daniel Miner, a distant cousin of Elias Smith, who helped organize a Separate church that declined to follow the logic of the revival all the way to exclusivist adult baptism.[25] The formation of these religious groupings provided new bases for community organization; reborn congregations would move virtually in a body to recently opened towns in New Hampshire, Vermont, and western Connecticut—as Ebenezer Mack and many in his church did to Marlow, New Hampshire, only a few miles from Alstead, where Samuel Thomson grew up. It was therefore not only kinsmen and fellow townsmen who provided the basis for the group migrations characteristic of the New England diaspora: religious persuasion was now also a factor, which in turn has much to do with the nascent New Light political culture of the upper Connecticut River Valley (Goen 1962, 252).

The effects of this evangelical perfectionism on the orthodox establishment could be devastating, as in the case of the Second Congregational Church of Lyme (East Lyme parish) under the pastorate of the Reverend George Griswold, member of a prominent local family, and a graduate of Yale who at first supported the revivals, only to find his church disintegrating in consequence of evangelical defections. An unknown but obviously Tory hand remembered this time.

> There were causes in operation, even before the revival ceased, calculated to produce evils in the church. There, as in several churches in this region, many began to grow weary of the order customarily observed in congregational assemblies, and "heaped to themselves

teachers having itching ears"; or, as was the case in some instances *aspired to become teachers themselves.* These all ultimately left the church, and either became Ana-Baptists, as they were called, or Separates. The consequences, in respect to this church, were diminished strength, discouragement, and at length desolation. Mr. Griswold continued to labor until his death in 1761, and was loved and respected by the few, who remained attached to the regular dispensations of the Gospel. The church had, however long before this, begun its journey into the wilderness.[26]

Some of the defectors went over to Mack's church, while others, among them most of the Ransom family, went over to Daniel Miner's, where we again pick up Elias Smith's own story, including his first (albeit involuntary) involvement in the controversies over infant baptism, which were to engage much of his early ministerial career. Stephen Smith and Elisha Ransom were Baptists; the rest of the Ransoms were New Light Separates, who retained the traditional Congregational allegiance to "pedobaptism," or the baptism of infants as a sign of their provisional incorporation into a covenanted community of church-goers. Separates defended this practice by appealing to the analogy of Abraham's circumcision of the infant Isaac. The so-called Anabaptists were, in a more neutral terminology, actually antipedobaptists. (The term *anabaptist,* when used by conservatives who recalled the excesses of the German Reformation, had much the same connotation as *democrat*—which is to say, "anarchistical enthusiast").[27] The families differed on this score, and Irene found herself caught in the middle between Stephen Smith and an elder brother Elisha Ransom, on one side, and her eldest brother, Richard, on the other, over what should be done with Elias. With the gift of hindsight, Elias remembered the controversy over his baptism as one of the decisive moments of his childhood.

Elias's father somewhat surprisingly agreed to let his son be sprinkled, and so Elias was taken off to the service. Upon finding what was actually in store for him, the eight-year-old Smith ran from the church and only by force underwent the sacrament.

> Notwithstanding all my exertions, I was brought in front of the bason, and was so confined, hands and feet, that I was obliged to receive what they called the seal of the covenant. I felt such malice

against the minister and my uncle, that had my strength been equal to my desire, we should all have been like Sampson and the Phillistines, with the house about our heads. My mother was greatly mortified at my stuborn[n]ess, and I at that which caused it. I wiped off what they called the seal, in such a manner as convinced all the spectators that the compelled was greatly enraged. This account of sprinkling a child by force, has a very different appearance from that recorded in the New Testament, where we read that believers in Christ voluntarily submitted to him, when buried with him in baptism, and raised to walk in the newness of life. Many children have shewn the same opposition to this invention of men which is soon to perish in the using. (26–27)

The sprinkler was Daniel Miner, who in the course of time was forgiven for the atrocity perpetrated on Smith in his youth. On his trip back to Lyme in 1787 Smith now found Miner, though misguided in the matter of baptism, always to have been a true Christian. On the same trip he also heard Ebenezer Mack's successor, Jason Lee, preach "in the spirit, and with power"; he reminded Smith of "the old disciple with whom some of the apostles once were to lodge" (101–3, 229).[28] Lee is remembered as having restored the health of the church after the factional dispute that led to the departure of Mack and his party over the issue of open versus closed communion (Mack favored the latter); under Lee's ministry the Baptists increased in numbers and influence, while Griswold's local Congregational church "grew weaker and weaker, until, it is said, there were but two aged women left members" (Graves 1952, 8). From such men as Lee and Miner, Elias Smith himself learned the art of preaching.

Shortly before the departure of his family for Woodstock, Smith had occasion to hear another Baptist who was to influence his life— William Grow of Pomfret, Connecticut, a powerful preacher with "a melodious and commanding voice" who on two occasions had the misfortune to run afoul of his own congregations over questions of money and women. At his ordination Grow had been given the right hand of fellowship by no less a figure than Isaac Backus, who, more than any other man, led in the fight for Baptist liberty in New England. Backus remembered Grow's ordination thus: "He gave such a clear and distinct account of his conversion, his call to preach, and call to take the charge of that people, that I could not but say, *the thing proceedeth from the Lord*" (1979, 2:960).[29] In happier times Grow's fame spread to Lyme, and the twelve-year-old Elias Smith went out of his way to hear him preach a sermon entitled "The Glory of Christ, as the Judge of the World." As Smith recalled, "The solemnity which these things brought on my mind remained long; and were never wholly worn off, until I found peace in believing" (31). Following a dispute in Pomfret precipitated by his fathering a child by a young woman of his congregation ("terrible!" exclaimed Backus in his journal), Grow moved north to Bridgewater, Vermont—Abner Jones's town—to take over a pastorate first occupied by Elisha Ransom (Dana 1980, 374).

In 1789, at age nineteen, Elias was baptized by Grow in the Queechee River, which runs through Woodstock to the Connecticut. As Smith remembered, Elder Grow spoke on the occasion "and then led me into the river, and baptized me in the name of the *Father, Son* and *Holy Ghost;* after which we both came up out of the water, following the example of our blessed Lord." Smith was declared a member of the Second Baptist Church in Woodstock (later to be called the United Baptist Society of Woodstock and Bridgewater) but later had occasion to question the Calvinist principles to which he then assented without proper understanding (30, 114–15). As for Grow, he had no better luck with his Vermont church than he had in Connecticut. The Woodstock town historian reported that "great trouble and disaster fell upon the church in the midst of . . . prosperity, owing to the imprudence of their pastor, Elder William Grow. He was accused of immoral conduct before the church; and at length, after much contention and bitter strife, a council was agreed upon, by which, after protracted hearing, he was deposed" (Dana 1980, 378). Though Smith himself, as far as is known, was spared direct accusations of sexual impropriety within his own churches, he did—as was so commonly the case in New England—become involved in contention with them over money and doctrine; such conflicts were often enough expressive of a pervasive and enduring local political factionalism coming into focus through disputes over the pastor's fitness.[30] Like Grow, Elias Smith would find evil reports dogging his footsteps.

Evangelicals such as Grow, Ransom, and Smith were linked by complex ties of faith, community, family, and place of origin. William

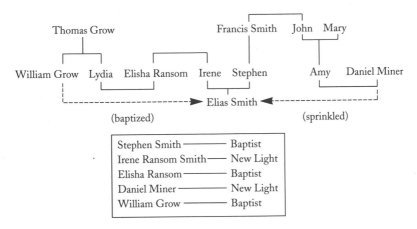

Fig. 5. Ecclesiastical connections

Grow's sister married Elisha Ransom; the Smiths and Miners were also related. All of Elias Smith's immediate family followed a course similar to his own toward the Christian Connection or beyond it to universal salvationism. One of his sons became a Universalist pastor; another who began as a Universalist ended as a defector to an ultra-orthodox Congregationalism. (See Fig. 5.)

Such regionally based familial networks provided the scaffolding for democratic sectarian movements conjoining the perfectionism of the reborn with apocalyptic hopes sparked by the Revolution.[31] This ideological transformation was possible because of the widely shared American understanding that God's hand was on the tiller of history and that if prophecy were rightly interpreted, it would be possible to determine where the ship was headed and when it would arrive. The problem was to situate the Revolution and the nation it created in this apocalyptic scheme, a hermeneutical exercise that turned out to have an intimate association with emergent partisan convictions.

For Elias Smith, first came the basics. Out of the air he breathed, Elias assimilated the fundamentals of what it was to be a pietistic Baptist: a conviction of sin and estrangement from God; belief in the necessity for absolute surrender to Christ as mediator; an assurance of salvation gained through a passive indwelling of the Spirit; and finally, social recognition of salvation granted through credible public testimony to the experience of saving grace. Only after all this could there be baptism by immersion, in imitation of Christ's baptism in the Jordan, as sign of regeneration through him; only then could there be full acceptance into a reborn Baptist congregation, covenanted together to observe God's New Testament rule and to provide mutual watch and ward over one another as a visible community of the invisible church. For the future preacher there were added tests: whether the call was truly of God or of one's own vain imaginings; whether there was indeed an evident capacity to transmit his word and a readiness of others to receive it; whether fellow Baptist pastors would recognize the doctrine as sound and the vehicle through whom it was transmitted worthy of inclusion among them.

The course of humanity's fall and the hope for salvation were documented with exemplary Calvinistic rigor in one of the works that Smith recalled reading as a young man, Thomas Boston's *Human Nature in Its Fourfold State* (1796)—by which Boston meant the primeval state of innocence, the state of utter depravity after the fall, the state of grace brought to the elect through Christ's atonement, and the state of utter happiness or misery following the last judgment.[32] As the sin of Adam was imputed to all his descendants, so in this Augustinian view all humanity, with the exception of Christ, fell with him—"Adam, our common father, being corrupt, we are so too; for, *Who can bring a clean thing out of an unclean?*" As Christ was the only person born regenerate, so his righteousness is imputed to all those whom God has elected from all eternity to be reborn and saved through him. Who the elect actually are, however, is always a matter for doubt, since only God himself knows for sure; "so we preach *Christ* to all, and shoot the arrow at a venture, which God himself directs as he sees meet." Even though all are enjoined to repent and seek God, a person alone is entirely incapable of finding him: "Hearken then, O unregenerate man, and be convinced, that as thou art in a most miserable state by nature; so thou art utterly unable to recover thyself, any manner of way. Thou art ruined" (Boston 1796, 91, 141, 133). In later life Elias Smith would reject this view, and with it all the works of "that dark African priest," St. Augustine. He likewise found unscriptural and renounced the doctrine of Christ's imputed righteousness (1812a, 222).

As Smith said of his own quest, "Self was not the subject, but God, Christ, and the things revealed by the spirit" (59). In saying so, he walked in the footsteps of those generations of Puritans who, like Thomas Boston, had already worked out in considerable detail what Edmund Morgan has called "the morphology of conversion" into God's true church and thus provided a model for the experience of those who followed them and for a literary art-form—the spiritual autobiography—based on it.[33] The process of conversion begins with a conviction of sin and personal unworthiness, which in itself may be a provisional sign of election (while complacency about one's spiritual state surely is not). As for the elect, "When the Lord is about to change their nature, he makes the sin of their nature lie heavily on their spirits. When he minds to let out the corruption, the lance gets full depth in their souls, reaching to the root of sin." Hence the classic anguish of the Puritan pietist—the certainty of damnation and sense of utter helplessness in the face of one's own irremediable evil and righteous condemnation. Yet for the truly elect this is but the darkness before the dawn; unlooked for while in the depths of despair, God may miraculously transform one's entire being in a blinding stroke. "Well may we say, when we see a man thus changed. *This is the finger of God!*"[34]

Thomas Boston, and like him Jonathan Edwards, expressed a view that was, by the time Elias Smith embarked on his own spiritual pilgrimage, a New Light and evangelical Baptist orthodoxy; each step in the morphology of conversion came to correspond to clearly marked denouements in the stereotypical spiritual autobiography, as in the classic scenario of Smith's *Life, Conversion, Preaching, Travels, and Sufferings*. Spurred by the untimely death of two young women in Woodstock from "canker rash," Smith was led to solitary reflection in the forest and there came to a conviction of his own utter depravity. "Every wrong ever committed, whether in thought, word, or deed, appeared before me, and things which before appeared small, now rose like mountains between me and my Creator. It appeared to me that I was a criminal brought to the bar, and proved guilty, and deserving death, without one plea in his own behalf." The stain on Smith's soul colored his perception of the world at large. "The day appeared dark, and every thing seemed to mourn around me." Still in despair, and once more in the snowy Vermont forest, he unexpectedly had his moment of transfiguring grace.

> Not long after those things passed through my mind, I went into the woods one morning after a stack of timber; after taking it on my shoulder to bring it to the house, as I walked along on a large log that lay above the snow, my foot slipped and I fell partly under the log, the timber fell one end on the log and the other on the snow, and held me, so that I found it difficult at first to rise from the situation I was then in. While in this situation, a light appeared to shine from heaven, not only into my head, but into my heart. This was something very strange to me, and what I had never experienced before. My mind seemed to rise in that light to the throne of God and the Lamb, and while thus gloriously led, what appeared to my understanding was expressed in Rev. xiv 1. "And I looked, and, lo, a Lamb stood on the mount Sion, and with him an hundred forty and four thousand, having his Father's name written in their foreheads." The Lamb once slain appeared to my understanding, and while viewing him, I felt such love to him as I never felt to any thing earthly. The view of the Lamb on mount Sion gave me joy unspeakable and full of glory. (53–54)

As his soul was transfigured, so darkness became light. "Looking around me, every object was changed, and a bright glory appeared on every thing. All things praised God with me." Though he would veer to and fro from hope to doubt, the experience Elias Smith had on that day changed the course of his life. Looking back on the event from the perspective of 1816, when he published the first edition of his *Life*, Smith saw the epiphany of 1785—when he was but sixteen years old—in terms of his later anti-Calvinist free-will theology, wherein "God is ready to save them that believe" (62).

These New Englanders encountered, just as their Puritan forefathers had, the implications for public order of a faith that stressed private and even visionary experience, and they reaped in full measure a concomitant harvest of new reformations and heresies. Just as the orthodox Congregationalists found many Baptists the embodiment of antinomian anarchy, the Baptists themselves would find sectarians and cultists further to their left who would also have to be rejected or disavowed. Elias Smith himself proved to be one such. Later, with the emergence of the "Christians" as an organized movement, they too would find him moving toward the fringe of acceptable doctrine and then beyond it to Universalism.

Smith's own particular education guided him toward a fascination with grammar and words, particularly the language of the Bible, and hence with the doctrine the words expressed. He made a practice of recording what he read and the effect it had on him. This habit, in addition to what is known of the contribution of individuals such as William Grow, Elisha Ransom, and Thomas Baldwin, and of the evangelical New Light culture that they shared, make it possible to follow the development of Smith's thought as it matured toward a fusion of religion and republicanism and a comprehensive providential interpretation of American historical experience. The New Testament was the foundation for it all, supplemented by works that Smith recalled as being especially influential on his intellectual development such as Thomas Dilworth's *New Guide to the English Language,* Isaac Watts's *Improvement of the Mind,* John Frederick Osterwald's *Compendium of Christian Theology,* Boston's *Fourfold State,* and Jonathan Edwards's *History of the Works of Redemption.*

By the decisive year of 1785 Elias was attending a school in Woodstock taught by his uncle Elisha, who, learning that he had been taught in "the Connecticut fashion," determined that now Smith must learn grammar. Here Elisha Ransom and Stephen Smith locked horns over the utility of such an academic subject, the latter believing arithmetic to be more useful. Irene took her brother's side on the issue, and worn down by this determined opposition and the entreaties of his tearful son, Stephen, as seems to have been his habit, finally gave in. Elisha victoriously declared that "you now consent to that which will be worth more to your child than all your farm"—prophetic words in their own right, which Elias remembered with gratitude: "I am to this day more indebted to him for knowledge of letters than all other men on earth" (46).

The grammar in question was Dilworth's *New Guide*, which remained the standard American text until supplanted by the works of Noah Webster. Smith proceeded to commit to memory, reading it and other books sprawled before an open fire to the extent of damaging his vision (45–46; Ellis 1979, 176–77). To give such matters less than full attention was, as Dilworth asserted, to do less than one's duty; it was willfully to abdicate, through ignorance of language, the fundamental responsibility of the Protestant Christian to read and understand the Bible for oneself.[35] Like most of the works that Smith mentions, Dilworth's was an eminently pious treatise; it led stage by stage in a question-and-answer format to an understanding of word structure and grammar via increasingly complex stories and verses, each containing its inevitable homily.

In Dilworth's view, the true meaning of words must be carefully sought out and examined so that they might be correctly conjoined into propositions and correctly understood when heard or read. Such was God's intent in transmitting his revelation to human beings, and such the preacher's function in explaining it. Smith came to view it as human presumption to take the plain divine word at anything other than face value, which led him into an extreme form of theological literalism as well as to total rejection of the central Calvinist doctrines of predestination and election. As Dilworth said of words, they "are given us by the alwise God, as a means by which not only one man may make his thought known to another, but that we thereby may also arrive to the knowledge of the will of him our *Creator*, revealed in the sacred oracles of his divine word" (1789, ii).

When Smith first learned of the existence and function of the dictionary, it came to him as an almost miraculous revelation.[36] Then, heeding advice found in Isaac Watts's *Improvement of the Mind*, he began the practice of carrying a dictionary with him wherever he went and immediately looking up the meaning of any unfamiliar word encountered in a sermon (he particularly recalled what a help Watts was with respect to improving his memory) (76, 84). Watts, an English dissenter, hymnodist, and philosophical disciple of John Locke who stressed the virtues of observational knowledge, also pointed out that "scripture is the best interpreter of scripture" and advised his readers to "not content yourself with mere words and names, lest your laboured improvements only amass a heap of unintelligible phrases, and you feed upon husks rather than kernals. The greatest and most common danger is in the sacred science of theology, where settled terms and phrases have been pronounced divine and orthodox, which yet have had no meaning in them" (Watts 1821, 70, 114–15).[37]

That point was reinforced once more by the work that Smith drew on more than any other for general theological background: Osterwald's *Compendium of Christian Theology*. According to Smith, "This book I read for several years, until I committed every chapter to memory. This was the beginning of my studying *divinity*" (110). Osterwald, a moderate Swiss Calvinist, recommended recourse to the Scriptures on all debatable points and the acceptance of certain things, such as why God chose to save only a predestined elect, as mysteries beyond human comprehension ("to leave to God the things that are hidden, and to acquiesce in what he hath revealed"), thus leaving aside abstruse theological concerns for the practical work of personal redemption through Christ. Osterwald, like Watts, also concluded that "the best exposition of scripture, is by scripture, and the Holy Spirit is the best interpreted of itself," and that "the right of interpreting Scripture, belongs to every one who has a right to read it, i.e. every one of the faithful" (1788, 163, 79, 81). Smith kept Osterwald with him as a constant companion, until he came to reject all systematic divinity in favor of the word of the New Testament alone.

Uncle Elisha, quoting Paul, also stressed the importance of determining the meaning and intent of biblical language, telling Elias: "Let no man deceive you with vain words" (Eph. 5:6). Smith elevated this aphorism into a principle of scriptural interpretation: "Remembering what my uncle said, that there were many words used, not in the scriptures, I have taken particular notice of the words used to describe doctrines, which are not in the bible, and have endeavored to point them out in speaking and writing, which has greatly enraged many who consent not to wholesome words, even the words of our Lord Jesus Christ" (235).

Thus were planted the seeds of Smith's most seditious work, the *New Testament Dictionary*, based on a radical attack on "sectarian"

Calvinist theology via a literalist interpretation of New Testament language. As Elias put it later, "However much the meaning of a word may be varied, it is certain that the original meaning of the word is the true meaning" (235), and so he went back to the beginning to discern the intent of those who uttered them. Elias's efforts were not unlike those of Noah Webster, who also sought to purify the American language, making it a fit vehicle for the thoughts of a democratic people; but whereas Webster became a self-consciously reactionary old Federalist (Ellis 1979, 161–212), Smith maintained his faith in the people and in the power of plain language to peel away the encrustations of human tradition from the pure gospel of Christ. "Searching the Scriptures to find the original meaning of particular words, led me to see that many scriptural words were used among men to convey very different ideas from those communicated in the same words by the Prophets and Apostles of Jesus Christ. I am certain that if all Christians understood the scriptures alike, they would be united, and the only way to understand them, is to know the meaning of the words used there to describe those things which the Spirit led the Apostles and others to write" (1812a, 3, 7).

Smith was also drawn to prophecy and was aided in this area by the acquisition of a quotation Bible that allowed him to compare New Testament fulfillment of Old Testament predictions. Around 1790 he encountered Edwards's *History of the Works of Redemption,* which he read "with attention and pleasure" and henceforth carried with him along with Osterwald on his early itinerant labors (125, 127). The influence of Edwards's *History* is hard to gauge, as is his influence more generally. Smith does not much cite him and, after becoming a "Christian," no doubt found Edwards's Calvinism uncongenial. But Smith shared his view that a direct encounter with the Holy Spirit totally transforms one's world and is the only reasonably sure sign of redemption, that the course of history is an expression of God's redemptive plan, and that "a remarkable outpouring of his Spirit" in the form of revivals of religion has accompanied "every remarkable new establishment of the state of his visible church" (1968, 114).[38] In this last regard Edwards was thinking of what came to be known as the Great Awakening, the beginnings of which were evident at the time he wrote what became the *Works of Redemption* as discourses for his revived congregation in Northampton. Smith in turn reached his maturity in the time of the so-called Second Great Awakening, namely, the revivals accompanying the turn of the eighteenth century, and what was to him the by no means coincidental victory of the Democratic-Republicans under Jefferson.

According to Edwards, "Where scripture history fails, there prophecy takes place; so that the account is still carried on, and the chain is not broken, till we come to the very last link of it in the consummation of all things" (1968, 97).[39] Elias Smith habitually attempted to fit the political events of his day into a prophetic framework. Such was a long-standing New England tradition, particularly in times of crisis. When, in the quieter times of 1739, Edwards wrote concerning the meaning of the passages in Revelation that describe angels pouring out seven vials of wrath preparatory to the destruction of Babylon and Christ's second coming, he was unsure as to the relation of the prophecy to secular history. He was reasonably certain that the pouring of the fifth vial "upon the seat of the beast" (16:10) meant the onset of the Reformation and the beginning of the fall of the Roman antichrist, but he saw little to suggest that the pouring of the sixth vial "upon the great river Euphrates; that the way of the kings of the east might be prepared" (16:12) had as yet occurred. On the meaning of this hermetic passage Edwards would only say, "It seems to be something *immediately preparatory* to the destruction of spiritual Babylon" (1968, 214, 237).

During the Revolutionary War, England itself supplanted Rome in the role of Antichrist, and thereafter it retained this role for many. But for the more conservative it was supplanted by revolutionary atheist France and its American supporters, while England itself paradoxically moved into the role of defender of Christ's kingdom (Bloch 1985, 77).[40] By 1805, in another time of war and domestic political agitation, Smith was convinced that the destruction of Babylon was imminent and that Thomas Jefferson could well be the sixth angel of the prophecy. As the Anglo-French conflict deepened and brought with it an increasing threat of American involvement, the end seemed still nearer: "When Jesus Christ spake of his coming, he told his disciples of the signs of his coming, by which all might know when the time was near. What people ever saw such a day as we see in this year, 1808?" (1808a, 85–86).[41] By now Antichrist and the Federalists had become one in his eyes, whereas in theirs he became one with dark satanic France and its Democratic-Republican allies—a spirit of infidelity and anarchy set loose in the new land.

Such was the world into which Elias Smith was born: a world of convictions deeply rooted in the English Reformation, framed by the propositions of Calvinist theology, and invigorated by the Great Awakening. It was a dynamic society grappling with new circumstances through adaptations of old religious and political ideas. What from one point of view could be seen as a continuation of the Puritan revolution on American soil via the awakening, the formation of new sectarian groups, and a broadening of the concept of religious liberty could from another be regarded as the inevitable birth of a plural society brought about by rapid demographic and economic change accompanied by incipient class formation and the progressive collapse of old Calvinist certitudes and sense of limits.

Nevertheless, even within this changed world, every event—from visitations of the northern lights to earthquakes, revolutionary war, revivals of religion, and the current election—still contained a transcendental lesson for those attuned to hear it. It was still a world of wonder. When just a boy, Smith was terrified by an aurora because those around him, young and old alike, thought it was a sign of the apocalypse. This experience later gave him occasion to reflect on the true light of the world. Smith wrote, "Light has come into the world, and men, young and old are condemned, because they love darkness rather than light." Nor, he significantly added, "are the nations left in the dark as many suppose" (23). For him, political salvation and personal salvation were becoming aspects of one and the same providential design— "For God sent not his Son into the world to condemn the world; but that the world through him might be saved" (John 3:17).

2
THE FIRE NEXT TIME
Religion and Republicanism

Behold, this dreamer cometh.
GENESIS 37:19

LIKE THE CHANCE CIRCUMSTANCES that brought Elias Smith and John Snelling Popkin together in 1792, another fateful irony brought Smith together with the Reverend Joseph Buckminster of the First Church in Portsmouth, New Hampshire, in the wake of a catastrophe that destroyed half the town. On the day after Christmas 1802, fire swept through the densely packed central section of Portsmouth, leaving many homeless in what should have been the most joyful time of the year. Joseph Buckminster, as was his duty, attempted to explain to his people what lesson could be drawn from this sad event, what salutary message this manifestation of God's displeasure had for Portsmouth. Knowing that "from the nature and perfections of God, it cannot be otherwise, than that he should be concerned in all the events that take place in the world," Buckminster looked about him to determine what circumstances in the life of the town could possibly be correlated with divine wrath. In *A Discourse Occasioned by the late Desolating Fire*, Buckminster found the answer to lie in a divisive party spirit and inroads of the pernicious doctrine of universal salvation. The party spirit to which he alluded was that between Federalists and Republicans, and in Buckminster's view had reached such a pitch:

> as to separate man from man; to burst relative and social ties; to generate hatred, envy, slander, backbiting, falsehood, confusion, and

every evil work: to prevent, in many instances, the common offices of neighborly kindness; and to influence and direct the course of municipal and civil affairs; to the neglect, if not to the injury, of the public good. God has kindled a fire of a different kind among us, in which, in the loudest accents, he proclaims his displeasure against us, and calls us to great searching of heart, for our intemperate divisions." (Buckminster 1803b, 24)

Buckminster had already expatiated on this theme in 1798 in the wake of that year's political excitement brought about by the quasi-war with France and the Alien and Sedition Acts of the Adams administration, seemingly targeted directly at Republican newspapers. Political turmoil was accompanied by a summer heat wave and crop damage from drought, all of which Buckminster associated with "those destructive demons, FACTION AND DISCORD"; happily, President John Adams had so far had been tempering God's disfavor by keeping these Francophile Republican demons at bay (Buckminster 1798). In 1802, with Jefferson in possession of the presidency, Buckminster had no such consolation.

Elias Smith, having settled in Portsmouth only a fortnight before the fire, found himself without a hall to preach in because of it; he had left the Baptists and now, speaking as a Christian—"without any sectarian name added"—had begun the work of assembling a congregation subscribing to the word of the New Testament alone. In the early part of 1803 he and his fellows, then only five in number, worked to draft articles for the constitution of their church on the model adopted the year before in the statement of faith and church-building of the Christian Convention in Sanbornton (Smith et al. 1802). As time went on, Smith's preaching in Portsmouth and surrounding towns resulted in increasing numbers leaving their former "anti-Christian" affiliations for his pure gospel order, which Smith hastened to associate with the purity of American republicanism. These defectors included members of Joseph Buckminster's First Church, and in the years to come its pastor would have occasion to reflect on what message God might have in allowing this new evangelical conflagration to spread from below within the body of the church itself.

From what, then, did it arise? The particular answer is that it arose from the Christian Connection and those who, under the influence of Smith's evangelical populism, adhered to that loosely organized body at the expense of Buckminster's church, the Calvinist Baptists, and other more established sects; the general answer is that it arose from a widespread revulsion against Calvinism in the years following the Revolution, and against formally constituted church bodies perceived as organized upon antidemocratic and anti-Christian hierarchical principles. An evolving folk republicanism and the exigencies of personal fate coalesced into a new and widespread democratic reformation known as the Second Great Awakening. In Smith's case the achievement of the requisite ideological synthesis amounted to a reorientation of his life that—for all his subsequent theological vacillations—proved to be enduring.

Following his encounter with Christ in the snowdrift, Elias Smith became convinced that he had been chosen for a special work, a revelation that came to him in a dream reminiscent of that had by the Old Testament patriarch Joseph, who had aroused the enmity of his brothers by dreaming he had been chosen above them (Gen. 37:6–19). Just so with Smith, who dreamed that an angel descended and granted him a vision of the fate of two young neighbor men who had recently shown such strong evidences of conversion that Elias was led to doubt the reality of his own. "You and they," the angel said, "are to be tried by fire, and those that endure the trial are right, and those who do not will not stand." The angel put two sticks into the ground and laid a pole across their tops. He then took three pieces of bark, which represented Smith and the other two young men, draped them one by one over the pole, and set a fire under them. The first and second burned through and fell to the ground. The third, though badly scorched, was saved from falling by the angel, who kept throwing water on it until the fire underneath went out. In his dream Elias wept copiously at the sight of this, and as he did so, the angel came to him, put his right hand on his shoulder and said, "Weep not at this, the Lord has appeared for you, and will preserve you, for he has a great work for you to do in the world" (Smith 1816). Smith awoke with his pillow wet from tears.[1]

It is a curious thing that Elias Smith saw fit to recount this vision in the first edition of his autobiography in 1816, when he was forty-seven years old, but not in the second of 1840, when he was seventy-one; though Smith changed the second edition in small ways to reflect the changing circumstances of his intervening life, he made no significant deletions, except this one large passage. Although we cannot say with certainty what this means psychologically, we do know that Smith saw a full measure of trouble and woe—scorched indeed, but not broken—in the years between the two editions of his *Life*. Perhaps from the perspective of 1840 he saw his interpretation of the angel's promise as overly sanguine or his bygone hopes as mere hubris.

In any event, during the period 1785–90 Elias was busily assimilating the heterogeneous stock of knowledge available to him out of the small local Woodstock fund of theology, geography, grammar, and the popular press—on which narrow base he began in his eighteenth year to teach school himself, "though I was almost as unfit for an instructor as those who came to be taught" (78, 75). Nonetheless, as he said, "when other young people were spending their time in amusements to no profit, mine was taken up in gaining something that might be useful in a future day. They called me a fool; this did not trouble me, as their opinion was only what was my own; and a fool appeared to me, such a disagreeable being, that it was my determination, if possible, to get rid of that which made me one, which was ignorance and folly" (79).

His drift away from the life of farm and woods was marked by his increasing teaching obligations and flirtation with the ministry. Elias taught in a classic rough-hewn school, the light for which was provided by windows covered with oiled sheets taken from *Spooner's Vermont Journal*, the only window on current local and national events that any of them then had (82). There was a family connection to that newspaper as well. Smith's maternal uncle Richard Ransom married the sister of Alden Spooner, the owner of the *Journal*—published in nearby Windsor—Vermont's first newspaper and an identifiable influence on Smith's own later journalistic career. Following the emergence of the party system, the *Journal* not surprisingly espoused Democratic-Republican sentiments. In 1783 the first issue of Spooner's *Journal* had the lead motto "From Realms far distant, and from Climes unknown,

We make the knowledge of Mankind your own." In 1808 Smith adopted this same motto for his own *Herald of Gospel Liberty,* changing only "knowledge of Mankind" to "Knowledge of our King" (Forbes 1905). Alden Spooner later became an agent for the sale of the *Herald* in the Windsor region, while Richard Ransom, Jr., took up the same chore in Woodstock.[2]

Following his first stint at schoolteaching in Woodstock, Elias went south on foot and whatever rides he could hitch back to Lyme, during which time he formed his unfavorable impression of the be-wigged orthodox clergyman in Springfield. Back in Connecticut he took up a school in East Hartford for some months and refined his theological skills in disputation with a local Episcopalian. When finished, he had enough money to buy cloth for the makings of a great-coat, which he hauled with him back to Woodstock. Soon thereafter he was baptized by William Grow in the Queechee. Even though convinced that he "was destitute of every qualification requisite for that great and glorious work," Smith was now groping for a sign that he was indeed called to be a minister of Christ (117). He sought out Baptist preachers and heard some whom he took to be unqualified for their office; of one such delivery he said that "a man of sense would have been ashamed to deliver such a discourse to a score of idiots in a *pig's pen!*" But Elias had not yet preached himself and did not know whether God would favor him with the spirit to do so. In this quandary he found it increasingly difficult to work at home and was repeatedly urged by friends to test out his preaching gifts. Much troubled, Elias determined to ask the advice of Grow in Bridgewater; "as he was considered a man of knowledge, and a great preacher, I concluded he could learn me to preach" (121). Smith was given some works on sermonizing and then went to unburden himself to Elisha Ransom, who gave encouragement and the decisive admonition to "let no man deceive you with vain words."

Elias recalled that at that doubt-ridden period, "sometimes I wished a bible had never been put into my hands; sometimes I felt a strong temptation to throw my bible away and drown myself, or starve in the woods." Around this time he made the fortunate acquaintance of a Baptist elder and tailor, John Peak, with whom he would have much to do in the period to follow: "Mr. Peak was low in the world, and in his own esteem, and the Lord looked to him then." Peak was "then an inquisitive man, desirous to learn"—before, as Smith added, Calvinism cooled his dedication to Jesus and his ardor in freely preaching the gospel (131, 195). John Peak invited Smith to go with him on a long journey to various Baptist meetings across the Green Mountains into the "waste howling wilderness" of western Vermont, and thence south to an association meeting in Adams, Massachusetts, in the Berkshires. On this trip they met many prominent Baptist elders who had gathered from as far afield as Kentucky. Smith and some of his companions then doubled back to a meeting in Vermont, and after a trip of three weeks he returned home to his school. Stimulated by his intercourse with all these preachers, and now twenty-one years old, Elias found that "the duty of speaking publicly, pressed harder on me than before." At last, in July 1790, he determined to yield and finally appointed a meeting in Woodstock at which he would preach.

His text was John 5:39: "Search the scriptures; for in them ye think ye have eternal life: and they are they which testify of me." In 1802, when mired in theological confusion over the merits of Calvinism and Universalism, he returned to these words once more and helped found the Christian movement in doing so. "Drop them both," a small voice would say, "and search the scriptures!" (142, 157). The other central element in the Christian platform emerged in 1792 in a sermon that Elias Smith gave before the First Baptist Church in Boston, shortly before his own ordination as a Baptist preacher and shortly after crossing over the Charles from Cambridge, where John Snelling Popkin had just delivered his commencement address at Harvard. This time the text was from Colossians 3:11: "But Christ is all, and in all," the same passage Smith used in the 1820s when constructing the diagram (see Fig. 1 in the Introduction) illustrating the one doctrine of Christianity about which all believers must agree—*Christ is all!*—which was a doctrine with the power to dissolve all sectarian differences into the ecumenical faith of the primitive Christian church. As Colossians states, "There is neither Greek nor Jew, circumcision nor uncircumcision, Barbarian, Scythian, bond nor free." Just as with the passage from Acts that tells us in the context of Peters Dream that the first followers of Jesus in Antioch were merely called "Christians," Elias selected a text for this important occasion that implied that the only legitimate form for the visible church of Christ is a pure democracy without distinction of class, race, or nationality. When Smith came to learn of Democratic-Republicanism, he extended that proposition into political life.

Smith successfully explicated John 5:39 in the point-wise fashion of a classic Puritan discourse, causing many hearers to wonder where this stripling formerly so shy of speech had acquired his knowledge and power. He was increasingly asked to preach, and with a growing local notoriety Smith again traveled with John Peak in Vermont and New Hampshire. Still in doubt of his calling, however, he resumed his schoolteaching once more and ceased speaking in public lest he judge himself a hypocrite and be so judged by others. At this point William Grow intervened and went to the house of Elias's parents and asked Irene what her son thought he was doing teaching school when his true vocation was preaching. Reinforced by Grow and a further dream message, Elias responded to a summons to preach in Piermont, Vermont, where he spoke with extraordinary success. Indeed, "the enlargement of mind, freedom of thought, ease in communicating, and power of truth which was then felt by me and many others, served at that time to remove all my doubts respecting being called of God to preach the gospel of Christ." On the strength of this evidence Elias Smith bade farewell to his scholars and "then took my leave of parents, brethren, sisters, friends, house and land, and the town where I had endured and enjoyed more than in any other place on earth; and from that day to this [1840], it has never been a home to me" (154–55).[3]

Smith soon became a minister himself and stayed at it for nearly ten years in charge of the Baptist churches in Salisbury, New Hampshire, and in Woburn, Massachusetts. In the end, however, he again encountered his "old trouble, discontent" and concluded that growing restlessness in settled office was due to his own deviation from the path to which he had first been called. Looking back on the time when he wore ecclesiastical black himself and took money for it, he recalled that "when my mind was right in preaching, it was led to travel and preach as Christ and the apostles did," concluding that "a minister of Christ ought always to be free from all men" (237–38). Henceforth Elias Smith tried to walk in freedom and judged those—like Thomas Baldwin and John Peak—who undertook the salaried care of settled churches as apostates from the pure apostolic doctrine of Paul. In 1805 John Peak, for example, finally succumbed to the temptations of Babylon and accepted the call of a Baptist congregation in the Congregational and Episcopal stronghold of Newburyport; he paid the price for it through a factionalism among his flock so severe that he was excommunicated by a part of his own church, which in turn was excommunicated by the group that supported him.[4] Commenting on this "want of harmony and rectitude which is but too apparent among professors of christianity at the present day," Peak attributed his church's troubles to a "want of sanctification"—all that can be expected short of a future paradise where "our union shall be compleat, and our bliss perfect; not a jarring note or discordant sound shall be known in all the heavenly concert" (Peak 1814, 19). Elias Smith hoped for the accomplishment of this on earth and blamed failure to achieve it on sectarian division, rather than on the hopelessly fractious streak in human nature more realistically postulated by the Calvinists.

The Calvinistic Baldwin went on to occupy peacefully for thirty-five years the pastorate of the Second Baptist Church in Boston, where, as Elias put it in 1816, he "is styled Rev. Thomas Baldwin, D.D. and wears a dress something like that worn by the ancient *pagan priests*." From that high-priestly station Smith's former friend lectured in favor of the doctrine of special election as though the survival of Christianity depended on it. The careers of men like Peak and Baldwin did not at all match Elias Smith's ideal of gospel liberty. When the "world" (i.e., wife, family, financial obligations) finally claimed him, he looked regretfully back on his younger days of republican virtue, when "I *then* enjoyed a kind of independence from men, not because of so much, but because I could live upon so little" (214–15).

In 1791 and 1792 Elias traveled extensively in the eastern part of the region, down to the coast at Salisbury, Massachusetts, and the environs of Haverhill on the Merimack. During this time Smith met Dr. Samuel Shepard, the Baptist pastor of Brentwood, New Hampshire, who preached Thomas Baldwin's ordination sermon in 1783. Shepard officiated at Smith's first wedding and later repudiated him when Elias questioned the scriptural legitimacy of the doctrine of endless punishment (143; Chessman 1826, 23). But in early days Elias was profoundly influenced by Shepard, though later counting him as one of those who went only part of the way toward foundation of the true New Testament church. "When they saw where it would end, the greater part went back, and apologized for their conduct" (264). Shepard was called by some the Bishop of Brentwood, a place characterized by a contemporary Baptist historian as the "Jerusalem" of a growing number of associated congregations arising from their parent (Benedict 1813, 1:320–21). Like Abner Jones, Mark Fernald, and many other itinerant ministers of his day, Samuel Shepard was a physician who derived much of his income by serving needs carnal as well as spiritual.[5] Among other things, Shepard was partially responsible for the conversion of William Plumer, a future governor of New Hampshire and a leader in the ultimately successful fight for religious disestablishment in that state.

With this preparation, and with eminently respectable patrons to recommend him, Elias became known by a number of Baptist congregations that took an interest in extending a call to him to be their pastor. With prospects of a formal appointment now in sight, it was necessary to be ordained, and in July 1792 Elias Smith journeyed to Boston, thus passing by the festivities at Harvard with which this story began. After he crossed over the Charles to the great bustling city, he sought out "my brother, Thomas Baldwin, whom I loved above all men on earth" and was immediately given an invitation to preach at the Second Baptist Church. Soon thereafter he met Dr. Samuel Stillman, pastor of the First Baptist Church, from which, in the previous generation, the Second had split because of the lack of encouragement that awakened New Lights received from Stillman's reactionary predecessor (Wood 1899, 238).[6] But with these disputes now resolved, both these churches and their respective pastors were on good terms and both gladly welcomed Elias Smith to their fold and to their pulpits.

Though Thomas Baldwin, a son of outer New England, began his career modestly enough, Samuel Stillman and the church he served were of quite a different stripe. The First Church was an old one, organized in 1665 in the face of Congregational resistance and legal disabilities imposed on dissenters by the Puritan establishment. By 1792 all that was past, except the general legal requirement that all ratepayers be taxed in support of the recognized Protestant church of their choice or, failing that, the standing Congregational church of their parish. Stillman was born in Philadelphia in 1737 and first preached in South Carolina. He studied at Harvard, graduating in 1757. He was appointed associate pastor of the Second Baptist until called to the First Church in 1764, where he remained until his death in 1807. Stillman's preaching was Calvinist, carefully reasoned, and delivered from notes though in an engaging extemporaneous style. His reputation led to his being invited to deliver an Election Sermon before the General Court (the state legislature) of Massachusetts, to which body he was also several times appointed chaplain. According to *Sibley's Harvard Graduates,* Stillman was "more a child of the authoritarianism of Calvin than of the anarchy of the Anabaptists" (Sibley 1968, 223). On the occasion of their first meeting, Elias Smith recollected that Stillman's "appearance struck me with awe. He was a small man, but he looked large to me. He was dressed in black, wore a large white wig, and three cornered hat. He looked as neat as is easy to be in a dirty world" (197). Stillman lived to oppose unequivocally both slavery and the consequences of the French Revolution and to have a major role in the foundation of what became Brown University. With the emergence of parties, Baldwin, a Republican, and Stillman, a Federalist, amicably divided the Boston Baptist flock among themselves. By 1792 these Baptist churches were as established as any non-Congregational bodies could be under the circumstances, and as such would each face the radical wing of the Second Great Awakening.

Baldwin seemingly was drawn in a conservative direction by Stillman's powerful influence, an ingrained Calvinism of his own, and the respectable denominational status of the Boston old Baptists. As it had with Stillman, the General Court called this now eminently acceptable pastor to deliver an Election Sermon (in 1802) and several times to be its chaplain. Reflecting on the revivals that accompanied the turn of the century, the historian of the First Church observed that together the two Baptist pastors "seemed especially raised up of God for that peculiarly critical time in the religious history of Boston" (Wood 1899, 285). On his death in 1825, it was recalled how hard Baldwin had worked to overcome the disadvantages he labored under in sophisticated Boston because of his rural upbringing and poor formal education (Chessman 1826).

In 1803 Baldwin was awarded the degree of doctor of divinity by Union College in New York, and some time before an M.A. by Brown University, whose foundation Smith took to be a sure sign of Baptist decline into the camp of the orthodox establishment. Such dubious accomplishments helped lay the foundations for Elias Smith's later contempt of Baldwin, whom he came to treat with the same scorn he had formerly reserved for the Harvard-trained Congregational clergy. Perhaps just because of their former friendship the relationship between Smith and Baldwin became rancorous and bitter (at least on Smith's side) once Elias rejected Baptist worldliness and departed the fold for the Christians; if Thomas Baldwin was "a man of peace," Elias Smith assuredly was not.

That was yet to be, and in 1792 the young Elias happily basked in the glow of these urban luminaries and rejoiced in the prospect of joining their company in the ministry. His place in the world seemed set, and in January 1793 the twenty-three-year-old Smith married the nineteen-year-old Mary Burleigh, daughter of Josiah Burleigh of Newmarket, New Hampshire, near Portsmouth. Elias wrote mainly of his spiritual experiences and public activities, very little about his private and domestic life, and so he never said much about Mary except to mention indirectly the cross she had to bear in marrying him: "We lived together but a small part of twenty one years; as my work was to travel and preach, I was gone from home a considerable part of that time. We lived in harmony through the whole time, and she was a faithful friend to me, the children, my interest, reputation, and the cause of religion, and endured through many scenes of trouble which we were called to experience in the course of twenty one years" (214).[7]

After repeated requests from the Baptists of Salisbury, New Hampshire, Elias accepted their call to settle among them for six months; and so, with the help of Mary's father, he and Mary set up a household there in April 1793. Salisbury lies about ten miles north of Concord, the state capital, and Elias preached in a circle of adjoining towns with such success that "through that summer, the work of the Lord went on gloriously." So well, in fact, that it produced defections from the local Congregational church, which involved Smith in disputation with its minister, who—in the first of many such episodes in Smith's career—publicly insinuated that Smith was simply an ignorant usurper (217).

The church to which Elias was called came into existence through a schism among local Baptists over where a new meetinghouse should be constructed in relation to the part of the town they happened to reside; it had existed as an independent body only since 1789, and in 1793 was in need of a resident pastor.[8] Like other congregationally organized churches, its constitution had the form of a covenant containing a profession of faith and an agreement among the signatories to bind themselves to one another in mutual watch and ward. The Salisbury Covenant was a document jointly based on the 1648 Cambridge Platform of the Massachusetts Congregational Churches, the Inalienable Rights of Man, and John 5:39. The signatories declared that "we ought, stripped of all prepossessions of opinion and sentiment, to *search the Scriptures,* to find out and know ourselves, what is good, and practice accordingly, realizing we must shortly be accountable to him, that is ready to judge the quick and the dead." Having done so, the covenanters determined that in good conscience they could only be Baptists: "We, therefore, as men, amidst all the controversy of religionists and the errors of the times, would assume our natural rights in the choice of a religious sentiment for ourselves [and do therefore] choose and prefer what is called the strict Anti-Pedobaptists sentiments of religion, and do hereby make said sentiments of religion our own, taking it upon candid examination, according to our best light in the Holy Scriptures, to be the most agreeable thereto" (Dearborn 1890, 173).

By "strict Anti-Pedobaptists," these people meant not only that they were Baptists insisting on adult rebirth and baptism but that they refused to admit anyone to their communion who had not had this experience and the public ritual acknowledging it; in the language of the day, they were "close communionists," a stance that often led to bad feeling and accusations of holier-than-thou exclusivity among those who were willing to give the benefit of the doubt to all who appeared to be among the faithful, even if already baptized as an infant.

The records of the transactions that brought Elias Smith to Salisbury are still to be found in the Baptist church where he preached, which stands to this day as the premises of the Salisbury Historical Society. On April 1, 1793, the church met and voted to accept Smith as their preacher and to provide a house for him. In addition to the house, the church contracted to pay Smith £60 for a year's preaching, to be proportionally raised among the congregation according to the tax rates. Smith made a good impression during this probationary period, and so the church resolved to continue his services for another six months, later extended through 1795–96, along with a raise to £80 per annum.[9]

But by 1797 the relationship was going sour, and even as early as 1796 Smith was "very unhappy and discontented in my situation in Salisbury, though the people were ready and willing to support me if I would continue to preach with them" (234). The Salisbury church was already experiencing some hints of the internal dissension that would later tear it apart under Elias Smith's successor, Otis Robinson. The town historian records that, after the "reformation" that led to Elias's call to the pulpit, there was increasing disaffection between liberals and orthodox Calvinists, to the extent that "there was no union of sentiment or belief to hold them together" (Dearborn 1890, 177). Smith himself noted that "the reformation abated, and a difficulty arose in the church concerning doctrines. Some of the members were strict calvinists, and others free. This caused great trouble, as I felt a necessity of being decided as to one side or the other. The consequences at last were serious indeed" (233). In 1826 controversies of this and a more personal type, which together often inflamed endemic local factionalism into open war, led to the secession of forty members of the church and the creation of a body that styled itself the Religious Calvinistic Baptist Society and called for a new minister in place of Robinson. Future pastors would prove reluctant to take up charge of a church so divided.

The troubles of the Salisbury Baptist Church were a microcosm of the political and doctrinal troubles of many New England churches throughout this period, which included arguments over open versus closed communion, over baptism, over the Trinity, over the relative merits of Calvinism and Arminianism (predestination versus free will), and over the very specific merits and demerits of the pastor. Out of such a climate, and exasperated with doctrinal controversy in general, the Christian movement was born. For Elias it came to a head in the suburban Boston town of Woburn.

Even though well established in Salisbury, Smith was nonetheless drawn toward Woburn, where the Baptists had extended him an invitation to preach part of the year, which he accepted for the winter of 1796–97. Elias attempted to reconcile himself to his lot in Salisbury but became increasingly depressed over it. In the midst of his promising preaching career and what should have been domestic bliss, "there was a lack, which increased upon me," which he came to see as lack of the freedom that he had once enjoyed as an itinerant but had now exchanged for the bondage of a settled ministry. This of course was in retrospect, and since he shortly took up another settled ministry in Woburn, it can be supposed that at the time the fundamental problem of this restless man was merely boredom, exacerbated by Babylon's siren song—the call of Boston and his intellectual idols Stillman and Baldwin. Smith later admitted that "one object in going to Woburn was to gain useful knowledge, by having an opportunity to converse with such knowing men as I considered Dr. Stillman and other baptist preachers to be." In the end, finding his mentors also wanting, Elias set out on his own (242). Caught in this spiritual travail Elias asked himself: "Is it right for me to keep bound in unrighteousness? The answer was, no. Why may I not be free? You may. When? Now.—What followed was this: 'I AM FREE.' There my bondage ended. The next step was to tell the people [of Salisbury] I could not stand to my agreement, and must be disengaged from it, come life or death" (239).

Notwithstanding his wife's displeasure at moving and that of his Salisbury congregation in losing him, Elias Smith had firmly resolved to depart. By 1797 the mutual disaffection of Smith and the Baptist Society was appearing in the church records, which record a vote on March 21 requesting "that Elder Smith should proseed to shew or offer some reason why he with drew and as he has returned how he will stay with us or on what conditions." They tried to keep him, but it was futile, and so in November chose a committee to negotiate with Smith about the fate of the house and land they had deeded him. There was also the question of letters of dismissal and recommendation, required when a member wished to transfer to another town or parish church. Because of the contractual nature of the church covenant through which a person was bound to a particular church society, that society could refuse to grant such letters if the departing member was judged to be morally unworthy or if the reasons for leaving were insufficiently grounded; it was therefore necessary for Smith to satisfy the Salisbury church on both counts—which he did in fact manage to do and so obtain his letters. But he remembered the episode with distaste, saying that "here I first felt the strength of the cords of sectarian bondage," an attitude at the root of his later rejection of the notion of the covenant itself, and hence of the fundamental constitutional principle of the congregationally organized churches of New England. Smith came to see that any such practice was of its own nature "contrary to the perfect law of liberty" (242).

And so, in January 1798, Elias and Mary Burleigh Smith left Salisbury in company with their daughter and their second child—a boy, Daniel Drown Smith, who was born in June 1797.[10] The church to which Elias was now called had come into being because of disaffection within the Woburn town parish, whose inhabitants (as in the rest of Massachusetts) were legally compelled to support the Congregational establishment unless they could demonstrate a legitimate affiliation to another recognized Protestant church. Some parishioners were dissatisfied with the edification they were receiving in Woburn and began to attend the Baptist church in West Cambridge (organized 1781).[11] Under the leadership of the Cambridge Baptist pastor, Thomas Green, the defectors sued for the recovery of their taxes on the grounds that they were now members of a legitimate church in an adjoining parish; the suit was successful, and in consequence the Woburn residents in 1790 constructed a church in proximity to their own homes for which they retained Green on a part-time basis.[12] This arrangement lasted until 1793, when Green departed the area, thus necessitating the search for another pastor. This turned out to be none other than John Peak, who preached (again part-time) through 1795 with occasional assistance from Baldwin and Stillman until Elias Smith eventually took over (Sewall 1868, 485–87).[13]

Smith was now among old friends and far from the rural country of his recent youth. In his *Life* he devotes much attention to the dandified figure he cut under the influence of Stillman and others, and to the degree he was compelled to follow the dictates of the state in becoming—through that "*man made anti-christian ceremony* called by its makers, *installation*"—a legally recognized minister of the Commonwealth of Massachusetts. Yet installed he was, with Stillman giving the sermon and Baldwin the right hand of fellowship. Stillman advised him to wear the clerical band so that he might appear respectable among the sophisticated company he would have to keep in the environs of Boston. Smith in 1840 remembered that he had refused to go so far, and that "from that day to this I have held as abominable, the *band, surplice,* and the other part of the clerical, anti-christian attire of the mother of harlots, and abominations of the earth" (246). But in the 1816 edition of his *Life* Smith makes it clear (in a passage omitted in 1840) that he had in fact worn the band and later blamed Samuel Stillman for the hypocrisy into which he was forced in doing so: "This was a piece of clerical foppery I always hated, and when I walked with it on, I then thought I acted with it as a pig does when he is first yoked. I should not have worn it that day, but Doctor Stillman, who was as fond of such foppery as a little girl is of fine baby rags, brought one and put it on me." All in all, recalled Smith "I became quite *too* respectable for a minister of Christ" (1816, 280, 282). His tone both in 1816 and 1840 is apologetic: that of a wiser, sadder, and older man accounting for his youthful excesses.

Smith lasted in Woburn only until 1801. Not only was he disappointed with his newly respectable status, but serious doubts were at last creeping in about doctrines that the Calvinist Baptists held most dear: specifically the Trinity and special election. He noted that even Stillman and Baldwin differed somewhat on theological questions and that his own preaching on election had the opposite effect to that which was intended: namely, it drove his listeners, particularly the young, in the direction of fatalistic hedonism. Since he had neither read deeply in theology himself nor had the advantage of Max Weber's observations on the vitalizing antinomies of the Calvinist soul, Smith questioned what he was doing in telling his flock that all their actions, no matter how morally dubious, had been preordained from the beginning of the world. To Smith's dismay one auditor, convinced that he must be damned anyway, went straight from church into dancing school. Baffled by such response, Elias told John Peak that his religion had boiled down to only two precepts—believe right and do right—whereupon Peak concluded that a man with such vague theological principles could only be a deist or Universalist (252).

Unfortunately Woburn was a more difficult place to leave than Salisbury, though for different reasons. In lieu of part of his salary Elias had accepted a loan of $1,000 from his congregation, which he used to establish a partnership with two others to help found a small mercantile company and open a shop in Woodstock. So when he finally managed to depart, Smith was pursued by debt and an ill rumor, which would bedevil him for years to come, about questionable financial practices with respect to the Woburn church. In 1801 the company opened another store in Salisbury, to which town Elias resolved to return and preach no more. He told the unwilling Thomas Baldwin of his intentions, complaining, "My mind and body were never designed for such narrow limits as my situation there fixed me in." And so, "having settled my affairs in the month of September, 1801, I took my everlasting leave from installations and hireling plans, such bondage as I had endured there, and sat out in a chaise, with my wife and three children, one of which was born there [in Woburn], April 22, 1799, for Salisbury, N.H." (255).

Smith took with him a political consciousness newly awakened during the 1799 election campaign through the newspaper writings in the *Boston Independent Chronicle* of a man known by the pseudonym of Old South—Benjamin Austin, an ardent and effective Republican publicist. With this awakening and with his theological doubts enhanced by further exposure to Universalism through his younger brother Uriah—a temporary convert to that creed who later also became a "Christian"—Elias Smith's religious and political sentiments began rapidly to elide into the synthesis achieved by his resolve to "search the Scriptures" and leave behind the works of men. As he did so, others were unknowingly preparing to join him.

✠

Of these Abner Jones was the most immediately important. Like Smith, Jones had followed the usual path into the evangelical ministry:

Plate 3. Abner Jones (1772–1841): cofounder of the Christian movement, doctor, and evangelist. Courtesy American Antiquarian Society; reprinted from A. D. Jones, *Memoir of Elder Abner Jones* (Boston: William Crosby, 1842).

conviction of sin followed by an experience of saving grace and the slow realization he had a preaching gift.[14] He was baptized by Elisha Ransom in 1793 and during this period also developed an interest in medicine, which he elevated into a trade paralleling his preaching work. Around the same time he began finding differences between what was preached in church and what the Scriptures actually seemed to say; his first and greatest shock was the realization that there is no biblical sanction for the name of his own denomination, the Baptists, and that the only scripturally ordained name for the followers of Christ is simply what they were called at Antioch in the beginning.[15]

Much else followed, such as anti-Trinitarianism. anti-predestinarianism, and doubts about the reality of eternal punishment—thus far all accomplished quite independently of Elias Smith. In 1801, the same year that Smith left Woburn and the Baptists behind forever, Jones commenced his preaching career in Lyndon, Vermont, in the far north of the state near St. Johnsbury. He believed that this was the first time that a church had been gathered acknowledging the name of Christ alone. As Jones's son recalled: "From the first he announced his determination to stand alone, and acknowledge the authority of no church or set of men. He and about a dozen others, laymen, and residents of Lyndon, covenanted together in church form, and called themselves CHRISTIANS; rejecting all party and sectional names, and leaving each other free to cherish such speculative views of theology as the scriptures might plainly seem to them to teach. This was probably, the *first* FREE, CHRISTIAN Church ever established in New England" (Jones 1842, 49).[16]

Jones went on to become an itinerant preacher working from a new home-base in Lebanon, New Hampshire, across the Connecticut River east of Woodstock. In 1802 he gathered the second Christian Church in neighboring Hanover, the seat of Dartmouth College. In the same year, the year of the great fire, Jones went on to join Elias Smith in Portsmouth, where the latter had himself raised a church on similar principles at the expense of the local Baptists and Congregationalists; together the two men "had glorious times, for they were *then* kindred souls, and fellow-workers" (Jones 1842, 63).[17]

By the time Jones began to preach, Smith was still passing through the fires kindled by his departure from hireling bonds in Woburn. In addition to the debts he carried with him, Elias's mercantile ventures were not doing well; a temporary lull in the war between England and France drove down the high prices induced by disruptions in transatlantic shipping, and in so doing nearly drove his company out of business. Under the influence of his younger brother he had been wrestling with Universalism just as he had earlier with Calvinism; finally he became convinced of the error of them both and resolved to desist from preaching, "being at a loss what to preach to be consistent" (258). With all these theological and financial difficulties Elias believed himself near death; as before, however, this was but the darkness before the dawn. Doubtful over just what he should think, and exhausted with sectarian conflict over fine points of theology, Elias Smith—like Abner Jones not long before him—picked up his Bible once more to peruse Acts 11:26.

> In the spring of 1802, having rejected the doctrines of *Calvin* and
> *universalism*, to search the scriptures to find truth, I found the name
> which the followers of Christ ought to bear; which was CHRISTIANS,
> Acts xi.26. My mind being fixed upon this as the right name, to the
> exclusion of all the popular names in the world . . . I spake upon this
> text; I ventured for the first time, softly to tell the people, that the
> name CHRISTIAN was enough for the followers of Christ, without
> the addition of the word *baptist, methodist,* &c. It was in this meet-
> ing that I first, in a gentle manner, spake against the catechisms, as
> an invention of men. (262)

In July he spoke again on this subject in Portsmouth before an audience that included Joseph Buckminster, who came perhaps out of
courtesy to a fellow preacher, perhaps out of curiosity about the new
phenomenon in their midst. That same month a Christian Conference
was convened at Sanbornton to draw up the *Articles of Faith and Church
Building,* a document that, with the assistance of Samuel Shepard,
Elias largely drafted himself. The conference declared that the followers of Christ could only be called Christians and that their only rule for
faith and practice would be the New Testament; so far as church organization went, they were to withdraw into themselves and exclude
everyone from their community who had not undergone conversion
and adult baptism. Theologically, their de-emphasis of the Old Testament was an important step, in that it stressed the primacy of the Spirit over the law in a country increasingly attuned to the conjoining of
spiritual and political liberty. Also important was their unitarianism
and consequent belief that Christ, as mediator, is a subsidiary being
rather than an aspect of the Godhead; by this means Jesus was brought
closer to humanity, humanity closer to God. More conservatively, these
early Christians still held to the doctrine of endless punishment and
the inherent sinfulness of human beings.

Though radical in some respects, the signatories to the *Articles*—
who included Samuel Shepard and Uriah Smith—acted in an otherwise quite conventional way (Elias acknowledged that Abner Jones had
already gone well beyond them in some respects) (281). They drew up a
statement of church faith and practice and entered into a compact
whereby, "being united in the doctrine of Christ, the whole church are
bound to one member, and one member to the whole church; and they

are thus engaged to bear each others burdens, and so to fulfill the law of Christ." This was the usual congregational mode of gathering churches, and in the emphasis placed on "separation from the world," they were just following in the same footsteps the earlier New Lights and Separate Baptists had taken as a logical consequence of the Great Awakening's spiritual perfectionism; as yet the Christians failed to see any inconsistency between their own exclusivity and the notion that "party names" dishonor Christ by creating division among his followers.

At this time Elias Smith and his friends therefore still thought in the traditional terms of creeds, covenants, and close-communion church organization. And they still adhered to the position they had always held on adult versus infant baptism. Infants should not be baptized at all, since only believers are the subjects of baptism and infants are not in a position to believe. According to Smith (1802), "If any person will deny this, it is evident that he must be a friend to *anti-Christ's* baptism, and not *to Christ's!*" But now this doctrine was used to attack the orthodox churches frontally in a very specific manner, as in Elias Smith's first published work, *A Sermon on Baptism,* delivered at the immersion of a Mrs. Stokes, where a taste of his future confrontational and satiric style emerges in his denial of the validity of *any* baptism administered by ministers who have not themselves been born again (ibid., 18). In a later sermon Smith asked how a person shall know he or she is born again—to which he answered in the pietistic rhetoric of the first awakening: "By the Spirit he is made a new creature, and by the Spirit *is begotten again to a lively hope, by the resurrection of Jesus Christ, to an inheritance incorruptible, undefiled, and that fadeth not away, reserved in heaven.* This is done in an instant, and not progressively, as some ignorant people vainly imagine" (1804d, 5). Therefore, whoever wished to join the Christians, but who had already been baptized according to anti-Christian principles, would have to be rebaptized as a condition of membership. Under the stimulus of such preaching, Joseph Buckminster (now doubting his own spiritual gifts) found a revival underway in Portsmouth and its environs that, with all the enthusiasm of a new awakening, forcibly urged true Christians to abandon him and those like him in favor of the renewed gospel of the primitive church. Again it had come to Elias in a dream: "In the night it was made manifest to me, I believe by the spirit of truth, that God would work in Portsmouth, and that I should see a glorious reformation, and turning to God among old and young" (267). And so it proved.

Evoking some of what Buckminster must have gone through, William Bentley (1962) of Salem reported what happened when the Christian evangelists came into his town. "Smith & Jones preach constantly & even sing in the streets & accost people by asking how it is with their souls." Bentley also commented on the religious scene in general and Elias Smith in particular: "Sects are in all their glory in New England & through the United States. They are as thick as the gulls upon our sandbar, as hungry & as useless. I have lately seen a work of Elias Smith, the Itinerant Free Willer, as he is called, but he prefers the bare name of Christian. This man has a kind of head quarters at Portsmouth, but he is to & fro in the Earth" (entries for July 19, 1807; Dec. 27, 1805). Here the reference is to Job 1:7, where the Lord asks Satan "Whence cometh thou?" and Satan answers, "From going to and fro in the earth, and from walking up and down in it." As Satan went forth to tempt Job to renounce God by visiting unwarranted torments upon him, so (it was implied) Smith went among the churches to sow discord and chaos by attempting to wean formerly good Christians away from their lawful affiliations.

This movement had two inseparable dimensions: theology and ecclesiology. There was a systematic assault on Calvinism, as well as a sweeping away of all forms of church organization not specifically sanctioned in the New Testament. Theologically it all came down to a few basic issues: anti-Trinitarianism, an attack on the concepts of predestination and election, and a revised vision of the nature of Christ's atonement. Given their implicit antielitist and democratic thrust, each of these revisions was of far greater significance than might at first appear on theological grounds alone.

The visible church was to be organized on the basis of the strictest congregational principle of free association: no Presbyterian synods, no Methodist bishops, no Baptist associational meetings, no interference of the state in religious affairs, no centralized authority at all—precisely what had led seventeenth-century English Presbyterians to accuse the

New England Congregationalists of anarchy in church government. Later came a far more radical step—no creeds, catechisms, or covenants: no organizational form departing from that of the primitive church. The fundamental though profoundly ambiguous principle of this movement would be just what Elias Smith preached before the First Baptist Church in Boston in 1792: Christ is all and in all! If entered into in the right spirit, the church will take care of itself.

In speaking of Smith as a "free willer," William Bentley alluded to the sect that, more than any other, was the direct precursor of the Christian movement in New England: the Free-Will Baptists, founded by Benjamin Randal of New Hampshire, who was heavily influenced by the Nova Scotian radical pietist Henry Alline (Bumstead 1971; Rawlyk 1984). Bentley identified Smith and the Free-Willers as "Arminian Baptists," an accurate label because their Arminianism is in large measure what separated them from their Calvinist Baptist brethren; but he also identifies the Free-Willers with the Christians, which is misleading, since they were separated over the issue of party names. Yet the Christians and Free-Will Baptists recognized their mutual kinship and often preached before one another's congregations. Abner Jones, for example, writing of the Free-Willers, found that "his heart was strongly drawn towards them," but that he could not accept their unscriptural name (1842, 50). Likewise Ephraim Stinchfield was baptized by Randal at his home base in New Durham and later ordained by him before Stinchfield rejected "every thing unscriptural" and went on to become one of the principal Christian evangelists in Maine (Stinchfield 1819b).[18] Joseph Boodey, Jr., was born into Benjamin Randal's Free-Will church in New Durham, where his father, Joseph, Sr., succeeded Randal as ruling elder in 1785. Joseph, Jr., was ordained to the ministry by Randal himself and yet affiliated early with the Christians (313; Buzzell 1827, 286). By 1816 he was a member of the New Hampshire House of Representatives, and (by then a Universalist) there gave a forceful anticlerical address as part of a general campaign to finally disestablish religion in New Hampshire.

Elias Smith wrote of Benjamin Randal as "this good man" who founded a church that is "nearer the scripture rule, than any denomination on earth. They have no creed, or platforms, and they consider the new testament as their only rule" (1805b, 40). In 1805 Elias visited

Randal in New Durham following a swing into Maine, and in November 1807, near the end of his own life, Randal preached before Smith's church in Portsmouth (Buzzell 1827, 296). Though recognizing his spiritual kinship with the Free-Willers, Elias nonetheless gained some satisfaction (as reported in the *Herald*) every time a Free-Will congregation adopted the name of Christ alone and abandoned its old affiliation.

The Christians and Free-Willers were at one over the question of just who Christ had died for, answering that is was all humanity, not just God's predestined elect. This was the very issue that in 1780 led Benjamin Randal to depart from the Calvinists. Like Smith and Jones, Randal had come to the conclusion that he must leave human doctrines behind and let Scripture and the Holy Spirit be his teachers; in the wake of that fateful and increasingly common step, "he saw that all was harmony in the universal love of God to man and a general atonement" (Burgess 1889, 557–61).[19] He preached on that basis henceforth and gathered the like-minded around him into the core of a new denomination founded upon the universality of God's love and the belief that all those who accept Christ will in fact be saved: "*Free Grace* was his theme living and dying" (General Conference 1848, 55–58). This belief entailed the idea that a person is provided with the freedom to choose or reject Jesus as Savior and therefore that, though some will choose wrongly and be condemned, those who are saved or damned were not predetermined to this role from the beginning of time; all reap the consequences of their own acts without distinction or prejudice. Hence there *are* no elect, as radical an alternative as can be imagined to the standing faith of orthodox Congregationalism and the Calvinist Baptists—a faith that was enunciated with stark clarity in the confession adopted by the New England Congregational churches in 1680, declaring that none are "redeemed by Christ, or effectually called, justified, adopted, sanctified and saved, but the elect only" (Churches 1812, 10).

Only recently that doctrine had been powerfully reiterated in Samuel Hopkins's *System of Doctrines*, which advanced what Hopkins, Jonathan Edwards's disciple, called consistent Calvinism. Hopkins's system emphasized the infinite majesty of God and the corresponding worthlessness of human beings. The concept of infinity was persistently invoked so as to justify deductively the apparent harshness of God's eternal decrees: God is omniscient, omnipotent, and infinitely good; humankind is fallen, debased, and (being infinitely below him) worthy of whatever punishment God chooses to inflict. But out of his own love, goodness, and wisdom the Lord has graciously preordained that some will be saved through the sacrifice of Christ Jesus—and as fallen mortals, we should rejoice in his mercy, even though as individuals we may have been justly damned in the process. God, being perfect, created the best possible universe there can be. For Hopkins any doctrine challenging the Lord's infinite majesty is an invitation to chaos, an undermining of the only assurance we have that the universe is a stable moral order with any coherent meaning at all. According to Hopkins, "God has foreordained whatsoever comes to pass," and that whoever questions this "must fall into the most awful darkness, and horror. If it be once admitted that any evil, or any least event, may or can take place, which is not, on the whole, best, and therefore not desirable that it should be, it must with equal reason be granted, that nothing but evil . . . may take place. . . . If *this foundation* were taken away and destroyed, what could the righteous, the truly pious and benevolent do. They must be left without any possible support and sink into darkness and wo!" (1811, 93, 113–14).

This attitude was the basis of the anxiety felt by the orthodox in the face of novel theological and political doctrines; when radical sectarians such as the Shakers and preachers such as Randal, Jones, and Smith directly challenged these core beliefs, it was for many as though the foundations of the world had been shaken and devils let loose from the pit. With God diminished and human agency enhanced, what sure guidance can there be? As Thomas Baldwin said in a sermon before his Boston congregation, if we give up the idea that divine purpose underwrites all things, then "all will be plunged in uncertainty. All must then depend on the volitions of depraved man, which are ever changing" (1804, 13). In this same spirit the subscribers to the covenant of the Salisbury Baptist Church declared in the ominous year of 1789 that they were conscious "of One only independent, supreme, superintending, absolutely perfect, all-gracious Being; and therefore conscious of our dependence upon him, from whence naturally arises our obligation to him, as rational creatures, and therefore capable of moral government . . . without the knowledge of which *we are a riddle to ourselves*" (Dearborn 1890, 172–73, emphasis mine). Yet shortly they too fell victim to the tendencies of their times in which human agency itself became deified, the riddle internalized, the walls between the human and divine progressively undermined, and the Salisbury congregation hopelessly divided between liberals and Calvinists.

As for the doctrine of the atonement, this too was modified in humanity's favor. In the traditional Calvinist vision, Christ through his sacrificial death paid the debt that all humankind had incurred relative to God through the fall of Adam and Eve. According to the Congregationalist *Confession*, Christ "underwent the punishment due to us, which *we* should have borne and suffered" and in doing so "hath fully satisfied the justice of God, and purchased not only reconciliation, but an everlasting inheritance in the kingdom of heaven, for all those whom the Father hath given unto him" (i.e., the elect) (Churches 1812, 15). The Christians, Free-Will Baptists, and Universalists unequivocally rejected this notion; in place of the "economic" doctrine that Adam's sin had created a debt needing to be repaid through substitutionary atonement, these populist evangelicals substituted the idea that Christ's appearance on earth was a free gift to humanity so that we might be reconciled to God through the mediation of Jesus.[20] The Universalist Hosea Ballou spoke for them all in concluding that "the atonement made by Christ was the *effect,* and not the *cause* of God's love"; that (again following John 3:17): "God sent not his Son into the world to condemn the world, but that the world through him might be saved" (Whittemore 1854, 1:109).

Under the heading of *atonement,* Elias Smith's *Dictionary* also spoke for the opposition though its customary procedure of declaring unscriptural and hence invalid all doctrines not explicitly identified in the New Testament. Once more this was a democratic message; Christ died for all, and all can be saved through him if they so choose.

> Some tell us that Christ atoned the Deity; that he paid a debt; that he appeased the wrath of God; and some, that Christ died to reconcile his Father to man; with many such things not named in the Bible. God is the same now as before Christ came. God was love, or he had not given Jesus Christ, that men might believe and be saved.

> The *Atonement* is meant for the benefit of man, and not to reconcile
> or change the mind of God. . . . All who obey him, by repentance
> and faith—all who receive his testimony—all who come to God
> through him—all who receive him as their all—find forgive-
> ness. . . . This *atonement*, which is sufficient for one, is for another;
> and all who come to God, through him, or obey him, have the
> promise of eternal salvation. (1812b, 54; see also Marini 1982)

Finally, Unitarianism. Smith's *Dictionary* does not include the entry *Trinity*, because there is no such word in the New Testament; instead Elias found occasion to make his position clear on this subject
under the heading of *Christ:* "In all the glorious things said of Christ,
there is no mention of his divinity, his being *God-man*, his *incarnation*,
the human and divine nature, the human soul of Christ, his being God
the Creator, and yet the Son of the Creator; these things are the inventions of men, and ought to be rejected." Christ is not an aspect of God,
but a *mediator* between God and humankind, more than man but less
than divine: "one appointed to stand and act between the Creator and
creatures. It means one who stands in a middle place between two.
There is but one mediator between God and all men, this is Christ,
who gave himself a ransom for all. There are always two besides the
Mediator, as he is not the Mediator of one; but of two. The Mediator
is neither of the two, but is appointed by one, ready, able and willing
the help the other" (1812b, 95–96, 263–64).[21]

Again Thomas Baldwin spoke for orthodoxy, for the Trinitarian
view that Christ is very God of very God. In a sermon entitled *The
Supreme Deity of Christ Illustrated* (1812), Baldwin claimed that "a denial
of the supreme deity of Christ subverts the very foundation of our holy
religion, and renders it little better than a cunningly divised fable. We
must either admit the supreme Deity of Christ, or acknowledge that
the scriptures were not given by inspiration of God." Alluding to those
who preach "another gospel," Baldwin queried whether anything can
"be denominated *another gospel* with more propriety, than that which
exhibits another Christ as the object of our faith, so different, and so
inferior to him *who is over all, God blessed forever?*" To reduce Christ to
something like a human level is simple blasphemy, arrogant hubris, the
ruin of souls.

Baldwin was responding to the anti-Trinitarianism of the *New Testament Dictionary*. Smith himself struck back at Baldwin directly in a series of letters to his one-time friend that undertook a chapter-and-verse examination of the biblical passages taken to establish conclusively that Jesus is a created being, a mediator, son of God the Father. and that Baldwin was "destitute of understanding" on the subject. Elias deployed numerous passages to disprove Baldwin's assertion that God and Jesus are one being, for example, John 5–8. According to Smith, these chapters declare no less than fifteen times that Jesus was sent to earth *by* God. And yet, now addressing Baldwin, Elias said that "you come forward and declare, that he was the God who sent him." This was of course antiscriptural nonsense, and so Elias was forced to declare, "I must consider your doctrine not of God, but from the *merchants of mystery, Babylon, the great, the mother of harlots, and abominations of the earth*" (1812b, 12, 25). Baldwin never responded.

Such doctrinal controversies should not be construed in overly abstract terms. The problem that Smith and the others had with orthodox Calvinism was simply that they found the doctrines of the Trinity, predestination, election, and substitutionary atonement incredible and unbelievable because they were inconsistent with their democratically biased scriptural interpretation of the nature of divine righteousness. God is not a moral accountant but an all-loving father with a paramount interest in the well-being of his children. How *could* such a God have decreed infinite punishment for finite sins?[22] How *could* he have predestinated much of humankind—including blameless infants—to eternal fire when the New Testament plainly says that Christ was sent into the world so that people should be saved. Elias Smith and others came to the conclusion that, since it was based on a radical misconception of the nature of the Deity, Calvinism can only lead to fatalistic despair; what they should be preaching is hope, since hope is what God has offered us. Abner Jones wrote of how his spirits lifted when he discovered the great truth that all men may be saved, and of how with this glorious knowledge "my mind was brought out of a dark narrow prison, into the clear sunshine of a free gospel offered to all men" (1842, 32).

The controversies sparked by Hopkins's "New Divinity" were part of the stormy theological weather when Elias began preaching in 1791, and as he pointed out in his autobiography, he was well aware of them. Later, in parody of Samuel Hopkins's usage, Smith described as "Consistent Christianity" what he believed it was he had all along been attempting to achieve (351–55). However, it is doubtful whether he ever had much real sense of what Hopkins was talking about—or for that matter had even taken the trouble to read him at all.[23] That too is somewhat beside the point, for Elias and those like him were mainly responding to their understanding of what emanated from orthodox pulpits, not to systematic divinity as such. Theirs was a visceral reaction to what they heard in person, read in a stridently partisan press or a booming pamphlet literature of theological disputation—in which epithets such as *Hopkinsian, Arminian,* and *Jacobin* referred as much as anything to the party affiliations of those against whom they were directed.

By 1800 their reaction to current events was based on a new reading of Scripture in the context of reawakened millennial expectations and a highly charged political atmosphere in the country at large and in the highly factionalized communities where they preached. In 1791 Elias Smith was a Calvinist because his brethren were; in 1802 he was something quite different. Between those years the tide had changed, and in different parts of the country many were reaching similar conclusions about the constitution of God's true church and of society in general. William Bentley accurately noted this epidemic of sectarianism, and (as seen above) it is a fact that later Christian historians would themselves comment on with wonder, as did Abner Jones's memorialist:

> The rise of the Christian Denomination presents . . . a new and singular moral phenomenon. No religious change or movement was ever more spontaneous, or less the result of mutual agreement. We are accustomed to spontaneity in the natural world, but seldom meet such as this presents in the moral. With no more designed concert, with no more mutual agreement than there is among the flowers to introduce the spring, or the stars to adorn the sky of evening, or the rivulets to make the river, these men by a spontaneous movement aimed to revive Primitive Christianity. (Hathaway 1861, 5–6)

Between 1780 and 1810 the Free-Will Baptists founded one hundred churches in New England. By the time of their Third General Conference in 1829, the Free-Willers reported the existence of about three hundred churches with some thirteen thousand members concentrated heavily in the Maine and New Hampshire heartland, but now spreading into western New York and Ohio along with the Yankee diaspora—remaining however a predominantly northeastern denomination (McLoughlin 1971, 2:727–28; Freewill Baptist Connection 1859). The movement to the South and West associated with James O'Kelly of Virginia (a Methodist apostate), and particularly with former Presbyterians Barton Stone and Alexander Campbell of Kentucky had greater numerical success and regional spread. Elias Smith would later have much to do with the Virginia Christians, while Stone was one of the signatories to "The Last Will and Testament of the Springfield Presbytery" which Smith quoted in the first number of the *Herald of Gospel Liberty* as an indication of the spontaneous impulse of their movement; like Smith and Jones, Stone and O'Kelly thought the only legitimate name for the followers of Christ is merely *Christians*.[24]

Alexander Campbell, a transplanted Ulsterman, founded the Disciples of Christ, a denomination that—later united to Stone's group—survives and prospers to this day as the only substantial direct descendant of the broadly based Christian movement. As with Smith, Campbell's chosen vehicle for the spread of his particular word was a newspaper—the *Millennial Harbinger*. All recognized their spiritual kinship with Smith in his Christian phase and the importance of the *Herald of Gospel Liberty* in fusing their disparate efforts into a common cause; all were also agreed on the radical deficiencies of Calvinist theology and agreed that the early church should serve as their model for ecclesiastical organization, holding that "the primitive church was fundamentally democratic, while the creeds and traditions of history were essentially un-American" (Hatch 1980, 68–78; Hughes and Allen 1988, 105).[25]

This elision of pietistic evangelicalism and populist democracy marks the difference between the First and Second awakenings; the great sea change was in large measure political, a product of the creation of the new republic. The conflicts that developed over its nature and direction were echoed in the theological controversies of the day; conversely, political perception and action were shaped by a highly politicized reading of Scripture. Whereas the evangelicals turned for guidance to prophecy and the book of Revelation, the conservatives took up those sections of Acts and the Epistles that tell of false prophets, of "wolves among the sheep," and of the dangers of factionalism within the church (and by implication the state) in the absence of firm lines of authority.

Thus the lines were drawn. William Plumer, a future governor of New Hampshire (and sometime ally of Smith), remembered those fervid days of the late eighteenth century in which "the spirit of party ran high, divided families, neighborhoods, towns & states; & blind to public interest, embittered the sweets of social life, & hazarded the rights of the nation" (quoted in L. W. Turner 1962, 66).[26] By 1799 most of the Congregationalist clergy were staunchly Federalist and frequently preached against the supposed infidelity of Thomas Jefferson and his indifference to the concerns of New England mercantile society; later came the infidel Madison and his exceedingly unpopular and divisive war with Britain. With attitudes like these to oppose, an attack on established religion was automatically a direct assault on the Federalist party and the aristocratic principles that both were seen to represent.[27]

Meanwhile, Elias Smith had been reading the works of Benjamin Austin ("Old South"), whose political columns appeared at interval in the *Boston Independent Chronicle* (and in 1803 were compiled into a book called *Constitutional Republicanism in Opposition to Fallacious Federalism*). Even as late as his time in Woburn, Elias had given no thought to politics as such. Through Austin's articles Elias learned that the pronouncements of the established clergy were part of a complex class-struggle in which the forces of republican democracy were pitted against those of Tory reaction. Given the obvious fact that much of the clergy supported the Federalist cause, Austin commented that "the pulpit in many instances has been a political theater, and days set apart for religious worship, have been converted to party rant, and defamation." In his view a perfidious and conspiratorial Tory remnant composed of a plutocratic cabal, their clerical camp followers, hireling Federalist press, and much of the legal profession had conspired to alarm and deceive the people by spreading tales about Francophile republican infidelity and anarchy. He could only conclude that "in a republican government, it is an alarming idea, that an aristocracy is operating among the clergy to check the spirit of republicanism" (1803, 73, 107, 271).

Having been a Baptist and hence a member of a sect with a long history of struggle against an oppressive establishment, Smith was already familiar with the part of the equation having to do with freedom of religious worship; however, only now did he realize the grander democratic implications of the faith in which he had been raised and of the New Testament, which sanctioned it. Now armed, thanks to Austin, with a satisfyingly consistent theory to unify his preexisting religious opinions, class biases, and recently aroused political sentiments, Elias Smith was set on the path to the ideological synthesis that he worked out during his years in Portsmouth as an evangelical preacher and journalist.

Smith endlessly reiterated republican doctrine in his discourses and in the *Herald of Gospel Liberty*. But he added something of his own to them. Benjamin Austin had little to say about religion except that his Federalist opponents were abusing it and that the true doctrine of Christ and Democratic-Republicanism have much in common (as Jefferson himself believed). Smith, however, regularly juxtaposed Scripture to American political documents and used the one to gloss the other, showing that the freedom promised to humanity through Christ was the selfsame freedom guaranteed in the Declaration of Independence, the Constitution, and the Virginia Declaration of Religious Liberty. "Men certainly are born free, and they are as certainly born equal. This Christ preached and this he established in his *kingdom*." Now convinced that American democracy represented the only secular order in human history compatible with the kingly government of Christ, Smith took aim at what vestiges remained in the United States of anti-Christian institutional hierarchies and un-American elitist attitudes.[28] The first target proved to be the college-educated clergy, upon whom Smith began in 1803 to heap his scorn in a four-part satirical diatribe—*The Clergyman's Looking-Glass.*

And so the gathering rivulets of a great evangelical flood swept toward the unsuspecting Joseph Buckminster; when it arrived in the train of the Christmas fire of 1802, he knew that an evil had been let loose in the land as God's righteous judgment on the sins of his town and his country, and perhaps even on his own. Considering what later befell, it may well have given him pause that, in the summer before the conflagration—a time with renewed visitation of the yellow fever—a madman appeared in the streets of Portsmouth prophesying death and destruction. Furthermore, "The fire spread just where he travelled and cried, and the last building that was burned was St. John's [Episcopal] Church, on the steps of which he sat down and ceased his crying. He afterward travelled through the streets and prophesied, 'Peace and Good Will,' before the great reformation under the labors of Elders Elias Smith [and] Abner Jones" (Fernald 1852, 35). Upon seeing the devastation in mid-January 1803, the Free-Will Baptist leader Benjamin Randal was led to reflect "O, How uncertain are all things here below!" (Buzzell 1827, 237).

3

FREE RADICALS
Federalists, Republicans, and the Second Awakening

Try the spirits whether they are of God.
I JOHN 4:I

THE PERIOD OF FERMENT NOW known as the Second Great Awakening spanned some thirty years. First noted among Connecticut Congregationalist youth in the 1790s, the geographic scope of this renewal was coterminous with the ever-expanding boundaries of the United States. It affected white, black, rich, poor and middling, members of established denominations, the completely unchurched, urbanites, rural people, more women than men—but many of both. Churches formed at a dizzying rate, as did new communities in the West. Local awakenings could take the form of giant ecstatic camp meetings among rural Presbyterians—as at Cane Ridge, Kentucky, in 1801; or a more sedate deepening of piety and expansion of church membership among town-dwelling Congregationalists—as at Andover, Massachusetts, in 1831–32; or among urban Methodists aroused through the efforts of their clergy—as in Baltimore in 1828–30; or among artisans and laborers in Portsmouth, New Hampshire, in 1802 (Birdsall 1970; Conkin 1990; Shiels 1985; Bilhartz 1986). Awakenings sometimes began among the laity, and then the clergy found themselves obliged to catch up with its momentum; traveling evangelists were later able to set the pace themselves, thus turning revivalism into an organizational strategy.[1]

Given its historical span and the great diversity of its manifestations and social appeal, it is difficult to assign this tendency ("whose complexity eludes precision") an essential defining quality except the name retrospectively assigned to it (Mathews 1969). Nathan Hatch has focused on democratization as an aspect of much of what was going on, the co-opting of American Christianity by ordinary people taking it upon themselves to fulfill the promise of the Revolution in their spiritual lives. Hatch and others have pointed out that the general result was not so much the rejuvenation of old churches but the creation of an entirely new pattern of church affiliation, a "splintering" of American Christianity into rival sects, which paradoxically made America more Christian in terms of active church allegiance than it had ever been before (1989, 226; Mathews 1969, 26, 37).

Another outcome was a great burst of organizational activity, including the emergence of middle-class revivalism accompanied by the formation of missionary, tract, and Bible societies, a vastly expanded religious press, and a variety of movements of moral uplift, such as Sunday schools, temperance societies, and women's mutual aid associations. As one historian puts it: "The Second Great Awakening remains the moment of institutional and ideological flux out of which grew the characteristic liberal-protestant-bourgeois synthesis of nineteenth-century America" (Birdsall 1970, 363; see also Butler 1990, 268–88, and McLoughlin 1978, 98–140). If, on the one side, it was a populist movement of the marginal and dispossessed and, on the other, the font of bourgeois respectability, then clearly different strata of the population were differently affected by it (or, what is equally likely, something is radically wrong with its definition). Jon Butler has called the First Great Awakening an "interpretive fiction" invented after the fact to link nineteenth-century revivals with those of an earlier age (1990, 165). Both "awakenings" prove to be terms without definite referent. (See Cooper 1992.)

That something profound was going on during the period of the Second Awakening, no one doubts; but It has been said that there are more generalizations about the awakening than solid information about what it was actually like (Hatch 1989, 220; Shiels 1980, 415). This and the following chapters should help to improve the situation. The revival that Elias Smith helped spark in Portsmouth in 1802–3 reveals some sense of how local life began to take on an increasingly national character in a complex web of mutual interdependencies. At least one thing is abundantly clear: Smith's revival was as much a political as it was a religious movement, an application of Jeffersonian principles in spiritual life, "the Revolution at work in religion" in the guise of a return to primitive Christianity (Mathews 1969, 35).

Portsmouth first began to prosper on the timber resources of the New Hampshire hinterland. Before American independence it was a major shipbuilding center and supplier of naval stores to the Royal Navy. It is a place where a river—the Piscataqua—meets the sea, providing in eighteenth-century terms up-country access, a protected harbor, fishing grounds, and opportunities for both local and transatlantic commerce; beyond, past Kittery on the north shore of the river, were the deeper forests of the District of Maine, then a part of Massachusetts, and a rocky indented coast that channeled human activity to and from what would become the Canadian Maritime Provinces of New Brunswick and Nova Scotia.

In 1802 Portsmouth was a city of some six thousand souls largely dedicated to trade, fishing, and the maritime crafts. During his famous travels Timothy Dwight described it as built on a beautiful peninsula but laid out without any sense of regularity; however, the manners of the citizens he found polished and pleasing, though upon surveying the town's closely built wooden houses could not "but shudder at the thought of their exposure to a conflagration" (1969, 311–14). The town had origins unlike the other coastal cities of New England, being settled not from religious motives but because of the advantages that the excellent harbor offered for trade and fishing.[2]

As a local clergyman said, "The religious element, having had no place in the settlement of New Hampshire, was at no time so strongly characteristic of our population as of that of Massachusetts," noting further that the history of the place had led to the formation of a society not entirely immune to "many of the frivolities and lighter dissipations of the gay world" (Peabody 1857, 9). Even so, there was no lack of religion: in 1802 Portsmouth had two Congregational parishes (North and South, the former Buckminster's), an Independent Congregational Society organized by New Lights dissatisfied with the looser ways of their sister churches, a well-established and prosperous Episcopal church (St. John's) under the ill-fated Rev. Joseph Willard, a languishing Universalist group, Elias Smith's Baptists (or so the local ecclesiastical historian called them), and finally a Sandemanian Society—followers of Robert Sandeman, an immigrant Scots Presbyterian who developed his own idiosyncratic version of primitive Christianity (Alden 1808).[3] There were two newspapers in Portsmouth, the *New Hampshire Gazette* and the *Oracle,* the former Republican, the latter Federalist; the *Oracle* carried reviews of plays and other such frivolities, while the *Gazette,* which published Smith's writings and announced his appearances in pasture and meeting hall, fulminated against the elitist decadence of the opposition party.

Born in 1763, Joseph Buckminster was the son of a Massachusetts Congregationalist pastor; his mother was a first cousin of Jonathan Edwards (Dexter 1903). Prefiguring his difficulties in Portsmouth, he lost his position as class tutor at Yale to Timothy Dwight, who would later become president of the college and one of the instrumental clerical figures in the Second Awakening. Following his studies, in 1799 Buckminster was called to the North Church of Portsmouth, where he stayed until his death in 1812. He aligned himself "with the Calvinists of the *old school*" (Parker 1812, 15).[4] Prone to depression, he periodically fell into fits of despondency about his own worth and the success of his pastoral calling. It began while he was a student and recurred to the end of his life (Lee 1851, 66). For such a man to be visited with the likes of Elias Smith was added torment to an already troubled mind.

Joseph Buckminster's daughter, Eliza Buckminster Lee, recalled Smith as "a zealous and effective, but very violent, Baptist preacher" who made a strong impression in Portsmouth, "dividing the congregations and taking from Dr. Buckminster's society some of his most valuable friends and church-members." In a eulogy for Buckminster the pastor of the South Church mourned the loss of one who had stood up against the agents of sectarian division: "In this part of our country, where divisions and animosities are breaking up our churches, the loss, which we are called to deplore, is no small calamity" (Parker 1812, 20). It proved to be a greater calamity than was imagined, for within three years of Buckminster's death his own church was itself now so divided over gospel principles that a faction could not tolerate the preaching of his successor and withdrew from the congregation, joining the South Church, which as a body went Unitarian.

Smith's evangelical success gave Buckminster "much pain and perplexity," because it was a success he had to own as real, even though he still questioned the methods through which it was accomplished (Putnam 1835, 175–76). Buckminster's equivocation is evident in a discourse he delivered on the new Baptist presence via a commentary on Luke 9:49–50, a passage in which Jesus—having commissioned his disciples to cast out devils—finds that others are doing likewise without his authority; John reported to him: "Master, we saw one casting out devils in thy name; and we forbad him, because he followeth not with us. And Jesus said unto him, Forbid him not: for he that is not against us is for us." In this context, the unauthorized exorcist is Elias himself, and the general subject the 1803 revival—launched after Abner Jones, and indirectly Benjamin Randal, helped reveal to Smith the nature of "the true light that lighteth every man that cometh into the world" (281).

> A society of the denomination of Baptists is opened among us and numbers appear to be seriously impressed under the preaching of their leader. And notwithstanding the ground we have to doubt, to fear and debate, we must do the justice to acknowledge, that a change appears to have taken place upon the minds and manners of some, more gross enormities are amended, and some profess to be turned from sin to the Lord. Many fear that it is only a temporary impression upon the passions, that will eventually leave the subject 'worse for mending.' The past experience of professed revivals in this denomination in this vicinity, gives reason to fear it. But we hope this will be an exception. (Buckminster 1803a, 72)

As things developed, Buckminster had to conclude that this was no exception after all, and he reluctantly rose to do battle with this wolf among his flock. It must have troubled Buckminster deeply that, in spite of his pulpit eloquence and what was remembered as "the imaginative and poetical turn of his mind," nonetheless he had not presided over a revival during his ministry (Dexter 1903). Why, then, was Elias Smith so favored?

Reinforced by the free gospel of Abner Jones and soured by a threat of legal action resulting from the hireling bonds he had entered into with his former congregation in Salisbury, Elias claimed that he had privately resolved to repudiate the Baptist connection and speak as a simple Christian as soon as it should seem feasible. Nevertheless, he still believed as strongly as ever in the necessity of adult regeneration and baptism, and this would prove to be the focus of his conflict with Buckminster. Elias was simultaneously redefining his position in relation to his former Baptist associates; hence when Smith shortly began publishing *The Clergyman's Looking Glass*, it would be implicitly aimed every bit as much at Thomas Baldwin and Samuel Stillman as at Buckminster himself, and constitute a radical class-based critique of the local elites to which the settled pastorate of whatever denomination belonged. The looking glass into which the clergy were invited to gaze provided a counter image of the purity, democracy, and equality of the primitive church against which "the reverend Doctors, D.D.s" could judge just how far they had departed from the original Christian ideal. If they wanted an example closer to home, they might well also consider the fellowship of Smith's own church.

The records of the Christian Church in Portsmouth begin on Saturday evening, New Year's Day 1803. At this first meeting Elias Smith and a few of his associates heard the evidence of spiritual rebirth on the part of four who wished to be admitted to the ordinance of baptism. The clerk records that "this our first meeting was attended with a divine harmony, which was peculiarly pleasing to all who attended."[5] With the great fire in recent memory, half of Portsmouth in ashes, and many undoubtedly still mindful of Buckminster's admonition that the calamity was the voice of God, this first Lord's Day of the year—Sunday, January 2—was a truly extraordinary occasion. Elias Smith preached "to a crowded solemn assembly" in the South School House on Luke 12:32: "Fear not little flock; for it is your Fathers good pleasure to give you the kingdom." As always with Smith, such commentaries should be set in their scriptural context. In Luke 11, Jesus condemns the hypocrisy of the Pharisees, scribes, and lawyers for their pride of place, for stressing outward form over the work of the Spirit. In chapter 12 Jesus again condemns the Pharisees and now also speaks against covetousness: "for a man's life consisteth not in the abundance of the things which he possesseth" (v. 15). After the sermon, continues the record, they "went to the water, by the tide mill, where three where [*sic*] baptised, in presense of a large number of people. This being the first time this ordinance was ever known to be administered according to the Scripture rule in Portsmouth, curiosity & other things, brought a great concourse of people together, it was judged there were nearly three thousand who attended. Considering it was a new thing, the people conducted with as much decency & candor as could be expected on such an occasion."

For a time the kingdom was theirs. In February they agreed to embody themselves as a Christian church and sent to Samuel Shepard and other elders to help them in this; having done so, "the remainder of the evening was taken up in singing, exortation & prayer. Membership in the church grew rapidly from the first few to a total of fifty-six men and ninety-eight women by early 1804.⁶ But even by the end of 1803 typical signs of declension were already emerging that would cause Elias Smith considerable grief later.

Following his work with Smith in Portsmouth, Abner Jones pushed on for Boston, where his innovative doctrines triggered a final parting with the Baptists for him and Smith alike. Meanwhile the revival he helped precipitate in New Hampshire was generating problems in Buckminster's First Church, where some were renouncing the old baptism for the new, thus leading on August 4, 1803, to an action against them for breach of covenant in language worth repeating:

> Whereas our sisters Sally Lowd and Betsey Barnes did a number of years since, voluntarily desire admission into the First Church of Christ in Portsmouth, and did there profess their faith in Christ and subjection to his precepts and institutions, assenting at the same time to the form of Covenant used in that Church and promising submission to its watch and discipline, and whereas they have since withdrawn themselves and forsaken the Communion of the church and without asking a discussion from the Church or seeking a release from their Covenant engagement have joined themselves to another denomination of Christians, which in our view is a manifest

violation of their Covenant vows. Consider how you will answer not only for renouncing *your infant Baptism* but your violating express voluntary promise to walk in communion with us and to *Submit* to the watch and discipline of the Church.[7]

Sally Lowd and Betsey Barnes had simply followed the injunction laid down by Smith (1802) at the baptism of Mrs. Stokes in 1802: "Those who are not rightly Baptized, are not Baptized at all." Barnes and Lowd went all the way with this logic, and the record shows that—"having the reason of her hope"—Betsey Barnes was baptized into Smith's church in March 1803; Lowd joined and therefore must have been baptized, about the same time. Other orthodox churches in nearby towns experienced similar problems. By 1808 Smith's preaching created a schism in the Congregational church of neighboring Greenland, while in Hampton Falls trouble was already afoot as early as 1803 that led in 1809 to the exemption of part of the congregation from ministerial taxes and, because of inability to cope with "the divided state of the town," the eventual resignation of the minister himself. Looking back on all this, a Congregational Church historian ruefully observed that Smith's "influence in this work seemed to be no less efficient as a political partizan than as the leader of a religious sect" (Lawrence 1856, 59 and elsewhere).

Close communionism accompanied rejection of unbeliever's baptism; not only did Elias's people withdraw from fellowship with their former churches, they would not allow members of those churches to commune with them. Smith justified his position in response to a Methodist critic who asked, "Why cannot you commune with us, seeing we are willing to commune with you?" Elias's answer was that he believed any other course to be inconsistent with what is declared in Acts 2:41, that the early church admitted only those who had been baptized as adult believers after evidence of spiritual rebirth; we therefore cannot, Smith argued, admit those who have been baptized oppositely to the New Testament plan. In a sermon on New Testament Baptism, Elias maintained that anyone believing otherwise "must be a friend to *anti-Christ's baptism, and not to Christ's!* " (1807b, 10; see also 1803d). Immersion baptism of reborn believers is the only acceptable public sign of incorporation into Christ's true church; furthermore, "no man out of the Kingdom of Christ, can be authorized to administer this ordinance. This work belongs to an officer in Christ's Kingdom, and no other. A man who is not born again, cannot administer this ordinance. A man who is born again and unbaptized, cannot administer this ordinance. He must be baptized and appointed by the church; being *separated unto the work whereunto the Holy Ghost has called him*" (1807b, 17).

There were other reasons for separation. Though other churches most certainly have reborn members, we ourselves (said Smith) have no direct evidence of it; and since these same churches also have members who most certainly are *not* converted, there is no basis for communing as a body with churches of such spiritually heterogeneous composition. Furthermore, if the ministers of these churches themselves show no signs of being born again, why should it be assumed without further evidence that the churches they lead are any better than those who lead them—especially when, "instead of living godly in Jesus Christ, and suffering persecution for such a life, they are in general the first gentlemen of the town"? (1803d, 13)—presumably the likes of Joseph Buckminster, a man remembered by his friends for the artistic inclinations he had to overrule in himself for the sake of his calling.

Buckminster thought mode of baptism a matter of relative indifference; addressing the apostate members of his own church, he "could not but regret that you should, with so much precipitancy, renounce your early baptism, and sacrifice, in the passionate and party feelings of the moment the inestimable privileges which God has bestowed on the infant seed of believers" (1803c, v).[8] This brought the matter clearly into focus, for what Buckminster was supporting was the time-honored Congregationalist belief—fought out (but not quite resolved) during the Half-way Covenant debate of the seventeenth century—that the baptism of infants by sprinkling of water is intended to serve, on the model of Abraham's circumcision of Isaac, as a sign of provisional admission of the children of believers into the community of the saints, bestowing by this means "a relative and federal holiness." The clarity of Buckminster's expression reveals just how profoundly antithetical his view of the constitution of ecclesiastical and civil society was to the alternative vision rapidly evolving among Elias Smith's Christians and those like them.[9]

The Old Testament concept of the covenant was the pivotal organizational principle of the Congregational churches, and in its use the New England clergy were walking in the path marked out by tradition and the 1648 Cambridge Platform of Church Discipline, which describes just what a visible church of Christ is: "a company of saints by calling, united into one body by a holy covenant, for the public worship of God, and the mutual edification of one another, in the fellowship of the Lord Jesus." The platform also describes how this fellowship should be constituted and what sanctions it may bring to bear against those failing to attend properly to the sanctity of their covenant obligations (see Banner 1970; Fischer 1964; Kerber 1970). The Hebraic conception of a conditional contract between God and humankind could be put to such uses because of a typological hermeneutics establishing parallels between the Old Testament and the New, a correspondence of type and antitype: just as the Lord made a covenant with Abraham, marked by the circumcision of Isaac, that his seed would be blessed and become the holy nation Israel ("the covenant of works"), so a "covenant of grace," marked by baptism, binds the followers of Jesus into a holy people of the Spirit. This new covenant is described by the 1680 Confession of Faith as the means "wherein [the Lord] freely offereth unto sinners life and salvation by Jesus Christ, requiring of them faith in him that they may be saved, and promising to give unto all those that are ordained unto life [i.e., the elect], his holy spirit to make them willing and able to believe" (Churches 1808, 22). As God chose to save Noah and his family "by water," so also we have the New Testament antitype, "whereunto even baptism doth also now save us . . . by the resurrection of Jesus Christ" (1 Peter 3:21).

Those who subscribe to the covenant in a particular church (and this is the only way in which church membership is possible) have voluntarily bound themselves together into an organic body-politic and in doing so are henceforth subject to its collective authority. Such a polity must have rulers and ruled just as the early institutional church did after the passing of Christ and his immediate disciples. "It is manifest that an organic or complete church is a body politic consisting of some that are governors, and some that are governed in the Lord" (Churches

1812, 13). Such a government is a "mixed government," a kind of classic republic resembling a democracy in respect to the brotherhood of the church, an aristocracy in respect to its governing body, a monarchy in being subject to Christ as King. The platform does not set aside any great place for the minister as such; his only scripturally sanctioned duty is merely "to attend to exhortation, and therein to administer a word of wisdom." In practice, the pastor's role was much more consequential; even so, he was not in a position to administer discipline—of which excommunication was the ultimate threat—without a collectivity or at least a voting majority behind him, as many a pastor found to his cost when he failed to attain it and was dismissed, or himself asked to be dismissed before he was fired.

For their part, "Church members may not remove or depart from the church, and so from one another as they please, nor without just and weighty cause, but ought to live and dwell together. . . . Such departure tends to the dissolution and ruin of the body, as the pulling of stones and pieces of timber from the building, and of members from the natural body tends to the destruction of the whole." If a member wishes to transfer to another church, the proper procedure is to ask for letters of dismissal and recommendation, so that the sister church cannot easily be deceived about the character of the new member it is asked to take in—a procedure that Elias Smith was obliged to follow when he transferred from Salisbury to Woburn, but that Sally Lowd and Betsey Barnes ignored when they bolted without warning from Buckminster's flock. When the First Church acted against these two women, it therefore had considerable precedent to draw upon in its dealings with them.

Buckminster's beliefs exemplify a federalist worldview; it was corporatist, hierarchical, fearful of leaders whose Christian principles were considered suspect, antipathetic to Jefferson and all his works, profoundly suspicious of appeals to personal liberty unconstrained by recognition of community obligation and the wisdom of the natural rulers of society—namely, the prosperous, the educated, and the godly (Churches 1812, 38–40). The federalist clergy equated recognition of one's duties in respect to the church to those with respect to civil society; as the church is a republican body created by a social contract (i.e., a covenant) and sustained by just division of powers and a virtuous leadership, so also the United States is a mixed republic created by constitutional contract and, with the consent of the people, sustained by the government of the righteous. Buckminster was certain that "though men are born free and equal," they are otherwise diverse in capacity, and that therefore the hierarchy of ruler and ruled is decreed by God on the model of his own spiritual government: "For, as order is heaven's first law, and civil government is become absolutely necessary to the well-being, and even existence of Society, in the present state of man; so some must be clothed with power and authority to administer government: and others are bound to be subject to its regular administration" (1796a, 11).

For ecclesiastical federalists the concept of a viable secular republic was an absurdity because virtue is the only possible basis for such a polity and Christianity is the only possible basis for virtue. Buckminster, for example, lauded America's advances in religious liberty but wondered if this degree of freedom was meant to exclude altogether from public life the general principles of religion; he thought not and concluded that no oath of office can be secure without evidence of such a principle on the part of the officeholder (1796a, 18–19). John Snelling Popkin stated the case for virtue as trenchantly as any from his pulpit in Newbury: "Let the temples of religion go to ruin, and how long will there be virtue enough to save us from rapacity and wretchedness. Public order, peace, and prosperity depend on public religion. The Church is the strongest fortress of the state, and the pious the ablest defenders and supporters" (1806a, 11). Sectarian division is subversive of both political and religious institutions in that it brings about the threat of that greatest of horrors, "the rage of an uncontrolled and inflamed multitude" (Popkin 1814, 5).

Joseph Buckminster could have only breathed "amen!" to exemplary sentiments he himself expressed repeatedly. In 1800 on the anniversary of George Washington's death, he had already delivered a sermon entitled "Religion and Righteousness the Basis of National Honor and Prosperity," one curiously timed to coincide with the election campaign of that spring in which the incumbent Federalist governor of New Hampshire was facing stiff opposition—largely because of his involvement with a chartered bank that was striving to maintain its monopoly against the attempted inroads of a group of Republican merchants in Portsmouth.[10] Likewise, in 1804 Elias Smith delivered a political sermon—"The Whole World Governed by a Jew"—the night before Jefferson was sworn in for his second term as president. It is here that Elias identified Jefferson with the sixth angel of Revelation. Smith reckoned that, to the rage of the "*law religion* people," his discourse had a palpable effect on New Hampshire politics in that the governorship passed into Republican hands on that day (308; Smith 1805e).

❧

Just as Smith, Jones, Fernald, and Thomson were representative of the populist evangelicals, their opponents—men of a common stripe like Popkin and Buckminster—represent the federalist clergy, the public voice of a more widespread conservative sentiment. To this latter voice should be added Thomas Andros and David Osgood, men also obliged to do public battle with these new radicals and who, in having done so, reveal once more the common attitudes they shared; through their troubled sermons and discourses they also indirectly shed light on the divisions within their communities to which the evangelicals gave voice.

Berkley, Massachusetts, in the southeastern part of the state near Taunton, was founded in 1735. Its first pastor was the Reverend Samuel Tobey, who held that post until his death in 1781, whereon he was succeeded by Thomas Andros. The church to which Andros fell heir renewed its covenant in 1788, and the signatories—after assenting to the central doctrines of their common faith—promised, "to forsake all iniquity & to proceed daily in holiness in the fear of God, & in dependence upon the assistance of Christ to take up our cross & to follow our great Redeemer, to renounce this vain world, its riches, amours & pleasures & to make God our joy & everlasting portion."[11] As always, this was not to prove easy.

Thomas Andros had been briefly a soldier in the Continental Army, following which he joined in a privateering expedition out of

New Bedford that resulted in his capture by the British and incarceration on a prison ship in the East River off New York. Andros wrote of his escape, of the guilt that his search for profit through violence entailed, of the illness that followed upon the privations endured during his flight, of an early flirtation with universal salvationism, of his discovery of the true Christ while on the brink of death, and of his "entire moral helplessness and dependence on the Spirit of God, to give a new heart and power to live a new life" (1833; see Emery 1853, 2:150–63). Thus reborn, and leaving the frivolity of youth behind, Andros engaged in theological studies through apprenticeship with a Connecticut pastor; though not college educated himself, he learned his lessons sufficiently well to engage passionately in pamphlet disputation on some of the most pressing religious questions of the day—work that, along with care of his family, his farm, and his pastoral and educational duties in Berkley, would occupy him most of his long life.

Andros took the conservative side of every issue: in defense of the Trinity against novel theological systems (1813);[12] in defense of God against the idea that he could or would directly motivate a person to sin without the agency of secondary causes; on the necessity that republican leaders be men of virtue and prayer; on the function of the orthodox clergy as defenders of the social order and bulwarks against anarchy; on the necessity of public support for religion (1809a, 1815, 1817, 1820). For Andros, *philosopher* and *Jacobin* were equivalent terms, and the American anti-Federalists little better than "those philosophic fiends who guided [France's] destiny under the abused name of republicans (a name now almost become synonymous with falsehood, tyranny and crime)" (1814, 47). He looked with favor on Washington and Adams, with loathing on the infidels Jefferson and Madison, and thanked God that America had been spared the excesses of the French Revolution—"the most pestilential fume ever exhaled from the bottomless pit"—since it represented not liberty but anarchy, "despotism in its most frightful form."[13]

When it finally came again to war, Andros was near despair that the conservative revolution, which had thus far spared them these horrors, had been commandeered by radicals who plunged New England into conflict with England, the only power now standing between Christian civilization and dark, satanic, atheistic France. In the face of this imminent apocalypse Andros made an anguished appeal to prophecy, to the past, and to the Massachusetts Way: "Through these awful scenes no power can guide us with safety but the word and Spirit of God. Inquire then diligently for the good old paths. Cling to the religion of your fathers, the good old policy, laws, and customs of Massachusetts. Intrust the management of your public interest in the hands of our good old puritanic fathers, not to striplings perverted by French wisdom, or turned mad by the spirit of desolation gone out into the world. Fight under the banner of the cross. Thus living near to God we shall escape the ruin coming upon the ungodly" (1812, 18). In the end Thomas Andros was cut adrift from his own past, deposed by his congregation over questions arising from the Cambridge Platform about what rights individuals have in relation to the church covenant and what authority he had as pastor. There was a foretaste of what was to come in 1816, when Elias Smith arrived in the Taunton area and visited on Andros's church a portion of Buckminster's fate.

The situation of David Osgood, pastor of the Congregational church in Medford, Massachusetts, parallels that of Andros. Osgood was close to the centers of power in Boston and personally connected to many influential in state politics; he vigorously defended the rights of the clergy to pronounce on political matters, a function that he thought no less than his duty: "to whom [after all] can the farmer, the mechanic, or the tradesman apply for information with so much confidence as to his minister?" (1810, 9). This function was especially important in a time of agitation and disarray, when the lower orders were pulled this way and that by sectarians and political radicals who demanded that, whatever the character and virtue of their rulers, they must be Republicans—no matter, said Osgood, whether they be deists or polytheists, "the friend of Jesus Christ or of Thomas Paine." Such crowd-pleasing Republicans he found to be like their French equivalents, "so many infernals, broken loose from their chains in the pit below, and now appearing in this upper world under the shape of men, but still thinking and acting as demons." *Sibley's Harvard Graduates* relates of Osgood that, "the Essex [County] Federalists used to invite him to pray because they knew that he would employ 'the most bitter invective' against the Jefferson administration" ("David Osgood" 1975, 576–77). In 1802 newly elected Federalist senator William Plumer of

New Hampshire paid a courtesy call on the president and had his darkest suspicions confirmed by finding in attendance "that outrageous blasphemer," Tom Paine, who behaved toward the shabbily dressed Jefferson with "the familiarity of an intimate and an equal!" Plumer asked himself, "can virtue receive sufficient protection from an administration which admits such men as Paine to terms of intimacy with its chief?" (1857, 242).

Osgood believed himself and the rest of the established clergy to be above sectarianism and faction; rather, he saw ministers of religion as "a bulwark *against* the spirit of faction, and *for* the preservation of order and union" (1798, 21). Therefore when, in a discourse delivered to Harvard College, Osgood likened George Washington to King David and Thomas Jefferson to David's rebellious son Absalom, he thought himself to be speaking the simple truth—that Jefferson had seduced the people away from the true course charted by Washington and Adams (just as "Absalom stole the hearts of the men of Israel" [2 Sam. 15:6]). Jefferson would never have been elected in the first place if only the voice of the clergy had been heard, but since it had not, the people "have brought upon themselves the displeasure of Almighty God, the effects of which they are now suffering."[14]

Osgood was no less forthright when it came to the affairs of his own parish. Early in 1804 he confronted a society of close-communion Baptists that had set itself up in neighboring Malden at the expense of his own church. Like Buckminster, Osgood thought mode of baptism a matter of no particular consequence ("Doth water commend us to God?" he asked); but though it was not offensive to the inhabitants of ancient Judea, nor would it be offensive to the "uncultivated and uncloathed inhabitants" of present-day Africa, Baptist-style immersion certainly would not do for Massachusetts people, who were "accustomed to polished manners." Somewhat missing the point, Osgood asked of the Malden Baptists the same question that Elias Smith was asked in Portsmouth: "Why are you not willing to commune with us, since we are willing to commune with you?" He seems to have received the same answer: "Baptism is a token of spiritual regeneration, not a question of mere water; we will not commune with you as a church because you are not known to us to be collectively regenerate." Osgood, evidently struck by the Baptist claim that their preaching was due to direct inspiration of the Holy Spirit, saw fit to demonstrate to his own congregation that he was capable of such delivery himself; therefore, to prove that Baptist spontaneity either was "no proof of inspiration" or that he was at least as inspired as they were, Osgood delivered an extemporaneous sermon without aid of notes attacking the embargo imposed by the Jefferson administration on commerce with the British ("David Osgood" 1975, 577).

Osgood noted, probably rightly, that the Baptists regarded every convert they could wean away from other churches as "recovered from a state of heathenism" and called into question the way in which they went about their work of conversion: "They creep into houses, and lead away silly women; throwing darkness upon their understandings, and prejudices and evil surmises into their hearts. Their substance, as well as their popularity and the estimation to which they aspire, depend upon their success in sowing discord among brethren, stirring up a party spirit, making divisions, and thereby advancing the cause of superstition and bigotry" (1804, 27).

If those brethren recently drawn into the Baptist fold have in truth newly acquired principles of grace and holiness, how much better it would have been for them to stay with their original affiliations and by good example help guide others to the same state of grace they have found for themselves. "To the peace and welfare of the town," Osgood said, "to the interests of civil society, as well as those of religion, continued union would be exceedingly beneficial." But no, it transpires that some will rest content with nothing but separation. Given that the New Testament roundly condemns schism, those who preach division should be judged according to the advice of 1 John 4:1: "Try the spirits whether they are of God."

Elias Smith read Osgood's discourse and did not like it; nor did he like Joseph Buckminster's *Discourse on Baptism* of the previous year. Accordingly they became the principal targets of *The Clergyman's Looking Glass*, numbers 3 and 4. The process that led to these literary outbursts and the steady stream of sermons, discourses, and polemics that followed hard upon them is obscure; it is as though, after a long and slow gestation of passive reading and reflection, something, now expressed in the form of an obsession with the printed word, burst forth in Elias, just as he earlier had discovered that he had a preaching gift.

Smith himself said that "in the course of the summer of 1802, new and strange things were made manifest to my understanding" (267). Meditating on the opposition he was receiving in Portsmouth from Buckminster and his kind, it occurred to Elias that *all* the clergy were preaching oppositely to the New Testament plan, and that the plan the clergy themselves supported had precisely the qualities that the New Testament describes as motivated by the spirit of Antichrist. Once he realized this, the word *clergy* became in Smith's usage a term of utmost opprobrium and scorn. He remembered that following upon this realization, "Here I first began to write" (268).

In Elias's second published work, a discourse delivered on Thanksgiving Day 1802, on a prophetic text from Daniel (pertaining to the politically loaded topic of Nebuchadnezzar's Dream) he declares that for his purposes the word *clergy* means "unconverted ministers of every denomination who are upheld by human laws. And the expression *Anti-Christ's ministers,* means the same thing" (1803c, 11). All explicit New Testament references to Antichrist occur in the first and second epistles of John. Ironically, the most telling of these (1 John 4:3) follows directly from the admonition in verse 1 to "try the spirits whether they are of God." These verses, when combined, establish criteria for determining which spirits are of God and which are not.

The writings of Benjamin Austin and biblical texts like 1 John were the basis of the revelation that Elias Smith experienced in the summer of 1802, whereby Smith found it possible to gloss what was happening around him it terms of biblical precedent and so articulate his heretofore poorly defined opinions into a conscious faith. The key passage in 1 John is perhaps the following:

> Hereby know ye the Spirit of God: Every spirit that confesseth that Jesus Christ is come in the flesh is of God: And every spirit that confesseth not that Jesus Christ is come in the flesh is not of God: and this is that spirit of anti-christ, whereof ye have heard that it should come; and even now already is it in the world. Ye are of God little children, and have overcome them: because greater is he that is

in you, than he that is in the world. They are of the world: therefore speak they of the world, and the world heareth them. We are of God: he that knoweth God heareth us; he that is not of God heareth not us. Hereby know we the spirit of truth, and the spirit of error. Beloved, let us love one another: for love is of God; and every one that loveth is born of God, and knoweth God. He that loveth not knoweth not God; for God is love. In this was manifested the love of God toward us, because that God sent his only begotten Son into the world, that we might live through him. (4:2–9)

Such a passage, and everything it implies, contains the essence of all that motivated Elias Smith's preaching and writing in the years immediately to follow. During this time he developed a populist creed glossing this passage, which I paraphrase as follows:

We are reborn through Christ, and so know the spirit of truth; those who know God listen to *us.* Those who do not listen to us listen to *them:* the clergy, the creatures of the world. *We* are the 'little children,' apparently powerless, and yet more powerful than the mighty because the spirit of Christ is in *us* not them. *They,* born of Harvard College but not the Holy Ghost, speak of the Law and not the Spirit; *they,* the settled ministry which gains its income through state imposed taxation, are the creation of Law Religion, not the religion of Jesus. *They* are the Pharisees, the tories, the secret monarchists, the apologists for the rich, the Federalists, the vilifiers of that champion of the weak and the defender of the poor, Thomas Jefferson. *We* know by the number of such pharisaical representatives of Anti-Christ abroad in the land, and by the titanic struggle underway between the nations of Europe, that the prophetically foretold dawn of the Second Coming is at hand (1 John 2:18).

Seen in this way, 1 John 4 and similar passages become the scriptural basis for a class-conscious apocalyptic reading of the current American political situation, incidentally, one quite in keeping with Smith's characteristic tactic of turning the statements of his enemies back on themselves. For Smith the concept of Antichrist was a condensed multivalent symbol of all he believed to be wrong in the life of the new nation; but though he had resolved to read the scriptures for himself and forsake human tradition, Smith's interpretation of Antichrist's identity already had quite a respectable ancestry and impeccable revolutionary credentials—dating back well beyond the English Civil War. It had been used by opponents of the papacy, later by Puritans of the left and right against King Charles I and the Anglican episcopal establishment; in America it found similar employment against Britain during the Revolution, and later against the established churches of various states (Bloch 1985; Hill 1971). Occasionally the tables were turned, and similar invective was used against revolutionary republicanism. As Christopher Hill has pointed out, "Emphasis on Antichrist has its advantage in time of acute crisis because of the simple Manicheanism of the doctrine; the world is divided into black and white, Christian and Antichristian" (1971, 170)—or, in the present instance, Republican and Federalist.

Traditional Protestant hermeneutics identified the Antichrist of 1 John with the "man of sin" mentioned in 2 Thessalonians 2:3, in a context pertaining to how it shall be known that these are indeed the last days; first there will be a "falling away," after which "that man of sin be revealed, the son of perdition; who opposeth and exalteth himself above all that is called God" (vv. 3–4). Elias accepted this equation but went far beyond the words of the relevant biblical passages to broadly define *Antichrist* and *the man of sin*—already protean ideas in any event—as whatever and whoever represents "a spirit of opposition to the simplicity that is in Jesus Christ," a simplicity that he found to be betrayed by political and religious hierarchy and by denominational factionalism.

> Anti-Christ is that which does not allow that Christ is the only Saviour, Lord, and Lawgiver; but pleads for many more laws than he gave, and laws contrary to his. Denying the right of *private judgment,* and setting up a system of doctrine, and code of laws, is *Anti-Christ* at *Rome, Constantinople;*—among the *Lutherans, Calvinists, Episcopalians, Presbyterians, Baptists, Methodists, Quakers,* and all others who do not own Christ as all, and in all. Every *name, title, office, creed, platform, confession of faith, discipline,* or *covenant* made by men, is in its nature as really *Anti-Christ,* as the superstitions and fooleries of the Church of Rome. (1812b, 41–42)

The accomplishment of that great work was Elias Smith's singular mission, and it is hardly surprising that a man with such a radical democratic and libertarian message was seen by his enemies as a wolf among their sheep and a menace to society at large—and also not surprising that they would array their own selection of biblical passages against him to prove that he was "a spirit not of God"; "a false prophet showing great signs and wonders"; "a deceiver (were it possible) even of the very elect"; a man who "crept in unawares, an ungodly man turning the grace of God into lasciviousness"; a "false teacher who will seduce many into following his pernicious ways"; a "liar in the Lord's name."[15]

Smith helped provoke this response by identifying the clergy with the "many antichrists" of 1 John 2:18, through whose presence we know that these really are the last times: as, for example, he did in the *Clergyman's Looking-Glass No. 2; being a History of the Birth, Life, and Death of Anti-Christ*—wherein Elias documents, in mock scriptural parody with chapter and verse, the career of Antichrist down to June 1, 1803, and the latest appearance of the "man of sin" in the form of Joseph Buckminster's observations on baptism (which for some reason Buckminster published without using his titles). "One of Anti-Christ's servants shall endeavor to make the people believe that Jesus Christ is his master, and that he requires parents to sprinkle their children. . . . (And for fear that he shall be considered Anti-Christ's servant, he will leave out the titles Anti-Christ gave him; which is Rev, and A.M. This he will do to conceal himself, that he may serve Anti-Christ in disguise)" (1803b, 36–38). In contrast, Elias styled himself merely "preacher of the gospel" or "servant of Jesus Christ" (Plummer 1842, 149).

Smith had only lately come to this detestation of the regular clergy; there is no sign that he had gone this far in his own settled ministerial posts in Salisbury and Woburn. The vitriol that Elias poured into his anticlericalism was not in any direct way a natural product of his own Baptist upbringing. To be sure, the New Light Separates and Baptists of Lyme had a history of antiestablishment opinion and occasional open conflict, but Elias makes no mention that either he or his family had any particular difficulties with the local establishment as such. Neither was there a history of controversy with the other churches of Woodstock, where, in that recently opened country, there really was no establishment of religion at all. Therefore, a frontal assault on the ministry was part of the revolution of sentiment that Elias underwent in 1802 3, and of deepening party antagonisms throughout society at large that Elias found himself able to articulate and address through his attacks on the clergy. But more personal factors were surely contributory elements, specifically a fair element of class resentment toward those who claimed specialist knowledge through their access to higher education and who would not give self-educated men like Smith the time of day because of what was taken to be their rustic crudeness and ignorance. That, in any event, is an interpretation easily gleaned from Elias's introduction to *The Clergyman's Looking Glass No. 1:*

> It has been my lot for twelve years past, to be opposed by the clergy, from whom I have received the most abusive treatment I ever met with; no other class of men have written and reported so many false and scandalous things about me as they have. The clergy in general, have never been willing that I should have any place to preach in, wherever I go, there [*sic*] language is to this amount, "prophesy not here, go into the land of Juda and prophecy and eat bread; but prophecy not here, for it is the kings chapel." I have always found the clergy as a body great backbiters; it is a rare thing that I ever can have an opportunity to see them or converse with them, though I have often desired it, and it is rare that they hear me; it is an uncommon thing for me to be admitted so near as to speak to them yet they are often biting my back; speaking hard things about me, though not to me. They often call me a wolf, and as often act the part of a hireling in fleeing, and keeping out of sight. (1803a, iii)

By July 1803, Elias—having read in 1 Peter 4:17 that "the time is come that judgment must begin at the house of God"—was including the Baptist clergy in his condemnation of the anti-Christian worldly ministry, and said as much in a letter to a brother in Boston that soon, as evidently it was intended to, reached the eyes of Thomas Baldwin. In his letter Elias wrote that the judgment mentioned in 1 Peter could only mean "punishment inflicted on professors of religion for leaving their first love, and conforming to the world in their manner of worship and appearance" (284–85). Elias claimed that he meant no harm to anyone through this, but Baldwin drew the conclusion that the strictures in the letter pertained to himself and responded accordingly in a return note to Smith, who reported of Baldwin that "the clergyman's looking glass displeased him" (1804a). As well it might have, for what Elias had done was to implicitly condemn his former friend for what he had become since moving to Boston—a hireling who followed the lead of fashionable clergymen in the wearing of the surplice, band, and "other *Popish* or *Babylonish garments*," and who accepted money for preaching before the General Court of the Commonwealth. Baldwin reciprocated by accusing Smith of attempting to incite a party spirit among the brethren and of setting up out of pride his church in Portsmouth as the ideal for all others to follow. Elias responded by declaring that Baldwin had gone into Babylon but that if he behaved as he formerly did when they were both country preachers, there would be nothing to divide them. "When Mr. Baldwin lived in Canaan [N.H.], he called himself a minister of God's word. When he came to Boston, he laid aside the title Jesus gave him . . . and received a worldly title . . . which was, A.M. When I saw this . . . I could not forbear saying, '*How hast thou fallen!*'" (Smith et al. 1804).

The events in this active period of Elias Smith's life are complex, the patterns shifting; however, what followed is clear enough—a definitive repudiation of former Baptist associates, a clarion call for no mere revival but another reformation, and to that end the creation of the *Herald of Gospel Liberty* as an instrument of God's will in America. Abner Jones by now was already active in Boston and, according to his son, quite at one with Baldwin and Samuel Stillman, even though it must be assumed that he already differed from them considerably on theological points. There was a vigorous revival underway among the Boston Baptists by the autumn of 1803, a time that the historian of the First Church looked back on as one in which Unitarian defections were creating problems among the Congregationalists; in this version of history, the Baptists stepped into the breach to preserve the old orthodox Calvinist faith and indirectly help steel the resolve of those Congregationalists who could not abide the Unitarian heresy (Wood 1899, 294).

It was a heated atmosphere. Jones's son thought it was Elias who stirred up the trouble that led to a final parting between the Christians and the Boston Calvinist Baptists. In later life Abner Jones said that Elias Smith always had him "in hot water" during the period of their close association. Jones's son thought Smith was Abner's "evil genius," provoking him to do things he might not have done otherwise, and was at pains to show that in fact it was Jones who was the first free Christian in New England, not Elias Smith (Jones 1842, 65-67).[16] Be that as it may with hindsight, the immediate result was that Jones was excluded along with Smith from Baptist pulpits and vestries and by July 1804, had constituted his own Christian congregation in Boston out the debris left behind by the schism he and Elias had provoked among their former friends and by whatever outsiders were picked up along the way.[17] On Smith's side there were other factors that led to all this; one was a declension in his Portsmouth church that spilled over to foul the waters in Boston, another the unwillingness of the Boston Baptists to have a black brother named Thomas Paul preach before them.

Charles Peirce was one of the original members of Smith's flock in Portsmouth, though still claiming an affiliation to Stillman's church in Boston. But by August 1803, he led a faction that wished to replace Elias because they regarded him as a "public nuisance" and believed that the rest of the town shared that view. The first sign of the difficulty appears in the record for August 28. At a meeting of the church, it was decided to appoint a committee to wait on Peirce and admonish him for his "disorderly walk." A woman named Underwood seems to have been an accomplice, for the rest of the church undertook disciplinary action against her for absenting herself from their communion and for having accepted without evidence certain unspecified accusations against Smith, which one must assume originated either with Peirce or with Elias's creditors in Salisbury and Woburn.

In September Peirce himself was formally admonished for having broken his covenant engagements, which evoked a violent reaction suggesting a flux in local opinion about the basic principles of church organization. Peirce claimed that there *was* no covenant because, when he put forward the idea that there should be one in order to regularize their proceedings, Smith retorted that it was not desirable to do so because "that was only tradition and it would be coming directly into the old Congregational track, and that he knew of no other way of adding to the church than by Baptizing people, and the moment they were Baptized they were members of the Church." They nonetheless agreed to have a few words said about the nature of their fellowship before they sat down at the communion table together; but Peirce believed that the members admitted in this early period did not consider themselves to have entered into any binding agreement by this act. He reasoned that, in the absence of a proper covenant, Smith's church was scarcely in any position to sanction a member for violating it. As for the elder himself, Peirce made it quite clear that he took exception to what Smith had begun to preach and publish since the church was first gathered at the New Year.

Smith's party claimed that they had signatures assenting to the doctrines of the New Testament and promising to walk according to the New Testament rule. Their view was that Peirce, in agreeing to this and to the articles of faith and practice drawn up by the Christian Conference in 1802, had indeed entered into an engagement with them that he was now violating by trying to undermine their elder and even to replace him with a Methodist minister "or some other man." That accusation was more than enough for Peirce, and the correspondence closes with an angry letter in October accusing his erstwhile brethren of "barefaced cruel treatment" and declaring that under these circumstances he would be selling the house and land he had recently purchased at auction (to house Elias?) unless the church immediately came up with the money it owed him. This nasty business soon drew in Samuel Stillman's First Church, to which the Portsmouth congregation wrote with an account of Peirce's dealings with them accompanied by copies of all relevant correspondence—including the threat to sell the house and land that, in their view, clearly showed Peirce to be "an enemy to the power of Religion among us."

That was a long way from the fellowship of January. Stories were flying about between Portsmouth, Boston, Salisbury, and Woburn that together caused Elias considerable embarrassment. "My enemies in Portsmouth were numerous and violent, my friends were few and the greater part young people. In Boston the baptists were displeased at my writings, and evil reports were in general circulation" (289). He chose to fight back by publishing under one cover—with appended editorial remarks—the letters pertaining to his dispute with Thomas Baldwin, a letter to Stillman complaining of the treatment he was receiving at the First Church (including evil reports spread by Peirce), and letters between himself and the Woburn church concerning the nature of their mutual difficulties. In the letter to Stillman of May 2, 1804, Elias now began dealing explicitly with the theological differences that separated them and, in raising the question of Thomas Paul, also struck on a theme to which he would return many times: his utter antipathy to discrimination against people of color—slavery, of course, but no less the treatment that Smith believed Paul was receiving from the Boston Baptists.

Thomas Paul was born in 1773 in Exeter, New Hampshire, of "respectable" free black parentage. In the early days simply the presence of a "colored" preacher was enough to draw crowds to hear him out of curiosity; but Paul was also a successful evangelist remembered for a "pleasing and fervent address." In the 1820s he labored for a time in Haiti under the auspices of the Massachusetts Baptist Missionary Society, though without particular success given his ignorance of French. Around 1810 Paul was influential in the establishment of the Abyssinian Baptist Church in New York, while yet remaining affiliated with Boston, where he spent his last years until his death in 1831 (Dowling 1849). Not much more is known about this man. William McLoughlin has noted that "surprisingly little has been written about Thomas Paul although his was the first independent Black church in the North, and he was the first Black pastor in the Baptist churches of New England" (1971, 2:766n).[18] His is a story remaining to be told.

In the letter to Stillman, Smith accused his former patron of having "opposed brother Paul's preaching in the vestry, on account of his colour." According to the history of the First Baptist Church (1899), many blacks had been baptized during the 1803 revival, thus swelling the numbers of their race already present in the congregation; by this account there were now sufficient black Baptists to ask for dismissal from Stillman's church in order to gather one of their own—the First

African Baptist Church of Boston. Permission was duly granted, and in 1805 Samuel Stillman preached the installation sermon for the new Baptist pastor, Thomas Paul (Wood 1899, 297). Writing in 1804, in the midst of these dramatic and portentous events, Elias Smith put quite a different light on the situation of the black Baptists by linking it to the ill treatment he and Jones were receiving themselves.

Baldwin, for example, is reported to have been reluctant to allow Jones to conduct baptisms in his church; "he did this [or so said Smith] to prevent a minister of Christ, from obeying his Master's orders." By March 1804 Smith and Jones had been excluded from preaching in the Baptist vestries because of open conflict over central points of Calvinistic doctrine and the fervent style of their preaching. Their exclusion immediately led to the formation of the first Christian Church in Boston under Abner Jones and the emergence of the Christians as a self-consciously radical movement in the same year that the black Baptists gathered an independent church of their own (293).

Smith recalled that Baldwin had concerns about the possible effects of taking blacks into his congregation and shared with Stillman reservations about allowing Thomas Paul to preach before them.

> When Thomas Paul came to Boston, Dr. [Stillman] told him it was *Boston*, and that they did not mix colours; or words of that import. He was not even willing he should preach in the vestry. Mr. Baldwin told me about these words, as near as I can recollect, "There are some of my congregation, who would leave the meeting, if Paul should preach here; on the whole (said he) we are too *proud* to have him preach; and as long as there are other white men to preach, I do not think it best for him to preach here." According to this, Jesus ought to be informed, that the ministers, and some others in Boston, are so *proud*, that it is not best for him to send any but *white-faced* preachers there, for they will not receive them. (Smith et al. 1804, 18)

Stillman's church advised its fledgling offspring that it should not admit whites, lest their intention to become an African church be compromised (McLoughlin 1971, 2:765).[19] Elias Smith, for his part, was quite certain that the treatment he, Jones, and their black brethren were receiving just added to the accumulating evidence showing how far the Baptists had lost sight of their origins and descended into Babylon. Given this, Elias predicted that in not many years *"Boston will be the same to the Baptists,* as *Rome* was to the catholicks—the Mother of Harlots" (Smith et al. 1804, 29).

Smith had great sympathy for the African Baptists. Though he was not above using what he took to be black dialect when it suited him in his writings to illustrate the principle that simple people often understand things their betters mistake, his attitudes toward blacks reveal much about himself and the emerging platform of the Christian Connection insofar as he was in a position to determine it. Elias once observed "a coloured labouring man" sitting beside his wheelbarrow, and on the side of the barrow was painted a sign saying "United with all Religious Societies in America." Smith asked him the meaning of this and in answer was told that the man considered himself united with all those who feared God. Elias suggested that he write this comment on the inside of the wheelbarrow, but the black man responded that it was not necessary, since the sentiment was engraved on his heart and "that is the best place for it." This agreeable response gave Elias cause to reflect that the faith of such a man was closer to the religion of Jesus than that of all the "D.D.'s, Parisees, and Hypocrites" in the world (*HGL* 3, no. 75 [July 5, 1811]: 299).

In 1805 Elias commenced his first experiment in periodical journalism, the *Christian's Magazine (CM)*. In the first issue he made clear that the purpose was to "diffuse useful knowledge among my fellow men, and particularly among those who love our Lord Jesus Christ." In that same year he was present at a baptism conducted by the Reverend Thomas Paul and described his experience for the magazine.

> I was exceedingly delighted with the performance. I went to see black people baptized; but when I saw them all dressed in white, all appearing to have heaven in their souls and joy on their countenances, and appearing to rejoice with the white robed company which came out of great tribulation—I thought if, they were black, yet they were comely; and seeing that God was no respecter of persons, and that Ethiopia was stretching out her hand, and that a son had taken them by the hand. I thought we might say of this company: *"Thou are beautiful O my love, as Tirzah, comely as Jerusalem, and terrible as an army with banners."* (*CM* 1, no. 2 [1805]: 66–68)

Elias Smith and his Portsmouth church were true to their principles, for in January 1808 they heard the experience of "Levi Johnson, a Man of Colour, concerning the reason of [his] hope." Mr. Johnson was duly baptized and numbered with the church in February, the record proudly noting that "he was the first male member of colour, that ever was added or baptized in this Town, agreeable to the New Testament." This particular conversion did not work out as well as might have been hoped, since Johnson was expelled the following year for "disorderly walk"—accused of drunkenness, lying, and stealing a brass kettle and a pair of andirons. This latest evidence of the fallibility of human nature did not affect the principle of the thing in the slightest. Elias remained firm to the last in his belief in the natural equality of all those reborn in Jesus, and later equated the abolition of slavery in New York State with the repeal of its medical licensing laws as examples of progressive democratic enlightenment. But when Thomas Paul came to be ordained a Baptist pastor, Elias commented acidly that, having once been free, Paul had become a slave to Stillman and Baldwin, his masters in Boston, by whom he "is soon to be adorned with POPISH ATTIRE" (*CM* 1, no. 4 [1806]: 155).

In September 1804 the Woburn church informed Smith that they had withdrawn the hand of fellowship from him because he had withdrawn from them without good cause. He answered this charge in a statement of his new beliefs via the public letters to Baldwin, Stillman, and others. He no longer considered himself a member of the Woburn congregation, but of the "Church of Christ" in Portsmouth: "If you wish to know what denomination I belong to, I tell you, as a professor of religion, I am a Christian; as a preacher, a minister of Christ, calling no man father or master; holding as abominable in the sight of God, every thing highly esteemed among men, such as Calvinism, Arminianism, Freewillism, Universalism, Reverends, Parsons, Chaplains, Doctors of Divinity, Clergy, Bands, Surplices, Notes, Creeds, Covenants, and Platforms, with the spirit of Slander, which those who hold to these things, are too often in possession of" (Smith et al. 1804, 24).

No more covenants, at least for people other than the Jews, whose agreement with the Lord remains in effect. No more trappings of established religion. No more controversy over doctrines not named in the New Testament. Therefore expunge the covenant of grace, the Trinity, eternal punishment, predestination, and special election because they are "a part of those *fables* which men turn unto, when they turn from the truth of the gospel" (1812b, 118). Expunge the traditional hermeneutic of Old Testament type and New Testament antitype, and hence the spurious parallel between Jewish circumcision and Christian baptism upon which the orthodox draw to justify the sprinkling of infants.[20] Though "the Old Testament is profitable for doctrine, reproof and instruction in righteousness, and was written for our learning; yet the New Testament contains the compleat rule of our faith; and there is no one thing required of a christian, but what is found in the New Testament" (Smith et al. 1802, 3).

As for particular churches, there are to be only three criteria for membership, none requiring formal assent to any doctrine or creed (except an implicit but total rejection of Calvinism): "First. That the person gives an evidence that he is born again. Second. That he has been *buried* in baptism after believing. Third. That he lives a new life." So far as practical worship is concerned, the New Testament authorizes preaching, praying, exhorting, singing psalms, and breaking bread; it does not specify the order in which this is to be done, and so the only order necessary is that "as will be most to edification of the whole." In almost all modern churches (Free-Will Baptists, Quakers, and certain Methodists excepted), there is a set order of service dominated by the minister; but in the Christian churches—as in the primitive church— "every one has a right to *preach, pray, exhort,* or *sing* one by one." Women, though denied a governmental role, were nonetheless allowed to pray and prophesy in the early church, and therefore (said Elias) "so it is now" (*CM* 1, no. 3 [1805]: 87). As for relations between these new purified churches, the only connection there need or should be is "through fellowship of the spirit"—through common recognition that Christ is all (1805b, 41).

4 A THIEF IN THE NIGHT
Prophecy and Politics

*He revealeth the deep and secret things: he
knoweth what is in the darkness, and the
light dwelleth with him.*

DANIEL 2:22

IN AN 1805 SERMON CONCERNING THE Day of Judgment, Elias
Smith suggested that the recent reappearance of the northern lights in
New England was a portent of the last days (1805a). For Smith and
many others, the signs of their time suggested that the struggle between Christ and Antichrist was approaching its eagerly anticipated
conclusion.

We read of commotions and signs in the skies,

The sun and the moon shall be cloth'd in disguise;

And when you shall see all these tokens appear,

Then lift up your heads, your Redemption draws near.

(SMITH ET AL. 1804, 7)

The country was alive with would-be prophets eager to give an
interpretation of what was afoot to all who would listen to them. No
matter where one stood, there was a cultist or visionary further beyond.
This millennialism was an important aspect of the opening phases of
the Second Awakening. Not only was there a new century, there was a
new political order brought about by the 1799 election of Thomas Jefferson. Abroad there was war, and at home partisan strife. In 1798 the
republic had barely avoided official hostilities with France, and now
conflict loomed with Britain. Apocalyptic expectation added spice to

domestic politics, and prophecy was easily enlisted in the service of more secular causes.

Millennialism, though often correlated with political events, was not necessarily driven by them. Prophecy was readily available to anyone with a taste for the arcane; as the 1840s Millerite agitation would prove, biblical chronology could also suffice for the derivation of millennial predictions. Social historians are now engaged in plumbing the depths of folk occultism and charting the distribution and significance of millennialist thought in colonial America and the early republic. In the light of such research, it is plain that Elias Smith was a man of his age. In addition to his millennialism, Elias put great stock in veridical prophetic dreams, while the herbalist Samuel Thomson found himself accused of wizardry and, though otherwise materialistic in his approach, personally believed in clairvoyance.[1] When such beliefs are combined with institutional flux, the overseas political situation, a radical republican mode of thought, the expansion of population, and the sectarian fervor of the early nineteenth century, it is no marvel that this was a time for the shaking of the churches, the competition of personal visions in a buyer's market.

Benjamin Randal, for example, had persistent troubles with internal dissension induced by the antinomian perfectionism implicit in his free-will doctrines; he had to argue with members of his own connection who held that, once saved, it is impossible to sin again. On one occasion Randal faced a schism led by a renegade preacher whom he had himself ordained but who now cultivated wild enthusiasms in his meetings and founded an Angel Society among those who believed that they were totally released from Satan's grasp (Buzzell 1827, 177–78).[2] In 1788 the Free-Willers also had the unfortunate experience of a massive defection to the Shakers among the brethren in Canterbury, New Hampshire, where the apostates founded a commune that until recently housed some of the last remaining followers of Mother Ann Lee, and whose buildings remain to this day as a Shaker museum.[3] John Buzzell, Randal's biographer, noted that the Shaker success on that occasion emboldened greater efforts and the foundation of still more of their societies in northeastern New England (or as Smith put it, "in breaking up families and endeavoring to invert the order of nature, and depopulate the country" [*HGL* 4, no. 5 [Oct. 25, 1811]: 330). Buzzell ruefully observed of his former Free-Will brethren that "by over driving, they got into some extravagances" such that they believed themselves to have achieved a state of spiritual perfection (1827, 109–10).[4]

Likewise Ephraim Stinchfield, himself ordained by Randal in 1799 before going over to the Christians, encountered a strange sect in Kennebunk, Maine, which by 1817 had spread as far afield as Gray, Saco, and Portland. It was led by a prophet named Jacob Cochrane, who was making inroads into the flock of one Joseph Smith, ordained a Christian evangelist by Elias Smith and Mark Fernald in 1810 (*HGL* 3, no. 58 [Nov. 9, 1810]: 232).[5] According to local folklore, Joseph Smith had attempted, on the biblical precedent of Samson pulling down a Philistine temple, to physically overthrow the local meetinghouse through the power of his word alone. Even though failing in "this egregious folly, the zeal of the followers of Smith was in no degree abated" (Bourne 1875, 633). When Cochrane arrived in 1815, he thus found a fertile field already prepared for him. Cochranite theology remains obscure, but he was able to convince his followers that he had the power to deliver them completely from evil, and he was apparently able to induce religious ecstasies at will. Stinchfield found the claim of the Cochranites to have attained absolute liberty to be a mere excuse for licentiousness; by his account marriage bonds were dissolved and new "spiritual" alliances consummated among the believers, who, following the practice of the early church, were to have all things in common (Stinchfield 1819a, 7–8).[6] "Cochrane pretends to have the power of life and death in his hands, and frightens his pupils into a compliance with any of his injunctions, by threatening to stop their breath in a moment; but which means he takes females from their parents, and carries them to his brothel. He declares that he has the keys of the kingdom of heaven, and pretends to open it for, or shut it against, whom he sees fit" (ibid., 11).[7]

A town historian found Joseph and Elias Smith equally ludicrous and derived considerable satisfaction from the fact that—bad leading to worse—the Cochranites were able to overthrow the Christian Connection in Kennebunk (Remich 1911, 276). Nor was the local historian alone in associating Elias and his associates with the more extravagant religious phenomena of the time. Thomas Andros, in detailing Smith's "abominable heresies," compared them with "the diabolical fanaticism" of Ann Lee, the Shaker prophetess (1817, 25). Gilbert McMaster, a Presbyterian clergyman in eastern New York State, on observing the local prominence of Nancy Gove Cram, a Christian evangelist closely allied to Smith, associated her with Jemima Wilkinson, Ann Lee, and King Ahab's wife, Jezebel (1815, 109–10).

Mark Fernald ran into the same problem as had Ephraim Stinchfield, in no less a form than the man who had preached death and destruction the summer before the great Portsmouth fire. This was Elliot Frost of Maine, who believed himself to be on a mission from God as evinced by his own personal immortality.

> So far did this delusion run, that Frost, in the greatest apparent joy and happiness, at one time undressed himself entirely, crossed what is called Great Works River, in South Berwick, passed through the main street of the village, in the open day, while brother Silas Goodwin bore his clothing after him, supposing they were obeying God and exposing the nakedness of the people spiritually. This was the commencement of my trials with honest but deceived Christians. O! Delusion: O! Fanaticism. I could only weep, pray, and preach truth, and wait the trying event of the prevailing delusion. (Fernald 1852, 35)

Fernald attempted to convince the Christians of South Berwick that Frost was "religiously deranged." Given a widespread local belief, however, that Frost was indeed sent by God, Fernald could only mournfully recall that "this brought heavy trials on the young church, and laid the foundation for its overthrow in 1833." In 1819 Fernald ran into another such group in Gilford, New Hampshire, which held that its prophets could pronounce forgiveness of sins, heal the sick, and work miracles. "Good Lord," he wrote, "deliver Zion from the many wild notions in the world about religion." The "perfect law of liberty" proudly proclaimed by the Christians was a mixed blessing with respect to the deportment of the churches that subscribed to it.

The Jeffersonian proto-psychiatrist Benjamin Rush, who had am-

Plate 4. Mark Fernald (1784–1851): Christian preacher in Maine, early associate of Elias Smith and keeper of the faith when Smith lost it. Reprinted from Mark Fernald, *Life of Elder Mark Fernald* (Newburyport, Mass.: Geo. Moore Payne & D. P. Pike, 1852).

ple experience in such things, noted that madness may result from "researches into the meaning of certain prophecies in the Old and New Testaments . . . most frequently from an attempt to fix the precise time in which those prophecies were to be fulfilled, or from a disappointment in that time, after it had passed" (also noting a correlation between madness and the acquisitive commercial ethic of the age) (1835, 35; see also Watts 1987, 139). Though deeply involved in apocalyptic readings of history, Elias Smith did not attempt to set an exact date for the Second Coming (that would be left for William Miller and the next generation of Christians). Yet he was convinced it must be soon: "From the present state of the world, we have reason to believe that the end of all things is at hand" (*HGL* 6, no. 6 [Nov. 12, 1813]: 543). As to the day and hour when Christ will return in glory, "no one knows; but we may know the signs of his coming, and if we only look to the heavens and earth at the present time, we may see signs in great abundance" (ibid. 1, no. 6 [Nov. 10, 1808]: 23).

What were these signs? The darkening of the sun and moon in the year 1780, wars, pestilences, earthquakes, the distress of many nations, general human perplexity, the hunger of the artisans of Manchester, England, turned out of their factories for want of work—and perhaps above all, the present situation of the Jews.[8] Could it even be that Emperor Napoleon, who had done so much for their liberation in Europe, would see fit to return them to Palestine? If so, "the attentive Christian will see, in this age, a rapid fulfilment of Scripture prophecy, and that things are in a train of preparation for the introduction of the Millennium" (*HGL* 1, no. 7 [Nov. 24, 1808]: 26). That was for the future to tell; meanwhile Ephraim Stinchfield reported making three converts on the day after a considerable earthquake shook the region around Kennebec, Maine.[9]

The signs were meaningful only in relation to prophecy and God's will; otherwise they perhaps would be frightening or ominous but lacking in clear significance. Though Elias Smith and his friends devalued the Old Testament in their 1802 confession of faith, Smith persisted in using it as a prophetic guide to the meaning of present events—as he believed he was entitled to do on the authority of such texts as 2 Peter 1:19–21, which declares that "prophecy came not in old time by the will of man: but holy men of God spake as they were moved by the Holy Ghost." Isaiah, after all, speaks of the coming of the Christ, and the followers of Jesus turned to Isaiah when weighing the possibility that he was truly the Promised One.

Identifying Old Testament prefigurations of the Messiah was a commonplace in biblical hermeneutics, no less for Smith than the more orthodox of his contemporaries and for the early Christians who started the business.

> Isr'el in ancient days,
> Not only had a view

Of Sinai in a blaze,

But learn'd the gospel too:

The types and figures were a glass

In which they saw the Saviour's face.

(JONES 1804)

Elias appealed to the prophet Hosea to demonstrate that the Lord may speak in "visions" and "similitudes" (Hos. 12:10); he was therefore able to claim that the golden bowl shown by an angel to the prophet Zechariah in a vision is a figure of Jesus (Zech. 4:2–3), and that the seven lamps of the candlestick upon which the bowl was placed represent the manifold unity of those reborn in Christ. In pursuing this exegesis, Elias arrived at the congenial (although far from obvious message) that "there is not one thing required of us to believe or practice, but what is in Christ, the golden bowl" (1809a, 32). One of the more surprising "similitudes" of this type that Smith identified is "the plant of renown" (Ezek. 34:29) that the Lord will one day raise up for the nourishment of his chosen people. Elias later glossed Ezekiel's "plant" as a metaphor both for Jesus Christ and for *Lobelia inflata* (Indian Tobacco, or "Pukeweed"), an emetic herb at the center of the Thomsonian medical system (1812b, 383).

Second Peter speaks of prophecy as "a light that shineth in a dark place." Although warning that "no prophecy of the scripture is of any private interpretation," Smith nevertheless employed these passages as introduction to his 1808 book *Sermons Containing an Illustration of the Prophecies,* which Elias used to advance his characteristic biblical literalism. The light *is* clear not dark, and prophecy obscures only because people make it so. Those who seek for symbolic meanings behind the plain word of Scripture are doing what Peter warned against, engaging in private interpretation. As a Methodist critic rightly said, "It seems you would have a system of religion without any mystery" (Merritt 1807, 6). Nevertheless, Elias—seemingly unaware of his own inconsistency—succumbed to the temptation to read prophecy symbolically when he used the consummately obscure and oracular (and hence everpopular) books of Daniel and Revelation as interpretive guides to contemporary politics, thus allowing him to discern "what the hand of God has wrought for us." It is one thing to say that the "new heaven" and "new earth" of Revelation 21:1 should not be taken figuratively but literally—that the weather will be better after the Second Coming, that the New Earth will have a continuous surface with no sea, and that men and women will walk this New Earth, not as spirits, but as embodied immortals (Smith 1808a, 238–48). It is rather another thing to say that Thomas Jefferson is the sixth angel of Revelation 16:12, who poured out his vial upon the great river Euphrates "that the way of the kings of the east might be prepared," that the great red dragon of Revelation 12:3 represents partisan clergymen, and that the body of the fourth beast of Daniel 7:19–27 signifies "a form of government where religion is a part of the constitution" (1805e, 77, 51; *HGL* 3, no. 64 [Feb. 1, 1811]).

Even when Smith did not directly use prophecy as a gloss on current events, he continually used the Bible in his sermons and discourses to situate contemporary America relative to the mythic paradigms of sacred history—as he did in his most political discourse, *The Loving Kindness of God Displayed in the Triumph of Republicanism in America,* delivered July 4, 1809, on the village green in Taunton, Massachusetts. Elias framed this discourse as a commentary on Psalm 107, showing that the love mentioned there is the same as that currently being displayed toward the new republic, even in the face of Federalist plots to overthrow it. The psalm sings of a nation gathered out of the winds, wanderers in the wilderness that the Lord delivered and settled, humbling the powerful who wished to oppress them and setting the poor on high in their place: "Whoso is wise, and will observe these things, even they shall understand the lovingkindness of the Lord" (v. 43). For Smith, the loving-kindness of God toward the United States was just as obvious as it had been for Israel "when Moses hoisted the standard of liberty, and marched out of Egypt."

It was always the genius of Smith and his fellows to address their audiences in terms readily accessible to them. In the present instance one senses the type of audience Elias addressed and the political ambiance in which he did so through an ironically toned report sent in by a Taunton correspondent to the Federalist *Columbian Centinal* of Boston. "The 4th of July was celebrated here by both parties. Each had a dinner contiguous to each other on the Green—each an Oration.— The Federalists upwards of 300—democrats 250.—The latter were honored with the company of Mr. *Elias Smith,* who had much to say. The greatest order was preserved by both parties" (July 8, 1809, 2).[10]

What Smith had to say concerned the things for the wise to observe regarding the loving-kindness of God. The nature of the Federalist oration has not been recorded, but Smith's appeal can be understood in relation to the sentiments he was addressing among his own auditors when he attacked the opposition group simultaneously holding forth at the other end of the common, in effect accusing them of being a faction working in secret for the dissolution of the nation and betrayal of America to England and Spain. Smith selected his texts carefully and searched for a resonance with his Taunton audience when invoking Psalm 107, which also sings of "they that go down to the sea in ships, that do business in great waters; these see the works of the Lord, and his wonders in the deep" (vv. 23–24).

In September 1816 Elias himself, then only a year away from his conversion to Universalism, had the opportunity to employ these powerful maritime images in a dramatic service held on the banks of the Taunton River, perhaps before some of those who heard him seven years previously. Here Elias—speaking from the scaffolding of a ship under construction at the river bank—preached from Isaiah of a time when "the glorious Lord will be unto us a place of broad rivers and streams; wherein shall go no galley with oars, neither shall gallant ship pass thereby" (Isa. 33:21). Smith illustrated the gloriousness of the Lord, that he is the place of broad rivers and streams, a boundless ocean upon which no ship is needed to sail if only one believes in Jesus as Savior. He reported to the *Herald* that "the similitude was before the people, and each one might see the meaning, by looking at the river then running within a few feet of the place where they sat."

> The Bible is my chart;
> By it the seas I know;
> I cannot with it part,
> It rocks and sands doth show;
> It is a chart and compass too,
> Whose needle points forever true.
>
> (SMITH ET AL. 1804, 59)

Others then spoke of one church and one baptism, "of the importance and truth of that religion, which destroys all party distinctions, and makes men one in Christ."

The previous February, the church of Thomas Andros in nearby Berkley had sad occasion to excommunicate Sister Polly Hatheway for subscribing to Elias Smith's "heretical doctrines," for violating her covenant vows, for preaching as though she herself were an apostle, and for "attending the ministrations & upholding & encouraging heretical & schismatical preachers, seeking to overthrow the truth & regular worship & order of the Churches."[11] Knowing all this, Smith took critical note of Andros in a preface to his account of the meeting at Taunton River: "The minister is considered a Calvinist. I once heard him and to me, he was a confused man. His discourse was to me like the reading on a page of an Almanack; sometimes one thing, then another, and then the same again. I am told that he does not allow his people to hear the Christian preachers. In this town, some who do not belong to his order, have seen their property taken by force to pay his salary" (*HGL* 8, no. 2 [Oct. 1816]: 67–70).[12]

Happily, Elias said, many in Berkley had escaped the coils of law religion and gathered a church of their own choosing under Elder William Whitten. Like Mark Fernald, Whitten had been a sailor. As with the rustic boatman John Snelling Popkin encountered in Newbury, it is possible to gain access through him to a sense of the attitudes and callings of those drawn to the Christian movement and the eschatological hopes upon which it drew: farmers, artisans, sailors, a transient urban population of day laborers, some free blacks, and a good many none-too-rich women of uncertain employment—persons well situated to respond viscerally to the antielitism of Jeffersonian Republicanism as enunciated in apocalyptic scriptural terms by the populist evangelicals.

❧

Anecdotally supported inference about the composition of the early Christian movement is supported by the lists of church membership that survive from Elias Smith's church in Portsmouth, from Abner Jones's church in Boston, and from Daniel Hix's church in Dartmouth, Massachusetts, a rural agricultural town in the southern part of the state near New Bedford (Hutt 1924, 709).[13] The most important general fact that emerges from the lists, and from the known activities of the Christian evangelists, is that this movement was not unidimensional, not restricted to only one social context or stratum. True, these people were usually of modest to middling background and means, and all were undoubtedly attuned by virtue of their own evangelical heritage to respond favorably to messages rationalizing political choice by religious principle. Beyond that, however, they were a mix of townspeople and farmers who were differently situated with respect to economic situation, local class relations, and the theological and political controversies of the time—and who accordingly became Christian adherents for somewhat different reasons.

Some were drawn in through the persuasiveness and power of the class-conscious rhetoric of the evangelists. But Smith's analysis of contemporary society, for example, was entirely consistent with that advanced by the general run of republican orators, while his born-again Baptist perfectionism was merely the latest manifestation of an American evangelical style around since the First Awakening; Elias's talent lay in fusing the two. Most Baptists—for that matter, the members of all the nonestablishment sects of New England—were likely to be Democratic-Republican in sympathy, if only because of their fervent desire (in the words of Jefferson's famous letter to the Danbury Baptists) to erect a "wall of separation" between church and state such that they could never again be oppressed by a governmentally supported ecclesiastical establishment (McLoughlin 1971, 2:785). Class, occupation, and former religious affiliation are therefore only approximate predictors of who would join the Christian movement. Other factors, harder to grasp, were equally if not more important in specific cases.

Many Americans were discomfited by the first outbreak of what would come to be seen as perfectly normal party antagonism and, whether Federalist or Republican, blamed the opposition for creating it. Some were convinced that the problems of the time were indeed due to a plethora of warring sects and parties, and that the only way out was to return to the Scriptures and emphasize the unity of the primitive church and hence the hoped-for unity of the new nation. Such was the case with Daniel Hix, who in addition to his pastoral duties was a prominent farmer rather than some crazed itinerant Jacobin. Just as with Smith and the Warren Baptist Association, Hix moved past the range of doctrines generally acceptable among his Baptist colleagues of the Groton Conference and, after a period of soul-searching, concluded that all creeds, covenants, and denominational names were merely human works and should be rejected. His congregation was already liberal, characterized by Smith as free-will and open-communionist in sentiment (319). Daniel Hix first met Elias in 1805 and apparently was impressed enough to name a son after him: Daniel Elias Hix. By 1807 he had taken virtually his entire church with him into the Christian fold. In this case it was not so much the spontaneous appeal of evangelical preaching that did the job, but rather the moral influence of a respected pastor (Andrews 1880).

In the first number of the *Herald,* in September 1808, Smith announced that Daniel Hix would soon speak in Boston, and reference to Hix's work appears regularly in Smith's paper thereafter. In October Hix himself reported having baptized no less than 232 reborn souls since January 1807, and of his belief that "every person born again is in Christ's church"—the only proper name of which is *Christian,* the only organizational principle of which is the voluntary association of the regenerate without the artificial human conventions of *articles* or *covenants.*[14] In the *Herald* of July 20, 1810, he wrote that he had now baptized over 1,000 but also of the treatment he was receiving from the Baptists by virtue of his questionable association with Smith. Elias had already himself encountered the attitude of what he called the "great ministers" of the Groton Conference. Once when attempting to preach before them, he found that rather than listen, they retreated out into the rain, "as though they thought some pestilence was about to spread among the people; they fled, as hirelings do when they see the wolf coming" (*CM* 1, no. 4 [1805]: 248). Soon the relationship between the Baptists and the First Christian Church of Dartmouth was terminated unmourned, and in a letter to his former associate Daniel Hix wrote that, "although the conference has dropped us, Jesus has not" (Andrews 1880, 92, 115). Much the same thing happened in nearby Freetown, Massachusetts, a place Elias had visited on a number of occasions, where both of its Baptist churches went over to the Christian Connection in the same period. A letter to the *Christian's Magazine* from a Freetown correspondent tells of how many there found the name *Baptist* contrary to New Testament practice and of how, following the occurrence of a revival among them, they now resolved "to call themselves CHRISTIANS, and to consider Christ their only Master, and the new testament their only rule" (*History of the Town of Freetown* 1902, 43).[15]

The rolls of the Dartmouth church contain a total of 250 members who joined the fellowship in or before 1825.[16] It has been possible to trace fifty-six of these names through probate records, which in turn enable a tentative sociological portrait of what kind of people these were. Of the thirty-seven men found in the records, no less than twenty are explicitly described as Yeomen, or may be supposed to have been mainly farmers, given the property they left behind; of the remainder one is a "mechanic," one Daniel Hix himself, and fifteen of unknown occupation.[17] Fewer women were traceable; of the nineteen recorded, three were "singlewomen," one married, seven were widows, and the rest of unknown status.

Sally Lawton of Dartmouth, singlewoman, left a total estate of $169.73 distributed to various siblings. Patience Faunce, another singlewoman, was able to leave eleven acres of land to a nephew, son of brother Thomas, who was also a member of Hix's church. Thomas himself left a house in New Bedford to his seven daughters and possibly had already deeded his farm to a son (John Faunce, again a church member) before moving to town in retirement. John's own son, Loun, grew up on his father's farm and later became a successful cabinetmaker and contractor; he married the daughter of "yeoman" Abiel Davis, deacon in Hix's church who died "strong in the faith" in 1840. Unlike the singlewomen, Mercy Tripp of Fall River, widow of Benjamin Tripp, farmer and carpenter, left a substantial estate of $7,800 in real property and $250 in personal. Both she and her deceased husband were church members. Their son, Howard Tripp, left the family farm for a stay in California before finally returning home to purchase a farm of his own. The history of Bristol County remarks that by then (1899) there was a Second Christian Church in Dartmouth, of which Howard and his wife were active members.

A number of the men had estates comparable to that of Benjamin Tripp, but some did not. For example, William Ashley's estate of homestead, woodlot, and half interest in a sawmill came to $1,650, while Samuel Sabins left only six beds, some furniture, and $0.75 worth of pewter and Britanniaware for a total of $23.62. The sum left by these men varies up from that figure to a maximum of $9,550 in real estate and no less than $20,663 personal left by John Chace in 1859. More moderate but still substantial was the estate of a different Howard Tripp (probably a brother of Benjamin, after whom the younger Howard was named), who left $8,329 to his daughters and sons. Richard Collins and his son Barnabas were both church members. Richard was a deacon along with Abiel Davis; Barnabas was ordained to the ministry in 1838 but perhaps never actively served and died intestate in 1888. Barnabas's son John spent "his entire life in tilling the soil" and married the daughter of Edmund Wordelle, yet another church member. Lewis Gifford left his pew to his children, as did Pardon Wordelle to hers. John Millard, whose homestead adjoined the "Hix Meetinghouse," provided in his will for funds to ensure that his widow had "decent conveyance to meeting on the saboth [*sic*]." Sally Collins, widow, left $200 out of a total estate of $2,220 toward the support of the ministry of the Christian Church and Society, "so long as said Church shall continue as a Christian organization."[18]

That their church was central to the lives of these people is obvious enough, and what emerges from all this is just how unexceptional the members of Daniel Hix's congregation actually were. They are distinguished only by their membership in a body that others in other places construed as radically sectarian in nature, and by the negative features mentioned above that serve to separate them from members of more conservative denominations. They were not Federalists, merchant oligarchs, or descendants of Old Light Congregationalists; they were yeoman farmers and artisans, married women, singlewomen, and widows. They lived in close proximity to the long-established Rhode Island tradition of religious dissent. They were making do in life and sometimes better, though sometimes less. They intermarried and they worshiped together; their sons and daughters were respectable members of the community, as they themselves had been. Just as with Smith himself (who might just as well have stayed a Baptist or become a Methodist), what must be looked for in providing a satisfying account of the country folk who became Christians is not just class or occupation but also ties of family, of broader social networks articulated through the churches, and the idiosyncrasies of personal and local history that affected the religious and political attitudes and affiliations of particular people and those close to them.

Things were rather different in the towns. In her detailed survey of the relationship in Boston between social standing and denominational affiliation for the period 1790–1820, Anne Rose has suggested that "rising groups joined marginal or new denominations in order to exercise an autonomy in religious affairs which doubled as an assertion of social power" (1986, 244). The Baptists and Methodists of Boston were concentrated toward the lower end of the economic scale in relation to the orthodox Congregationalists, the Unitarians, the Episcopalians, and the Universalists. A majority of the members of the Baptist congregations were laborers and artisans, and many seem to have been transients, since their names cannot be traced in city directories, a fact Rose tentatively associates with "mobility, poverty, and youth." The Baptists and Christians permitted their lower-class communicants a voice that they could not have found in the more hierarchical bodies; women also found greater liberty with them and actively participated in church government.

A list of church membership and a brief history of that body survives from the Boston church that Abner Jones founded in 1804. The history speaks of the role of Jones and Elias Smith in the 1803 revival and of the primary cause—Smith's revolt against Calvinism—that led to separation from the Baptists. July 4 was a significant day for the Christians, and on that day in 1804 Abner Jones baptized seven persons in the Charles River, organizing them into a church following the New Testament rule. "Their platform and creed was then and still is: The bible our creed and discipline. Christian our name. And, all converted Souls our brethren." In the first year of its existence the church admitted twenty-two men and twenty-four women, and in 1805 seventeen men and thirteen women; with the waning of the revival, admissions declined.[19]

After being excluded from the Baptist churches, Jones's people met in a hall in Boston and in the upper story of a house owned by a member of the congregation from Charlestown; in the latter venue they were substantially bothered by rowdies "who went there for sport," such that the city selectmen were petitioned for redress. "Why is this Church more disturbed than others? We answer, that it is the fate of all new sects. Why were Christ and his followers treated in the same manner and worse, when they first made a public appearance? Why did the Apostles and their followers share the same fate?" (Jones 1842, 185). Smith made much the same point when referring to his treatment at the hands of Baldwin and Stillman: "The two baptist ministers in Boston have conducted in the same manner towards me, that the Jews did towards the Apostles," claiming that his old friends had stirred up this rabble by "their words or conduct" (316). Jones himself stayed in Boston in 1807 and then moved to Haverhill; it seemed to Jones's son that "Elder Smith, who ever seems to have been his evil genius, was at the bottom and cause of it." He and his family stayed there for two years, largely it would appear for business reasons, and then went to Salem for a more lengthy stay during which Jones resumed his regular preaching (Jones 1842, 69–70).

These Christians were much like the Baptists in a relative social anonymity, as again shown by their absence from city directories and tax records.[20] Therefore not much is known about them, except that there seems to have been a certain instability in church membership. Of the original cadre of forty-six souls admitted in 1804, no less than seventeen were eventually excommunicated; the reasons for this are unfortunately not given but—on the basis of the experience of other churches—reason for this action could range from doctrinal heterodoxy to moral turpitude, to absenting oneself from the Lord's Supper without good cause.[21] As in Portsmouth, the Boston church was prepared to admit people of color, though, perhaps because of the presence of Thomas Paul's African Baptist Church, it did not do so in any great numbers; the Boston roll shows that a "coloured" man named Lolo Octon was admitted in 1805, and two "coloured" women in 1821.

Smith's own church in Portsmouth presents a still different picture. Of the 270 people (105 men and 165 women) who, according to the church list, joined the Portsmouth Christians in 1805 or before, 111 (63 men and 48 women) have proven traceable through local probate and tax records. We see through these records a pattern driven by the range of trades available in a mercantile port town still actively engaged in shipbuilding. Of the 30 men in the sample whose occupations are known, virtually all were artisans or involved in service trades; only 2 were characterized as yeomen. John Locke is representative of the upper range of the communicants in Smith's church. He was a glazier and one-time boss painter at the Portsmouth Navy Yard; by 1850, when he died, Locke owned five houses and a shop valued at $5,300 in addition to personal property of $1,775. He was a member of the St. John's Lodge of Freemasons and was a member of the Associated Mechanics and Manufacturers, a self-improvement and friendly society that also functioned to certify apprentices—and to which at least eleven members of the church belonged, many as charter members since its founding in 1804. Smith's friend Daniel Drown, after whom Elias named one of his sons, was a goldsmith and a member of the Associated Mechanics; he was an active Mason in later days, served in a variety of civil offices in Portsmouth (justice of the peace, town clerk, inspector of lighthouses), and was for a time in the 1830s a New Hampshire state legislator. Drown became legal guardian of the children of at least two other members of the church and briefly edited in 1815 a newspaper called the *People's Advocate,* reflective of internecine regional disputes within a now overwhelmingly Republican New Hampshire establishment.[22] He died in 1863, but by then his debts apparently outweighed his assets, since the probate inventory lists a house and lot valued at $2,150 and yet declares his estate insolvent.

Henry Bufford, founding member of the Associated Mechanics, owned a carriage- and sign-painting business; he too was prominent in the civil affairs of Portsmouth, serving as assessor of taxes in the 1830s and later as city clerk. When he died, he owned two houses and a shop worth $4,799 and a personal estate of $954. Benjamin Carter was a baker, Overseer of the Poor in 1827, and sometime trustee and president of the Associated Mechanics. Thomas Treadwell was a hatter and founding member of the mechanics who died with an estate of $4,053; his obituary lists him as an "esquire" and recalls that he filled many public offices. One more example of this social type is Hanson Hart, joiner and founder member and sometime president of the Mechanics in addition to service as Overseer of the Poor in 1829 and active involvement with the Masons.

William Hoit represents the low end of the scale. In the probate records he is listed as a laborer alias yeoman; Daniel Drown was appointed as his guardian because of "drunken[n]ess, idleness, and debauchery." When he died, he owned half a house and was worth $439. Benjamin Chevers was a currier who, according to the 1807 tax lists, owned no taxable property. Likewise impecunious were John Crosby, Hunkin Lowd, and Samuel Lowd, all coopers. Samuel Lowd's wife, Sally, in company with Betsey Barnes, had been excommunicated by Joseph Buckminster's First Church in 1803 for breach of covenant because they had allowed themselves to be rebaptized by Elias Smith; when Samuel died, another church member, Samuel Woodbury (cordwainer), was appointed administrator of his estate. Another Lowd, Solomon, had no taxable property as of 1807 and, though he lived until 1834, is missing from the 1821 city directory. Lowd married Sally Dame in Buckminster's North Church and both joined Smith's congregation in 1803; Lowd left behind an extraordinary confession that details the salutary effects of Elias Smith's preaching before Solomon was ruined by devotion to rum. Josiah Downing (trade unknown) inherited a farm from his father, but at his own death in 1846 he was worth only $333.62 and was declared insolvent; among his debts was a loan from Smith of $32.75.

There is a considerable range of crafts and trades represented by the men of Smith's church: a carriage- and sign-painter, baker and grocer, coach and chaise maker, hatter, two printers, a carpenter, watchman, goldsmith, cabinetmaker and chairmaker, sailmaker, two cordwainers, five coopers, a butcher, three joiners, a truckman, and a ropemaker. Two men were shipowners. Joseph Ayres was a merchant who in 1807 had twice the taxable property of any other church member except the troublesome Charles Peirce. Ayers was a dealer in molasses, rum, and sugar imported from the West Indies and South America. During the War of 1812 he was part owner of John Paul Jones's ship, the privateer *Ranger;* his second wife was the aunt of the prophet of the great fire of 1802, Elliot Frost. Former mariner William Shaw had an interest in nine ships, and in partnership with his father and uncle operated two privateers during the war. Mary, the sister of former mariner and now Christian Elder Mark Fernald, was also a church member.

Charles Peirce is a special case, but one of considerable importance in light of Elias Smith's subsequent journalistic career. As we have seen, he was a member of Samuel Stillman's First Baptist Church in Boston in addition to his membership in Smith's new church in Portsmouth. He and his brothers, Nathaniel and Washington, were printers and booksellers. Charles published the *Oracle* between 1793 and 1801, and his brothers were publishers of the *Portsmouth Gazette*, in which the doings of Elias Smith frequently appeared; they also printed a number of Elias's pamphlets, first in Exeter, and then in Portsmouth. Charles Peirce had the highest tax assessment in Smith's church. Robert Foster was another printer who had a sideline in the sale of medicinal elixirs ("Foster's Balm of Life"). He published the *Gazette* from 1813 to 1823 and, following Smith's defection to the Universalists in 1817, published the successor to the *Herald of Gospel Liberty*, renamed simply the *Christian Herald*.[23] The first issue contains an open letter to Elias Smith from Joseph Burgin, now clerk of the church, which attacks the announcement of conversion to the doctrine of universal salvation that Smith made in the last number of the old *Herald*. Burgin was a "trader" and partner in a grocery business with church member Benjamin Carter; Daniel Drown assumed the guardianship of Burgin's children upon the latter's death in 1820.

So far as the records indicate, none of the women in Smith's church were of any particular financial or social prominence. A few were "singlewomen," and at least one (admitted in 1807) was black— Candice Whidden, wife of Cesaer Whidden, who appears to have remained a member of Buckminster's First Church. Communicants often joined the church with their spouses; in any event they often had family ties of one sort or another within it. As in Daniel Hix's Dartmouth, various members were connected by siblingship and affinal bonds. Peter Bonnen, a man of little property, married Lucy Dickson. Amos Dow, joiner, married Lydia Fabyan, sister of Elizabeth, also a church member. Joseph Moulton was the son of Thomas Moulton, both church members; Joseph married Mary Brown, the daughter of William Brown, one of the organizers in 1805 of the Christian Church in Hampton Falls, which was built from the wreckage of the local Congregational establishment.[24] John Davis married Mary Moses, the sister of Thomas Moses, ship carpenter and boatbuilder.

Their daughter, another Mary, wed Robert Neal, a ship captain, sailmaker, and in 1834–35 president of the Associated Mechanics and Manufacturers; he was in charge of the seacoast defense militia during the war, in 1827 was Worshipful Master of St. John's Masonic Lodge, and (having risen in the world?) owned a pew at St. John's Episcopal. Noah Perkins, joiner, married Hannah Mitchell, sister of Robert Mitchell; in 1834 Hannah was president of the church's Female Benevolent Society. Hannah's sister, Sarah, married Moses Safford, later elder of the church in Kittery Point and half-brother to Thomas Safford, a coach and chaise maker who died in 1834 with the considerable total estate of $5,493.03. Samuel Remick was a shipwright who named his first child Elias; Dorcas Kennard married Samuel's brother, William, a farmer in Elliot, Maine. Mary Ayres was the sister of Thomas Trickey, the only early member of Elias's church characterized as a yeoman upon his death; he left thirteen children and an estate valued at $579.90.

There were similarities between the Christian churches of Dartmouth, Boston, and Portsmouth, but also important differences. The relative prominence of certain members of the Dartmouth and Portsmouth churches is balanced by the obscurity of the membership in Boston. Many in Dartmouth were prosperous farmers, while many in Portsmouth were artisans and tradesmen who, given their prominence in public office, were well connected to the predominantly Republican civil establishment. By virtue of their involvement in the Associated Mechanics and the Masons, these men in their own eyes were forward-looking progressives; they were archetypal Jeffersonians, members of a rising urban class that had little time for claims to deference made on the basis of superior breeding, college education, inherited wealth, and anachronistic appeals to classic republican theory.

In sum, the records of the Christian churches in Dartmouth, Boston, and Portsmouth suggest a complex picture. The members of the Dartmouth church were very much like others in the older settled areas of New England and evidently became Christians for reasons largely rooted in local circumstance. As I have noted above, the Christians and Free-Will Baptists have been characterized by some as marginal "rural pietists"—natural supporters of religious liberty and a revivalistic Arminianism by virtue of the open quality of the hinterland societies that gave them rise. However, this generalization does not quite capture the Christian appeal in long-settled rural Dartmouth and in cities such as Boston, Portsmouth, Philadelphia, and Norfolk, Virginia; nor does it properly address how Smith's congregations heard what he was saying about the relation between democracy and salvation in the context of current political debates and the class structures of their own communities as they perceived them. Country folk these people may often have been by origins, but their experiences were colored by the specific qualities of the urban political and economic milieu and by the class dramas acted out before them on the town streets and in church on Lord's Day.

When Smith evoked imagery of a corrupt, self-serving clergy and of the town gentry that supported it, his audience knew what he was talking about, since what they took to be the evidence was there before them. But when Elias spoke of plots, and of the infamous Essex Junto, an imaginary Federalist cabal in eastern Massachusetts, how would it have been taken? Such invective was stock rhetoric of the time, a prototypical example of the famous paranoid style in American politics— an interpretation of social ills in terms of identifiable social groups working in secret, rather than with reference to the more abstruse workings of politics and political economy (Wood 1982). When he spoke of oligarchic conspiracies, was Smith pointing the finger at the wealthy merchants and shipbuilders of Portsmouth going off to worship at St. John's Episcopal and Joseph Buckminster's First Church, or was he merely speaking in the generalities of the latest political campaign? Elias had little to say about bankers, merchants, lawyers, land speculators, and moneylenders. The only human targets he habitually identified personally were members of the regular clergy, and this must have pleased his audience or it would not have been so consistently repeated; though he constantly inveighed against privilege, the only flagrant social abuse he regularly condemned was state supported religion and, later, slavery (though while resident in Philadelphia and attempting to reach a national audience through the *Herald*, he equivocated even on that).

Smith hit a chord when associating his listeners with the original followers of Jesus and identifying those who opposed and ridiculed them—who deemed them a "swinish multitude" (a phrase to which Elias constantly returned)—with the hypocrites and Pharisees of Bible times. Those attracted to Smith's message knew what was said about them in the Federalist press and from the pulpit by such clerics as David Osgood and John Popkin. Benjamin Austin struck back at just such "time-serving clergymen" in his columns for the *Independent Chronicle*.[25] In an address to "the Cossack priesthood of Massachusetts" written from England for publication in Boston, William Cobbett (1815) accused the clergy of opposing the Republicans only out of fear of losing their sinecures. His address was prefaced by "an epistle to certain priests" by "Jonathan, one of the people called Christians" (perhaps Elias himself) who held up Osgood as an example of the type Cobbett was addressing; this Jonathan recommended Cobbett's diatribe to the public as "a kind of *looking-glass*" in which the images of the Massachusetts clergy "are faithfully reflected."

In his own *Clergyman's Looking Glass No. 1; or, Ancient and Modern Things Contrasted*, Smith examined the status of the clergy in these latter days by contrasting their doings with the work of the apostles, doing so in effect by ridiculing their class standing. He divided his pages into two opposed columns, one headed ANCIENT, the other MODERN, and then gave an apposite New Testament passage on the left, and a parody rendition on the right pertaining to the regular clergy, as in Figure 6.

Smith later used much the same contrastive style when, as a Thomsonian physician, he opposed himself and all those using "natural" remedies to the orthodox doctors relying on chemical "poisons" to ensure their profit at the expense of the health of their patients. Elias brought this all home with his comments on the ordination of Joseph Buckminster, Jr., in 1805. Joseph, Sr., delivered the sermon, in which he spoke of the dangers of introducing ignorance, infidelity, impiety, or fanaticism into the sacred office (Buckminster 1805, 14); the service

ANCIENT	MODERN
"And how shall they preach except they be sent?" (*Rom. 10:15*)	"And how can they preach except they are sent to college?"
"Who also hath made us able ministers of the new testament, not of the letter, but of the spirit, for the letter killeth, but the spirit giveth life." (*2 Cor. 3:16*)	"Which (the college) also hath made us popular ministers of the old testament, not of the spirit but of the letter, for the spirit giveth life but the letter killeth."
"For God who commanded light to shine out of darkness, hath shined in our hearts to give the light of the knowledge of the glory of God in the face of Jesus Christ." (*2 Cor. 4:6*)	"For men who commanded a college to be built have made us shine, to give the light of the knowledge of the glory of human learning in the face of us who profess to be masters of arts."
"The elders which are among you I exhort, who also am an elder, and a witness of the suffering of Christ, and also a partaker of the glory that shall be revealed: feed the flock of God which is among you, taking the oversight thereof, not by constraint, but willingly; not for filthy lucre, but of a ready mind; neither being Lords over God's heritage, but being ensamples of the flock; and when the chief Shepherd shall appear ye shall receive a crown of Glory which fadeth not away." (*1 Peter 5:1–4*)	"The reverend clergy who are with me I advice, who am also a clergyman, and a D.D. a member of that respectable body, who are numerous, and 'who seek honor one of another,' and a partaker of the benefit of it: feed yourselves upon the church and parish over which we have settled you for life, and who are obliged to support you whether they like you or not; taking the command, by constraint, for filthy lucre; not of a ready mind, as lords over men's souls; not as ensamples to them, and when commencement day shall appear, you shall receive some honorary title, which shall make you appear very respectable among the reverend clergy."

Fig. 6. The ancient apostles vs. the modern clergy (from Smith's *Clergyman's Looking Glass No. 1*)

concluded with Ralph Waldo Emerson's father offering the right hand of fellowship to the new pastor. In the *Christian's Magazine* Smith took note of Buckminster's exalted view of the ministry and condemned it as "Anti-Christian Trumpery!": "hypocrisy . . . outwardly beautiful; but inwardly full of rottenness and dead men's bones!" (*CM* 1, no. 1 [1805]: 22–25).[26]

These direct attacks on the class standing of the regular clergy were supplemented by assaults on the theological doctrines that Smith saw as the ideological props of invidious class distinction. Elias's attack on the Calvinistic doctrines of predestination and special election must therefore be understood in the context of the populism characteristic of the various numbers of the *Looking Glass* and his writings in general. The result was an elision of theology and American constitutional principle.

Elias concluded that, except for the Jews as a people and Christ and the apostles as individuals, no person whatever has been preordained by God for any particular fate or station—not for salvation or damnation, not for privilege or penury: these outcomes are human responsibilities. Therefore, when Smith attacked the notion that, since before the foundations of the world, some men have been "predestinated unto everlasting life, and others foreordained to everlasting death" (Churches 1812, 10), he was simultaneously engaging in a radical political critique that swept aside the pretensions of the Federalists, the town gentry, the hireling clergy, and all the self-styled "elect"—those with a vain hope appropriate only to unregenerate "hypocrites, deceived persons, fatalists, atheists, deists and epicureans" (Smith 1805d, 31). It is a superb irony that a doctrine that Calvin and other Protestant Reformers originally propounded to magnify the glory of God at the expense of the Roman Catholic hierarchy and its claim to mediate the process of salvation was in turn maligned by the Christians as an antidemocratic travesty of the real biblical doctrine of free grace to all who accept Jesus as Savior.

With the example of American democratic elections before them, Elias Smith and Abner Jones returned to the Scriptures to determine the true meaning of predestination as contained in the key passage justifying the orthodox position: "For whom he did foreknow, he also did predestinate to be conformed to the image of his Son, that he might be the firstborn among many brethren. Moreover whom he did predestinate, them he also called: and whom he called, them he also justified: and whom he justified, them he also glorified" (Rom. 8:29–30).

They concluded, in the words of Smith's *Dictionary*, that the pre-destined elect referred to in passages such as the above are "such as are chosen of God to some particular work, for the benefit of those that are *not* elected" (1812b, 153), a theme reiterated in Elias's *Three Sermons on Election*, where he said that "whenever one or more are *elected*, it is for some public employment, to do something too [*sic*], or for those who are not elected to the same thing. This is the way *election* is considered among men; so it stands in the scriptures. There is not one place in the scriptures where *election* is considered in any other way" (1808b, 17). As Abner Jones saw it, just as the president of the United States is elected "for the benefit of the community at large," so Christ was "the first and great elect of God . . . for the benefit of the world at large." The fact that some are elected to high office while others are excluded does not entail that anyone should be deprived of the benefits accruing from the services of those chosen as political representatives in their place. As Christ represents the church as a whole, the president of the United States represents the people as a whole. Jones followed this logic to the interesting conclusion that, just as the election of the president does not exclude the general population from the benefits of his constitutionally established office, so God's "election" of Christ as Savior "does not reprobate others from the benefits that arise from this election, which is, SALVATION TO 'WHOSOEVER WILL'" (n.d., 17). Elias commented that if the president of the United States (James Monroe, say) were to behave like the God of the Calvinists, he would remain in office no longer than it took for the people to "get to him, to remove such a wretch, and place a merciful ruler in his stead" (*Herald of Light and Immortality* 1, no. 3 [July 1819]: 91 [henceforth *HLI*]).

In 1804, Thomas Baldwin delivered and published a sermon on Romans entitled *The Eternal Purpose of God, the Foundation of Effectual Calling*, in which he argued the orthodox line that God has preordained from the beginning all that will come to pass, and that (as this entails) those called to him by the Spirit are brought "according to his eternal purpose" (1804, 12). Baldwin, as had Samuel Hopkins before him, held that this metaphysical determinism is in no way incompatible in any practical sense with the existential freedom of a person to choose or reject the truths of the gospel: "the one under the influence of sovereign grace, willingly receives the gospel; the other under the influence of depravity, as freely and heartily rejects it" (ibid., 6). Politically, however, it was not clear who in this new democratic nation would now be willing to deal with a God who had seen fit to construct a universe on such radically amoral principles.

For the Free-Willers it was all irrational fatalism, and its mirror opposite—universal salvationism—was even worse, because without the threat of hell as a consequence of choosing wrongly, human depravity would have no check at all. Smith believed that Baldwin's sermon was associated with the inroads that he and Jones were making among the Boston Baptists, and with their consequent exclusion from pulpit and vestry.[27] When looked upon as slogans, "salvation according to the eternal purpose of God" does indeed, whatever the theological subtleties, have a different political ring to it than "salvation to whosoever will." Smith spelled out what he took the difference to be in his response to Baldwin—*A Man in the Smoke, and a Friend Endeavouring to Help him out*—a homily that identified the root of a Calvinist propensity for alternating fits of religious euphoria and despair. Elias thought Calvinism the logic of the betting shop, and the whole question of predestination and election a nonscriptural muddle demeaning to both people and God. "This plan says to me, It is determined from eternity how many will be saved; so many will be saved, and no more. You must *repent* and *believe,* and if you are one of the *elect,* you will be saved, and if not you can be but lost. If you are lost, you will have this for your comfort, you tried to be saved;—but observe, the minister sells the ticket!" (1805d, 31).

In a nutshell, the issue for Smith was that no one has the right to dictate to another the conditions for admission to paradise. God, through Scripture, has plainly revealed what these conditions are: all else is pretense and delusion. Those who freely come to him will be saved according to his promise; all others will be condemned.

> Freedom and reason make us men;
> Take these away, what are we then?
> Mere animals, and just as well
> The beasts may think of heav'n or hell.

Know then that every soul is free
To choose his life and what he'll be,
For this eternal truth has giv'n,
That God will force no man to heav'n.

This my free will for to believe,
Tis God's free will me to receive;
To stubborn willers this I'll tell;
It's all free grace and all free will.

(SMITH AND JONES 1805,

231, NO. CCXVI)

By now Smith was acquiring something of a reputation. In a sermon delivered to combat Elias's inroads into his church and perhaps to assuage his own self-doubts, Joseph Buckminster anticipated that the liberal interpretation he wished to give concerning the proper mode of baptism would meet with a harsh response from his opponent; if so, he would—since he had no such weapons at his own disposal—engage in the dispute no more and leave the "champion of reviling, railing, and slander . . . undisputed master of the field" (1803c, vi). In the *Looking-Glass No. 3* (subtitled "the champion of reviling, railing, and slander, left undisputed master of the field") Elias surmised that he was the champion in question, and that, if so, "my reviling is telling the truth about the wicked clergy." As for Buckminster himself, "I think I do not envy, but I pity the man, and those who are blinded by him. I hope that though the blind is leading the blind, that their eyes will be opened before they both fall into the ditch" (1804a, 6, 33).

Portsmouth was a small town in which much was widely known that might better have been kept secret. The slashing attacks that Elias mounted against Buckminster and the rest of the orthodox clergy, coupled with endemic rumors about his dubious character, ensured that when an anonymous pamphlet appeared alluding to sexual improprieties on the part of the Reverend Joseph Willard of St. John's

Episcopal, it would be widely believed that Elias wrote it. The printer, one Mr. Whitelock, was accused of libel by Willard and incarcerated in the town jail. Elias was out of town when this piece was printed, and his return was greeted by a letter, again anonymous, suggesting that tar and feathers might be of service to him, and by a mob that seemed all too likely to administer the prescription. The day following, June 4, 1805, he described as:

> the most trying day I ever saw; that evening it appeared to me that there was five of six hundred people gathered round the meeting house conducting in a riotous manner, I was obliged to go guarded to the meeting house, and a guard stood in the door while I was preaching, and then went home with me. This is what Paul calls being in a tumult. This rage lasted all the week. Through all this the Lord delivered me, and an hair of my head did not fall to the ground. Glory to his name for this kind preservation. The members of the church conducted with zeal and boldness, being willing to lay down their lives for me. (*CM* 1, no. 3 [1805]: 106–7)[28]

Joseph Willard, another Harvard graduate, had come to St. John's in 1795 and shortly after was ordained an Episcopal priest by the bishop of New York (Adams 1825, 308). The pamphlet for which Elias was blamed contained accusations about the unfortunate Willard on the part of an unnamed woman in collusion with Whitelock, the printer. With the help of his friends—notably Thomas Treadwell and Henry Bufford—Smith escaped the wrath of the mob and was able to convince the wardens of St. John's that he was innocent in this affair (307). But it did not end there. A letter to the Republican *New Hampshire Gazette* on June 11 wondered why, if Smith had indeed demonstrated his innocence, crowds persisted in causing disturbances around his meetinghouse and throwing rocks and brickbats in through the windows to the danger of those worshiping there. The writer intimated that some "gentlemen" and "gentlemen's sons" were behind it and suggested that Portsmouth was deserving of no less than the fate meted out to Sodom for the inhospitable reception it had accorded to the patriarch Lot. Another letter, to the Federalist *Portsmouth Oracle* on June 15, took exception to the previous comments in the *Gazette*, which claimed that Elias had been unequivocally exonerated. "We have no hesitancy in saying this is totally FALSE, is groundless. We can easily conceive that any character however desperate may wish to rid itself of any concern in a production, which must consign the author and his abettors to everlasting scorn."

Nor was Smith's meetinghouse the only target, for—again on June 15—the wardens of St. John's placed the following advertisement in the *Oracle:*

> Whereas certain malicious persons, under the influence of the most disgraceful passions that can corrupt the heart of man, have for a considerable term of time, combined their exertions to calumnate the character, and in various other ways to disturb the peace of the Rev. JOSEPH WILLARD and his family. A reward is hereby offered of FIFTY DOLLARS to any person who will bring to light the Villain or Villains who entered his Dwelling House on Monday night last, and there wasted and destroyed his Property, so that the perpetrator may be brought to condign punishment. We further engage to pay the sum of ONE HUNDRED DOLLARS to the Person or Persons who will bring forward legal and satisfactory evidence of the *Real Author* of a late scandalous publication relative to himself and Parish.
>
> Thomas Brown   Samuel Larkin
Wardens of St. John's Church

Evidently this notice brought no immediate result, for the wardens republished it on June 22.

This cycle of violence was perhaps not just the product of small-town gossip and public scandal. Elias thought it all political. He noted that it was widely held that his discourse *The Whole World Governed by a Jew*, which he had delivered in March 4, 1804, on the occasion of Jefferson's second inauguration as president, had some impact on the New Hampshire gubernatorial election. The new Republican governor, John Langdon, was sworn in—"to the great grief of the *tories*"—on the same day that Smith was mobbed in Portsmouth (308). March 4 was a Jeffersonian holiday throughout the country and thus a particularly galling time for the opposition. In his earlier discourse, Elias had condemned John Adams by comparing him unfavorably with the second Adam, Jesus Christ, and thanked God that Jefferson—the sixth angel of Revelation—had been raised up for the good of the nation in place of his "retrograde" predecessor. In those Federalist years of darkness now happily past, "*Democracy* has been trampled under foot. *Aristocracy* has been raised as a beacon on the mountain for all to look at, and steer by." But now "*republicanism* is triumphing in almost every state in the union . . . declaring that all men are free and equal; that the foundation of a righteous government stands on these four pillars, *liberty, equality, unity* and *peace*" (1805b, 72).

The year 1805 was a busy one for Elias. He had commenced the *Christian's Magazine* and published sermons and discourses on various subjects; he had also traveled and preached extensively beyond Portsmouth—for example, among Daniel Hix's flock and among the Baptists of adjoining Freetown. He was becoming known as a Republican agitator, an evangelical Benjamin Austin. Following his experiences in the Willard matter, however, Smith briefly put on the cloak of martyrdom and, in conclusion to the third number of the *Magazine,* alluded to having been ridiculed by "children, federalists, and bastard republicans" and then bade farewell to his adopted town forever (*CM* 1, no. 3 [1805]: 108).

In fact Elias stayed in Portsmouth until 1810. It was Joseph Willard who left, a town historian recording that "the pastoral relation between St. John's Church and the Rev. Joseph Willard, was dissolved by mutual consent the 20th day of March [1806], and Mr. Willard removed to Newark, in New Jersey" (Adams 1825, 338). Smith observed that Willard, though bringing charges against the perpetrators of the slanderous pamphlet, had never let the matter come to court.

Even in the midst of such a sordid affair, Smith framed the situation in prophetic terms. Following his good-byes, Elias announced to his readers at the end of the *Christian's Magazine* (no. 3) that "I have been informed, that 20 Jews in England have lately been baptized, and that one of them is preaching the Messiah to others." Apocalyptic hopes—like the image of the Antichrist—are a constant hermeneutical resource in unsettled times, arising in response to the current political climate and the more insubstantial vicissitudes of public mood. This would be the experience of the Christian Church in Dartmouth in response to the Millerite excitement of the early 1840s, as it had been in the context of millennial expectation that Elias Smith helped fuel in 1804.

Daniel Hix died in 1838, and his place taken on a yearly basis by Elder Howard Tripp. In this fervid period, "prayers, hymns, and sermons on the prophecies were heard until nature was exhausted." Elder Tripp, who had been ordained in 1824 with the help of Mark Fernald, flirted with these new ideas himself, but wiser heads prevailed, and he was persuaded to hold himself aloof from public commitment to the notion that the world would end in 1843, as predicted by William Miller on the basis of his interpretation of biblical chronologies and publicized all over the United States by Elder Joshua Himes, one-time preacher in Abner Jones's First Christian Church of Boston (Fernald 1852, 182). Just as their parents had been stirred by the republican apocalypse of Elias Smith, Miller's predictions animated the children of the sedate Christian flock of Dartmouth with millennial dreams of imminent glory; such would be the case with many Christian congregations throughout New England and beyond into the westward Yankee diaspora. But the local consequences were divisive, and in the wake of the failed prophecy Hix's church slid into a prolonged decline lasting until the next great revival in 1857 (Andrews 1880, 161–66). By then abolitionism, prohibitionism, Spiritualism, and universal salvation were on the agenda of a nation dominated by perfectionist hopes and now on the edge of a cataclysm totally unforeseen when Elias Smith invoked the perfect law of liberty in 1802.

Following Smith's departure from Portsmouth in 1810, his church fell into periodic declines and renewals. The record of the church meeting of September 20, 1813, speaks of the resolution of certain difficulties that "for a number of years have existed between us the Subscribers." John Rand, who later took upon himself the unpleasant task of condemning Elias's conversion to Universalism, was one of those affirming this resolution, as were Hanson Hart, Joseph Burgin, Smith himself, and Abner Jones, who had been serving the church as pastor during this latter period with the occasional help of Mark Fernald and the unattached Free-Willer John Colby.[29] The record for November 19, 1817, notes that "the Church being satisfied that Elder Elias Smith had embraced the Universal Doctrine came to the following Decision:

That they do not approbate the Preaching of Elder Elias Smith, nor can they receive him as a preacher so long as he preached the Doctrine of Universalism."

In 1826 the Portsmouth church was completely reorganized; by this time it was known as the First Baptist Church but once more had fallen into disarray and was badly in need of repair, such that "church disipline [*sic*] has been neglected, and that now it is difficult, if not imposible [*sic*] to ascertain who are proper and worthy members of it." Of the members of the original church, now only Thomas Treadwell, Edward Call, Polly Carter, and widow Sally Marden remained. A footnote to this record appended in 1838 shows that the reconstituted First Baptist Church was henceforth to be called the First Christian Church.[30] The following year the congregation split in two, the original body remaining in Chestnut Street, the new one under Elder David Millard, a prominent minister among the second generation of Christians, moving to Pleasant Street.

The Chestnut Street church did not survive, and by 1858 the Pleasant Street church had taken over the building of its parent; again there were difficulties suggestive of former problems, in that the one-time church clerk at Chestnut Street, on being asked for the records, responded that no one would get them while *he* was alive and that furthermore the silverware had been sent to another church in the West. In the interim William Miller had come into town in 1840 to give a series of lectures on the imminent second advent of Christ, and by 1853 there was an Advent Baptist Church in Portsmouth formed at the expense of the other evangelical bodies. Miller's teachings also created a schism among the Christians of nearby Exeter, where Smith's preaching in the early days had created a rift among the Baptists and deepened a personal one between himself and former ally Samuel Shepard. Following Millerite inroads, the Christian society of Exeter withered away, and around 1860 its meetinghouse was closed forever (Bell 1888, 205).

5

PREPARE YE THE WAY
Smith as Christian Communicator

In the beginning was the Word, and the
Word was with God, and the Word was God.
JOHN 1:1

ELIAS SMITH CONSTANTLY PREACHED about simplicity: the simplicity that is in Christ (2 Cor. 11:3), the simplicity of the early church, and the corruptions to which it has since been subject. He judged his fellows, himself, and the institutions around him in relation to that standard. "Simplicity" is a complex idea that unifies Smith's attitudes concerning politics, medicine, and the constitution of the church. Not that Elias ever thought it out in philosophical terms; the metaphysics is implicit, inherent in a particular eschatological notion of history, an idealization of the natural, and a realist approach to language.

History is what has occurred and what will occur between Genesis and the postmillennial world of liberty, equality, unity, and peace promised by the Apocalypse of John—the perfect republic of Christ in his dual aspect of King and Priest. The ideal church is the social form described by the Gospels and the Acts of the Apostles, involving a mutual breaking of bread without invidious social distinction. The language of the Bible is what it originally meant when directly inspired by God, not what human artifice has since added to it by way of interpretation. The human body was created in the image of God, and in the beginning the products of nature sufficed for its well-being and health; just so now, though once more that truth has been obscured by artifice, and the body itself corrupted by overly refined foods, artificial stimulants, and chemically derived drugs.

Spirits that are not of God (Isaac Braman, Rowley, Mass., 1810); *An Essay in Vindication of the Fundamental Doctrines of Christianity against Socianism, including A Review of the writings of Elias Smith, and the claims of his* FEMALE PREACHERS (Gilbert McMaster, Schenectady, N.Y., 1815); finally, *The Scriptures Liable to be Wrested to Men's own Destruction, and an Instance of this found, in the Writings of Elias Smith* (Thomas Andros, Berkley, Mass., 1816).

As Elias had summarized the essentials of his belief in such works as the *Dictionary* and *The Age of Enquiry,* so Cornelius Everest of Windham, in a mirror image of Smith's views, summarized the essentials of those held by the Hopkinsian Calvinists. He concluded that the most important of the doctrines essential to salvation are "the universal and perpetual obligation of the moral law; the total depravity of mankind; the divinity of the Lord Jesus Christ; election; the covenant of grace; and the future endless misery of the wicked" (1819, 5). Doctrine was not the only concern however; each of the above-mentioned pastors explicitly addressed his own flock about the dangers of following the itinerants down the garden path to hell—and, perhaps more to the point, the divisive consequences for the churches of giving their spurious doctrines any credence whatever in place of the counsel offered by the regularly ordained, settled pastorate.[5] For them Smith and his followers were "a host of itinerants spreading poison and death"; "the societies though which such men have passed wears the visage of a natural landscape overthrown by a whirlwind, all peace and order gone"; "their success in our time is the best evidence for the natural depravity of man"; "the chaos which they sow is a prophetically foretold sign of the impending millennium"; "their emphasis on 'liberty' (a great cant word with them) is a ruse to elevate the pride of man at the expense of the grandeur of an infinitely perfect God"; "the elect are those who cannot possibly be deceived by such as these": *"Go not after them! Fulfill your covenant vows. Live as a band of brethren!"*

The practical consequences of not heeding such advice are known for a number of churches: Joseph Buckminster's, of course, but also Stephen Porter's Presbyterian Church in Ballston, New York, near Saratoga

Springs, and Thomas Andros's Congregational flock in Berkley, Massachusetts. What befell Andros is particularly interesting in this context, because language was at the center of it.

Andros, though not college educated, was skilled at formal theological disputation. Before encountering Smith, he had already engaged in controversy with a self-styled "Orthodox Clergyman" who objected, as Elias did, to creeds cast in other than purely scriptural terms. The "Clergyman" found confessions based on such human inventions "a forcible and unjust invasion or seizure of the rights of conscience and christian liberty," and seemingly agreed with Smith's view that the New Testament is the "perfect law of liberty." He argued that "all more than this, is an addition to what [Christ] has commanded; all short of this, is taking from what he has commanded. Every addition of *creeds, covenants, confessions of faith, disciplines,* &c. is an attempt, (directly or indirectly) to *diminish* the authority of Christ" (*HGL* 3, no. 63 [Jan. 18, 1811]: 249). In much the same spirit the Orthodox Clergyman implied that what individuals make of a seemingly orthodox creed based on scriptural language should effectively be their own business, a private matter that ought not to disrupt fellowship with others holding to a different opinion.

As one of a long line of Puritan divines whose task it was to explicate texts in the framework of Calvinist theology, Thomas Andros could not abide this. Why? Because it would allow egregious heresy to creep into the churches, heresy concealing its true face by democratic appeals to liberty of conscience and the rights of the individual:

> A creed drawn up wholly in texts of Scripture, affords every one an opportunity to assent to it, in the sense in which he understands the passages of which it is composed. Take what texts you will, and form them into a creed without affixing any definite meaning, and not only this orthodox clergyman, but Arius, Socinus, Swedenburg [*sic*], and even Jemima [Wilkinson], would readily assent to it. A most cunning device indeed! It opens wide the door of the church to the grossest heretics, not to creep in, but to come in openly, under the name of orthodox good Christians. (1814a, 19, 23)

That Andros's church was in danger of the fate he described above may be seen between the lines of the anxious discourses he then delivered before his own congregation in 1816–17 in the wake of a revival sparked by the Christians, during which Elias gave his memorable sermon on Psalm 107 from the ship scaffolding at the Taunton River. In these discourses the old Federalist conservative spoke for most of his ministerial colleagues in citing the dissension created in the early church by those pretending to be Christians, yet introducing spurious doctrine of their own invention (Andros 1817, 3). For Thomas Andros, the Enemy is always the same, as are the divisive effects of his inroads, whether in the early church or in Berkley. Andros's simple duty as Christian watchman was therefore to point out to his congregation "the real nature and character of that essential corruption of christianity, which is now attempted to be established in this place"— namely, a church of the Christian Connection in part gathered from schismatics who had left Andros's own congregation (ibid., 9).

Andros associated Smith with the "diabolical fanaticism" of the Shaker prophetess Ann Lee and took particular exception to one of Elias's followers, Jabez King, who believed himself to no more have an immortal soul than his horse did. "What think you," Andros asked, "of such a gospel as this? Would you have such a teacher for your children?" As Smith wrote in the *Dictionary*, "all said of the *Immortal never dying soul &c* is unscriptural, as it is not named in the Bible" (1812b, 221). Equally heretical was Smith's belief that when sinners go to the final judgment, they will not be condemned to eternal damnation but rather destroyed altogether, burnt up like chaff from the winnowing. Likewise offensive were Smith's strictures on the Trinity, a doctrine that Elias had condemned as "an impossibility, a contradiction, a jargon of unmeaning words . . . not a MYSTERY but a MISTAKE!" (*HGL* 3, no. 77 [Aug. 2, 1811]: 304). Andros concluded his homily by commending the parents in his flock "for their quick discernment, in distinguishing between a wild, irrational fanaticism, and the genuine operation of the Spirit of God, and the zeal and firmness with which they resisted the introduction of the contagion into their own families" (1816, 27).

Andros also spoke to his people of "the innumerable, though hitherto vain attempts that have been made to seduce you from the primitive faith and order of the gospel," and of how to distinguish true from false revivals of religion; he noted expectantly that a pouring out of the Spirit must precede the onset of the Millennium, and that it is at just such a time when Satan will "exert himself with all power and craft, to defeat this great end, and to destroy the credit of true revivals, by introducing such as are spurious." Specifically, of course, the one recently sparked by the Christians, which among its other faults exhibited verifiably satanic origins through its employment of female evangelists: "Wherever you find a female public teacher, there in general you will find a jezebel, who comes as the advocate of some deadly corruption of Christianity" (Andros 1816, 167, 169). The consequences of all this were as seen—proceedings within the Berkley church for breach of covenant against those "with itching ears" who frequented unauthorized assemblies.

Andros echoed the usual conservative reaction to female exhorters, who, in the words of a Presbyterian clergyman, "forsaking their proper business . . . justly expose themselves to the animadversions of such of mankind, as retain any sense of decency and propriety. If in the age of apostolic purity, some were seduced by the arts of Jezebel, why should it be deemed strange, that, in what many reckon a more degenerate time, there should some be found the victims of the seductive address, of the female heralds of *Smithite Christianity?*" (McMaster 1815, 109–11). For their own part, the Christians were proud of the relative equality accorded to women in their meetings and in their evangelical work.

The power and influence of women within the Christian Connection was dramatically evident in the mission of Nancy Gove Cram, who, in league with C. W. Martin and Jabez King, two Woodstock evangelists, came close to overthrowing Steven Porter's church in Ballston. Little is known about Nancy Cram; all that she appears to have left the world, other than the antipathy of the opposition and the fond memories of those she converted to Jesus, is a small but highly revealing hymnbook (1815), itself intended to be a kind of catechism, exposing "the doctrines of men, by showing them to be absurd" (like Thomas Paul, she is a person who deserves to be better known). A Christian historian remarked in 1921 that his church had long known "that in the great moral machinery of the world there are strings which only woman's touch can start vibrating" (Burnett 1921, 7–8). A Christian preacher who had seen Cram speak in Ballston was thankful that his fellows were free of the "Oriental bigotry" that denied women their proper place in the church.

Nancy Cram, foremost among the first generation of Christian women, was born in Weare, New Hampshire, in the south-central part of the state. She married a man named Cram who was remembered as having been so dissolute that she left him. So far as Gilbert McMaster, a New York Presbyterian, was concerned, domestic life was uncongenial to her, "perhaps being better pleased with the service to which she is called [by Elias Smith], than with the society of her husband and children." McMaster also found occasion to comment on Cram's approach to preaching: "She is abundantly gifted with that spirit of her head, which opposes literature, order, and whatever christians usually have considered, as of vital importance to the interests of religion. She indeed does not profess to entertain her audience with anything like what well informed men call a regular discussion; she never studies, and *compliments* her Maker with being the author of her crude invectives. She exhibits her discourse, as it is given her from above! Such, it is said, is her language" (1815, 100).

In a later age Nancy Cram might have caught the attention of a Henry James, but in this one she was a powerful evangelist who began her evangelical career with the Free-Will Baptists, then missionized with the Oneida Indians, and later came into contact with the Christians in Woodstock, whom she visited in the course of one of their general meetings. Her ministry lasted only the four years from 1811 to 1815, when she died at the young age of forty (Burnett 1921, 9). Jabez King, who in Berkley would equate his own soul with that of a horse, became a party to this work. His background was similar to Elias Smith's; emigrating in the 1780s from Bridgewater, Massachusetts, the King family were among the first settlers in the southern part of Woodstock, and Jabez engaged at times in a tanning business, perhaps helping to supply what Stephen Smith needed in his shoemaking trade (Dana 1980). Cram's account of the work needing to be done in New York roused King to help in it, and he spent parts of 1813–14 preaching in the general area of Saratoga Springs. In 1814 Elias itinerated westward from Woodstock, reaching Ballston in September (348). Nancy Cram went into Ballston shortly afterward, and as Elias reported in the *Herald*, "her praying, singing, and speaking, took great hold of the minds of old and young. Hundreds attended to hear; whether the meetings were in *school-houses*, the *court-house*, or the orchards or groves." Since Cram was not empowered to baptize, Jabez King joined her in Ballston in order to reap the harvest she had sown (*HGL* 7, no. 174 [June 23, 1815]: 701).

These developments aroused the Presbyterian pastor, the Reverend Stephen Porter, to deal via a commentary (1814) on Jude 4 with the serpent that had crept into their midst: "For there are certain men crept in unawares, who were before of old ordained to this condemnation, ungodly men, turning the grace of our God into lasciviousness, and denying the only Lord God, and our Lord Jesus Christ." Porter's disquisition was cut from the same cloth as Thomas Andros's. The particular drama of the occasion arises from the fact that Jabez King was in the audience, prepared after the meeting was over to sing a hymn written by C. W. Martin and later published in Nancy Cram's hymnal under the title "The Whole World Turned Upside Down":

> When Paul came to Ephesus,
> Who died to redeem us,
> From an indignant frown;
> They knowing not the stranger,
> Once cradled in a manger,
> Cry'd out our craft's in danger,
> They turn the world upside down.

> Priests follow this example,
> That they should on us trample,
> And turn us out of town;
> But when a soul engaged,
> Exhort the young and aged,
> The Clergy cry enraged,
> They pull our churches down.

The Church that's on Christ founded,

Although by hell surrounded,

Can never be confounded,

Though earth and hell may frown;

But those of men's invention,

Built on some paper notion;

Are quite turn'd upside down.

In the time of reformation,

The Clergyman's vexation,

For loosing their taxation,

They often sue the town;

They hate a gospel preacher,

And cry out a false teacher,

Turns our church upside down.

(CRAM 1815, 21)[6]

King's message in song was not well received; according to Smith, he was collared in order to get him to shut up, and otherwise threatened by personages taken to be friends to Mr. Porter, including "one Esquire [who] did not behave so much like a Christian as he might have done" (*HGL* 7, no. 174 [June 23, 1815]: 701). According to Christopher Martin, who answered Porter's discourse in pamphlet form, King's performance turned the meeting into "a perfect *hurly-burly*. One man threatened to run *Elder Jabez King through* with a sword, provided he had one. Another man, running his *fist* into Elder King's face, accosted him with these words, '*well you lie, you rescal!*'" (Martin 1815, 43). For Martin, all of this bore "the mark of the beast": the wrath that proclamation of the truth always arouses in Satan's minions, whom Martin identified as the "Esquires," the town gentry and their hirelings the learned clergy.[7]

In taking note of episodes like this and the burgeoning literature of anti-Christian polemics, Smith reversed their logic to show that it was not he but his opponents who were the false teachers. Did they not take money for what the apostles did free of charge, from their love

171

of Christ? Were they not the followers of Samuel Hopkins rather than Jesus, of philosophy rather than plain Scripture? Are they not "dry wells which contain no water"? (*HGL* 4, nos. 84 and 86 [Nov. 8 and Dec. 6, 1811]).

This brand of class-conscious evangelical populism had practical and dramatic effects in a variety of contexts, which further research must detail. Smith's writings were widely distributed and apparently widely read. Armed with his forceful writings and moved by the force of his example, Smith's fellow workers were now independently engaged in the restoration of pure Christianity, and so the message moved westward along with those who would become the dominant force among the second generation of Christian preachers and evangelists. Elias himself recognized that there were still more effective ways of doing this, and so in 1808 the *Herald of Gospel Liberty* was born. To understand that effort, it is necessary to consider the circumstances in which it was founded.

In 1807, when he wrote *The Age of Enquiry*, Elias Smith was thirty-eight years old; he and Mary had by then five children—two boys and three girls. In that same year, the Universalist Hosea Ballou moved to Portsmouth and further complicated Joseph Buckminster's already troubled life. Thomas Jefferson was near the close of his second term in office. After steady growth in their electorate, the Republicans gained control of the New Hampshire legislature in 1804 as a result of the election upon which Elias believed himself to have had an influence through his disquisition entitled *The Whole World Governed by a Jew*. Republican John Langdon was chosen governor in 1805, and by 1806 the New Hampshire congressional delegation was also Republican. Langdon would be voted out in 1809 in reaction to the vastly unpopular trade embargo imposed earlier by the Jefferson administration against Britain in the hope of ending its harassment of American shipping and the impressment of American sailors into the Royal Navy (Cole 1970, 22). But he was to be back once more in 1810 with the repeal of the embargo. New Hampshire was under increasingly firm Republican control while Federalist fortunes progressively withered, as

Plate 5. William Plumer (1759–1850): governor of New Hampshire, sympathetic to Smith's demands for religious liberty and leader of the fight for disestablishment in his state. Reprinted from William Plumer, Jr., *Life of William Plumer* (Boston: Phillips, Sampson, 1857).

did those of the conservative clergy that supported their cause—one such being Joseph Buckminster, who had backed the successful Federalist gubernatorial candidate, John Gilman, in 1800 but found himself increasingly marginalized thereafter.[8]

The question of religious establishments continued to simmer in all the New England states except Rhode Island. In New Hampshire it was usually possible to evade taxes supporting the local establishment by proving, as the law allowed, that one was a member of a legitimate alternative church body and therefore should not be taxed for the support of another denomination (usually Congregationalist) that happened to be dominant in a given town. William Plumer, longtime religious libertarian, former Federalist United States senator, and now a reborn Republican, announced his shift of party in 1807 and attained the governorship of New Hampshire in 1812 with religious disestablishment near the top of his agenda; he too was out in 1813 as a result of the unpopular war with England. But in the pages of the *Herald* Elias would endorse Plumer's 1814 candidacy for governor under the heading of "principles not party"; for that reason or others, Plumer was reelected (see Cole 1970, 27–31; L. W. Turner 1962). There were still statutory provisions for the maintenance of the churches, and formal disestablishment did not come until 1819, when, through the efforts of Plumer and the Republicans, it was at last legislatively determined through the Toleration Act that, in New Hampshire, government on any level cannot have the power to compel the support of religion.[9] But in 1807 Smith reckoned he still had his work cut out for him with respect to the religious liberty issue. And 1808 was a federal election year.

In the spring of 1807 Elias was spending much time in the vicinity of New Bedford in company with Elder Hix and others of their connection. He also journeyed into Rhode Island and, while preaching in Little Compton, met the local congressman—Isaac Wilbour—who proposed that Smith, with the financial aid of himself and several backers among his colleagues in Washington, should undertake a "religious newspaper" aimed at enlightening a people who had "a better understanding of *civil* than *religious* liberty." But Wilbour was a Quaker and a Federalist; the former plus his Rhode Island venue no doubt account for his opinions on religious liberty, but the latter must have been a matter of some disquiet to Smith who was by now unequivocally Republican in sympathy.[10] Elias was tempted by the offer, since he was struggling financially, but decided against it because he did not want to have to truckle to anyone about what he should and should not publish. Instead he determined to start his own subscriber-funded paper, which turned out to be guided by this striking syllogism: "Almost all who are converted to the Lord are Republicans. Why is it so? Because, converts are redeemed with righteousness; and of course are right in things political as well as things religious" (326–27).[11] There could therefore be no contradiction in supporting a political party in the pages of a supposedly religious newspaper (and equally Smith could frequently condemn his evangelical rivals, the Methodists—who, as one protested, "are republicans to a man"—because in his opinion

their adherence to episcopal hierarchy is nothing less than covert Tory-
ism) (Merritt 1807, 16).[12]

Thus the *Herald of Gospel Liberty* came into the world—and
would be published under that name by the Christian Church until
1931, with only a brief period under a different title following Smith's
Universalist apostasy.[13] This was Elias Smith's most important work
except perhaps the *New Testament Dictionary.* hrough it he reached far
beyond New England into the country at large and for nearly ten years
brought to it his distinctive views about the constitution of the church
and society, and in so doing provided a medium through which he and
his increasingly far-flung comrades corresponded and became aware of
each other and their common cause. Again It was as it had been when,
as a youth, Elias dreamed of being tried by fire. Now the dreamer was
a Vermont woman who dreamed of stars fighting in the firmament,
one remaining unmoved while the others seemed to combat it, until all
moved as one off to the Southwest. The angel told her that all were
ministers of Christ and that the one that was originally unmoved had
converted the others such that they united with him, "so the gospel
will have a glorious spread in the world." As Elias wrote in 1816,
"Whenever I see the truth of a dream, I am bound to believe it. The
truth of this dream I have seen and do see. Many who in the year 1808
were opposed . . . have now not only ceased to oppose, but are actually
fellow-laborers" (333–34).[14]

With the assistance of the *Herald* the Christian message moved
south and southwestwards—as had the stars in the Vermont woman's
dream—via the U.S. Mail and powerful fellow-traveling local evangelists. According to Smith, "The *Herald,* by different means, was carried
into various parts of the United States, and in consequence of this in a
few years, I became acquainted with Christians in almost every state in
the union. At this time God raised up several young men to preach the
gospel; some from the free-will baptists, and other denominations who
become united with us to spread the name of Christ only" (337).
Nathan Hatch observes that "by striking down all normal lines of authority in the name of the people, dissenters such as Smith exalted the
printed page as the primary means to convey a sense of direction to
widely dispersed congregations each groping to find its own way" (1983,
269). The efficacy of this strategy is witnessed by what a Georgia cor-

respondent wrote to Smith in 1812: "About eighteen months past, the *Herald of Gospel Liberty* fell into my hands by the means [of a Kentucky brother]. I conceived, that it was one of the most glorious means to disseminate gospel news, that I had seen; accordingly I advised a number of the brethren to subscribe to it" (*HGL* 5, no. 10 [Jan. 8, 1813]: 455). In New Hampshire itself William Plumer subscribed to the *Herald* and corresponded with Smith on the subject of religious liberty.[15]

Volume 1, no. 1 appeared on Thursday evening, September 1, 1808, with the epigram Smith adapted from *Spooner's Vermont Journal*—"From realms far distant, and from climes unknown: we make the knowledge of our King your own." But, with volume 4 in August 1811, Elias replaced that dictum with a more appropriately prophetic extract from Jeremiah. (See Fig. 7.)

Elias began volume 1 with an "Address to the Public" in which he outlined his intentions in publishing a religious newspaper, which, as he said, is "almost a new thing under the sun; I know not but this is the first ever published in the world."

> This is my design, to have a steady and persevering regard to truth, and the general good of men; and to treat every thing in a fair and manly way; not scandalizing any, or doing any thing by partiality. Should any scandalize themselves by bad conduct; let them not charge it to me. If men do not wish to have bad things said of them, let them not do bad things. It is my design in the following numbers to give a plain description of the rights of men, and to shew the principle on which they are founded, and likewise to shew the opposite.

By his own lights this is just what Smith did every other week from the first number to the last under his editorship, volume 8, no. 8, published in Boston in October 1817. Given his experience of the power of the *New Hampshire Gazette* and the *Boston Independent Chronicle,* Smith had taken note of the fact that the press was a principal bulwark of the democratic cause; he regarded the political battles between Republicans and Federalists as effectively a contest between their respec-

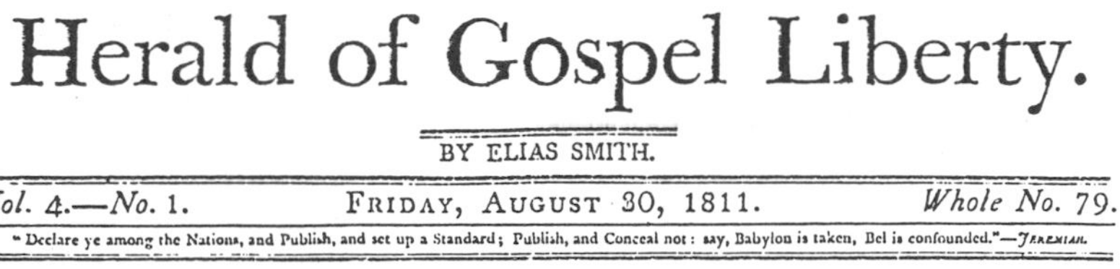

Herald of Gospel Liberty.

BY ELIAS SMITH.

Vol. 4.—No. 1.   FRIDAY, AUGUST 30, 1811.   *Whole No.* 79.

" Declare ye among the Nations, and Publish, and set up a Standard; Publish, and Conceal not: say, Babylon is taken, Bel is confounded."—*JEREMIAH.*

Fig. 7. *Herald* masthead

tive newspapers. "Under kings, men fight and kill each other; and often rise against their government. Here we do not fight. Our newspapers do the fighting, and those who read them, see the battle. Under monarchies, they shed blood; in a republican government, they shed ink. We destroy paper;—they men" (*Morning Star and City Watchman* 2, no. 4 [1828]: 90–91 [hereafter *MSCW*]).[16] In order to forward the Republican agenda, Smith's communicative strategy was therefore simple and effective, rooted in three basic considerations: distribution, style, and content. In his initial issue Smith recognized the political utility of newspapers and then commented, "I do not see why the knowledge of the Redeemer's kingdom may not be promoted or increased in the same way."

The terms for subscribers were one dollar per year "exclusive of postage," half down in advance; letters to the editor were to be sent through Daniel Drown in Portsmouth (because of Smith's frequent itinerancy). Elias then lists twenty-two agents for the paper, all in New England—one of whom was his cousin, Richard Ransom, Jr., of Woodstock; another was the unfortunate Joseph Smith of Berwick, Maine, later brought low by a combination of his own folly and Cochranite zeal.[17] Though still heavily concentrated in New England, the last full list of agents for the *Herald*, which Elias provided from Philadelphia at the end of volume 4 in August 1812, contains eighty names distributed from Maine southward to Virginia and South Carolina, and from Boston westward to New York State, Kentucky, Ohio, and Indiana Territory.[18] If the list of agents is any guide, Smith was therefore eminently successful in the propagation of his message, and even more so if one takes into account the fact that any one issue of the

Herald very likely had more than one reader, perhaps many more. Smith said he began the paper with a mere 174 subscribers, and that by 1815 it had grown to about 1,500 (334). Plagued by local "Smithites," Steven Porter of Ballston took note of the number of agents Elias had recruited to distribute his newspaper, suggesting to his congregation that these "Iscariot bands of Infidelity, are employing [the *Herald*] as one of the means of their united exertion, to betray the Saviour with a kiss!"—to spread heresy and discord under the banner of pristine Christianity (Porter 1814, 49–50).

֎

Even with such growth, it was difficult for Elias to sustain the effort because of problems in collecting from his subscribers, and so as early as the beginning of volume 2 on February 2, 1810, he put out an appeal to them and his agents to submit their remittances so that the printer and the paper supplier could be paid, "or the *Editor* suffer that which neither he nor his customers would be willing he should experience." Such appeals appear periodically thereafter as, for example, in March 1811, in a notice that "those people in Vermont & Maine, indebted to the Editor for Books and Papers, who were to pay in Country produce, are requested to convey the same to the Editor . . . immediately, as he must have it, or Money" (*HGL* 3, no. 66 [Mar. 1, 1811]: 264). In 1812 Smith wrote about hard times and how especially hard it is "for a man to scatter his property over the country for the benefit of others, and not receive help from them in return" (ibid. 4, no. 21 [June 5, 1812]: 396). It was the same thing near the very end when, in the penultimate issue of volume 8, Elias once more asks his debtors to pay up, observing that "they that use a Lamp must supply it with OIL!" (ibid. 8, no. 7 [Aug. 1817]: 252). In the final issue Smith announced his departure and the beginning of the new *Christian Herald* under Robert Foster in Portsmouth. He demanded immediate payment for what is owed, or by implication, more drastic measures would be taken.[19]

It is a wonder that Elias managed to keep the *Herald* going at all. Certainly he had occasional help in the form of gifts, most notably assistance in 1810 from "several of my friends in Portland" in the purchasing of a complete printing office, which he ran with the help of a young man, John Colcord, who would give him considerable grief later (340–41). It might be supposed that Elias's ability to reach out to the evangelicals with a consistently Republican message was seen, in the early days at least, as a political advantage worthy of subsidy by party organizers and sympathizers and those directly involved in the campaign for religious disestablishment. Given the perennial difficulties that Smith had in securing payment from his debtors, extra funds or at least a line of credit must occasionally have become necessary to sustain himself, his growing family, his printing office, and John Colcord.

An essential key to the success of the *Herald* was its style and content; it presented a particular worldview to its target clientele in an accessible and agreeable format worthy of support by those with the capacity to offer it. The religion of Smith's adult life, whether Christian or Universalist, was always political: religion in the context and cause of freedom, a pairing of democratic republicanism and gospel liberty. For him republicanism was just the political application of the Golden Rule. A republic functions for the benefit of all equally, not as in an aristocratic government, which is meant to benefit only a few at the expense of the many: "A *Republic* is like a healthy body, where every member, great or small, honorable, of dishonorable, is an equal sharer, with the rest; and where each member has the same care one for another. If one member suffer, all the rest suffer, and if one member is honored, all rejoice" (*HGL* 3, no. 61 [Dec. 21, 1810]: 244). A true republic, hence the American republic, is therefore the logical equivalent of the fellowship of the primitive church.

Gospel liberty was not to be construed as the spirit of individual license and excess manifest among the antinomian fringe, which so plagued the evangelicals and divided their churches, just as the evangelicals had divided the churches of the orthodox, and Gnostic radicals the counsels of early Christianity. The fundamental New Testament principle is embodied in 2 Corinthians 3:17, which states: "Where the Spirit of the Lord is, there is liberty." But this liberty—attained at such expense through the crucified Christ—is not the freedom to do whatever one likes; rather, it is freedom from sin, death, and corruption, the liberty to do only good and the will to accomplish it. As Elias himself said, the religious law of liberty "was given by Jesus Christ, the one Lawgiver . . . which makes free from the law of sin and death" (*HGL* 4, no. 1 [Aug. 30, 1811]: 313). Romans 8:21 foretells that we "shall be delivered from the bondage of corruption into the glorious liberty of the children of God.," while James 1:25 adds the essential caveat that faith must be accompanied by works: "Whoso looketh into the perfect law of liberty, and continueth therein, he being not a forgetful hearer, but a doer of the work, this man shall be blessed in his deed."

Smith's old Baptist associate John Peak, with whom he had crossed the Green Mountains so long ago and who now served a troublesome church in Newburyport, had occasion to use James 1:25 in a sermon in Philadelphia in 1811. Smith was apparently in the audience, and his comments later allow us to see how he understood this crucial passage. In comment for the *Herald* Elias observed that the epistle itself describes the "perfect law of liberty" in "a most beautiful manner," but that what Peak seemed to be speaking of in his sermon was actually the law of Moses, which had been terminated with the coming of Christ, just as British law had been supplanted by the sovereign acts of a newly liberated people. The law of liberty "is a law that frees bondmen, and after they are free, it keeps them so, as long as they obey the Lawgiver." Elias strangely referred to his former friend as though he had never heard of him before: "This man was from *Newbury Port* (Mass.). His preaching upon this verse put me in mind of the words of Paul concerning certain preachers of his day; 'desiring to be teachers of the LAW; understanding neither what they say, nor whereof they affirm [1 Tim. 1:7]" (*HGL* 4, no. 2 [Sept. 13, 1811]: 318).

As Smith wrote in the first issue of the *Herald*, "Religious liberty signifies a freedom to believe in God, and to obey him according to the manifestation which he has made to man, in his works, in the scriptures, and by the spirit of truth, the *manifestations* of which is given to every man to profit withal." A correlate of the belief that these manifestations are given to *every* person is that any attempt to use state authority to dictate what should be left to private conscience is contrary to the spirit of gospel liberty, and that therefore religious establishments of any kind are part of the kingdom of Antichrist. "The operations of the mind, are not, cannot be subject to the laws of men, no more than the light of the sun, the rain, wind, or seasons of the year can be under their controul." Elias was beginning to propound a form of radical individualism that evaded its own antinomian implications through the heartfelt belief that anyone who truly approaches the Scriptures in the spirit of meek inquiry can arrive only at a common conclusion, thus achieving through individual means a consensus transcending, in its spirit of truth, any attempt to legislate consensus through the force of law. "All doctrines *really* sacred must be clear and incapable of being opposed with success. If civil authority interposes, it will be to support some misconception or abuse of them" (*HGL* 7, no. 3 [Oct. 28, 1814]: 637). *Gospel* liberty can have no anarchy in it.

This was the religion of the commonality, empowered by both the Gospels and the political results of the American Revolution to seek out the truth personally; Elias Smith and the Christians believed that everyone has the inherent ability to discern that truth in whatever area of endeavor without the aid of mediating elites. The nature of the fusion that Elias accomplished between gospel liberty and the inalienable rights of which the Declaration of Independence speaks is nowhere better found than in the statement of personal faith—what he called the protest—that he placed at the end of both editions of his autobiography, and that first appeared in the *Herald* in 1811 (issue of Jan. 19) before his move to Philadelphia, as well as in the penultimate number in August 1817 just before the announcement of his conversion to universal salvationism in the final issue.

> I . . . assert that every *Christian* is under an indispensable obligation to *search the Scriptures for himself,* and make the best use of it he can for information in the *will of God,* and the nature of *'Pure Religion';* that he hath an *unalienable right,* impartially to judge of the sense and meaning of it, and to follow the Scriptures wherever it leads him, even an equal right with the Bishops and Pastors of the churches; and in consequence of this, I further *protest* against that unrighteous and ungodly pretence of making the writings of the fathers, the *decrees of councils and synods,* or the *sense of the church,* the *rule and standard of judging* of the sense of the Scriptures, as *Popish, Anti-Christian, and dangerous to the Church of God.*" (352)

Such an attitude governed Smith's editorial policy on the *Herald* from beginning to end, and so far as he was concerned, the pattern of his life as well; no matter what the changes he went through in his opinions, they were all due to the application of a common principle:

to follow the Scriptures wherever they might lead. In deliberate irony Elias dubbed these principles those of a "Consistent Christian." This was ironically meant because Samuel Hopkins had characterized his own radically predestinarian views as "consistent Calvinism." In Smith's hands, however, *consistency* was now to be defined in the terms of the ideal democratic citizen, secure in his or her rights, willing to accord those rights to others in the spirit of free inquiry and in the belief that out of such inquiry the truth will naturally emerge: "A man is only free from the spirit of *tyranny*, when he is willing others should have their *liberty*" (*HGL* 7, no. 160 [Oct. 28, 1814]). Consistent this may or may not have been, but at least Elias Smith consistently held to it through whatever particular changes he rang on the theme. The practical corollary of all this is implied in an epigram that Elias occasionally used for the Herald: "Intelligence is the life of liberty."

As for style, Hatch observes that the expansion and democratization of the press in the politically divisive years around 1800 also led to "communication strategies that conspired against any form of social distinction: blunt and vulgar language, crude oratory, and sharp ridicule of mediating elites such as lawyers, physicians, and clergymen" (1983, 257).[20] Benjamin Austin's caustic articles in the *Independent Chronicle* are a case in point, where particular notice was taken of the camp followers of the Federalist cause—the legal profession and the learned clergy. Another example is what became *The Clergyman's Looking Glass No. 2*, or the history of Antichrist, which Elias first published in the *New Hampshire Gazette* in 1803, and which he said "sorely grieved the friends of *Law religion*, and those who were attached to an *anti-republican government*" (278). In this parody of clerical Federalism, Smith wrote in barely disguised satire of how the Alien and Sedition Acts of the Adams administration were no better than the Inquisition, of how the Congregational clergy were no better than Roman bishops, and of how a proud "tower" had been set up in Cambridge to perpetuate the rule of the conjoined political and ecclesiastical elite so that they might hold their "places of office for life" and suppress the rights of the people to think for themselves (1803b, 14, 16, 29).

For ten years Elias reiterated these same themes in the *Herald*, varying his specific targets but always returning to a small number of general topics: the work of the increasingly far-flung Christian Connection in overthrowing the kingdom of Antichrist, the necessity for rebirth and adult baptism, missionary news from abroad, the evils of ecclesiastical and political hierarchy, electoral victories of the Republicans, the absolute supremacy of Scripture, the threats to democracy posed by anti-Christian aristocratic cabals, the virtues of the republican form of government and the evils of its opposite, the nature of the primitive church, the place of current events in the framework of prophecy, and above all the meaning of liberty. Any issue of the *Herald* could without exception be selected to illustrate these things, but numbers 101 and 102 (July 3 and 17, 1812) and 166 (Mar. 3, 1815) are of particular interest in that the former pair flank the beginning of the War of 1812 and the latter number marks its end; in this unsettled time the hermeneutical resources of Elias Smith and his collaborators were deployed to place the affairs of his nation and the world in relation to a perceived divine plan and thus to imbue them with morally compelling cosmic significance.

⁂

On July 3, 1812, number 101 of the *Herald* (now published in Philadelphia) begins with the thirty-fourth in a series entitled "The Preacher," which Elias devoted to his exegesis of particular biblical texts. This is followed by several items of "Religious Intelligence" pertaining to the affairs of the Christian Connection, in this case letters from Cedar Hill, Kentucky; Bristol, Rhode Island; and Candia, New Hampshire. The Kentucky correspondent remarks with wonder on the fact that "the *Herald* was, and is, the means of you and me, conversing together. You in the *East*—I in the *West*—Labouring and toiling under difficulties, neither knew any thing of the other's distress. The Lord delivers us both. The *Herald* tells us of it: makes us acquainted, and acquaints us with our brethren all over the Continent. If in this *material* and *mortal* body, such wonders take place, what may we not be fitted for in *Immortality!*"

The letters from Rhode Island and New Hampshire speak respectively of the withering of Calvinism in Bristol and of a general meeting at Candia where Mark Fernald spoke appropriately on Acts 2:42: "And they continued stedfastly in the apostles' doctrine and fellowship, and in breaking of bread, and in prayers." The section on religious intelligence is followed by remarks from the editor on the scripturally validated duties of the church deacon and on the prophetic meaning of earthquakes, namely, "the shaking and removing of earthly things, or things contrary to the kingdom of Christ." No. 101 concludes with the eighth installment of a letter from "Christianos" remarking on the conduct of John Wesley during the Revolution, conduct suggesting that not only had he been hostile to the patriot cause but that he had wished the British government to create an American bishopric for himself.

The lead article, "The Preacher, no. 34," is the most important. It is styled "A Sermon for July 4, 1812," and is a commentary on Ezekiel 21:27: "I will overturn, overturn, overturn it; and it shall be no more, until he come whose right it is; and I will give it him." Elias Smith judged that the prophet was speaking of two things here: (1) the kingdoms of this world, and (2) the kingdom of our Lord Jesus Christ. In this context "it" is the sovereignty that, with one notable exception, is currently usurped by despotic governments. The kingdom of Christ is one of "righteousness, peace, and joy"; when the kings of this world are overthrown, "it" will be vested in Christ as King and Priest as prefigured by Melchizedek, the priest-king of Salem ("Peace") in Genesis 14:18.[21] This kingdom is based on what Elias—as in his July 4, 1809, "loving-kindness" address on the Taunton town green—always took to be the central principles of republican government: liberty, equality, unity, and peace. America has the only extant government of this sort. The commotions to which the world is now subject are the product of nations ruled by kings and priests; if all the nations of the world were truly republican—ruled by Christ rather than human pretenders—all this disturbance would be at an end: "Were all nations under a government like ours, and each one as here, allowed to read and believe for himself in things of *religion*, there would be no *war* or *persecution*—All would be free."

The next issue of the *Herald* stands in ironic counterpoise to the preceding number. On July 8, 1812, President James Madison proclaimed a day of humiliation and prayer for the second Thursday in August so that God might be moved to grant victory to a repentant nation in its recently declared war with Britain. No. 102 begins with

"Liberty" no. 45, proceeds to a reprinted anti-Trinitarian sermon, then moves on to the "Religious Intelligence" section (a letter from Wood-stock concerning the recent glorious works of the Lord in those parts), a republication of Madison's proclamation, and an extract from the *Richmond Enquirer* concerning "ancient prophecy accomplished in America." It ends with remarks on the lukewarm response of Governor Caleb Strong of Massachusetts to the president's request for a day of national humiliation.

Strong's response was seen as being so hypocritical that any people from his state who saw fit to pray for national victory on such terms would endanger their own souls in doing so. (In 1814 Strong would be involved with the infamous Hartford Convention, at which dissolution of the Union was advocated as a step necessary to protect the interests of New England.) The piece on ancient prophecy attempts to establish that a prediction in Genesis 9:27 about the fate of the descendants of Noah's three sons—Shem, Ham, and Japheth—actually pertains to the Indians (Shem), the blacks (Ham), and the European emigrants to America (Japheth), who, as Scripture declares, "shall dwell in the tents of Shem, and Canaan [Ham's offspring] shall be his servant." The editor was at pains to emphasize that the author of this commentary did not mean to approve of what had occurred but merely to establish where it stood in relation to prophecy. "Liberty" no. 45 is a reprinted article on the inseparability of religious and political freedom, and the consonance of New Testament religion and American republicanism. The author ("Casca")—speaking of the relative virtues of aristocracy and democracy—implies that many of the clergy have reacted to the recent crisis so as "to weaken the energy of government," instead of in-spiring "the god-like *amor patria* which swells in every virtuous bosom" at a time when "the free-born sons of America are called upon to de-fend the altars and the firesides of this modern land of promise."

With the end of the war no. 166 is naturally different in tone. Publication of the *Herald* had itself been recently affected by political adversity. Elias was obliged to interrupt its appearance for several weeks in early 1815 because of his own travels and fear of British inva-sion of Portsmouth, where the *Herald* was again being published. In this issue Elias devoted himself to a commentary on Isaiah 32, inter-preting "the work of righteousness" to which the prophet refers. Insofar as "righteousness" refers to humanity, it pertains (so said Elias) to "the natural and unalienable rights of men; which belongs to every individual, and can never in justice be given or received by another." So far as this righteousness pertains to nations, it can pertain only to those nations that acknowledge that all are born free and equal, those nations governed by republican principles. The "work of righteousness" is the throwing off the yoke of tyrants; and so, even though true republics are pacific by nature, the War of 1812 was a just one. In consequence, "*America* has succeeded in preventing the tyrant from replacing his galling yoke upon us again!" It is true that many were disquieted by the late war, thinking that the new government had taken more upon itself than it could deliver; but now that the struggle is successfully concluded, harmony prevails among those who only recently had been, because of their political disagreements, "strangers while in sight of each other." Smith then evocatively describes the effect news of the peace had in Portsmouth:

> On the evening of the 22d of Feb. (1815) (an evening long to be remembered by thousands) the public buildings, and many others in Portsmouth, N.H. were *illuminated*, to the great joy of thousands. On the *Academy* the word PEACE shone—and the same on Mr. *Elwin's house*. On one *hotel*, was seen PEACE AND UNION. On two Bookstores—PEACE—UNION U.S.G.B. At another shone *America* and *England*; described by two men taking each other by the hand.— What gave pleasure to the inhabitants was the things these brought to their minds—Thousands of men, women and children were seen walking in companies through different parts of the town; this was right—the effect of *righteousness* was *quietness* and assurance; for each one was *certain*, they saw a good day, and each seemed to rejoice that a righteous foundation was laid for their future prosperity, and of their children they lead by the hand through the streets.

Elias concluded with his hope that now the "spirit of party" would die away and that the gospel of the Prince of Peace spread through the land. He then moved to religious intelligence, including a message from Freetown, Massachusetts, where a great work had been going forward with the help of Daniel Hix, who of late had baptized no less than thirty to forty souls. Letters follow from Coventry, Rhode Island,

and from Franklin Township, Indiana Territory, in which New Testament religion was spreading rapidly at the expense of unscriptural doctrines and the "unscriptural *denominations*" that supported them. The number concludes with a "SURPRIZING ACCOUNT Of a Child who Spoke and Sung when he was Eight days old. Certified by an eminent and learned Physician." The "physician" who related the story was St. Luke; the child in question was John the Baptist, a figure who appealed to Smith. As the Baptist had foretold the first coming of the Messiah, it was Elias's mission to foretell the second and to prepare the way for it.

By the end of the War of 1812 Smith had gone through many changes and much trouble; his affairs and opinions were building to the great crisis of his adult life in 1816. That denouement was taking shape in 1811 with the removal to Philadelphia of Elias, his family, and the editorial offices of the *Herald*. First, however, came an obscurely motivated move to Portland, Maine, in February 1810. All Elias tells us about it is that this was undertaken because of entreaties from the believers in Maine that he should come and join them; Smith came to regard it and the later move to Philadelphia as disastrous mistakes, "a foundation for such trouble as to that day we had been unacquainted with" (340). With the help of unidentified friends he acquired a printing shop of his own and the services of John Colcord. The contents of the *Herald* reveal little of what transpired in Maine, and Smith's autobiography next to nothing. One thing he did do while in Maine was to deliver a Fourth of July address in 1810 in Gray on the topic of government and religion (Smith 1810). In it he commented on the meaning of the biblical verse "render therefore unto Caesar the things that are Caesar's," concluding (accompanied by a few digs at David Osgood) that only a republican government has any legitimate claim on its citizens.

What little else we are offered about the stay in Maine suggests a familiar pattern. Six months after he arrived in Portland, Smith wrote an open letter to the ministers of that town, remarking that though they seemed to treat him as below their notice, "yet I do not consider you *above* mine," and challenging them to debate him in public on the scriptural validity of the heresies he was supposed to be propounding (*HGL* 2, no. 49 [July 6, 1810]: 193). There is no sign they responded, but Elias did publish the observations of a sympathetic correspondent ("Detector") who found that the opposition, except some of the more enlightened Methodists, had in fact wondered how anyone "could bear to hear such an abominable wretched monster [as Smith] preach." The central problem seems to have been Smith's already questionable reputation and his views on the destruction of the wicked (ibid. 3, no. 60 [Dec. 7, 1810]: 239). In the next issue (Dec. 21) Smith published a letter of commendation from his Portland church—John Colcord among the signatories—stating that all the calumnies that have been so widely spread about by his enemies are totally without foundation, and that anyone who should meet Elias on his forthcoming journeys ought to receive him "as a man eminently qualified to be extensively useful in society." The July 5, 1811, issue of the *Herald*, then, was published in Philadelphia.

The move to Philadelphia is somewhat easier to interpret. Elias long had associations to the south with the Christians of Virginia, with whom he had been in correspondence since the foundation of the *Herald*. Philadelphia was still the metropolis of the nation, and Pennsylvania had a long-standing tradition of religious freedom since the time of the Penns. By situating himself between North and South, Smith and his supporters believed he could better reach out to the nation at large and serve, as he had always intended, as a clearinghouse for the movement. The ground was already prepared by Frederick Plummer, a New Englander who had traveled more widely than most of his brethren. At Plummer's behest, and that of a local man, John Hunter, Elias uprooted his family and brought them to Philadelphia in August 1811. Once more Smith later looked back in regret on the misfortunes this move brought down on him. He realized only too late that he had too little capital to accomplish what he had hoped; furthermore, his family "was discontented and unhappy" but now had little choice but to endure it (341–43). The *Herald* was published in Philadelphia until February 1814.

During this period Elias traveled as far from the scenes of his childhood as he ever would, accepting invitations to preach and attend meetings in Caroline County, Virginia, and in the Shenendoah Valley.

Smith spent much of this period traveling, and one senses that in practice the editorship of the *Herald* was often in other hands. It was not a good time for him, and 1813 a particularly difficult year in which Elias "had continued scenes of trouble to pass through." His wife and eldest daughter were both sick, and his debts were getting the better of him. That year also saw the beginnings of a controversy that would drag on until after Elias finally left Philadelphia, and that would involve him in an inquiry by his own brethren into what some took to be irregularities in his financial dealings.

Smith had affiliated himself with a church of which John Hunter had been a principal organizer. It called itself the Christian Church Mount Zion in Southwark. But in order to act as a corporate body with respect to church property, the voting majority decided to incorporate under the laws of Pennsylvania, an act that precipitated a schism over whether such a move is compatible with New Testament principles. Elias thought not, and so he, in company with twenty-nine other members of the congregation, set themselves up as a separate body, declaring that "it is contrary to command of Christ for his Church to be an *incorporated body*, by laws made by men" (*HGL* 5, no. 116 [Feb. 5, 1813]: 462). Smith published the constitution of the putrescent body from which they had seceded so that the readers of the *Herald* could judge for themselves just how far Mount Zion had departed from the equality of the primitive church. In his opinion, incorporation was a manifestation of "law religion . . . the old *Tyranny* in a new form," the lineal descendant of the beast mentioned in Revelation 13:1: "having seven heads . . . and upon his heads the name of blasphemy" (ibid., no. 117 [Feb. 19, 1813]: 466).

This was characteristic Smith. But it emerged that there was more to it than a difference of constitutional opinion when certain charges were circulated that April concerning just why Elias had left Mount Zion; these accusations were published in two Philadelphia newspapers, and Smith took passing note of them in a number of the *Herald* otherwise devoted to an analysis of the meaning of the word *Christ*, and (in "Liberty," no. 51) to an account of why the American war against England was a just one. Elias wanted to leave it at that but evidently was not given the chance, for shortly afterward the Mount Zion church published a circular addressed "to the brethren of the Christian

Churches in the United States" detailing certain supposed defects in the character of Elder Smith (*HGL* 5, no. 124 [May 28, 1813]: 496).

Elias responded in a long-suffering letter to the *Herald* from Portsmouth, where he was away on a visit. It now becomes apparent that the main accusations against him originated with his printer, John Colcord, accusations that began with events that took place when they were resident in Portland: specifically that Smith had made unfulfilled promises that Colcord would one day come into possession of their printing shop and that Smith had misappropriated funds meant for others. For Smith, the actions of the publishers of the circular proved them to be "not only enemies to me, but enemies to 'the perfect law of liberty,' given by Christ" (*HGL* 5, no. 127 [July 9, 1813]: 503). The affair dragged on until January 1814, when, after an inquiry by the Christian brethren and elders at a meeting held in New Bedford, Elias was absolved of the charges of financial improprieties (taking money from letters not addressed to him) and of himself generating the schism in the Mount Zion church contrary to the spirit of Christian charity (ibid. 6, nos. 141–42 [Jan. 4 and 21, 1814]). As for charity, the brethren asked what charity there was in the fact that John Hunter sued Smith for his board "after he had, as a brother, freely and pressingly invited him to his house?"[22] Insofar as Elias was guilty of anything, they found that it was in "acting inexpedient" (though not from ill intent) because of the press of his business affairs.

Elias's writings for the *Herald* were beginning to change in tone. He now included pieces on envy, hypocrisy, and slander, as well as fillers on "parental duty" and "filial obedience," which perhaps has some bearing on the tenor of his personal affairs (Colcord supposedly had been like an "*equal* or a *favourite son*" to him) (*HGL* 5, no. 129 [Aug. 6, 1813]: 513).[23] According to Elias, "Slanderers are like flies, they leap over a man's good parts to light upon his sores." Smith was becoming reflective. In September 1813, he visited Lyme for the first time in thirty years and wrote to the *Herald* with some "thoughts from the sea shore." Elias recalled how as a child he had once thought a large rock at the shore must one day be washed away by the waves, but here he was, now older, and the rock still stood untouched. Awash in metaphors, Smith likened the rock to the truth and the waves to the wicked; the rock to the government of the United States and the waves to its opponents; finally, the rock to the saints of all ages and the waves to the agents of their martyrdom (ibid. 6, no. 132 [1813]: 526). In November Elias became seriously ill for the first time in his adult life; far from home and laid low by "the symptoms of a distressing fever" (which he later described as typhus), he reflected on death and how it holds no terrors for the true Christian (ibid., no. 137 [1813]: 548). Worse followed. Still in New England recovering from his own illness and now again editing the *Herald* from Portsmouth, he resolved to bring his family back north and wrote them to prepare for it. But he received word from Frederick Plummer in Philadelphia that his wife and eldest daughter were themselves dangerously ill.

Mary Burleigh Smith died on February 27, 1814, and Elias mourned her passing in the pages of the *Herald:* "What but the religion of Jesus can support in such a time as this! She is gone a little while first, we must all follow soon—Though she is dead, yet she lives in the memory of hundreds and thousands with whom she had been acquainted for many years. Though gone, yet we sorrow not, as they that have no hope—The dead in Christ shall rise first.—The Lord prepare us all to follow when called" (*HGL* 7, no. 145 [Mar. 18, 1814]: 577). Perhaps in this time of trouble Elias was moved to recall words from his 1804 hymnbook.

> Precious Bible! what a treasure
> Does the word of God afford!
> All I want for life or pleasure,
> Food and med'cine, shield and sword;
> Let the world account me poor,
> Having this I need no more.
>
> (SMITH ET AL. 1804, 14)

This was the lowest point of Smith's life. In his autobiography (which speaks hardly at all of the time in Philadelphia, and nothing whatever of the Colcord affair) he wrote of this trying period that "for

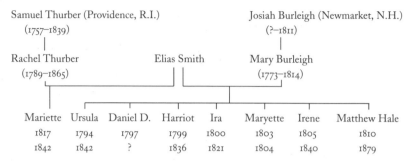

Fig. 8. Elias Smith's family

some time I thought my mind would sink under the additional trouble which this brought me into; and from which I saw no way for deliverance. I was left with six children. One only was married, the others young and strangers in a strange land" (349). By the end of the year Elias was married to Rachel Thurber of Providence, Rhode Island—a woman twenty years younger than he—and unknowingly set in motion the events that would lead to the loss of another son. (See Fig. 8.)

Rachel was the daughter of Samuel and Mehitabel Thurber, members of the liberal Fourth Baptist Society of Providence. In the earlier edition of his *Life,* Elias describes her as "a rich man's daughter," who nevertheless had nothing but the "fruit of her own hands" when she left her father's house to marry Smith (1816, 401). Perhaps she married without her father's approval. Smith's 1816 remark about Rachel's being a rich man's daughter has a tone of resentment about it; in any event Elias chose to strike it from the 1840 edition. As for wealth, it would seem that the Thurber family was indeed relatively prosperous, as indicated at least by the size of the Thurber family burial plot, in which both Elias Smith and Rachel would be finally laid to rest.

Samuel Thurber founded a paper manufactory where both of his sons, Isaac and Dexter, worked in their youth. Rachel's brothers became prominent persons in their own right. The *Providence Directory* for 1841 shows that by then Dexter Thurber was a founder and member of the Board of Directors of the Roger Williams Bank of Providence, capitalized at half a million dollars. It also shows that in the same year

Elias Smith was now resident in Providence and a practicing "Botanic Physician" (pp. 194, 188). The Thurber paper mill (among other things, printer of bank notes for the Roger Williams Bank) later converted to cotton spinning and became noted for "the production of cotton checks and stripes." Dexter Thurber set up a cotton manufactory of his own in Manchaug, Massachusetts, and became a Providence city alderman in 1832 (*Providence Journal*, May 24, 1871). Isaac Thurber also had once worked in his father's mill and later became superintendent of the Franklin Foundry. Isaac (like many of those who belonged to Smith's church in Portsmouth) was active in civic affairs, local business enterprise, and self-improvement societies. He delivered a lecture entitled "Hydraulics and Dynamics" before the Mechanics Association in 1831 (in which Dexter was also active) and in 1850 became a director of the Providence Mutual Fire Insurance Company. In religion, Isaac was a man of "clear and positive" religious convictions who took a keen interest in God's work as manifested in physical nature (*Providence Press*, June 1, 1866).

This connection to a prominent family did Smith no immediate good, and by the end of 1815 Rachel was selling dry goods out their home in Portsmouth, while Smith continued on with a trade in his own books and other works of service to the connection, which now by his own count included among its number no less than forty-three ordained preachers and their congregations in New England alone.[24]

6
PHYSICIANS OF VALUE
Medicine for the People

*They that be whole need not a physician,
but they that are sick.*

MATTHEW 9:12

THE BOOK OF REVELATION TELLS OF the river of the water of life
flowing down from the throne of God. On each side of the river stands
a tree of life yielding a crop of fruit for each month of the year, and
whose leaves serve for the healing of the nations. This is the tree from
which Adam and Eve were forbidden to eat, lest—having already eaten
from the Tree of Knowledge and being put under God's curse because
of it—they eat and live forever. In the postmillennial paradise that
John describes in his vision—when "all accursed thing shall disap-
pear"—the children of God will see him face to face for the first time
since the beginning of the world and, by implication, at last enjoy the
fruit of the tree of life.

The prophet Ezekiel spoke of another plant that the Lord will
create for the benefit of his people: "I will raise up for them a plant of
renown, and they shall be no more consumed with hunger in the land,
neither bear the shame of the heathen any more" (Ezek. 34:29).[1] This
passage refers to the return of Israel to its patrimony, to the earth freely
yielding her increase, a covenant of peace, and of the reappearance of
David as Israel's shepherd. Following the logic of type and antitype,
Christian hermeneutics has interpreted the text as referring to the condition of the world upon the return of Jesus Christ; Ezekiel's "plant of
renown" therefore becomes a figure of the Messiah, who will renew all
things.[2] Elias Smith—already steeped in prophecy—saw Ezekiel 34 as

a promise of "a new heaven and a new earth," of Eden restored (1805e). Smith conflated this plant of renown with the herb at the center of the Thomsonian medical system—Indian Tobacco, *Lobelia inflata*—which, as promised, God has provided as a panacea for the healing of the nations. Christ suffices for the spirit, and *Lobelia* will suffice for the body until illness, death, and time itself are no more.

> Come then to this Physician,
> His help he'll freely give;
> He makes no hard condition,
> Tis only—"look and live."
>
> <small>(SMITH ET AL. 1804, 19)</small>

Elias Smith's mature philosophy was fully embodied in his adaptation of Samuel Thomson's medical system: Disease arrived with the fall of man, but it is God's intent to restore all of creation to him, to which end he has provided his creatures, human and beast alike, with the means to sustain and heal themselves within the limits of mortal existence. Nature should therefore be our guide, not human artifice— the false systems and harmful drugs of the medical pharisees, the regular doctors.

Smith's illness, the death of his first wife, his desperate financial straits, and the needs of his still young family forced upon him an end to his itinerant existence. He was also once more in theological doubt about the message he was preaching. This combination of circumstances led to a synthesis that shaped Elias's life and activities henceforth. A mixture of necessity and personal experience led to the adoption of this trade from which many evangelicals derived much of their income—medicine. But the form of medical practice that Smith adopted was no longer just an unpretentious ad hoc expedient serving the needs of a dispersed rural society. Thomsonian herbalism, like the Christian Connection itself, was taking on the character of a populist crusade.

Once Smith had moved back to Portsmouth after the disastrous experience in Philadelphia, he suffered an attack of the "bilious colic,"

which led him to reflect seriously on the nature of the healing art. Beleaguered by debt, forty-seven years old, and with a family and new wife to support, the simplicity, ideological consistency, and growing popularity of Thomsonian medicine proved an irresistible attraction. Smith needed steady employment, while the semiliterate Samuel Thomson needed Elias's proven skills to spread abroad the word about his system.

Illness was an admonition and a warning. In earlier more hopeful days, Elias himself had been brought all too close to death by an epidemic of "canker rash" in March 1786, soon after he began teaching school in Woodstock. A young man near Elias's own age died of this affliction, and in dying cried that, being without Christ, he was undone for all eternity. As Smith recalled, "the news of his death, and what he said . . . was like a fire, and spread alarm wherever it came." The youth's view that he was undone led Elias to think that maybe he was as well, and so he resolved to live a better life than he had done before. The canker rash struck again near where Elias had been teaching, ushering still others to an early grave and proving once more that "all men are mortal, and that life is always uncertain" (49–50). Very soon afterward, Elias Smith had his vision of the Lamb of God on Mount Zion while his body was stuck in a snowdrift in the forest under a bindle of firewood.

Community life was strongly affected by collective experience of illness and the fear of it. What are now rare infectious diseases previously laid whole families in their graves in a matter of days, striking indiscriminately throughout all ranks of society. Elias Smith was probably correct when he reported that the sickness he suffered from in November 1813 was typhus. He was, as he said, "taken with a violent pain in my head, with all the symptoms of a distressing fever" (*HGL* 7, no. 138 [Dec. 10, 1813]: 551). These are in fact the signs of typhus, a disease spread by body lice. A combination of questionable personal hygiene, exposure to the elements, close living conditions, inadequate nutrition, and contaminated water rendered infectious illness a constant companion and imminent mortal threat from cradle to an often early grave—as a casual stroll in any eighteenth- or nineteenth-century cemetery readily testifies. Elias's account of his family's poverty and of the diseases that periodically swept through the Woodstock area are testimony to the difficulties the settlers of the newer areas in particular had to endure.

The densely settled larger towns were the epicenters of misfortune. Recurrent epidemics in American cities produced scenes of panic and disarray rivaling the visitations of plague in Europe. The Philadelphia yellow fever epidemic of 1793 killed upward of four thousand souls out of a population of forty thousand and compelled the national government to flee. The "canker rash" that helped bring on Elias's epiphany in Woodstock was actually scarlet fever, a streptococcal infection whose symptoms are a red rash on the body and "cankers" in the mouth and throat. According to the bills of mortality for Portsmouth in the years 1801–20, scarlet fever was the most proportionately deadly of the infectious diseases after cholera and typhus; in September through December 1803, it rose to a clear peak. In those four months it accounted for 5 percent of all deaths that year, and an unknown total morbidity (Estes 1979, 115).

In the summer of 1802, the summer before the great fire, a pestilence descended on Portsmouth in fulfillment of the prophecy that Elliot Frost made that April when he wandered the streets crying out his warning of death and destruction. Beginning in June there was an outbreak of what Smith called "the yellow fever" or "putrid malignant fever," which the town doctors recorded as "bilious remitting fever."[3] According to bills of mortality, it seems that this disease had been around at a relatively constant rate throughout 1801 and accounted for about 10 percent of the total deaths in that year. However, it emerged into greater prominence in the summer of 1802, accounting for nearly 10 percent of the year's total deaths in the months of July through September alone. It was perceived as an epidemic by the townspeople and was referred to as such in a hymn composed by Smith's friend Daniel Drown, on the subject of "the judgments and blessings sent on Portsmouth," which Elias included in his first hymnal (1804):

The Lord on *Portsmouth sinners* call'd
About five years ago,
By the destructive pestilence,
To lay us rebels low!

The Lord again bid sinners stop,

Yet they refus'd to hear,

But they pursu'd their wicked lot,

Although it was so dear.

The Lord again did shew his rod,

By a tremendous fire!

Yet they did not perceive 'twas God,

When dress'd in this attire.

Drown gave baleful warning of the consequences for those who refused to heed the Lord's call—referring in a fourth verse to the revival that had started under Elias Smith's auspices in January 1803, in fulfillment of the remainder of Frost's prophecy, that following death and destruction there would be "peace and good will":

You who oppose this glorious cause,

Remember you must die,

Who have despis'd God's holy law,

That you in hell must lie!

(SMITH ET AL. 1804, 71–72)[4]

Again, there was no event without meaning—the more baleful, the more significant. Just as the fire was, in Joseph Buckminster's estimation, a visitation of God's terrible wrath on the town for political divisions, doctrinal heresy, and individual greed, so in the estimation of Smith and Jones the epidemic of yellow fever was sent both as chastisement and as a cautionary example of the evanescence of human life and the proximity of final judgment.

Woodstock was visited with spotted fever in the winter of 1810, which, according to the historian of the local Christian church, "swept many inhabitants into the grave as with a broom of destruction." Elder Frederick Plummer, who served the congregation in this period, cried out in the course of a baptism, "Woe, woe, woe to Woodstock!" as he stood in the stream awaiting the initiate on a cold November day. Plummer was remembered as a powerful preacher (Williams n.d., 4).

Similar experiences shaped the attitudes and the practices of two of Smith's foremost comrades in the Christian Connection, Abner Jones and Mark Fernald.

Jones knew the transience of human existence only too well; not only did he have the unavoidable experiences of illness characteristic of his day, he was, like many other itinerant preachers, a practicing physician himself. His father died of a "quick consumption," a child was lost to "a malignant typhus fever," and he himself suffered a bout of "rheumatic bilious fever" such that he thought himself to "have entered into the dark valley of the shadow of death." He was witness to the great influenza epidemic of 1824, which afflicted perhaps two-thirds of the population of Salem, where he then preached, and was widely prevalent in New England at large (Jones 1842, 19, 122, 131, 127). How Jones came to the doctoring trade is obscure, and how he practiced it still more so. Before his final calling to preach the gospel of Jesus (and still convinced that the call he felt to do so was at the prompting of the Devil), he instead "decided to pursue the study of medicine, wisely concluding that it could do him no harm, and might be of great service to him" (ibid., 25). It served him well afterward, since his remarkable works of healing around Deerfield, New Hampshire, during a spotted fever epidemic in the winter of 1815 led to widespread public perception of the efficacy of his cures. Thereafter he was known as Doctor Jones, and medicine often preoccupied him more than preaching did (though in the eyes of the opposition his activities were all of much the same order; for them Jones was "a fanatic in religion" just as he was "a *quack* in medicine").[5]

Spotted fever (again, probably typhus) was associated with the winter months, as yellow fever was with the summer. What Jones actually did about fevers is unknown. But it is recalled that "his treatment of the fever, was unlike that of most of the physicians, who resorted to depletives, with a most fatal effect"; this suggests that his system probably did not include the then-common practices of bleeding, blistering, and issues, all of which were aimed at drawing out a fever by depleting "hot" (or "phlogistic") bodily fluids either generally, as with bleeding, or locally, as with blisters (Jones 1842, 106). An example of the latter procedure was provided by Smith when writing about contemporary practice in dealing with typhus. After becoming a Thomsonian, Elias observed that a common way to deal with the problem was to "shave the head and blister it," which he thought a very dangerous practice because, by raising the heat on the outside of the head, it actually drives the cold into the brain, leading to delirium and death, whereas what is really needed is a raising of the temperature of the body in order to drive the cold out altogether (1837, 178).

Jones considered his curative techniques as private property, and even his son was circumspect when describing the nature of his father's practice after Abner's death. One reason was that Jones had what was regarded as a particularly efficacious cure for "cancer," or surface tumors. Other forms of what we now call cancer were most likely diagnosed as *consumption* if in the lungs, and something else if other parts of the body. Jones refused to disclose what this cure was, which contributed to accusations of quackery. His son responded that "it must be allowed that he applied a *secret* to the cure of a certain disease [but] he obtained the secret in such a way that he could not honorably or conscientiously divulge it. It was indeed no quackery, but an effectual and radical cure" (Jones 1842, 188–89).

The case of Mark Fernald is still more instructive, for his memoirs are replete with mention of illness—his own and that of others—and what they attempted to do about it. His mother died of a hemorrhaging cancer in her thigh, presumably the kind of thing that Abner Jones specialized in treating (and perhaps Smith's brother, Richard Ransom Smith, who possessed an obscure cancer cure derived from an equally obscure "Canadian" source). Fernald seems to have been decidedly eclectic in his own treatments, but at the center of it was a "medicine" that he came by "from study, practice, a revelation, or all" (1852, 107). Again, because of the secrecy of this proprietary medicine, whose nature Fernald never disclosed, one sees that doctoring was a competitive art based on a mixture of good luck, personal charisma, and the supposed efficacy of a particular system or theory. All Fernald tells us is that "the knowledge of God's vegetable medicine inabled [*sic*] me to give relief to many suffering bodies" (ibid., 137). This at least serves to place Fernald in relation to the orthodox medicine of the day, which relied heavily on bleeding to deplete the fever-producing sanguinary element and on the mercury-based compound calomel (mercurous chloride) to induce purging, which it did by irritating the gut. Fernald, in company with Samuel Thomson and Elias Smith, rejected such procedures as unnatural.

On at least one occasion, Fernald used blisters and issues on himself for what he called "a bad humor" and nearly died from the cure, for the issue (a small wound inflicted for the sake of the fluid that would be secreted from the infection) resulted in an injury that was slow to heal. His own demise from a wasting illness, perhaps stomach cancer, was probably hastened by a physician who prescribed "powerful vomiting" (Fernald 1852, 397). Fernald was certainly aware of the variety of treatments available in his day. He himself was once treated by Thomsonian methods and given "great relief" by that means. The same treatment was applied to the long-standing infirmities of his wife, and to Abner Jones (himself no Thomsonian) for "rheumatic bilious fever" (ibid., 98, 299; Jones 1842, 131). Fernald also had ample experience of devastating epidemics. In 1815 he preached at the home of a man who had lost six of his seven children to the spotted fever in a space of eight days, and he remarks in 1849 on the proclamation of a national fast by President Zachary Taylor in heed of a disastrous visitation of cholera, a disease originating in India that had spread into the United States by the early 1830s (Fernald 1852, 385).[6]

To a thinking Christian all of this was cause for reflection, as expressed in a verse appearing in the coauthored hymnal published by Smith and Jones in 1805, and written by Jones during "a season of general sickness":

Around, how thick diseases fly!
The young, the gay, the hopeful die:
No age exempt, can life ensure,
No place, from death's attack secure.

The vig'rous youth on passions borne,
From all his flatt'ring prospects torn;

Warm with full strength, a victim falls:
No strength avails, when judgment calls.

The infant's bloom, with morning smile
Did late the parent's heart beguile;
Faded in death, now pale he lies,
And fills the parent's heart with sighs.

Deep on our hearts, that mercy write,
Our path illume with heav'nly light;
Long as thy guardian hand we see,
Help us, O Lord! to live to THEE.

(SMITH AND JONES 1805, 303-4)

Though Smith was drawn to Jesus through the salutary lesson of the canker rash, it was only much later that he entered medical practice as Christ's temporal ally with respect to the ills of the body. But he long had before him the example of Samuel Shepard of Brentwood, who along with the other itinerant doctors united "the characters, then not uncommon of physician and divine" (Plumer 1857, 25). In addition to his role as nodal figure in a network of evangelicals radiating out from his Baptist church in Brentwood, Shepard was a traveling physician who in all probability devoted most of his time to healing (Towle 1990, 300–301). It is not known what type of medicine this "doctor of physic" actually practiced, but again he was possibly a model for Smith, and certainly an example of how spiritual and physical welfare were often served in the persons of itinerants like Jones and Fernald.

What is certain is that an attack of "bilious colic" in 1816 led to a very substantial alteration in Smith's affairs. He had become convinced that only vegetable medicines would do for an illness of this sort, and he went home to Portsmouth to seek out a Thomsonian practitioner. Toward the end of his editorship of the *Herald* in 1817, Smith was beginning to include writings by Samuel Thomson, along with his own observations on the efficacy of herbal remedies and steam baths. Perhaps not coincidentally, Thomson was a Universalist. Within a year Elias was both Universalist and herbal physician.

The relations between Thomsonian medicine and the Christian movement were close from the start. Elias Smith's own association with Samuel Thomson had indirectly begun with a treatment from Thomson's agent in Portsmouth, Dr. John Lock. This appears to have been the same John Lock(e) who joined Elias's church as a charter member in 1803—the boss painter at the Navy Yard, and later president of the Associated Mechanics. Thomson allowed Locke 25 percent of the proceeds derived from the sale of patent rights, and remembered him as one of the few agents who dealt with him honestly (1835, 134). After attaining relief for his bilious colic from Locke, Smith suffered a relapse and turned next to Daniel Drown for help (358).

The connection provided Thomson with a social network for the propagation of his medical system, as well as an ideological nexus receptive to it. He and Locke went to Philadelphia in 1814 and sought out Elder Frederick Plummer, an early member of the Portsmouth church who had moved southward and who then was instrumental in getting Elias to follow suit. Plummer had joined Smith's church in 1805 and was ordained an elder in 1808 by Smith, Hix, John Rand, Zephaniah Crossman, and Joseph Boodey, Jr. (who in 1810 collectively attested to Plummer's character and denied rumors that he had been expelled from the Baptist and Methodist churches for "bad conduct") (*HGL* 2, no. 52 [Aug. 17, 1810]: 207).

Plummer arranged for Thomson to give a lecture on his medical system, which the latter remembered as an occasion in which he put in their place a couple of heckling medical students who held that overly great heat is the key to fevers and that bleeding is the means necessary to reduce it. Thomson responded that, if this is so, then "an animal that had the blood taken from it and was frozen, would be the liveliest creature in the world" (1835, 148: Smith 1840, 358). After the lecture, Thomson recruited sixteen new subscribers to his system. Plummer became one of Thomson's principal agents after the falling-out with Elias, as did the notorious freethinker Abner Kneeland, who allowed his paper the *Boston Investigator* to be used for Thomsonian attacks on Smith. By 1835 Plummer was manager of a "Thomsonian Infirmary" in

Philadelphia and was defending his system against charges of murder leveled by "a respectable physician of this City." Kneeland started as a Baptist, became a Universalist, and finally denied the existence of God, the divine inspiration of Scripture, and the personal survival of death; for publicly voicing such sentiments Kneeland was tried under the Massachusetts antiblasphemy law (the last person to be charged under this law). Thomson's system was evidently congenial to free spirits of all kinds.

Plummer, Locke, and other Christians referred Thomson to Smith, and by November 1816 the impecunious Elias was practicing the Thomsonian system under the personal supervision of its creator. Thomson reports having sold Elias a family right to his system in December and as having stayed "in his family during the winter, for the purpose of instructing him in the practice, to qualify him to attend upon the sick, and give information to others" (1835, 141). This Smith certainly did, but shortly Thomson would accuse him of attempting to undercut his prices and of misrepresenting the Thomsonian system as his own invention.

Samuel Thomson and Elias Smith were seemingly made for each other. Both were the products of the New England hinterland, both of Baptist parentage, and both born in the same year, 1769. They had common childhood experiences to look back upon (both detested farm life), and as adults both had ample occasion to develop their latent populist attitudes through exposure to the persecution of those purporting to be their betters: the regular doctors in the case of Thomson, the settled clergy in that of Smith. Thomson's antipathy toward farming was accompanied by a loathing of the strict religion of his Baptist father. Samuel once commented, "If my father's treatment of me was the effect of his religion, I never wished to have any" (1835, 18). Things improved with his father's conversion to Universalism, to a belief in God's free grace to all. On the whole, however, Thomson himself seems to have been indifferent about religion and instead dedicated himself to his evolving perceptions concerning the nature of health and disease, which he elevated into a full-time profession as itinerant healer in places also frequented by the Christians and Free-Will Baptists, such as Woodstock, Portsmouth, and the coastal towns of upper Maine. In the process he accumulated accusations that he was a wizard and dealer in love potions, being variously called "the Indian doctor; the old wizzard; and sometimes the quack" (ibid., 66–67, 94). Worse yet, he was accused of willful murder by a regular doctor and was unsuccessfully tried for that offense after spending an uncomfortable midwinter period in the Newburyport jail (he observed with satisfaction that the doctor responsible for this later ended up in the same place for grave robbing).

In later years, Dr. Oliver Wendell Holmes characterized the Thomsonian system as "the common sense scientific radicalism of the barn-yard" (quoted in Berman 1956, 562). Yet Thomson reveled in the charge of his opponents that he was a *mere* empiric and turned their accusations of quackery back on them precisely as Smith had often done against those who branded him a blackguard and a wolf among the sheep. "The opposition and abuse that I have met with, have been uniformly from those to whom I think I can with propriety, give the name of quacks, or ignorant pretenders; as all their merit consists in their self-importance and arrogant behaviour towards all those who have not had the advantages of learning, and a degree at college. This class compose a large proportion of the medical faculty throughout our country; they have learned just enough to know how to deceive the people, and keep them in ignorance, by covering their doings under an unknown language to their patients" (1835, 41–42).

Precisely this attitude made Thomson and Elias Smith such natural allies. Since about 1800, when he first discovered politics, Smith had been aiming just such diatribes at the orthodox clergy, the Federalist party, and elites in general; his new campaign for the democratization of medicine (and his own incidental profit) was merely the last link in a nearly complete ideological chain. As Paul Starr puts it in his account of early American medicine, "These ideas, medical and political, must be seen not only as related but as homologous. What they lack in originality, they make up in consistency" (1982, 52). Smith's proven journalistic skills as a Republican partisan and polemicist drew the herb doctor to him. Thomson said that he needed someone to serve his as general agent so that he could retire from active practice and have some security against his old age, and that "after considerable inquiry, I became acquainted with Elias Smith, who was recommended as a man in whom I could confide, and who was in every way qualified as a suitable person to engage in the undertaking. I found him in Boston, and in very poor circumstances; having been for many years a public preacher. . . . He readily engaged with me, and promised to do every thing in his power, to promote my interest and extend the usefulness of my system of practice" (1835, 148).

For Smith the regular doctors and the settled clergy were much of a piece in any event, since they used the same methods (spurious claims to specialist knowledge) and had the same goals (usurpation for their own profit of the inalienable rights of people to think and act for themselves: most importantly in religion, politics, and medicine):

> How selfish are the crafts combined,
> Engaged t' oppress the human mind;
> PHYSIC, DIVINITY, and LAW
> They chief of all our labors draw.
>
> The nests of college-birds are three,
> *Law, Physic,* and *Divinity;*
> And while these three remain combined,
> They keep the world oppressed and blind.
>
> All three of us as one agree,
> To take away true liberty,
> And keep it from such people's hands,
> As dare dispute our high demands.
>
> (THOMSON 1836, 18–19)

In the April 1817 number of the *Herald,* Elias appended an "Address to the People of the United States" by Dr. Samuel Thomson, commenting that "this is inserted here free, for the common good of our fellow citizens."[7] Thomson (or Smith on his behalf) wrote that:

There are *three* things which have in a greater or less degree, called the attention of men, viz. *Religion, Government, and Medicine.* In ages past, these things by millions were thought to belong to three class of men; *Priests, Lawyers* and *Physicians.* The *Priests,* hold the things of *religion* in their own hands, and brought the people to their terms; kept the Scriptures in the dead languages, so that the common people could not read them. Those days of darkness are done away; the Scriptures are translated into our own language, and each one is taught to read for himself. *Government* was once considered as belonging to a few, who thought themselves, *"born only to rule."* The common people have now become acquainted with the great secret of government; and know that *"all men are born free and equal,"* and that magistrates are put into authority, or out, by the voice or mind of the people, who choose them for their public servants.

With two of these transformations already accomplished by the Protestant Reformation and the American Revolution, only one in Thomson's view now remained to be achieved—the reformation and democratization of medicine, which unfortunately still "is in a great measure concealed in a dead language, and a sick man, is often obliged to risk his *life,* where he would not risk a shilling." Thomson proposed to remedy that state of affairs by making publicly known the pretensions of those who hide their ignorance under the cover of Latin, dispense chemical poisons under the guise of medicines, and then levy extravagant changes for killing their own patients. In its place Thomson would substitute a system of medicine based on products of native American soil and accessible to anyone who could read and was willing to pay a modest sum to learn of his patented discoveries.

In the next number of the *Herald* Elias began to contribute personally to the great cause of medical reform through a discourse explicating the text of Job 13:4: "Ye are all physicians of no value." He explained that in these latter days the "physicians of no value" are those who bleed, blister, and dispense poison masquerading as medicine, while those physicians who *are* of value are those such as Dr. Samuel Thomson, who use only medicines of vegetable origins, renounce chemical drugs and all other intrusive heroic measures, and open up the nature of their practice to the scrutiny of the common citizen (*HGL* 8, no. 6 [June 1817]: 205–8). In postscript to Thomson's address,

Smith had already produced a testimonial from Eastham, Massachusetts (signed by the local minister, two selectmen, a justice of the peace,
and the postmaster), concerning the efficacy of Thomsonian methods
in dealing with an epidemic of spotted fever.[8]

Many testimonials of that sort attested to cures attained by
Thomsonian methods, while taking note that those who relied on regular doctors went down to early graves. The republican populism of
Thomson's address suggests the ideological impetus behind his medical
system, as well as being a key to what would become its considerable
popularity throughout much of the nineteenth century: its simplicity,
accessibility, and low cost.

How the system worked can be illustrated by Thomson's own accounts of what he did about the spotted fever, for example, in the case
of the son of one Captain Alden of Portland, Maine. Alden's son was
taken with the disease very suddenly and brought into the house senseless; finding him this way, Thomson pried open his jaws and "administered a solution of Nos. 1, 2, and 6." Having by this means restored the
lad to his senses, Thomson then proceeded to give him a steam bath by
covering him with blankets and placing him over a pan of water into
which hot stones were dropped while administering another dose of
the medicine orally (sometimes these concoctions were administered by
"injections"—enemas—depending on the supposed locus of the problem). This had its usual salutary effect, and "the natural vigor of life and
action was restored." In the spring of 1816, Thomson was on Cape Cod
gathering his herbs and found the spotted fever (or "cold plague")
prevalent there. Again he demonstrated the efficacy of his system with
steaming and (this time) infusions of nos. 1, 2, and 3 (1835, 128, 143).

Thomson made no real secret of what these medicines were, since
what he had patented was not the medicinals themselves but, coupled
with steam baths, the combinations in which he used them. No. 1 was
the most important and the most original to Thomson himself (though
some disputed this), an infusion with wine or water of the dried and
powdered leaves and seeds of *Lobelia*—"to cleanse the stomach, over-
power the cold, and promote a free perspiration"; no. 2 was merely
cayenne pepper mixed with water, a remedy that Thomson hit upon by
trying some West Indian pepper sauce on himself and, finding it of

good effect, used thereafter "to retain the internal vital heat of the system and cause a free perspiration"; no. 3 was a mixture of various herbs, barks, roots, and berries aimed at clearing the bowels of "canker"; no. 4, bitter herbs and barks "to correct the bile and restore digestion"; no. 5, a syrup made of peach pits and cherry stones "to strengthen the stomach and bowels, and restore weak patients"; finally, no. 6 was a mixture of strong wine or brandy with myrrh and cayenne for use in preparing rheumatic drops "to remove pain, prevent mortification, and promote a natural heat" (1822b, 34–57).

That was the core of Thomsonian medicine, a system in which heat is life and cold is death (Thomson 1822b, 7). Thomson later cited Hippocrates to the same effect and invoked the Greek theory of the four elements—air, earth, fire, and water—in giving an account of why this is so. Yet Thomson wished it to be understood that he did not come by his system out of books but directly out of his personal experience (subsequently rationalized, and packaged with Smith's aid, into a theoretical system that formed the basis of the instructional material that he provided along with the sale of his patent rights). Thomson took pride in being condemned as an empiric. Given his unlettered rural background, he reckoned he could have been nothing else than naively empirical and that precisely because of this his eyes were wide open, whereas those of the regular doctors were blinded by received wisdom: "Two thousand years they boast of light, Yet deadly scales obstruct their sight" (1836, 5).[9] Earlier, Thomson explained his background and his personal development as follows: "Being born in a new country, at that time almost an howling wilderness, my advantages for an education were very small; but possessing a natural gift for examining the things of Nature, my mind was left entirely free to follow that inclination, by inquiring into the meaning of the great variety of objects around me" (1822b, 7).

The major result was the discovery of what became the center of his therapeutic regimen—Thomson's no. 1, a decoction of *Lobelia inflata*, which as a child he had accidentally discovered to be a powerful emetic (as indeed it is) and put to innocent amusement by inducing his playmates to try it. Thus *Lobelia* became known as the Emetic Herb, or more simply and evocatively, Pukeweed.

Th' Emetic number one's designed
A gen'ral medicine for mankind,
Of every country, clime, or place,
Wide as the circle of our race.

(THOMSON 1836, 23)

The use of *Lobelia* was perhaps not quite so simple a discovery as Thomson made out. Knowledge of herbs was widely distributed, in rural New Hampshire where Thomson grew up, no less than in the towns where apothecaries stocked many of what were the sometimes ancient herbal remedies that he himself later employed in his own system. His first childhood recollections of healing were of an old root-lady who lived nearby at a time when "there was no such thing as a Doctor known among us," and whose whole practice consisted of roots and herbs "applied to the patient, or given in hot drinks, to produce sweating; which always answered the purpose." She was a rank empiric; if one thing failed to work, she just tried another. She took Thomson out into the fields to help her collect medicines and so whetted the curiosity of the boy who as a man would become the inventor of the most widespread and influential system of alternative medicine abroad in nineteenth-century America (Thomson 1835, 16).

The reasons for the success of Thomsonian medicine can be assayed by the nature of the systems it opposed and the social attitudes it expressed in opposing them. With "nature for my guide, and experience as my instructer," Thomson had inductively concluded that cold "is the cause of *all* disease" and that therefore all disease must have only one cure: increasing the body's heat. Health is a matter of balance, and if this balance is upset, illness is the inevitable result. Cold produces obstructed perspiration and hence local putrefaction and canker; therefore one must remove the source of the chill, get rid of the canker, enhance heat where most needed, and restore a systemic balance by encouraging the natural flow of perspiration through steaming and hot herbal preparations. The Emetic Herb clears the system of cold and canker through vomiting; cayenne and other hot agents act to stoke the depleted fires of internal warmth, while sweating induces this renewed warmth to penetrate throughout the body, thus restoring good health. With this unicausal theory at his disposal, Thomson could therefore boldly attack disease in all its forms through a judicious selection from his sixfold pharmacopoeia.

Thomson derided the regular doctors for having no system at all. "Their practice is founded on visionary theories, which are so uncertain and contradictory that it is impossible to form any correct general rule as a guide to be depended upon" (1822b, 30–31). There was truth in this charge. The "irregular" practitioners were not the only dealers in proprietary nostrums; professional college-educated doctors were little better because of lack of agreement over the underlying principles of medical science. They were sometimes professionally organized, but their system of knowledge was not. Hence Benjamin Rush of Philadelphia could have a most unprofessional quarrel with his medical colleagues via the public press during the great yellow fever epidemic of 1793 over just what should be done about it (Rush 1818, 132). Rush himself was no less an "empiric" than Thomson's old root-lady when it came to dealing with emergencies; he too tried everything and found that by and large none of it worked: "Heaven alone bore witness to the anguish of my soul in this awful situation," he wrote. As for getting agreement among his colleagues, Rush observed that "a Mahometan and a Jew might as well attempt to worship the Supreme Being in the same temple, and through the medium of the same ceremonies, as two physicians of opposite principles and practice attempt to confer about the life of the same patient" (ibid., 126, 191).

Rush had come around to a unicausal theory of his own pertaining to the influence of a disordered circulatory system in the genesis of fevers. He concluded that, for all the various symptoms associated with fever, there is in fact only one underlying cause of them all. In his view, science should deplore the idea of multiple causes of disease, rejecting the supposition that different symptoms *must* be signs of different diseases. He found this assumption as repugnant in medicine as, for him, polytheism was in religion (Rush 1818). To this point his attitude and Thomson's were not dissimilar; each advocated looking beneath superficial appearances in order to arrive at a synthetic principle through which medical knowledge might be unified. So far as the cure of yellow fever went, Rush hit on the use of bleeding, in combination with purges induced by calomel and jalap to clear the bowels of the "corruption" that in his view had settled there by virtue of exposure to the fever-inducing "miasmata" originally emanating, not from mosquito-borne infection, but from an abandoned load of decaying coffee on the Philadelphia wharves.[10]

Here Rush and Thomson definitively parted company. Thomson had sought the favor of the Philadelphia doctors upon his return from Washington in 1813 after securing patent rights to his medical system. He too believed that fevers have a unitary cause, and this spilled over into the use that Elias Smith made of his mentor's system. For Thomson, however, fever is the effect, not the cause, of disease, the attempt of the body to throw off the cold that is at the source of internal obstruction. Yellow fever is most certainly *not* to be cured by bleeding and purges; the fever is produced by the body fighting the cold, a cold productive of cankers blocking the "gall" that, "instead of being discharged through its proper vessels, is forced and diffused through the pores of the skin" (thereby causing the jaundiced discoloration that gives the disease its name) (1822b, 13). The way to cure it is to expel the canker induced by the cold through the use of *Lobelia,* and then to raise the heat of the body through the use of sweats and cayenne infusions. Bleeding is an absurd practice because it depletes the source of heat and therefore actually serves as an ally of the disease. (Rush [1835], being convinced that irritated cerebral blood vessels are the cause of madness, regularly used bleeding to treat it.)[11]

When Thomson learned what Rush did about fevers, he stepped back in dismay from this type of medicine and those who practiced it. He was now convinced that excessive bleeding, far from being an efficacious cure, "would kill one half of those in health" (1835, 125). As for what Thomson and Smith took to be the correct procedure in such cases, Elias summed it up for yellow fever and spotted fever alike: "What is called the yellow fever, generally prevails in hot weather; and the spotted fever in cold weather. In the summer, the heat upon the surface, is too great for the heat of the blood; which causes it to putrefy. In the winter, the cold upon the surface, is too great for the heat of the blood, which is chilled, and becomes spotted. . . . The same cause will cure either. Raise the heat in the man above the heat on the outside, and he may be cured. Raise the heat above the power of the cold, and the disease is removed" (1837, 178).

Benjamin Waterhouse of the nascent Harvard Medical School (and himself an early practitioner of smallpox vaccination) was much attracted to Thomson's system precisely because it did not depend on injurious drugs. He observed that, when they first met, Thomson "had the strongest opinion of the *power of the Sun*. The source of light, growth, life and warmth he almost worshipped. The Sun was Thomson's God. By it, and through its evident, and its invisible influence, he accounted for every thing in the great machinery of Nature, and also in *Man*, who was the world *epitomised*. . . . He derided chemical *laboratories*, or workshops of the piddling chemists, and regarded only the chemistry of Nature."[12] For Thomson, the contrast between the two approaches was great indeed.

Our Father, whom all goodness fills,

Provides the means to cure all ills;

The simple herbs, beneath our feet,

Well used, relieve our pains complete.

While doctors rove in foreign parts,

And rack their powers, and skill, and arts;

Health's medicines grow upon our land,

They're ours, by stretching forth our hand.

(THOMSON 1836, 6)

Waterhouse believed that Thomson's appeals to nature were well taken and that instead of being considered a quack he should be seen as a champion of medical reform, and as a virtual martyr in its cause; he thought that Thomson had brought about significant reduction in the use of drugs such as opium, "nitre" (saltpeter), and calomel, and in harmful practices such "the depleting, or anti-phlogistic practice of Rush"—bleeding.[13] Whatever its other merits or defects, Thomsonian medicine at least had the virtue of being less harmful than the systems it opposed.

✵

Paul Starr has schematized the logic behind the affinity between Thomsonian medicine and Jeffersonian Republicanism as follows: "Disease is to life, as cold is to heat, as minerals are to herbs. The political ideology shares the same pattern: Learning is to common sense, as aristocracy is to democratic government, as physicians are to popular healers" (1982, 52; see Hatch 1989, 29). Thomson was no less an ardent Republican than Smith.[14] They both aimed at putting it in the power of the people "to become their own physicians . . . by making use of those vegetable medicines, the produce of our own country, which are perfectly safe and easily obtained; and which, if properly understood, are fully sufficient in all cases of disease" (Thomson 1835, 147).

Smith added a religious element to the equation. His calls for a return to the practices of the early church and his emphasis on use of the "natural" in medicine each convey an implicit millennialism; what Elias sought to achieve in this world is what John promised would obtain in the next. The central charge that the Thomsonians leveled against the practices of the regular physicians was precisely that they were unnatural. Nature has its own wisdom, and God has seen fit to provide natural herbs appropriate to each nation for the cure of animal and human ills. Smith wrote that "as man is made of what grows, is fed and clothed only with that which grows, it is certain that nothing can restore him to health, but what has grown out of the earth." Elias associated republicanism with a natural order of things to be restored with the Millennium, or at least when the Thomson-Smith reforms in medicine had completed the American Revolution.

Pursuing this arcadian theme, Thomson wrote of the "great plan which is dictated by nature" and protested that sometimes his enemies called him the Indian Doctor, even though his discoveries had nothing to do with Native American medicine (1835, 23, 94; see Albanese 1990, 129–33). It was commonly thought that native healers and herbs were efficacious by virtue of the naive wisdom bred of their closeness to the earth. For the early nineteenth-century medical sectarians, "Nature became the great healing symbol" (Albanese 1990, 122). Those who spread the Thomsonian system to Britain lauded its supposed American aboriginal origins, though when he learned of this, Thomson reiterated that it was all his own discovery.[15] Yet such imagery was pervasive (as it still is), and Elias Smith drew on it: "[One] reason why men generally ought to become acquainted with medicine, is, that the natives, the wild men of the woods are acquainted with it. How many people there are who, after trying all the Doctors, as they term it, have been cured entirely by some old Indian or squaw! They never think of giving poison to the sick to effect a cure. And who ever saw an indian bleed or blister a sick man to remove disease! A man cannot have a high opinion of his knowledge of medicine, when the beasts, birds and wild men use none of them" (1837, 227). It was therefore a pity verging on a crime that poisonous metallic compounds like mercury-based calomel were given to combat disease "instead of that medicine the Lord has created out of the earth, by which he heals men, takes away their pains, and makes peace through all the earth" (ibid., 223). Peace, however, was not Smith's lot.

✦

Following the death of Mary and his marriage to Rachel, Elias was dogged by poverty and by the debts he had incurred in Philadelphia and elsewhere. "My furniture in Philadelphia I sold, and parted with every article, down to knives, forks, and spoons. Besides all this poverty, I was several hundred dollars in debt, and could not pay because others who owed me, had not paid, and the greater part have not paid me to this day. With all this trouble, my three youngest children were in Philadelphia on expense, and I saw no way to get out of this trouble" (1816, 401; Smith 1840, 349). Smith's shift into herbal medicine allowed a reconstruction of his fortunes; his continued association with the Christian Connection was no longer necessary in a financial sense, nor was it perhaps expedient in relation to his newly acquired tastes in theology.

When Samuel Thomson first met Smith, the latter "was in very poor circumstances . . . in consequence of his often changing his religious principles and engaging in different projects in which he had been unsuccessful" (Thomson 1835, 149). In 1816 Thomson gave Elias instruction in his method by treating the Smith family, and as time went on, they established what amounted to a successful joint practice. However, in hindsight, Thomson had begun to notice things that led him to question Smith's character, most particularly that Elias and Rachel were behaving very badly toward Ira, Elias's and Mary's middle son. According to Thomson, Ira Smith had returned after a long absence but, instead of being gladly received at home, was, largely because of Rachel's antipathy, sent off to a boarding house in town. In despair the boy attempted suicide by drinking laudanum, which Thomson purged by administration of *Lobelia;* this unfortunate episode turned things around for a time, and Elias now tried to help his son out by establishing a herbal practice for him in Taunton. But when Ira returned to Boston a few years later, the old pattern of neglect repeated itself, and his next attempt at suicide was a successful one. As the *Columbian Centinal* reported, Ira Smith's body was found near the Bunker Hill Monument in Charlestown (ibid., 152–53).

But the actual rupture between Thomson and Smith was precipitated by Elias's behavior in regard to a book he had been commissioned to write containing a description of the Thomsonian system and an autobiographical memoir of Thomson's life.[16] The way in which Smith submitted the *New Guide* for publication convinced Thomson that his entire system was in danger of being pirated; it also seemed that Elias was attempting to co-opt the local patent holders into a new botanical society under his own direction, a suspicion that gained credence when Smith advertised the Thomsonian system in his new Universalist paper—the *Herald of Life and Immortality*—in such a way as to undercut seriously the price that Thomson had been charging for patent rights. The upshot was that Thomson took Smith to court for infringement, but the court decided that the specifications of the patent were insufficiently explicit in the first place and therefore that there was no case in the claim that Elias Smith had trespassed upon it (see Thomson 1835, 148–64).

The relationship between Thomson and Smith was at an end, though the echoes from this unpleasant affair reverberated for some time after. Fully ten years later, in 1832, "A Thomsonian" published a systematic account of Elias Smith's supposed wrongdoings to date in Abner Kneeland's free-thought newspaper the *Boston Investigator* (which also announced that Kneeland himself had become Thomson's agent in Boston). Among other things, the author said that Elias had slandered him by saying "that I was a man of no character; that I kept a prostitute, and boarded in a w——e house," that Smith told Hosea Ballou that Thomson had hired a man to go to bed with his own wife so that a bill of divorce could be filed against her. After listing a substantial bill of charges against Elias himself, the "Thomsonian" rhetorically (if incoherently) concluded: "Mr. Smith, what can you think of yourself? And what can your brother ministers belonging to all the denominations, where you have been on, and flew off the handle—where you have been received and turned out, and must henceforth remain wrong side out, as the basis of human depravity!" As late as 1828 Elias found it necessary to publish an open letter from his new Christian congregation in Boston to the effect that the rumors about his character circulated in the west by Samuel Thomson were quite without foundation (*MSCW* 1, no. 8 [Jan. 1828]: 188–89).

Smith fought back in the pages of his *Medical News-Paper (MNP)*, which he founded in 1822 primarily as a vehicle for extolling the virtues of Smith's own version of botanical medicine. Elias flanked the title of the *News-Paper* with profile heads representing "The Doctor" and "The Physician," personifying them respectively as practitioners of orthodox versus herbal medicine. Through this medium Smith launched attacks on the attempts of organized medicine to gain monopolistic privileges through such things as the formation of medical societies ("it looks to me like *monopoly* and *usurpation*," he said). Hostile note was taken of the rules of the Boston Medical Association—an "*Aristocracy* which has sprung up in republican soil"—which admitted only those who had medical degrees from Harvard or were certified by the Censors of the Massachusetts Medical Society (*MNP*, no. 15 [Aug. 20, 1822]: 63). This was yet another example of the attempts of the privileged classes in a spirit "contrary to the principles of republican government" to "put down wise men, and exalt fools; whether in things political, medical, or religious" (ibid., no. 4 [Mar. 19, 1822]: 14; no. 16 [Sept. 3, 1822]: 66).

To bolster his point Smith included whatever allegations he could muster that the proprietors of medical colleges and their henchmen were engaged in resurrectionism—grave robbing to provide cadavers for the college dissection rooms. In 1822 Elias reported that the selectmen of Boston had ordered watchmen to keep guard over the burying ground on the Neck; he then asked, "Would it not be well to set a Watch around the medical college, to see if any dead bodies are carried there by night?" (*MNP* I, no. 2 [Feb. 5, 1822]: 8). In the same year he also observed that a bag of body parts had been found floating past the Charles River Bridge and speculated as to how it came to be there (ibid., no. 6 [Apr. 16, 1822]: 22).

After their falling out, Elias attempted to undercut whatever claim Thomson had to patent rights by denying that the latter's system had any originality or was ever a coherent system at all. Smith distinguished his own system from Thomson's "imperfect discoveries of disease and medicine" by the elimination of sweat baths and a de-emphasis on *Lobelia,* which at first amounted to complete dismissal of its use on the grounds that it too is a dangerous poison (1822, 3).[17] By 1826, however, Smith was again maintaining that "in the wisdom of God *[Lobelia]* was as certainly designed for the relief of the sick, as food and drink was designed for the hungry and thirsty" (1826, 96). *Lobelia* was firmly back in Smith's favor as "the plant of renown," perhaps because its use really was the only thing to distinguish this form of medical botany from common backyard herbalism, and because of the still-growing popularity of the Thomsonian system itself.

Smith also reproduced trial records of the 1809 case in which Thomson was tried for having killed a patient with *Lobelia* and exulted with unholy glee when Thomson's patent was struck down in 1822:

SUDDEN AND JOYOUS DEATH!!!

DIED, suddenly, on Friday the 17th inst. between the hours of 9 and 12 o'clock, A.M. in Boston, (old Court House) not much lamented, Doctor Samuel Thomson's PATENT for the exclusive right of using herbs. The death of this *patent* must be more severely felt by the Doctor than would have been the death of his wife, whom he has divorced, being desirous to get rid of her sooner than death would remove her. This death must cause great and constant grief to the *doctor*, as it was expected it would be his companion, income, and comfort, after getting rid of his house, farm, wife and children, in the manner he has. But alas, it is dead, and no resurrection can rationally be expected. (*MNP*, no. 9 [May 28, 1822]: 34–35)

⚜

This conflict between Smith and Thomson over the legitimacy of their respective systems was one symptom of the sectarianism and incipient utopianism running through society at large. Formal institutions were still undeveloped, and a republican stress on the ordinary citizen supported the claims of individual prophets, entrepreneurs, and inventors that their innovations were as good as anyone's. Sectarians of all persuasions were busily engaged in patching together amalgams of prophetic teaching, personal revelations, Swedenborgianism, Masonic symbolism, popular science, mesmerism, alternative medicine, and restorationist primitivism, thus producing a characteristically American religious pastiche.[18] Thomsonian medicine itself had a strong Restorationist component in advocating a return to nature and to the simplicity that once obtained when the earth freely provided all that was necessary for human welfare. The profoundly democratic, antielitist, and perfectionist Thomsonian message was well suited to the public mood of Jacksonian America.

Samuel Thomson, a disappointed man, departed from this life in Boston in 1843. The movement he founded was meant to provide a simple and democratic alternative to the medicine of the day; his system was propagated through the sale of patent rights and at first was administered on an exclusive basis by "Friendly Botanical" societies, which were supposed to function as mutual aid associations bringing inexpensive medical care to families and local communities.[19] As time went on, the great scheme would prove itself to be exposed to a process of professionalization and internal sectarianism that—like the fate of the Christian movement—belied the goals of its founder. Thomson lived to see the founding of Thomsonian medical colleges and infirmaries that deviated substantially from his original system and ended up being little different from the elitist medical colleges that he and Elias had opposed a generation before. More than once, with very little he could do about it, Thomson found his methods pirated by former associates for their own advantage.[20] Like other movements of the early part of the nineteenth century, Thomsonianism began to coalesce with an ever-broader stream of popular radicalism manifested in new medical systems, communistic experiments, and religious innovation.

7 AGE OF MIRACLES
Smith and the Universalist Movement

All flesh shall see the salvation of God.
LUKE 3:6

IN THE PIVOTAL YEAR OF 1816 ELIAS published the first edition of the his *Life, Conversion, Preaching, Travels, and Sufferings of Elias Smith;* in May moved to Boston to remain there for almost the rest of his life; and entered medical practice under the personal tutelage of Samuel Thomson, for whom he incidentally functioned as publicist and ghostwriter. The *Life* was written to tell the world about Elias's own pilgrimage and about the Christian movement and in order to clear up certain misunderstandings created by the harsh things said about the Christians and about himself personally in David Benedict's 1813 general history of the Baptists in North America. This last was written in order (as Smith put it) "to fix on me a lasting reproach, at least among the baptists, to the latest generation" (1816, 399); perhaps Elias was right, for among other things, Benedict had said that "Mr. Smith is a man of popular talents, but unusually changeable in religious creed. He has propagated, at different times, *calvinism, universalism, arminianism, arianism, socinianism,* and other *isms* too numerous to mention" (1813, 411–12).[1] With his formal conversion to Universalism, Elias would soon have still more to explain.

The Universalist movement was a nineteenth-century American phenomenon. Extending the promise of democracy into the afterlife, this Christian progressivism appealed to a wide range of theological revisionists, utopians, and social reformers. Samuel Thomson was an ear-

Plate 6. Hosea Ballou (1771–1852): Universalist organizer and theologian, a great influence on Elias Smith's later career. Reprinted from Thomas Whittemore, *Life of Rev. Hosea Ballou* (Boston: James M. Usher, 1854).

ly example; in the next generation Universalists went about the founding of universities, communistic societies, newspapers, and popular museums. In the 1840s many of them would subscribe to the scientific religion of Spiritualism, which, through the revelations of spirit mediums, claimed to validate empirically the infinite march of progress. Universalism was an optimistic religion of the self-made person, putting great faith in reason and a reasonable God, on the power of individuals to accomplish their own salvation within the framework of divine purpose.

A skeptic once asked the theologian and organizer Hosea Ballou why it was that, if his universal doctrine really were true and scriptural, it had never been preached before the nineteenth century? In answer,

Ballou referred to the Father and Son, and confidently replied that "*love* rather than *wrath*" had "always been their teaching, no matter what human innovations had been added to the original message" (1852, 227, 61). Yet it was clear to many, and no less to Ballou himself, that something highly unusual was afoot in their new century. Imminent apocalypse was giving way to the idea of infinite progress. On earth, as in heaven, Enlightenment was seemingly on a triumphant march everywhere, in theology as in politics, telegraphy, and railway transport.

Some thought Elias Smith's slide into universal salvationism plainly evident when he rejected the doctrine of endless punishment in favor of the notion that at the final judgment the wicked will be utterly destroyed rather than consigned to eternal torment. Elias came to that belief through the influence of John Evans's *Sketch of the Denominations of the Christian World* (1804). This popular work outlined, in the name of religious moderation and tolerance, the beliefs of the various branches of Christianity, including the idea of several English divines who sought a middle way between "the system of *restoration* and the system of *endless misery.*"[2]

Smith was troubled about the same question that had exercised Hosea Ballou during his own passage to Universalism: How can a just God have decreed infinite punishment for finite sins?[3] It was absurd and unreasonable, and above all unscriptural. The logic that, in previous generations, had led Samuel Hopkins and Jonathan Edwards to marvel at why God should have shown any mercy at all to so debased a worm as the human being was now judged by these progressives (who looked back on a time just past when "Calvinism darkened the land") as plainly incompatible with natural justice and the actual promises of love and redemption offered so bountifully in the New Testament (Whittemore 1854, 1:39).

Ideological inconsistency made Smith uneasy: A loving Father of infinite wrath? A promise of the restoration of all things to the Lord in the last days, but eternal incarceration of the better part of humanity in hell thereafter? Predestination of some to eternal misery, and yet sublime justice in the fact that they have been damned for acts they could not have helped performing? The condemnation of multitudes to pain and slavery in this life for no apparent reason at all? The Father and Son *one* being, and yet the latter a *mediator* between humanity and an entity of which he is already a part? It was all absurdity compounded. Elias Smith needed a different God but was stuck with the one he knew, the strangely inconsistent deity of inerrant Scripture.

⚘

At first Smith could not accept that the end of the wicked is destruction rather than endless punishment, but finally with the help of Evans he came around to that idea after searching the Scriptures for himself. He kept the results private for a time, as he knew they would "disturb my brethren with whom I was connected"—and indeed he was right, for among others it at first disturbed Abner Jones, who, according to his son, never accepted the destructionist thesis for his own (304, 313; Jones 1842, 71).[4] As when he left the Baptists, Smith now felt constrained to speak his mind or "preach no more." The product of his reasonings appear in two 1805 pamphlets entitled *The Day of Judgement* and *The Doctrine of the Prince of Peace . . . concerning the End of the Wicked;* the latter, a treatise of seventy-two pages, was primarily an attack on Universalism, the "bastard child" of Calvinism. Smith believed that these two are intimately related, that Calvinism and Universalism are variants on the twin themes of predestination and election; they differ as to who will be saved or damned, agreeing that in the context of ultimate divine purpose, human freedom has little to do with the outcome. Elias concluded that "I believe *Calvinism* to be a dead carcass; and *Universalism* an unclean animal to eat it up" (1805c, 4).[5]

In rejecting the notion that salvation is for all, as the Universalists claimed, Smith simultaneously dismissed the "Platonic" idea of the immortality of the soul and the doctrine of original sin, "a sin invented but never committed"—the work of that "dark African priest," St. Augustine (*HGL* 1, no. 13 [Feb. 16, 1809]: 51).[6] According to Smith, body and soul are inseparable; sin is not the natural product of a hereditary taint but, rather, a willful rejection of Christ freely made by the individual sinner. With such "traditions of men" out of the way, Smith enunciated his characteristically materialistic postulate that "at the day of judgment, all who are found enemies of Christ, will be destroyed both soul and body, and be no more" (1805c. 11).[7]

The final product of this line of thought appears in the *New Testament Dictionary* under the heading of *Damnation,* a word that, in its most important biblical usage, Elias took to be synonymous with "everlasting destruction" (1812b, 124).[8] This exegesis, though reasonable to Smith, was troublesome to those who worried about the consequences of any doctrine that held that sins of this life might not be visited with eternal punishment thereafter. Such a doctrine was suspiciously close to the licentious Universalist notion that all will be saved, and if all will be saved, what disincentive is there to sin? Destruction— a brief moment of pain at the Last Judgment—is far better than the eternal fires of hell, and destructionism therefore only a shade better than Universalism in its implications for the preservation of social order.[9]

Such was the reaction of the Free-Willer John Colby on hearing this doctrine preached in Windsor, Vermont, by a Christian elder in 1808. "The particular sentiment he advanced, was that the wicked would be burnt up, and cease to exist, at or immediately after the day of judgment." Colby found that this message gave him such "disagreeable feelings" that he felt obliged to preach against it on the same day. "I told the wicked, if they were so senseless of their own happiness and of their duty to their Maker, as to live in sin, wickedness and folly, in this world, they might expect their condemnation, horror and sufferings, would be intolerable in the next" (1829, 37–38). One former Christian minister who had returned to the Baptists begged "the forgiveness of God and of man" for his deviation, proclaiming in repentance that the doctrine of the soul's mortality "is an idea of the Atheist and Sadducee" (Newman 1818, 4).[10]

Samuel Shepard of Brentwood undertook to answer Smith directly. He had written a letter of recommendation for Elias in 1804 affirming Smith's "Christian character" in the face of the scandalous reports circulating about him; yet Shepard and Smith had a falling out as early as 1805, when Elias reported in the *Christian's Magazine* that his old friend was involved on the wrong side of the sorry though obscure affair of Joseph Burley's excommunication from the Baptist church in

Plate 7. John Colby (1787–1817): Vermont-born Free-Will Baptist, Christian fellow traveler, and itinerant pietist. Reprinted from John Colby, *The Life, Experience, and Travels of John Colby* (Cornish, Maine: S. W. & C. C. Cole, 1829).

Exeter (295–96).[11] Burley was a cabinetmaker and chairmaker and deacon of the Exeter church who, as Elias supposed, was expelled for a variety of trumped-up charges, even though his real offense was that "he was friendly to the church in Portsmouth." Smith expressed his sorrow that "the Doctor has involved himself in any such thing in his old age" and suggested that his old friend had been stirred up against him by communications from Thomas Baldwin, who, after the falling-out, was organizing the opposition among the Baptists and corresponding around the Warren Association to the effect that "Mr. Smith and Mr. Jones had scattered a great deal of free-will stuff in Boston." Burley and his wife joined Elias's church in 1805; Smith and Shepard parted for good (*CM* 1, no. 2 [1805]: 63–65).

Shepard's reaction to Smith's destructionist preaching appeared in

1808 in the form of an epistle addressing Smith's two published tracts on the subject and arraigning his former ally for the sin of pride, the wresting of Scripture to suit his personal fancy. Shepard attempted to prove that the doctrine of original sin—the sin of Adam imputed to the human race at large—is indeed scriptural and not, as Elias claimed, a later Augustinian contrivance.[12] But the fundamental point for Shepard was that destructionism is a licentious doctrine. Smith's teaching would see set free "all the numberless millions of the fearful and unbelieving, and the abominable, and murderers, and whoremongers, and sorcerers, and all liars, with every description of the ungodly, not excepting those who have committed the unpardonable sin; no matter for that, your plan is laid to free them all from future misery after the day of judgment, by burning them all together into nonexistence like chaff" (Shepard 1806, 30).

Though fought out in biblical terms, such controversies over doctrines such as these—part of a shared Calvinist heritage—were as much as anything anxious wranglings over social ethics during a period of flux in which nothing seemed assured. Smith's politicized reaction to those upholding the doctrine of endless punishment is a case in point. Smith held that "the doctrine of eternal misery is the old pagan doctrine, christened with a scriptural name, and that, like infant sprinkling, it is an old wives fable, a plan of *ignorant, lazy priests*, who wish to keep people in ignorance, that they may rule them with ease" (1806a, 12). In short, it is a spurious dogma fit only for the defense of aristocracy, whether Episcopal, Monarchist, Papist, Calvinist, Federalist, Tory, or—Smith's specific target in the present instance—Methodist.

The rapid cycles of decline and renewal that enlivened the early nineteenth-century ecclesiastical scene felled some churches and gave birth to others. A revival swept through the vicinity of Cumberland, Rhode Island, in 1813, and Adin Ballou, who was then ten years old, recalled that the obscure group with which he and his family had once associated—a congregation of the Six-Principle Baptists—was displaced by a new church of the Christian Connection under the leadership of Zephaniah Crossman.[13]

Elias Smith, Daniel Hix, and Mark Fernald had preached in Cumberland in 1814, at which time Ballou's father was convicted by this new message. Adin in his turn was baptized into the church in 1815 following his spiritual experience and in that year heard Smith, Jones, and Hix preach at a General Conference of the connection in Massachusetts (*HGL* 7, no. 3 [Oct. 28, 1814]: 636). He noted that at the time of his conversion, "Elders Elias Smith, Abner Jones, and other influential leaders in our order had come out against endless punishment and in favor of absolute, final destruction or annihilation of the doomed impenitent. This obliged them to deny the innate immortality of the soul. These doctrines I readily embraced and made myself an expert in their scriptural defense" (Ballou 1896, 46–47).[14]

These doctrines helped carry both Smith and Ballou down the road to Universalism. But first, following a vision of a divine being who called him to the ministry, Ballou became a Christian elder, and in the course of his labors again heard Mark Fernald preach and visited Hix in Dartmouth. At this time Adin preached against Universalism, but in his heart were doubts about the fate of the wicked. Would they, as the Christians preached, be destroyed at the final judgment, or was it possible that all would be finally cleansed by passing through fire to eternal life?

He was already aware of the preaching of his distant cousin Hosea Ballou, who was what was then called an "ultra" Universalist, holding that the trials of the wicked are to occur in the flesh and that God has promised salvation to all in the next life, no matter the sins committed in this one. Caught between these conflicting positions, Ballou remembered that he "grew pale and wore an anxious, sickly look." In the face of this intense spiritual conflict, he sought refuge in prayerful solitude and in 1822 was granted another revelation that straightened out all his theological perplexities: "In a moment the heavens seemed to open above my head; an inexpressibly sweet influence flowed in upon my soul; the whole subject became luminous, every doubt vanished, a vision of the final triumph of good over evil shone forth in majestic splendor, and my heart was filled with transports of joy. My faith was conclusively sealed, and I have never since felt one serious doubt of the final universal holiness and happiness of all the immortal children of God" (1896, 85).

1792	Ordained a Calvinist Baptist minister
1792–97	Baptist pastor in Salisbury, N.H.
1797–1801	Baptist pastor in Woburn, Mass.
1801	Resigns the Baptist pastorate
1802	Declares himself a "Christian"
1802–10	Elder of the Christian Church in Portsmouth, N.H.
1808	Founds the *Herald of Gospel Liberty*
1810	Moves to Portland, Maine
1811–14	Resident in Philadelphia
1814	Returns to New England
1817	Announces conversion to Universalism
1823	Requests reaffiliation with the Christians
1826	Expelled by the Universalists
1827–28	Again a Christian elder
1828–31	Responds to charges that he is still a Universalist
1840	Received back by Christian Church in Portsmouth
1846	Dies in Lynn, Mass.; funeral service is conducted by pastor of the First Universalist Society of Boston

Fig. 9. Smith's theological career

To the consternation of his father and former friends in the Christian Connection, Adin Ballou became a Universalist; his permutation of the classical Puritan conversion experience was a twist that his associates could regard only as the product of satanic delusion or a deranged mind. Meanwhile Ballou had his cake and ate it too; he did not become an "ultra" like his cousin but rather became what was known as a Restorationist, a believer in the cleansing of sin in a reformed version of purgatory, rather than immediate entry into paradise. In 1811 Elias Smith condemned Restorationism as "a damnable doctrine, and a strong delusion" (*HGL* 3, no. 63 [Jan. 18, 1811]: 250), only to embrace it himself in 1816. In 1834 Adin Ballou—sustaining his point of view with full armamentarium of biblical chapter and verse—publicly debated Elias's son Daniel Drown Smith, an "orthodox" ultra-Universalist minister, and then pushed on to the foundation of the Christian socialist Hopedale community in Massachusetts and the infinite progressivism of the Spiritualist movement. Meanwhile Elias had gone from the

Christians to the Universalists and back twice over. (See Fig. 9 for a chronology of Smith's various theological positions.)

Hosea Ballou was another product of outer New England. Born in 1771 in Cheshire, New Hampshire, into the Calvinist Baptist church of his father, Ballou, like so many others, such as his mentor, Caleb Rich, had come to question the biblical grounds upon which the old faith rested, specifically the Old Testament ferocity of the God it worshiped. John Murray had independently come to similar conclusions before emigrating from England to America, where, beginning in 1779, he presided over a group of Congregationalist defectors in Gloucester, Massachusetts, and sparked yet another dispute over the distribution of tax money for the support of the churches. Adopting the same principles as Elias, Ballou became convinced that the only way out of theological perplexity was to search the Scriptures for himself; having done so he found to his own satisfaction "that the Bible affords no evidence of punishment after death" (1852, 48). Whereas at this time Smith held that the damned would be destroyed rather than eternally punished, Ballou concluded by an alternate reading that all humanity in fact would be saved and brought into eternal life.

In 1810 this issue still separated the two men. In 1801 Smith had flirted with Universalist doctrine while back tending store in Salisbury after leaving his pastoral charge in Woburn. His younger brother, Uriah, had made himself familiar with Universalist writings and preached on the inconsistencies of Calvinism; Elias, "being convinced that calvinism was wrong . . . concluded that of course, universalism must be right." He preached that doctrine for a brief period, but found himself so struck by its own apparent inconsistency with Scripture that he was forced into research, which led to his realization that Calvinism and Universalism are both nothing but unscriptural fatalism—by the realization that *Christ is all!* and that Jesus will accept all who freely acknowledge him (256–58). Thereafter he condemned Universalism in the *Herald* and elsewhere almost to the time of his baffling public conversion to that "doctrine of devils" in what amounted to virtual renunciation of everything he had apparently stood for and everyone he had been connected with since becoming a Christian.

There is no direct evidence that Ballou and Smith had any contact during the period from 1807 to 1810, when they were both living in Portsmouth. Yet certainly they must have, since they already had encountered one another in Woodstock in 1806 when Ballou was still Universalist pastor for the mid-Vermont region. As the story goes, Ballou once gave the Sunday sermon when Elias was in the congregation, the whole time with his "head bent forward and chin resting on his breast, not looking up once during the whole discourse." The Woodstock town historian recalled that the local Baptists were then in disarray because of the delicts of William Grow and the incompetence of Elisha Ransom. Elias entered the breach to confront the Universalist menace; "Smith was a man of native abilities above the ordinary, a vigorous speaker, and, like Ballou himself, always ready for a fight" (Dana 1980, 403). In the afternoon, one supposes by prearrangement, Elias answered Ballou by speaking from the text "Ye do err, not knowing the Scriptures" (Matt. 22:29).[15] The substantive content of their debate was not recorded, but each side claimed victory, and the event lived on in local folklore long after.[16]

Ballou and Smith at least had common ground in opposition to Joseph Buckminster, with whom Ballou had a brief controversy in 1809 after being warned where the evil tendency of Universalist preaching must lead on Judgment Day. Buckminster and Ballou exchanged letters on the subject of the latter's impending damnation, but Buckminster refused to do battle on the specific claims of Universalist doctrine. This was left to the Reverend Joseph Walton of the Independent Congregational Church of Portsmouth (a New Light church), who had heard Ballou speak at funerals to the effect that God had designed death for the *good* of humankind, rather than as punishment for Adam's primal disobedience.[17]

Things grew more complicated for Hosea Ballou with the coming of the War of 1812. Ballou thought the war necessary, but others within his congregation strongly disagreed with that opinion. His biographer, Thomas Whittemore, pointed out that the rich were more likely than the poor to oppose the war, and that the Congregational and Episcopal clergy were therefore usually to be counted among leaders in the opposition to it, whereas the evangelicals and most of the Universalists were its supporters. As Whittemore observed, on the day of Madison's declaration "some of the clergy absolutely ran riot . . . in denouncing the constituted authorities of the United States" (1854, 1:376). In response to such sentiments (emanating from David Osgood, among others), Ballou gave a "war sermon" that alienated a part of his own congregation, a society that "was composed of members of both political parties, a majority of whom, as to numbers, were Republicans; but there were a very respectable number, of the wealthiest and most influential of the members, who were of the other class" (ibid.).[18] Because of the friction caused by this division, Ballou moved to Salem in 1815, and then on to Boston, where Murray had also settled, and where his path would again cross that of Elias Smith.

After moving to Boston in May 1816, Elias for a time continued to follow the old road he had walked since founding the *Herald*. Apparently tiring of the whole venture, he concluded volume 7 of the *Herald* with an address stating that perhaps this will be the last time he would communicate to his readers through that medium. Since the Christian Connection was by now numerous and spread through the various parts of the United States, he felt his time had been well spent. Here Elias fairly summarized what he and the connection had together stood and fought for:

> One God—one Mediator—one lawgiver—one perfect law of Liberty—one name for the children of God, to the exclusion of all sectarian names—A Republican government, free from religious establishments and state clergy—free enquiry—life and immortality brought to light through the gospel—the reign of Christ on earth one thousand years—the new heavens and earth at last—the utter destruction of all who at the last day are found enemies to Christ—the eternal state of the righteous in the new earth. (*HGL* 7, 181 [Dec. 22, 1815]: 721)

Smith continued to edit the *Herald* until October 1817, in an expanded format issued bimonthly rather than fortnightly. But there was an eight-month hiatus between the end of volume 7 in December 1815 and the beginning of volume 8 in August 1816, under the banner of a new motto—"And knowledge shall be increased"—which Elias extracted from Daniel 12:4 ("But thou, O Daniel, shut up the words, and seal the book, even to the time of the end: many shall run to and fro, and knowledge shall be increased.")[19] The increase in Elias's own knowledge during this brief period took an unexpected direction, and his brethren were collectively dumbfounded—as he knew they would be—when he announced his conversion to universal salvationism and publicly resigned from editorship of the *Herald* in the last number.

This decision may have astonished his brethren, but it came as no surprise to the orthodox clergymen whom the Christians plagued with their radical message concerning the nonexistence of the Trinity, the mortality of the soul, the destruction of the wicked, and the human nature of Christ. One of the clergy explicitly pointed out what many had long suspected, that "a denial of total depravity is connected with a belief of universal salvation. If mankind are not depraved, they of course, possess a holy principle. But if they all possess this holy disposition, they will doubtless all be taken to heaven." Such was the doctrine preached by the Devil at the beginning; such is the doctrine preached by the Universalists now (Everest 1819, 17). Such, as it proved, was the logic that brought Smith to universal salvationism in 1817.

In his "Farewell Address" for the *Herald*, Elias said that for some two years past he had felt that his "testimony was in a great measure finished." He reviewed his career to date, beginning with his baptism by William Grow twenty-eight years before, then gave an account of his relations with the Baptists, his departure from their fold, and his rejection of Calvinism, the Trinity, and the doctrine of eternal misery for the wicked. Though he had continued to oppose Universalism until very recently, he had been brought short by a verse from Acts with this sentence: "For we are also his offspring" (17:28). For Elias this implied that we all partake in his holiness, whatever our mortal defects. Since the day when Elias realized that we *all* partake in God, his opposition to the universal system had ceased, and he had become convinced that it was God's intent to bring all humankind to glory.

Smith now thought that each of the various systems abroad in the Christian world is true in its own way: Calvinism, because God has in-

Plate 8. David Millard: like Joseph Badger, an influential western Christian, an academic who helped bring respectability to the movement. Reprinted from David E. Millard, *Memoir of Rev. David Millard* (Dayton, Ohio: Christian Publishing Association, 1874).

deed elected part of humankind (the Jews and Christ's immediate disciples) to a special purpose; Arminianism, because it is true that *all believers* will be saved; Universalism, because *all people* "will finally be saved from sin and death." If we are all offspring of the Creator as Acts seems to declare, could he have possibly intended the destruction or eternal misery of a part of his creation? No, a loving Father might discipline, but he could not destroy and remain the moral being we know him to be. There is no other way we can behold the sad spectacle that the world offers us and remain a believer in a just God. "How many we see born blind, deaf, dumb, lame, halt and withered. Many are born slaves, and others are made so. In different regions they suffer with cold, heat, imprisonment and famine. All these have a taste of life, and a strong desire for it; though many never enjoy life. When every child of Adam is one in Christ, and gathered there, then will their bliss be complete, having come out of these great tribulations, and made their robes white in the blood of the Lamb" (*HGL* 8, no. 8 [Oct. 1817]: 270).

It is indeed as St. Luke said: "All flesh shall see the salvation of God" (Luke 3:6). It is as St. John said: "For God sent not his Son into the world to condemn the world; but that the world through him might be saved" (John 3:17). Knowing what effect these declarations would have, Smith concluded his address with a plea that his former friends, the preachers and ordinary members of the connection, "judge nothing before the time." He hoped "that the blessing of heaven may attend the preachers while proclaiming Christ as the bread of God. All the help in my power to render according to truth, I am ready to afford, though I may never write again. My acquaintance through this medium has been large, and the fellowship with such as never saw my face, sweet. God grant we may keep the unity of the spirit, turn many to righteousness, and shine at last as the STARS, and as the brightness of the firmament forever." Smith followed this with a letter from David Millard, who had been converted by Nancy Cram, and who was now active in Ballston and having much success with the youth of that town. With a few additional notes concerning what little religious intelligence he had received lately, and an account of a lackluster meeting in New Bedford, Elias Smith was done with it.

A Christian historian remembered that "strong men wept at the announcement." A group of Christian ministers gathered in Portsmouth "to plan means for obviating inroads of a seemingly perverse faith only a step removed from an abandoned life" (Morrill 1911, 122). In the 1840 edition of his autobiography, and now again writing as a "Christian," all Elias had to say about his conversion to Universalism was that in 1816–17 he was troubled "as to the course I had pursued in preaching" and that (as he put it with considerable understatement) the announcement of his new conviction that all would be saved "made a great stir throughout the whole country; many were grieved, a few were enraged against me, and a very small number approved of the doctrine" (360).

John Rand left Samuel Stillman's First Baptist Church in Boston to become a Christian during the 1804 revival; he was the first preacher of the connection from Massachusetts, ordained in 1806 by Smith, Jones, and Joseph Boody, Jr.[20] It fell to Rand to address Smith's apostasy. Elias's plea for Christian forbearance had in this case fallen on deaf ears, for Rand wrote, "You have *guessed* right in supposing that what you have published in the last Herald would shock and surprise many of us. We are both surprised at your weakness and shocked with your presumption; for they seem equally manifest in almost every page, and in such a degree, that it is with difficulty we can believe you was [*sic*] in a state of sanity when you wrote" (1818, 2).

Elias had written in apology, "My mind has made several *advances* towards what I thought was perfection. These *advances* my friends and acquaintances have called *changes;* but such changes are only 'from glory to glory,' by beholding as in a glass the glory of the Lord" (*HGL* 8, no. 8 [Oct. 1817]: 254). Rand thought Smith's career to be just one of changes, rather than of advances in glory. In writing of the period around 1792 when attempting to get straight on the doctrines of predestination and election with the help of Samuel Shepard and others, Elias remarked in his autobiography that the "infection I [then] took broke out in *universalism*, about ten years after." This refers to the period around 1801, when Elias was going through the period of doubt that led to separation from the Baptists; the general problem then was fatalism, and the specific question was whether or not God had predestined all humanity to salvation rather than just the elect. Elias veered toward the former option, later saying that he managed to cure the "infection" of universalism only with "'the Root of Jesse' to the wound that it caused" (213). Now fifteen years later, John Rand suggested that Smith needed another dose of the same medicine: "and may the same good effects follow, and the cure remain permanent to the praise of the glory of grace.—Amen—Farewell" (1818, 16).

Joseph Badger, a prominent second-generation Christian who had settled near Rochester, New York, arraigned Smith for adopting a doctrine he had once so effectively opposed ("Zenas" 1819).[21] Elias received similar treatment from his old comrades in Portsmouth, in the form of disfellowship of him as a preacher so long as he should remain a Universalist, as announced in an open letter from the church clerk, Joseph Burgin, published in the first number of the successor to the *Herald of*

Plate 9. Joseph Badger (1792–1852): second-generation Christian, strong critic of Universalists, and a powerful influence in the West as the Christian movement crystallized into a new denomination. Reprinted from E. G. Holland, *Memoir of Rev. Joseph Badger* (New York: C. S. Francis, 1854).

Gospel Liberty, called simply the *Christian Herald (CH)* and edited by Robert Foster (proprietor of Foster's Balm of Life). Burgin turned Elias's old arguments against him in referring to the many times that Smith had previously condemned Universalism in all its forms. He asked how it was that Smith could have once reasoned so soundly and yet now reason so speciously in blatant disregard of the Word of God? "We are amazed and confounded, and know not how to account for such declarations from you, when these scriptures are as familiar to you as the letters in the alphabet." Burgin's condemnation of his former friend was comprehensive, and its substance repeatedly echoed from various sources to the end of Smith's life and beyond.

We should expect that your former experience would teach you the impropriety of hastily embracing any new and important doctrine; for your whole public life has been a scene of changes from one place to another—from one society to another—from one doctrine to another, and from one practice to another, until you have exhausted the patience of your friends, and they have grown weary of endeavouring to vindicate your conduct, and have in fact lost much of their former confidence that they had in you both as a man and a public teacher. And if you would candidly review your writing, preaching, and conduct for years past, you cannot wonder that it should be so. . . . Farewell. (*CH* 1, no. 1 [May 1818]: 7)[22]

Evidently Mark Fernald had some advance warning of what was afoot, for in August 1817 he "found my brother Elias Smith had sunk into Universalism. The effect of leaving preaching for men's souls, to doctor their bodies. Why will men leave God and get NOTHING?" (1852, 105). And so the Christians were through with Elias Smith as well; he was never fully accepted by them again.[23]

Smith may have gotten little of a spiritual nature from this change to Universalism, and certainly he garnered much abuse, but at least he managed to earn something like a regular income from his medical practice. The infection of Universalism that Smith took so severely on this occasion may well have been activated through exposure to Samuel Thomson and Hosea Ballou, but it was also a result of Smith's following the implications of his own religious and political beliefs through to their logical conclusion, for universal salvationism is more consistent with the secular utopia of Jeffersonian democracy than with any of the theological systems to which Elias had subscribed thus far. As orthodox critics recognized, Smith and those like him were making a human sense of natural justice the arbiter of God's intent.

The Universalists had high hopes for him, a hope "that Rev. Elias Smith would cease to be unstable, and become of use to the denomination. True, the hope was doomed to disappointment, but it gave comfort at first. But, alas! Elias Smith could not avoid change; like the apostle Peter before his Master's resurrection, he did not know how feeble he was" (Whittemore 1854, 2:325). At first things seemed promising, and after little more than a year's hiatus following his departure from the Christian Connection Elias was back in public view with a Universalist newspaper, the *Herald of Life and Immortality*, which first appeared in January 1819 and lasted until October 1820.[24]

During his short official career as a Universalist, including his role as pastor of the Third Universalist Society of Boston, Elias had to deal with the problems that had arisen because of his dispute with fellow Universalist Samuel Thomson. The difficulties were so serious that the latter found it necessary to call an ex parte council of prominent Universalists, including Hosea Ballou and Ballou's future biographer, Thomas Whittemore, to investigate the charges that Thomson was making against him. Among other things, the council investigated the charge that Elias and Rachel Smith had treated Ira Smith unkindly; it found that neither of them had, reporting that "it is a fact well known to an extensive circle of Mr. Smith's acquaintance, that he is a most kind and affectionate father, and that his present companion is a worthy, prudent wife, a tender and provident mother of his children." In order to clear up this disputed point, which seems to have assumed unusual importance, the council asked Elias to leave while it questioned one of his daughters by Mary Burleigh Smith, who was asked how the other children, including Ira, had been used by their stepmother. She answered "that they were as well used as they could have been by their own mother."[25]

In sum, this council of eminent Universalists found against Thomson, though (reiterating the decision of the Christian Council in the dispute between Elias and John Colcord) it stated that Smith, in some of his behavior, was probably not clear of blame himself (*MNP*, nos. 15–16 [Aug. 20 and Sept. 3, 1822]). A year later they too were done with him, and in 1826 the Universalists passed a resolution declaring Elias Smith no longer a member of their denomination because "he had renounced the faith" (Whittemore 1854, 2:325).

Mark Fernald reported that in 1823 Smith requested to be received back into the Christian Connection, pleading that he had been "lost" for the preceding six years because he had misconstrued Scripture to the advantage of the doctrine of universal salvation; in 1827 he "made another humble and tender acknowledgement of his departure from the truth to Universalism." In June 1827, Smith returned as a Christian once more; his literary vehicle this time became the *Morning Star and City Watchman,* which lasted through two volumes, until April 1829.

Elias's actions during this period, when he was trying to regain the favor of the Christians, caused a temporary split in the Boston church between those who were willing to admit him to their company and those who were not; he had a role in this himself through founding yet another church body, a step he considered necessary because in his view the other Boston congregation calling itself Christian had departed "from the original *simplicity,* recorded in the New Testament." Smith's new church was probably suspect all along because (as the "Orthodox Clergyman" had once advocated, to Thomas Andros's dismay) it refused to reject any person just "on account of different thoughts respecting any part of the doctrine of Christ" (*MSCW* I, no. 1 [June 3, 1827]: 13–14). In any case, Elias was soon back with the Universalists, and as David Millard said, "this put an end to it" (1874, 99–100).

In 1831 it became known that Smith had preached before a Universalist Society, and Fernald thus "felt bound in duty to declare him not with us, but wished he might get right once more, and if he died in three minutes after, I should not be sorry." In July 1837, Fernald saw Elias Smith for the last time, in company with Smith's brother Uriah, who had also veered again toward Universalism and sometimes filled the pulpit that Hosea Ballou had first occupied in Woodstock (Dana 1980, 404). The occasion that brought Fernald to Boston was to attend worship with Elder Joshua Himes, who in the morning led the Sunday school, where "a dozen or more colored children united their songs of praise with the white children." Later, after regular service, Fernald went to hear an antislavery address, "the first I had ever heard." Of Elias and Uriah Smith he said only that "they had both been great men, and supposed to be good, but had retired from the gospel field. The Christian Church in Boston had become two, but not in union" (1852, 169, 198, 284). Five years later Joshua Himes set the country on fire with his advocacy of Miller's apocalyptic prophecy.

In 1828 Elias Smith was answering charges, originating with David Millard, that Smith was a Restorationist masquerading as a Christian (*MSCW* 1, no. 12 [Apr. 1828]: 283). Elias, now fifty-nine and implying legal action in retaliation, replied that "it is not my wish to appear in public unless it is a duty, having a desire at this time of life to retire. I say with Mr. Jefferson,—'I am too old to buckle on the harness again, but wish to defend the truth.'—But it is rather disagreeable to be kicked by an ass." Whether or not Elias was a Restorationist at the period in question, he continued to veer toward and away from some version of universal salvationism to the end of his life. In 1840, he received a testimonial from a committee of the Christian Church in Portsmouth (among them Thomas Treadwell), to the effect that he had finally renounced Universalism, and that "this being done, the church therefore receive him as a member in good standing with them; and recommend him to all that may have an opportunity to hear him preach the gospel of the grace of god: and we in behalf of the church in Portsmouth, sign this recommendation to him, hoping and praying that God would prosper his ways, so that thousands may be converted to the Lord and live a new life, and be received at last to his heavenly kingdom" (361).

Nevertheless, Universalist pastor Henry Bacon, who wrote Smith's obituary for a church publication in 1847, claimed that by 1842 Elias, after an illness that nearly claimed his life, was again confessing his belief that everyone will be saved, and his opinion that even if some judged him harshly because of his changeability, at least he did not hide his doubts but faced them squarely like a man. Elias's 1840 renunciation of Universalism was seemingly as positive as anyone could wish, and yet Adin Ballou appears to have been quite correct in his conclusion that "Elder Elias Smith, who had been regarded as one of the two chief apostles of the 'Christian Connection' went over to the Universalists, in whose fellowship, after some vibrations to and fro, he finally died" (1896, 47).

Smith changed his residence in Boston a number of times. In the 1832 edition of the *American Physician and Family Assistant*, he "informs his friends and the public that he has taken that large and pleasant house, No. 54 High-Street . . . for the accommodation of the sick and lame, who may apply to him for help." He listed the following eight conditions of his treatment:

1. Nothing of a poisonous nature shall be given, on any occasion; such as *quick silver* under the names of *mercury, calomel,* corrosive sublimate, arsenic, antimony, nitre, opium, laudanum &c. No blistering, bleeding, steaming, or pouring cold water.
2. For boarding men, three dollars per week; women, two dollars per week, exclusive of washing.
3. For one course of medicine, two dollars and fifty cents; some deduction from the above, if paid in advance. Advice gratis.
4. All persons who come without recommendation from others that can be relied on, must obtain security if required, or pay a certain sum in advance.
5. Money due for board, must be paid every other week, unless an arrangement is made to the contrary, upon certain conditions.
6. No person received to be attended, to be out later than ten o'clock at night, or drink spirituous liquors.
7. People (who live in the city or country) who come to be attended once, and stay one or two nights, to pay three dollars for board and attendance.
8. Those who come or send their children or friends, may depend upon their being treated in a faithful and friendly manner. (Smith 1832, ix–x)

And so it went throughout the rest of Smith's stay in Boston: occasional changes of domicile, occasional innovations in his medical practice, and the usual criticisms of elite pretension in all its forms. For example, he branched out into dentistry in 1822 (*"Teeth extracted* in a safe and easy manner, at No 56, Middle-Street, at 25 cents each"), and into progressive medical practice in 1830 ("MEDICAL ELECTRICITY attended to at 156 Hanover Street—useful for those afflicted with Rheumatism, and many other complaints") (Smith 1822; Smith 1830, 18).

Having a little extra space to fill in the final pages of his 1840 *Life*, Elias once more gave a brief account of his herbal remedies, "such medicine as the Lord has created out of the earth, instead of resorting to the *poisonous minerals,* which produce disease and death" (370).[26] In 1841 he was gone from Boston, and now resident in Providence, where he continued to dispense his botanical medicines. In these years he experienced further personal misfortunes. In 1840 his daughter Irene— his sixth child by Mary, born in 1805, named after Elias's own mother, and now happily married to Joseph Ripley—died in Lynn, Massachusetts; her funeral was held in the Second Universalist Society of that town (Willis 1874). His only child by Rachel, Mariette Smith (perhaps named after another Mariette, who died as an infant and who was his fifth child by Mary), passed away in 1842 at the age of twenty-five. In that same year Elias became seriously ill and thought himself on the brink of death. It is also the year in which he drew up a will (witnessed by Isaac Thurber and his wife, Lucy) showing that Elias, though resident in Providence, still owned a house in Boston, which he bequeathed to Rachel for the duration of her life. Uriah Smith was to receive his clothing, while Daniel D. and Matthew Hale Smith were to be given his books. At the conclusion of his 1840 *Life* he wrote, "Soon I shall be done, with all things earthly, soon my race will be run, and my course finished on earth; and all you among whom I have gone preaching, will see my face no more. May we be prepared to meet the Lord in the air, to be ever with him—Amen" (363).

In 1846, Elias and Rachel were in Lynn, living near their son-in-law, Joseph Ripley. There on the twenty-ninth of June, twelve days after his seventy-seventh birthday, Elias Smith died of undisclosed causes. His funeral service was conducted by the Reverend Sebastian Streeter of the First Universalist Society of Boston (Willis 1874). In September, Smith's will passed through probate, and as Elias had prescribed, Rachel was declared his executrix. He was buried in Lynn, apparently in the Ripley family plot, but a year later was disinterred and his body taken to permanent rest in the Thurber plot in Providence, where his large though illegible gravestone, now broken and fallen over, may still be found near the stones of his brothers-in-law Isaac and Dexter Thurber.

Elias Smith's eulogists had their work cut out for them. Abner Jones predeceased Smith in 1841. Mark Fernald (who survived him), having had enough of Elias in this life, failed to note his passage into the next one. The task of formally acknowledging Smith's demise and evaluating its significance fell to Universalist pastors Henry Bacon and Lemuel Willis and to Elder Jasper Hazen, who, since 1816, had been pastor of the Christian Church in Woodstock first gathered by Elias himself and successively tended by Uriah Smith, Frederick Plummer, and John Rand (Williams n.d.).

Jasper Hazen was another characteristic early Christian; coming from an apostate Congregationalist family, he had been variously tanner, artisan, farmer, town selectman, schoolteacher, and preacher and in 1847 moved to Albany to become editor of Joseph Badger's *Christian Palladium,* a work at which he already had some experience through a short-lived editorial venture with Abner Jones in the 1820s (Dana 1980, 394–96). In December 1846, Hazen wrote an obituary of Smith suggesting that the problems of Elias's later life were mainly attributable to the financial exigencies that led to the abandonment of his preaching career in favor of Thomsonian medicine. Remarking, as so many had, that Elias's "instability was the great obstacle to his excellence," Hazen (1846) concluded, "I am inclined to believe had he been sustained in his labors, and saved from the necessity that carried him for the work, his course might have been far otherwise. That his labors unremitting might have been continued to the benefit of the cause, to the time of his death."[27] Universalist pastor Henry Bacon remembered of Elias that "crowds once attended upon his preaching, and thousands have felt the kindlings of a new spiritual life under the preaching of the word by him. His acquaintance with the Scriptures was remarkable, and a peculiar charm in his preaching was the happy use to which he applied Scripture language in conveying his ideas. In his prayers, the whole petition was Scripture linked with Scripture." Troubled by the general silence greeting Smith's passing, Bacon (1847) explained it by the fact that "with too many, the memory of his good works is lost in the recollection of his eccentricities." Yet, in this estimation, Elias's heart was sound and he died firm in a belief in universal restoration, a "trust dear to the heart of his surviving companion [Rachel]. May it be the fulness of comfort to her soul; and may the death be sanctified to the surviving children."

Lemuel Willis (1874), who had helped spread the word of God's universal love to Maryland, and who had an intimate acquaintance with Smith from 1824 to 1842, also remembered his friend:

> He was highly gifted with those elements of mind calculated to qualify one for distinction as a public speaker and writer. He had an unusually full and bright eye, which was a very striking feature in his fine expressive countenance. His personal appearance was good; and whoever looked upon him as he might pass in the crowd, would regard him as no common man. In stature he was large, having a large and well formed head, such as a phrenologist would like to examine; though he might regret, perhaps, to find so plentiful a lack of *firmness*. [Though he] was distinguished for his many changes in religious faith, I believe him to have been an *honest* man, honest in giving up one faith, or doctrine, and embracing another, and honest in his pecuniary transactions with his fellow-men. With regard to the last days of this man, who never lost faith in revealed religion, and was always loyal to Christian truth and the hopes of the gospel, it is a just occasion of thankfulness that he was established and joyful in the faith of the restoration of all things finally to God and heaven.

The generation was passing. Joseph Buckminster and his son Joseph, Jr.—"the wondrous pulpit boy" of the liberal Brattle Street Church in Boston, who was remembered for his profound religious feeling and glowing imagination, and whose Unitarianism had compounded the grief of his Calvinist father still further—died within days of each other in 1812.[28] The old Federalist David Osgood of Medford passed on in 1822, by which time almost all of the prominent families of his town were Unitarian. Thomas Baldwin, much lamented, died in 1825. In 1845 the stalwart conservative Thomas Andros—"a decided law and order man [who] had faith to believe that these were essential for the good of society"—died at the age of eighty-six. His eulogist alluded darkly to the problems that led to Andros's retirement ten years previously, "difficulties from which we have no desire to withdraw the veil of oblivion" (*Observance* 1888, 29; Emery 1853, 258, 261). In fact, Andros had been deposed by members of the congregation disturbed by their pastor's dictatorial attempt to impose absolute prohibition of alcohol on his flock. ("Total abstinence will save a drunken world!" he had declared [Andros 1830, 7–8].) The victorious rebels took revenge on Andros via an "independence-in-church-estate" clause that they had written into a revised church covenant in 1847 in order to defend their right to liberty of conscience in matters not pertaining to fundamental doctrine.

Adin Ballou began life as a Six-Principle Baptist, became a Christian when his family did, ended up a Restorationist, a Spiritualist, and cofounder of the Christian Socialist Society in Hopedale, Massachusetts. He died an old man in 1890, disappointed in his goals but secure in his faith of their eventual fulfillment.

Rachel Thurber Smith died non compos mentis in Providence in 1865, leaving the Boston house to a number of Elias's offspring, notably Daniel D. and Matthew Hale Smith, who bought out the minority legatees and took over the property as tenants in common. Rachel also left significant sums to the Old Ladies Home and the Coloured Children's Home in Providence, to the New England Antislavery Society, and (most interestingly) $200 "to the society now worshiping in the Music Hall in Boston . . . Rev. Theodore Parker . . . Pastor."[29] The "now" in question was 1858, when Rachel declared her will, and Theodore Parker was indeed established in the Music Hall as one of Boston's most famous personages. Formerly a Unitarian, Parker had become closely allied to the leaders of the transcendentalist movement (one of his closest friends was George Ripley of Brook Farm); having come to see official Christianity as a positive evil, Parker moved far beyond even what passed as Unitarian orthodoxy.[30] Of the Christian sectarians, he remained most sympathetic to the Universalists, a favor they could not reciprocate because of Parker's denial of the divine inspiration of the Bible.

In 1852 he moved into the Music Hall, and there delivered lectures, homilies, and sermons that eclectically drew from spiritual writings of all kinds. In 1858 he gave talks—which Rachel perhaps heard—on famous Americans. These were "designed to instruct and fortify the American people in the essential ideas of their institutions." But he was already afflicted with consumption and died in Rome in 1860 vainly searching for a cure. Parker had been a leading antislavery activist and supporter of John Brown; his eulogies in Boston were delivered by Wendell Phillips and William Lloyd Garrison of the New England Antislavery Society, which Rachel also remembered in her will. Garrison reflected a widespread sense of exhaustion with doctrinal controversy, when he said of "mere abstract theological opinions" that "the longer I live, the less do I care about them, the less do I make them a test of character. It is nothing to me that any man calls himself a Methodist, or Baptist, or Unitarian, or Universalist. Whoever will, with his theology, grind out the best grist for our common humanity, is the best theologian for me" (Frothingham 1874, 541). Parker was such a man.

Garrison was not alone in his exasperation. It was precisely an opposition to sectarian divisiveness that had motivated Elias Smith and Abner Jones when launching the Christian movement—and yet in the end their efforts only increased the fragmentation of American Christianity into a plethora of mutually antipathetic sects. As Gordon Wood says, "Nowhere in Christendom had religion become so fragmented and so separated from society. Yet nowhere was it so vital. By the second quarter of the nineteenth century, the evangelical Protestantism of ordinary people had come to dominate American culture to an extent the founding fathers had never anticipated" (1992, 333). But these ordinary people, so newly empowered, once more faced the same problems that Paul encountered when attempting to impose coherence of dogma and practice on the early church.

In 1808, God called the itinerant Free-Willer John Colby to go west. "Go unto Ohio, that great country, and preach in it the preaching I bid thee!" Ordained by the Free-Will Baptists in 1809, Colby was soon on his way and left vivid descriptions of the raw and godless new land through which he passed. He traveled by Jericho, New York, where "though I did not fall among thieves, yet I fell in among a parcel of hardened universalists." On to Owego, west of Binghamton, where he "was credibly informed, that there was not one Christian in the place, although it was a considerable village." The day after New Year's 1810, Colby entered Pennsylvania. In Canton he delivered to good effect a sermon on the text that Elias Smith had used before his newly gathered church in Portsmouth just after the Christmas fire of 1802: "Fear not, little flock; for it is your Father's good pleasure to give you the kingdom" (Luke 12:32).

In February Colby preached in the environs of Phillipsburg and Clearfield. He described one settlement he visited as "a noted place for drunkenness and other wickedness," but in expanding on the text "What shall I do to be saved?" he thought he had brought some to Jesus. At the end of the month he felt that "my work was done in that place." Being warned about prevailing sickness to the west, he nevertheless pushed on and made it to Ohio by the end of March. Colby got as far as southeastern Indiana Territory, then turned back to Dayton, where he found that the Christian brethren were sitting in conference. They allowed him to preach, after which a number of converts were baptized in the Big Miami River. He commented of his hosts that "these people, who call themselves *Christians,* though by others are called *New-Lights,* appear to be the most engaged in religion, of any denomination in that State." Now at the end of April and feeling sickly himself, John Colby was taken to taste the mineral waters—"supposed to be useful in almost all disorders"—at Yellow Springs, near the growing town of Dayton (Colby 1829, 79–80).

Colby made further excursions in the western country and finally returned to New England, where he established a semipermanent relationship with a congregation in Rhode Island and preached at least once to Elias Smith's old church in Portsmouth. But he had consumption and in 1817 died in Norfolk, Virginia, on a hopeful but abortive journey to South Carolina to recover his health. The second edition of his autobiography contains a eulogy by Christian elder David Millard, who wished "to heaven, that thousands might catch the spirit of Colby, and follow him as he followed Christ" (Colby 1829, 379).

The career of David Millard followed into the next generation the trail pioneered by Colby and the Ohio Christians. Millard, who, along with Joseph Badger, would be among the foremost of the second generation of Christian leaders, embodied the trends shaping his cause in the middle years of the nineteenth century, namely, the westward migration and the consolidation of a movement into a denomination. He was born in 1794 near Ballston, New York, of a family that had come from Massachusetts in the 1760s; he was converted in 1814 by Nancy Cram during the revival that caused Stephen Porter such pain and later took it on himself to condemn Elias Smith for being a closet Restorationist.

He too felt that he was called to bring the free gospel to foreign regions and, not knowing quite what to do, was advised by Elder Jabez King to trust the Lord and persevere. He soon heard that a number of people who had belonged to Daniel Hix's Christian Church in Dartmouth, Massachusetts, had settled in the vicinity of Middletown, west of the Hudson River town of Newburgh. For a time he preached to congregations in that area but then resolved to explore westward and was drawn to the same area near Rochester, New York, to which Joseph Badger had already gone, taking leave of his congregation in Gilmanton, New Hampshire, a place once within the orbit of Benjamin Randal and the site of some of Elias Smith's earliest labors while still a Baptist.

Millard married a young woman from Taunton, Massachusetts, and traveled widely for a time—to the developing Christian community around Norfolk, Virginia; to Salem to visit Abner Jones; to Portsmouth, where in 1824 he found that "zeal without knowledge" had undermined the integrity of Elias Smith's original church; to Kittery, where he met Mark Fernald, a man who "amidst the changes and speculation of the age has maintained but one course, and that is directly onward" (Millard 1874, 73, 168). But the focus of his labors continued to be the Rochester area, and in order to serve the region better, he became editor of a new periodical called the *Gospel Luminary*, later to be supplanted by Joseph Badger's *Gospel Palladium*.

Again he traveled: to Pennsylvania's Wyoming Valley, west to Cincinnati on the Ohio, still further to Indiana and Michigan. Yet for a time his attention was drawn to Portsmouth once more, where, as we have seen, he took over the old church in 1837. While there, he became involved with the antislavery and temperance movements until his health failed and he—the first of his generation with the ability to do so—went on a pilgrimage to the Holy Land to restore his health. As a result of his observations during a journey that took him from Egypt to

Beirut, he was appointed professor of biblical antiquities and sacred geography at the Meadville Theological School in western Pennsylvania, and from 1845 served there for twenty years until he retired and moved in 1868 to Jackson, Michigan, north of Hillsdale, where the Free-Will Baptists had founded a college in 1844. Like Millard himself, a large majority of those whom he brought to Christ "had been carried by the tide of emigration to the young and growing West" (Millard 1874, 264–65).

By the 1820s it had become apparent that the center of gravity of the Christian movement and the nation at large was rapidly shifting. In 1828 Elias Smith broadcast in his new Boston periodical the *Morning Star and City Watchman* a general address to the Christian brethren pointing out the fact, and how New England had declined in relative importance because of it.

> It is well known to the greater part of you that the first attempt made to be free from sectarianism, in New-England, was made in Portsmouth, (N.H.) and Boston, in 1802; and after. The number at first was very small. From that small beginning, the principal has spread *east, west, north,* and *south*. Our brethren in Virginia and other states began first, and beyond the Allegany [*sic*], not far from the same time. For many years, almost every thing appeared favourable. Within a few years, several things have taken place, apparently unfavorable to the churches in New-England. One thing was; the removal of so many of the preachers to the west, and other parts of the country.—This left many churches and congregations destitute of much preaching; and to this day, there are but very few who travel through the towns and cities to preach the word. (*MSCW* 2, no. 3 [1828]: 71)[31]

Smith had put his finger on it (and had the example before him of his uncle Elisha Ransom, who moved from Vermont to Indiana in 1813). Dayton, Ohio, where Colby found so many enthusiastic members of the Christian Connection in 1810, would in time become the organizational center of the movement and the editorial seat of the *Herald of Gospel of Liberty* well into this century. Soon the Ohio Christians would acquire land at Yellow Springs from a Cincinnati group of

Owenite socialists with Swedenborgian inclinations in order to found a college of their own.

For Smith and his friends, formal structures were anathema. For him colleges were a part of the kingdom of Antichrist, and the founding of one a sure sign of the decay that the Baptists evinced when they founded what became Brown University in Providence, which Elias was sure would become a Baptist Harvard—just another mill for the production of hireling priests. In this spirit Smith, in the *Morning Star*, published with approval a letter from a brother in New York State commenting on the proposal that the Christians should establish a seminary for the education of young preachers. This rural Jeremiah from upper New York wrote that, "having *seen* a people arise in America; with the naked Bible in their hand, declaring to take the New Testament for their only rule of faith, and practice," he now saw the church embracing worldly things like seminaries, contrary to the spirit of everything his connection stood for in the pristine time when their ministry consisted of "plain farmers, mechanics, and sailors" (*MSCW* 1, no. 11 [Apr. 1828]: 260).

But for a new generation of Christians, college building and the provision of an educated ministry was becoming an essential part of the denominational program; it was being done for the benefit of the youth, the prestige of the church, and the hope that a properly informed ministry would follow "the perfect law of liberty" in a more orderly way than the erratic visionaries of the previous generation. Milo Morrill, who served as pastor of the Woodstock Church from 1894 to 1904, and who published in 1911 the first (and still only) general history of the Christian Church, was well aware of the various problems that it had suffered in the past because of fluid organization and lack of adequate criteria for ordination of preachers (Williams n.d., 16–17).

Elias Smith's Universalist apostasy brought an organizational crisis of its own. The Millerite agitation brought on another such: "In an incredibly short time many ministers among the Christians were swept off their feet by Miller's views . . . and began to preach his and their own vagaries. . . . Vermont met with the greatest loss." Given the problem of wolves among their sheep, the collective wisdom of the Christian Church came to be that "protection must be provided, ministers must be accredited." Morrill noted how "observant men had seen [that] their sporadic unorganized movement laid both laity and ministry open to endless imposition, loss of prestige, and charge of abetting charlatans." What he was documenting was the process whereby a movement becomes a denomination, and its ministry a profession (Morrill 1911, 175, 121, 291).

The Free-Will Baptists founded Colby College in Maine and Hillsdale College in Michigan; Presbyterian and Methodist colleges appeared everywhere. The Universalists, with the help of Phineas T. Barnum and other luminaries, founded in 1853 what would become Tufts University in David Osgood's old town of Medford, Massachusetts. The Boston-based Unitarians, who had formally organized into an association in 1825, made common cause with the already active western Christians, who sometimes (to Elias Smith's dismay) allowed themselves to be referred to by the party name of "Evangelical Unitarians." This collaboration resulted in the foundation of the Meadville (Pa.) Theological School in 1844, which speedily passed under Unitarian control because their more evangelical collaborators, then riven by the Millerite excitement, could not find the funds to support it (Olbricht 1966, 185). Joseph Badger became one of the trustees of the Meadville Theological School, and David Millard one of its professors. According to Badger, "Nothing can be more degrading to a religious community, and nothing can more effectually retard their usefulness and prosperity, than an ignorant ministry" (Holland 1854, 338).[32]

The Christian Connection would open its own college at Yellow Springs, Ohio, in 1853. It was given the name Antioch after the place at which the followers of Jesus were first called Christians.

Badger's memorialist observed that "all great religious movements, however catholic in aim and spirit, do almost necessarily centralize themselves at last into denominational form" (Holland 1854, 170). Badger and Millard, men who transcended the limitations of their modest backgrounds, were able to deal with the sophisticated Boston Unitarians from a position of relative equality; they were the natural leaders around which a denomination could gain form, substance, and—perhaps above all—respectability. Their organizational accomplishments were in turn what a new generation of antinomian radicals could react against. And so it proved when the Christians were shattered by the Millerite movement. William Miller, himself a Baptist Vermonter, found fertile soil for his apocalyptic message in the area of western New York where Badger and Millard had settled—the famous "burnt-over district," so receptive to religious innovations of all kinds throughout these years.[33]

The second generation of Christian leaders, now themselves aging and having already seen enough of the consequences of human folly in their lifetimes, tried in vain to hold back the new flood of apocalyptic enthusiasm but had to content themselves with observing what happened when the prophecy failed. Badger wrote: "For thirty years past I have seen many false prophets and false religions rise and fall, and uniformly a vain, vaunting, self-righteous spirit has attended them all. But I have never witnessed more of it in any case than in Mr. Miller and his followers" (Holland 1854, 369). As usual, Mark Fernald went to the heart of the matter when he branded the entire episode "horrid nonsense and fanaticism" (1852, 338). Horrid or not, the excitement of 1843–44 led to the creation of still more new denominations (most notably the Seventh-Day Adventists), while the Christians and other groups affected by the prophecy tried to close ranks again, as they had once done against the Universalists and the Shakers.

Going against the sectarian tendencies of their age, Alexander Campbell and Barton Stone managed to bring their respective movements in western Virginia and Kentucky together under one roof in 1832, a union that Stone regarded as "the noblest act of my life" (Rogers 1847, 79). They were naturally loath to see their efforts at unification undercut by sectarians, but in testimony to the ambiguities of a movement espousing rejection of divisive party names, the individual churches that emerged from Stone's movement, the Campbellites, and the western Christians of the New England diaspora have variously known themselves as the Disciples of Christ, the Christian Church (Disciples of Christ), the Disciples of Christ (Christians), and sometimes merely the Christian Church. Historians of the Christians and Disciples have been obliged to point out that, though their movements are often confused, they in fact have separate historical origins (Morrill 1911; Garrison and deGroot 1948).

Many Christian churches of New England, the upper South, and the Midwest—the direct spiritual descendants of Smith, Jones, and Fernald—experienced a consummately ironic fate: union with the Congregationalists in 1932 to form the United Church of Christ. This union was the product of developments already in evidence when Badger and Millard flirted with the Unitarians (and that would emerge in another form when the Universalists followed suit in the 1961 creation of the Unitarian-Universalist Association). Though their churches were of radically different theologies and class alignment in origins, by the 1920s the leaders of the Congregationalists and Christians thought they had more in common than otherwise. In fact, what happened when the merger took place was that substantial numbers of the Christian churches in the North and Midwest hived off to become independent or to affiliate with fellow travelers such as the Disciples rather than accept such an unnatural marriage to their old adversaries. A skeptical historian of the merger described the outcome as "merely a cultural realignment of middle class churches" (Taylor 1981, 12). The Christian communions that accepted union were often urban and middle class with a college-educated pastorate; those that rejected it, often rural with what effectively was a lay ministry. The Christian movement in part arose out of hostility to upper-class antidemocratic pretension; but now reason for rejection of the Congregationalist merger, and separation from those who supported it, could be found within the increasingly heterogeneous Christian Church itself.

Elias Smith's legacy is therefore an ambiguous one. Much of what he hoped for came to naught; much of what he actually accomplished he would have judged harshly, had he lived to see what became of it. In any event, the effect of his presence on earth cannot be fully measured. Through this study of Elias Smith, however, I have sought to show how a cultural dynamic unleashed by the coupling of Revolution and unprecedented social change manifested itself in the course of one life. This particular life had unique features in abundance and yet possesses a representative quality in relation to the emergence of the ethos that it has been my purpose to track. The translation of perceived class conflict into a religious idiom was central to Smith's thought, and he was not alone in this. Equally important was the process through which fundamental notions about the person in relation to God and human society were modified by the consequences of political revolution.

In attempting to summarize the results of that Revolution, Gordon Wood has said that the idea of equality was "the most radical and most powerful Ideological force" let loose by it. He sees Elias Smith as an exemplar of this tendency, saying of his type that "such men were sick and tired of being dismissed as factious, narrow, parochial, and illiberal and were unwilling to defer any longer to anyone's political leadership but their own" (1992, 275–76). As for the effect on the churches, Nathan Hatch regards the collective efforts of men like Smith as having "delineated the fault line of class within American Christianity" (1989, 226). No longer was it possible to sustain any notion of church and society as a coterminous organic unity. Elias Smith constantly maintained that his goal for the Christian movement was the creation of a truly republican basis for the permanent establishment of liberty, equality, unity, and peace. Liberty and equality he got; ecumenical unity and peace were beyond his grasp.

Elias Smith had great expectations. Again, he was not alone in his hope; nor was he alone in his disappointment. But from the perspective of the year 1800, anything seemed possible. It was Smith's assumption that the mutually reinforcing effect of political liberty, freedom of personal conscience, and a correct understanding of Scripture would produce the basis for an ecumenical faith fully compatible with the principles of equality upon which the nation was founded. The personal practice of liberty would thus become an act of worship, and the reborn nation a church without walls. The Apocalypse of John predicts that, following the Second Coming, there will be "no temple [in the city]: for the Lord God Almighty and the Lamb are the temple of it. And the city had no need of the sun, neither of the moon, to shine in it: for the glory of God did lighten it, and the Lamb is the light thereof. And the nations of them which are saved shall walk in the light of it: and the kings of the earth do bring their glory and honour into it" (21:22–24).

Elias Smith saw the signs for the imminent accomplishment of this all around him. His fusion of millenarian Christian perfectionism and popular democracy is nowhere more obvious than in what he said in the first number of the *Herald of Life and Immortality* in 1819. It may stand for his epitaph, an epitome of his thought, and a summary of the ideological synthesis that it has been my purpose to examine:

> Such a time as the present was never known in America. The government of this country is universal; it is founded on principles that the whole world may in truth acknowledge, to their greatest temporal advantage and profit. It acknowledges that all men are born free and equal, that is, that they are all born in that liberty peculiar to the sons of God, and that as such, they have a right to worship him. The doctrine that proclaims the salvation of all men, agrees with the principles of our government; with the condition of man; with God's dealings with all nations; with the general testimony of all the scriptures; with the desires of the best men; and if known to all as true, would cause the greatest joy among all nations. Christ is said to be given a ransom for all, to be testified in due time—That time appears to be fast approaching, yea, is nigh, even at the door.

EPILOGUE

WHEN ELIAS SMITH DIED, THE UNITED STATES was at war with Mexico. In New England the Mexican War was taken as evidence of a southern plot to enhance its influence through the expansion of slavery to new territories. The abolitionist leader and pacifist William Lloyd Garrison publicly wished that the army of General Winfield Scott would suffer "the most utter defeat and disgrace." The opposite proved the fact, and the Americans advanced on Mexico City via a naval landing at Vera Cruz. With Mexico defeated, attention turned to Oregon.

The world in which Elias Smith's children grew to adulthood was one of ever more radical change. Little is known of Elias Smith's home life and, with the exception of Matthew Hale Smith, the youngest surviving son of Elias and Mary Burleigh Smith, little about the fates of his offspring. Elias was publicly reticent about his family beyond the pious observations that his marriages were harmonious and that his children were born. Yet one son was a suicide, and another suffered from a "disease in his head" beginning at an early age. Such an erratically managed household—during the Boston period one often shared with Smith's in-patients—cannot have been an easy one in which to live. Ira Smith's unfortunate destiny is known, but not much more about him. Of Daniel D. Smith, again little is known; he became a Universalist pastor and stayed in that connection throughout his active life. All that Daniel Smith left behind for the public record are published discourses on "domestic duties" delivered to the women of his flock in Portland, Maine, and the proceedings of a debate he had with Adin Ballou over the respective merits of ultra-Universalism and Restorationism.[1]

Matthew Hale Smith presents quite another story; through him a sense emerges of what the Smith household was like from the perspective of one who endured it. Matthew was born in 1810, and his mother, Mary, died when he was but four years old. Matthew therefore spent most of his formative years in Boston. He became a Universalist pastor like his brother, Daniel, but in the early 1840s underwent a crisis of faith brought about by reflection on the seemingly licentious results of the doctrine he preached. He now came to accuse the Universalists of harboring the same tendencies that his father had identified in them while still a Christian. Matthew's wife and all his closest associations were Universalists, and now in profound doubt about his vocation, Matthew knew not where to turn; caught in this horrible dilemma, he experienced a recurrence of what he called "a complaint, which, from my childhood, has been the bane of my existence"—which led to "an instability to my views and feelings that I could not control."[2] He was treated with the application of leeches to his head, but without effect.

While still serving a Universalist congregation in Hartford, Connecticut, Matthew underwent a mental breakdown, which presaged more the insane asylum than the relative success that came his way in later life. He renounced Universalism, set out in his chaise for Boston, and was found on the road in a dissociated state with no memory of what had just transpired.[3]

Matthew Hale Smith's strange pilgrimage bridges the theme of my first book, *The Passion of Ansel Bourne,* with that of the present one. Perhaps now it is easier to see the connection between exotic mental disorders and the cultural history of early America. In this study of Elias Smith I have concentrated on the cultural and ideological ferment of the early republic as evidenced in one intriguing life; the evangelical culture and social experience that Elias shared with many of his fellows, however, also set up acute psychological tensions. Their common faith, this religion of the twice-born, was itself predicated on an essential antinomy—the dialectic of sin and redemption—which gave rise to habitual soul-searching and ecstatic transformative experiences such as Smith's Vermont epiphany and call to the ministry, Adin Ballou's conversion to universal salvationism, Matthew Smith's dramatic renunciation of his father's faith and return to old-order Calvinism, and the extraordinary call that Ansel Bourne received in front of John Taylor's Christian congregation in 1857, which was precursor to his episode of multiple personality in 1887 where my work on this subject began.

We do not know how Matthew's "disease" was construed by his doctors and the others around him (as mania? epilepsy? hereditary instability?). By his own account, it emerged in childhood and therefore presumably had something to do with the exigencies of his upbringing. As an adult, he translated his personal unhappiness into a religious quest. Perhaps his father had also done so, but given what we know, it is impossible to say anything sensible about the roots of Elias Smith's curious instability. All I would venture is that Elias had what would now be called a romantic disposition. When young, his only access to the great world around him, the only outlet for his idealism, was provided through his eclectic reading and the example of his youthful idols—the Baptist preachers. His only obvious career choice outside of farming or shoemaking was to follow in their steps. Itinerancy provided Smith with experience of the world, while preaching and writing became the vehicles for his personal creativity. He was impressionable, and yet intellectual issues bothered him to the point that he was capable of radically changing direction in response to perceived inconsistencies of belief.

Whatever one makes of Elias Smith's striking personality, the changes he went through in his life were experienced by many others, to which they reacted in similar ways. In writing of the immediate post-Revolutionary generation, Joseph Ellis has said, "Men who live in an age that straddles a great divide in history are forced to graft new ideals to inherited assumptions in ways that seem to us, who possess the advantage of hindsight, highly paradoxical" (1979, 37). Following a similar logic, Clifford Geertz points out that "it is in country unfamiliar emotionally or topographically that one needs poems and road maps. So too with ideology" (1973, 218). The country into which Elias Smith and his fellows were venturing was unfamiliar indeed. Perhaps

Smith took a side road, but the point should be made that there was no clear road at all, except the one that we imagine leads to ourselves.

Leaving psychological questions aside (though they are far from irrelevant), one of the essential ideological tensions of Smith's time was that between conflicting demands for individual liberty and what conservatives took to be the organic needs of society. Elias Smith's stance is clear enough; he rejected the organicism of Federalists and former Baptist associates alike and wholeheartedly embraced the radically egalitarian message that he read into the Declaration of Independence and justified by reference to "the perfect law of liberty" promised in the New Testament. Smith put his faith in the belief that personal search for truth in light of Scripture will produce all the consensus needed for the survival of the republic. It would again be anachronistic to call this a "liberal" stance (It had little to do with economics), and yet it contains classically liberal elements in its focus on the ultimate value of the free individual.

Whether and to what degree this stance was a product of the evangelical heritage of Smith and those like him is not an easy question to address, much less answer. Perceived individualistic elements in evangelical Protestantism have borne a good deal of historiographic weight with respect to the interpretation of the Revolution and its consequences. (Whether the so-called Second Great Awakening is a viable construct, I will leave for others to decide.) Smith's religious heritage—in the form of such works as Dilworth, Watts, and Osterwald and the advice he received from people such as Elisha Ransom—put considerable stress on independence of judgment. But the essential feature of Elias Smith's thought is the blending he achieved between his faith and the promise of his new nation. Smith reinterpreted his faith in the light of his politics; neither is fully comprehensible without the other. Elias Smith therefore represents a variation on a republican theme, with the outcome for him being a specifically Christian republicanism growing out of a New Light evangelical heritage, conjoined with a rapidly evolving national political culture in a climate of strident partisan conflict.

The relationship between religion, class, politics, and conceptions of selfhood is an intricate one that would test any theory of ideology. Smith was raised in a theological climate demanding self-effacement;

as he said of his early religious experience, "Self was not the subject, but God, Christ, and the things revealed by the spirit." And yet he came to apotheosize the individual and magnify individual agency via his free-will theology. As transcendentalists and Swedenborgians internalized God and so brought him closer to humanity, Universalists turned the logic of salvation to human advantage with their hopeful claim that in God's great scheme, all people are equally worthy of eventual salvation. Emerging from this complex brew was a set of notions pertaining to the inherent divinity of the self and the power of the individual to effect indefinite physical and psychological self-improvement in fulfillment of nature's teleological plan—ideas affecting elements of American thought and practice to this day. One need only mention mesmerism, hypnosis, breakfast cereal empires, Christian Science, chiropractic, the "mind cure" practices that so fascinated William James, the variety of "power of positive thinking" and alternative medical movements current now.

However, Smith's brand of millenarian republicanism has not been much seen in these latter days, contemporary Christian millenarianism being weighted toward a pessimism about the ability of politics to accomplish any real improvement in the human lot (though still retaining a strong populist antielite bias). Yet American political life continues to be tinged by millenarian imagery, as may be seen in the invocation of the idea of "a new covenant for America" during the presidential campaign of 1992 by a candidate who explicitly associated himself with Thomas Jefferson. The line of descent of Smith's mode of thought is more obvious in the nineteenth century, in items such as the association of Universalism with a variety of reform causes, attempts to cope with an emergent industrial society through the foundation of religiously motivated socialist communities, the rise of Bryanite populism, the association of Seventh-Day Adventism and health reform, the strange conjunction of Spiritualism and progressivism accomplished by such figures as Andrew Jackson Davis, the "Poughkeepsie Seer."

This study of Elias Smith suggests refinements in the way in which the relation between social stratum, evangelicalism, and political opinion in early America should be conceived. One of the central points of this book is that the Christian movement, insofar as Elias

Smith was directly involved in it, was as much of an urban as a rural affair. The Portsmouth congregation, for example, may have been marginal in relation to the dominant culture—say, of the Federalist clergy—but equally it could be said that they and people like them, many of whom were or became artisans and shop owners, were in the process of becoming the dominant culture themselves. I suspect that if a church roll should prove forthcoming from the Christian Church, Mount Zion, much the same pattern would be revealed for Philadelphia, a city with a history of urban radicalism.

The venue in which Smith developed his distinctive constellation of ideas—Portsmouth, New Hampshire—is of considerable significance in its own right, but surprisingly little social-historical research has been directed at one of the most important seaport towns of the time. Portsmouth had a significant federal presence in the form of its Navy Yard, where a number of the communicants in Smith's church worked. This is only to say that there is a great deal I do not know that would have been helpful in this study. Large gaps also remain about what went on during Smith's time in Philadelphia; likewise awaiting investigation is the nature of the Christian presence in Norfolk, Virginia, another seaport town.

Nor is it entirely clear how the Christian message was received in particular communities and by whom (Portsmouth, Dartmouth, and Boston being only partial exceptions). It is known that Christian preaching *could* be disruptive, as was the case in Portsmouth, Berkley, and Ballston. But further investigation into local class relations and the local political scene is required to make sense of what made these communities so susceptible to such agitation. (Berkley is a particularly promising case because of the richness of local material pertaining to the question.) The Christian Connection became established in Dartmouth, however, without particular disturbance except separation from the regional Baptist Association. In Woodstock, the Christian movement virtually grew out of the soil itself but remained only one sect among several; here too, the relation between class, family, and religious persuasion awaits attention.

But all this is for another day. For now I heed the final admonition of the Preacher: "One further warning, my son: the use of books is endless, and much study is wearisome" (Eccles. 12:12).

NOTES

1. Throughout this book, page references in the text with no other identification are citations from Smith 1840. This remarkable work is an only lightly edited version of Smith 1816.

2. As Gordon Wood has observed, "For the revolutionary generation America became the Enlightenment fulfilled" (1992, 191).

3. Linda Kerber also calls attention to Popkin's representative status as a Federalist divine (1970, 6).

4. See Hatch 1989, 58. Frederick Jackson Turner wrote of how "the frontier is productive of individualism. Complex society is precipitated by the wilderness into a kind of primitive organization based on the family. The tendency is anti-social. It produces antipathy to control, and particularly to any direct control" (1962, 30). For further elaborations of this theme, see Bushman 1967, McLoughlin 1971, and most particularly Marini 1982. As far as religion is concerned, the question is that of how a common Anglo-Protestant cultural heritage was transformed by these hinterland conditions and coupled with rapid social change into a distinctive form of Protestant evangelicalism characterized by an emphasis on personal experience, by the revival as a recurrent ritual form, and by a pervasive, fractious sectarianism corresponding to the individualistic ethos of the region.

Such socioeconomic arguments undertake to explain these ideological developments by the general characteristics of the society that produced them, which somehow render them natural and even logical by-products of social conditions. Perry Miller, for example, wrote of the role of revivalism in a society in the process of a massive transformation from locality to nation, from the covenanted community to a mass democracy. He saw the end result to have been a reorientation of "American Protestantism within an uncovenanted piety" and observed that without knowing it, Americans of that time were "asserting the unity of a culture in pressing danger of fragmentation" (1967, 114). William McLoughlin, drawing on the work of anthropologists concerned with revitalization and millenarian movements, noted in the same vein as Miller that expansion, mobility, economic opportunity, and political friction gave rise to cultural and social tensions productive of an ecumenical revivalism that simultaneously redefined what it meant to be Christian and American (1978; see also Mathews 1969). Likewise, George Thomas in *Revivalism and Cultural Change* (1989) seeks for what gives such movements their content and power, the capacity to work change through modification of preexisting cultural categories in such a way as to make them more consonant with social reality as it is actually experienced: for example, to replace old elitist Calvinist notions of predestination and election with more appropriate conceptions focusing—though still very much in Christian terms—on the freedoms that were already being effectually exercised through the effects of such processes as economic expansion.

5. The concept of ideology is of considerable background importance here—if only because debates concerning its nature permeate the contemporary historiography on the development of republican thinking and political action in the early national period. The reason for this originates on one side with the attention an influential group of American historians has given to the works of the anthropologist Clifford Geertz; on the other with a compelling approach to the structure of republican thought advanced by the intellectual historian J. G. A. Pocock, an approach based on an analysis of political discourse utilizing the notion of paradigm—a term borrowed from the historian of science Thomas Kuhn (who, through Pocock, has also influenced Nathan Hatch). For Pocock, the term *paradigm* connotes a structure of concepts binding, limiting, but, under changed circumstances, also steering into new waters what can be said about the verities of political life (or anything else): "a reference point within the structure of consciousness, stable and durable enough to be used at more than one moment, and so by more than one actor in more than one way" (Pocock 1971, 280).

Under Geertz's influence the production of ideology has come to be seen as a culturally embedded symbolic process, and to this day an emphasis on ideology as culture remains at the center of the debate over the significance of early American republicanism. From a Geertzian point of view, ideology provides a symbolic template of the social order and consequently a guide for action within it. As Geertz said: "It is through the construction of ideologies, schematic images of social order, that man makes himself for better or worse a political animal" (1973, 218). This concept of ideology is distinguished from the more general notions of culture or of worldview in that it pertains to circumstances in which the nature of social reality has become dubious, when conceptual moorings have been slipped. Ideology, in this sense, is therefore not just a map of the sociopolitical world order but a response to an order that has become problematic to such a degree that it compels reflection: "It is, in fact, precisely at the point at which a political system begins to free itself from the immediate governance of received tradition, from the direct and detailed guidance of religious or philosophical canons on the one hand and from the unreflective precepts of conventional moralism on the other, that formal ideologies tend first to emerge and take hold. . . . It is in country unfamiliar emotionally or topographically that one needs poems and road maps. So too with ideology" (ibid.).

To what degree should American republicanism be seen as autonomous source of social action, as a creative power in its own right rather than as a cognitive reflex—a notion associated with more traditional concepts of ideology—of deeper sociopolitical forces and conflicts? Following a culturally based view of ideology, it might be said that, without the influence of British republican thinking, the perceptions that guided the actions of the Anglo-Americans would have been different from what they were, and that therefore the Revolution might not have occurred at all; nor, without this influence, might the political controversies following independence have assumed the virulently antagonistic form that they did. Likewise, a central question must be that of the degree to which the American branch of evangelical Protestantism prepared the way for revolution and for the class-based confrontations typical of the republic's early years.

Geertz's approach to ideology as culture concentrates on the rhetorical forms and emotionally compelling images available within given political traditions. This approach also recommends itself to Pocock, though from a somewhat different point of view. In his study of the evolution of republican thinking from Renaissance Florence to Revolutionary America, Pocock is concerned with the identification of the "conceptual vocabularies which were available for talking about political systems considered in their particularity, with exploring their limitations and implications and considering how these operated, and with examining the processes by which these conceptual systems, their uses and implications changed over time" (1975, 57). By implication these are the analytical procedures that might be applied to any political ideology at any time; however, republicanism offered Pocock a particularly fertile field to track how the elements of a particular ideological form were permuted and transformed over a considerable period in a variety of local circumstances. Reflection on the nature of republican constitutions and, more broadly, the nature of the state in relation to the citizen gave rise to a theoretical rubric through which the Florentines, certain British thinkers, and the writers of the American constitution attempted to conceptualize the political order. They had political "languages" at their disposal that were part of the common heritage of European thought, and Pocock wishes to show how these languages served as "paradigms in action." (ibid., 271).

6. Hatch describes the nature of this process as "a pervasive collapse of certainty within popular culture. From the debate over the Constitution to the election of Jefferson, a new and explicitly democratic revolution united many who were suspicious of power and many who were powerless in a common effort to pull down the cultural hegemony of a gentlemanly few. In a complex cultural process that historians have just begun to unravel, people on a number of fronts began to speak, write, and organize against the authority of mediating elites, of social distinctions, and of any human tie that did not spring from volitional allegiance" (1980, 561).

7. Joyce Appleby identifies this passage as a typical phrasing of the "anthropological" attitude of Bailyn and his followers toward the function of ideology: "Bailyn's understanding of the role of ideas in history rests heavily upon the work of Clifford Geertz, and Geertz's thinking on ideology flows from anthropological studies of small face-to-face communities" (1986, 26). Appleby's problem with this is that such an approach runs the risk of oversimplification relative to an already complex society such as that of late eighteenth-century America, when ideological forms were in considerable flux under the impact of innovators such as Jefferson. For similar points, see also Appleby 1977–78 and 1982.

8. Pocock thinks his work and Bailyn's bear a "special relationship," while Bailyn looks toward the "anthropological" approach of Geertz—theoretically a full circle. See Pocock 1981, 49.

9. "We *will*, that our power of making laws for the government of the church, and executing them by delegated authority, forever cease; that the people may have free course to the Bible, and adopt *the laws of the spirit of life in Christ Jesus.*"

10. Bailyn (1973) advances what he calls an anthropological view of the ideological background to the Revolution, finding it more satisfactory than its presumably discredited predecessors because "such a view of the central themes of the Revolution—neither whig nor tory, idealist nor materialist, liberal nor

conservative: a view that might best perhaps be called anthropological—helps one go beyond the immediate events of the Revolution itself and assess the most general meaning of the event in the broad sweep of eighteenth-century history and to isolate its impact on the overall course of American history." A central work on American republican ideology is Lance Banning's *Jeffersonian Persuasion: Evolution of a Party Ideology*. In describing the aim of his book, which built on Bailyn's by-now classic *Ideological Origins of the American Revolution* (1967), Banning argues that "a constellation of inherited concerns gave rise to the Republican party and its foes. It seeks to trace the process. In doing so, it tries to show that the Republican persuasion was a great deal more coherent than has formerly been thought" (1978, 17). Joyce Appleby's answer (and that of other more critics of the so-called ideological or neo-Whig historians) is that republican thought was, in fact, less coherent and monolithic than Banning and Bailyn would have it; Appleby focuses on the innovative quality of Jeffersonian ideology, while critics like Ernst (1973), Kramnick (1982), and Murrin (1980) believe that an emphasis on the autonomous effects of republican ideology has amounted to a covert dismissal of class analysis.

In the earlier flush of enthusiasm for the anthropological (i.e., Geertzian) approach, Banning found it possible to speak of "Republican minds" as manifestations of a more or less unitary vision of social reality (1974, 185). Later, however, a more pluralistic approach has emerged, as witnessed by a debate between Banning and Appleby in the *William and Mary Quarterly* over proto-liberal elements in the republican thought of the early national period (Appleby 1986; Banning 1986). Another sign of the continuing vitality of the problem is a special issue of the *American Quarterly* edited by Joyce Appleby and devoted exclusively to republicanism; in her introduction "Republicanism and Ideology," Appleby states that "the recent discovery of republicanism as the reigning social theory of eighteenth-century America has produced a reaction among historians akin to the response of chemists to a new element. Once having been identified, it can be found everywhere" (1985, 461).

More than any single work except Bailyn's *Ideological Origins*, J. G. A. Pocock's *Machiavellian Moment: Florentine Republican Thought and the Atlantic Republican Tradition* (1975) has set the terms of the general debate about republicanism. Pocock himself calls attention to the pluralistic nature of republican discourse: "I do not believe, and I never have, that there can exist only one hegemonic language at a time; on the contrary, everything I have written is concerned with the inconclusive contests for hegemony that go on, and the complex dialectics to which they give rise, between languages which compete, and argue, with one another" (1988, 817). Obviously such a view is of immediate relevance to an understanding of the various "republicanisms" current in the years following the Revolution. For important reviews of the state of republican historiography, see Shalhope 1972 and 1982.

11. When Smith cited Jefferson, it was generally only the Virginia Declaration of Religious Liberty.

12. Smith's *Letter* is specifically in response to Humphreys 1802, 15–19. Humphreys was a preacher in the small Sandemanian church in Portsmouth. Founded by a Scot, Robert Sandeman, this body advocated (as did the Christians) absolute separation of church and state, but also communalistic practices associated with the primitive Christian church.

13. The relation of Democratic-Republican to Federalist thought is a major historiographic issue, as is the relation between class and the various forms of republicanism. Even proponents of the most violently opposed views could call themselves "republicans," for which see Shoemaker 1966, which points out that in the political writings of the time, "republicanism" was commonly associated with representative institutions conducive to the maintenance of social order, while "democracy" was associated with turbulence and anarchy. As Linda Kerber points out, "A republican democracy was assumed to be a contradiction in terms; Democratic-Republican as a party label a non sequitur" (1970, 194). Such was the attitude of John Snelling Popkin, who can stand for the rest of the Federalist clergy in this regard. Howe calls attention to the rhetorical violence of political controversy in that period. Asking why so many should have seen so much at stake, Howe found the answer in the intellectual insecurity engendered by doubts about the stability of republican forms of government. "Indeed, the whole revolutionary era may be most profitably viewed as a continuing effort by the American people to decide what for them republicanism was to mean." But, once more, "republicanism, one quickly finds, is no easy concept to define" (1967, 153).

Both Banner and Kerber identify a concern with disintegrating standards of deference—i.e., concern with increasing refusal to recognize a natural aristocracy of learning, ability, and wealth—as one of the central features of Federalism. Banner, for example, writes of "the universal code of deference which helped cement Massachusetts society," before the onset of party competition in the waning years of the eighteenth century (1970, 10), while Kerber states that "all around them, the Federalists of the Old Republic saw familiar social habits decaying. The most obvious sign of changing social balances was the decline of deferential behavior" (1970, 178). With regard to the onset of the Revolution, Gary Nash attempts to place such antideferential attitudes relative to the class structures of the port towns: "Different groups, in sum, began walking the road to revolution in the port towns with different perceptions, rooted in prior experience and values, of what a new society should look like"

(1979, 350). Lemisch suggests that a tendency to see American society of this period as dominated by standards of deference is based on scholarly acceptance of what contemporary elites believed, while in fact during the revolutionary period "the powerless refused to stay in the places to which a theory of deference and subordination assigned them" (1968, 16; see Banning 1986, 18). In pursuing the same themes, Kirby suggests that, in the historical literature, "the strongest doubts about the deference theory center around the claim that most colonials shared the same values and assumptions concerning the proper workings of American social and political institutions" (1970, 810). Paraphrasing Lemisch, Kirby states that "ideas of social and political deference may very well have been considered the ideal system by the leadership elites of early America, but it does not necessarily follow, that other classes, excluded from participation in this elite, accepted the same ideology" (ibid., 828–29). Once again, running through this entire literature, may be seen the influence of Geertz and Pocock.

14. Bloch shows how prophecy provided an interpretive scheme for the New England clergy with respect to its understanding of political events. She also points out how the debate over pre- versus postmillennialism took shape and what its wider implications were for the development of American religion in the nineteenth century. It is observed, for example, that "the figures most involved in issuing this [premillennialist] doctrinal challenge to the Calvinist clerical establishment were usually Baptists and Congregationalist laymen removed from the intellectual center of American theological life. The various efforts to construct a premillennial interpretation of prophecy represented a kind of rebellion against religious intellectualism which would eventually lead to the emergence of Protestant fundamentalism in the following century" (1985, 135). Bloch believes that a literalist view of the Bible had more immediate intuitive appeal to the lower orders of society in any event; to be sure, Elias Smith's vision of the Millennium is highly concrete and even materialistic in nature. Marsden reviews the implications of the post- and premillennial views and suggests that the former could be construed as having optimistic and reformist implications, whereas the latter could be relatively pessimistic and rejectionist (1980, particularly 48–55). But Bloch points out that, though this may have been the later pattern, it had not yet emerged in the period of direct concern to her, that in the 1790s, "differences between premillennialists and postmillennialists did not correspond clearly to wider progressive and fatalistic world-historical outlooks. There were still both activistic premillennialists and pessimistic postmillennialists. But beginning in the late 1780s, postmillennialists and premillennialists were becoming distinct, self-conscious groups, and this new exegetical alignment revealed an emerging an-

tagonism between different parts of the American religious community. The conflict arose from social as well as theological origins, and may even have had underlying political significance" (1985, 131–32).

15. In writing of a "paradigmatic revolution" in American political thought that took place between 1740 and 1800, Hatch draws on Pocock for his theoretical framework: "These years witnessed a fundamental reordering of values that gave a profoundly new religious significance to the function of man as citizen, to the principles governing the civil order, and to the role of nations and political kingdoms in the scheme of providential history. Far from being a process that removed the political sector from the domination of religious symbols—a plausible inference from studies that treat this period of religious history primarily in terms of the separation of church and state and the rise of religious liberty—this intellectual shift saw the expansion of New England's functional theology to include republican ideas as a primary article of faith" (1977, 11–12).

16. Here I draw upon the work of Gillian Feeley-Harnik, whose study of food symbolism in the Bible stresses the use of culinary metaphors in defining and redefining social boundaries. She sees the Christian elimination of Jewish dietary taboos as an essential aspect of Christianity's universalistic message (1982, esp. 156–64).

17. Here an essential background work on the emergence of the Separate Baptists and separation in general at the time of the awakening is Goen 1962, esp. 198–295. Also see McLoughlin 1971, 329–99. The scriptural text quoted by Smith is Numbers 23:9: "For from the top of the rocks I see him, and from the hills I behold him: lo, the people shall dwell alone, and shall not be reckoned among the nations." This is part of the sequence involving the strange story of Balaam's speaking donkey, and the request made of the prophet Balaam by the king of Moab that he curse the invading Israelites. But instead of doing this, the prophet discovers that they are God's chosen people.

18. See Fulop 1992 for a recent study of Smith that also highlights the role of *liberty* as a driving concept in his life.

1. WHEN I WAS A CHILD: FROM LYME, CONNECTICUT, TO WOODSTOCK, VERMONT

1. "If a child died, his or her existence was perpetuated indirectly, for the same forename was normally given to the next infant of the same sex, especially when the dead child carried the same name as one of the parents" (Henretta 1978, 29). This practice can be seen on Smith's mother's side of the family; one

of Irene Ransom Smith's sisters, Lydia, died when only two; the birth of another daughter shortly followed, who was again given this name. And on Smith's own side, his sister, another Lydia, was evidently named after his father's first wife, who had died without issue.

2. Daniels's 1979 book is a valuable source for the foundation and evolution of Connecticut towns from the original settlement to 1790. He traces the history of town formation, the economic basis for settlement, as well as the development of local institutions such as town government and religious societies. The general drift of his argument is the tracing of the evolution of individualistic social and economic institutions in the eighteenth century.

3. In evidence of which is a deed of gift in the Lyme Land Records dated 1712, wherein Francis Smith gives to "my well beloved son Benjamin Smith my eldest son" 43½ acres; subsequently Benjamin engaged in land transactions with his brother-in-law, George Way. Through the efforts of Edward Little, an abstract of Francis Smith's will was uncovered in the New London Public Library, including Hezekiah's receipt for his portion of the estate. The executor of the will, Francis—his father's namesake—was presumably the one endowed with land, and Hezekiah's portion perhaps was a product of the sale of part of it. Obscurities remain; Hezekiah's will has so far not been located, and so we do not know what Stephen's share and that of his brothers may have been. I cannot imagine it was large, given there were three of them still living. Hezekiah did at least have some land dealings, it being recorded that in 1743 he purchased 15 acres of "upland and fresh meadow" for £257; in early 1746 he sold land "being by estimation 30 acres" to Elijah Chadwick of Lyme for £200, this Elijah presumably being a brother or other relative of his wife, Sarah.

4. "Ransom Genealogy" (typescript by Harry B. Ransom in the Connecticut State Library, Hartford).

5. This point is reiterated in more general terms for preindustrial America as a whole in Henretta 1978, which points out the age-stratified nature of wealth distribution in the farming population, whereby "the high rate of natural increase constantly threatened to overwhelm the accumulated capital resources of many of these northern farm families." See Rutman 1977 for an account of this process in New Hampshire.

6. James Henretta points out that, contrary to those who have seen such frontier farmers as economic individualists, in fact many social constraints of a familial and economic nature were inhibiting the development of a market orientation. As the career of the Smith family in Vermont shows: "Work was arranged along familial lines rather than controlled communally or through a wage system. This apparently simple organizational fact was a crucial determinant of the historical consciousness of this farming population. For even as the

family gave symbolic meaning and emotional significance to subsistence activities, its own essence was shaped by the character of the productive system. The agricultural family remained an extended lineal one; each generation lived in a separate household, but the character of production and inheritance linked these conjugal units through a myriad of legal, moral, and customary bonds." "The lineal family—not the conjugal unit and certainly not the unattached individual—thus stood at the center of economic and social existence in northern agricultural society in pre-industrial America" (Henretta 1978, 21, 32).

7. The general land quality in Lyme is among the poorest in Connecticut, achieving a productivity rating of only 2 out of a possible maximum of 12. Fully 75 percent of its land is listed as "very stony or mountainous," 15 percent of "hilly land of light-textured rapidly drained glacial till soils," 5 percent of "permanently wet muck," and only 5 percent of the most agriculturally desirable "valley land, level surface, of medium-textured soils over sand or gravel." By these reckonings only about one-fourth of Lyme's land has any agricultural potential to speak of (Daniels 1979, 186–90).

8. The area west of the Connecticut River was then under New York jurisdiction, which probably accounts for Apthorp's involvement.

9. The record of this transaction may be found in the Woodstock Town Hall.

10. "The Reminiscences of Daniel Ransom" (typescript in the Library of the Vermont Historical Society, Montpelier).

11. "In South Woodstock, for example, Stephen Smith, a pioneer farmer, tanned hides, taught his wife and children to make shoes, and had his eldest son Elias trained as a carpenter. He traded leather goods and his son's labor for help in clearing and fencing his land, for construction of a bark roof for his log cabin, and for flour after his first harvest fell short. Other neighbors contributed to the local economy by building furniture, framing houses, forging tools, loaning breeding stock, or repairing wagons and sleighs" (Roth 1987, 21).

12. Will and estate assessment recorded and preserved in the Windsor County Court House, Woodstock, Vermont.

13. "Reminiscences of Daniel Ransom." The spread of New Englanders to such places as Indiana is documented in Rosenberry 1962, which acknowledges its debt to the work of Frederick Jackson Turner and accordingly places stress on the democratic fluidity of frontier institutions.

14. Land transaction records in the Woodstock Town Hall (vol. 6, p. 149).

15. Abner recounted, for example, "My father's was the first family that moved into the town; it was therefore entirely a wilderness, excepting a small house spot, where the trees were cleared away, together with a few other trees such as were suitable for erecting a sort of shelter, which was called a log

house. It was in the month of March when my father and family arrived at our new habitation. Our house was erected without either plank, joist, boards, chingles, stone, brick, nails or glass; but was built wholly of logs, bark, boughs and wooden pegs in the room of nails. The snow then was about four feet deep, and the weather extremely cold; and many trees within reach of the house; we were two miles also, from neighbors. We were favored, however, with warm clothing, and solid provision, and enough of it; although our house and furniture, were not quite so delicate as some. The great plenty of wood which was nigh, was easily collected into a large heap before one end of the house, (the greater part of which was open) and set on fire; thus it was kept day and night, until the weather grew warm. What little household furniture we had in our new habitation, was drawn two miles on hand-sleds, by men on snow-shoes. This made a path sufficiently hard for my mother, and such of the children as were not able to assist in drawing the hand-sleds, to follow after. The object which stimulated my father to move at this period was, that he might make sugar on his own land; which was done by extracting sap from maple trees, and boiling it into sugar. This must be done in the months of March and April" (Jones 1842, 10–11).

16. According to Baldwin's memoirs, "In the latter part of 1781 I was baptized by the Rev. Elisha Ransom, then of Woodstock, Vt. This was a very trying, but on the whole a very joyful day to me. . . . When the day arrived, my mind was exceedingly dark; I thought that I should not be able to satisfy any one, that I had experienced a change of heart. . . . But as I had opened my mouth to the Lord, I dared not go back. During most of the public exercise, my mind remained still dark; but the preacher in addressing the audience, asked them this question: 'Have you not love enough to follow your blessed Lord into his watery grave?' This expression touched my heart, and in a moment I was bathed in tears; and thought I could say: 'Lord I will follow thee, whithersoever thou goest: through floods and flames, if thou willest me to go.' The dark cloud which had hung over me, was now entirely dispersed. I enjoyed great freedom in relating my experience of God's dealing with my soul. We all repaired to a pleasant river, to attend the solemn ordinance" (Chessman 1826, 20).

17. The work cited is the first edition of Smith's autobiography, with a later edition appearing in 1840. The two agree in most specifics, the 1840 edition departing from the original mostly with regard to changes wrought by time, people who have died since 1816, etc. There are a few more interesting differences however. For example, the 1840 reference to Baldwin (73–74) deletes reference to *pagan priests*, presumably out of respect for the departed.

18. According to Marini, "This massive encounter with the frontier was

unprecedented in New England and American history, and it introduced grave problems of social and cultural fragmentation to a generation already bent on establishing national and regional autonomy." Furthermore, "The hill town was a distinctly pluralistic social, cultural, and political entity from the beginnings of settlement and remained so through the early nineteenth century" (1982, 5, 29).

19. Roth summarizes the syncretism as follows: "People had become less willing to submit to discipline, to accept compromise, and to defer to authority. The valley's settlers were not as yet individualists, because they still denied the individual's right to place his or her interests, values, or beliefs above those of the community; but they had moved in the direction of individualism, by becoming more assertive of their rights and more accepting of the independence of others in moral, spiritual, and political matters. The social and political antagonisms that arose on the frontier had also made people less willing to live by a common communal and political ideal. The valley's settlers had not become pluralists or true partisans, but they had also moved in the direction of pluralism and partisanship, by championing particular views of what Christian communities and republican polities should be and by recognizing that denominational and party strife would persist, even though they detested that strife, denied their own contributions to it, and refused to confront the differences in experience, sensibility, and social condition that lay behind it" (1987, 78–79). Both Marini and Roth cite Henretta's influential essay (1978) on rural New England *mentalité*.

20. The country that Smith passed through on his 1787 trip to Lyme had been the center of Shays' Rebellion just the year before. As a result of legal action taken on behalf of Boston merchants to collect debts from a number of local farmers, Daniel Shays, a Scots-Irish Presbyterian from the Massachusetts hills east of the Connecticut, found himself leader of a revolt focused on disrupting foreclosure proceedings in local courts. The disturbance was put down by militia when the rebels attempted to seize arms from the Springfield Armory. Elias Smith makes no mention of this incident in his autobiography or, to my knowledge, anywhere else. Alexander Hamilton, however, noted it well and made such episodes a part of his argument for a strong national government and consequently for ratification of the Constitution.

21. "The sectarians constituted a typical and representative socioeconomic group in rural New England. They were not dispossessed, nor were they socially ostracized. They occupied a normal range of incomes and participated in town offices commensurate with their class. The constituency attracted by sectarianism was typical of hill country citizens in its social, political, economic, and religious characteristics" (Marini 1982, 95, 100).

22. "Wightman took the negative on three grounds: 1. Because there is no precept nor precedent for so doing in the New Testament. 2. Because so to do is what we would not be done unto ourselves. 3. Because the Lord requires only volunteers and not forced men in his service." Wightman, a descendant of English dissenters, had come to Groton from Rhode Island, and his church is remembered as having been "the first attempt to establish a departure from the Congregational church order in Connecticut." The next Baptist church to be formally organized, in 1726, was in New London, a town in close proximity to East Lyme (Jones 1861, 262). See also Bushman 1967, 165.

23. Following this episode Backus became convinced that he had a call to preach the gospel himself.

24. Joining the Baptists was the only way in which these separates could legitimately claim membership in religious societies already legally exempt from the taxes levied to support orthodoxy in the form of the Congregationalist pastorate. "The larger part of the Separate churches became Baptists, not because they preferred distinctive Baptist principles, but because the Baptists were Congregational in government, and for the most part in doctrine, and they, by calling themselves Baptist, could escape the oppression of double taxation. Indeed, the formation of those Separate churches, and the earlier growth of the Baptist denomination in this state, was little more than a practical protest against the prevalent violation of religious liberty" (Dutton 1861, 123).

25. Mack's own church went through upheavals on this score. As McLoughlin reports (Backus 1979, 3:1322), "The church had been founded as a Separate church in 1749 but was reorganized on open-communion, Baptist principles in 1752 under Elder Ebenezer Mack. Mack came to believe in closed communion and was dismissed in 1770. Elder Joshua Morse of Montville, Conn., tried to persuade the church to adopt closed communion, but the majority adhered to open communion and chose Jason Lee as its pastor on this basis."

26. Handwritten notebook concerning the history of the Second Church in Lyme (in possession of the New England Historical Genealogical Society, Boston). McLoughlin has explained the appeal of the New Light preachers as follows: "The New Lights preached a folk form of Calvinism and their preachers were the folk artists of their day. They brought the rarified intellectualism of Puritanism down to the level of the common man. This was the contribution of the frontier to the development of the American pietistic temper—fervent, anti-intellectual, popular, egalitarian, but often eccentric and flamboyant. . . . The New Light experimental rationale for Calvinism gave the common man knowledge through experience, and pietistic faith gave him the

sublime confidence to trust his experience against the traditions, learning, and laws of his 'betters'" (1967, 45).

27. An opinion expressed, for example, in Jonathan Edwards's *History of the Works of Redemption,* pertaining to the objections raised by Satan to the work of the Reformation via the instigation of "corrupt opinions": "The first opposition of this kind was by the sect of the *Anabaptists,* which began about four or five years after the Reformation itself. This sect, as it first appeared in Germany, was vastly more extravagant than the present Anabaptists are in England. They held a great many exceeding corrupt opinions. One tenet of theirs was, That there ought to be no civil authority, and that it was lawful to rebel against it. And on this principle they refused to submit to magistrates, or any human laws; and gathered together in vast armies, to defend themselves against their civil rulers, and put all Germany into an uproar, and so kept it for some time" (1968, 219). Edwards then follows with a description of *enthusiasts, Socinians, Arminians,* and *Arians*—all of which Elias Smith was accused in one way or another of being. On attitudes toward the Anabaptists that spilled over onto indigenous New Lights and Baptists, see also McLoughlin 1967, 58–59.

28. Lee was the son of Joseph Lee, who "was ordained over a Separate church in Lyme, Conn., . . . in 1752. Apparently a large part of the membership of this church was Indian. The church became embroiled in the question of antipedobaptism and open communion in 1753 and broke up" (Backus 1979, 1:288 n. 3). As for Jason Lee's abilities, Backus reported that after Lee was ordained pastor of this church, he "has had great success therein" (Backus 1871, 519).

29. See also Dana 1980, 37; Davis 1913, 378. Elisha Ransom was associated with Backus in the cause of liberty and was characterized by the latter as "not only . . . a successful preacher of the gospel, but also has earnestly contended for Christian liberty, against the ministerial tyranny which has been carried into that wilderness, from the States of Connecticut and the Massachusetts." Ransom carried the fight to the Vermont Assembly in 1795 in the form of a petition against public support of the clergy (Backus 1871, 548; McLoughlin 1971, 2:803–7).

30. It is reported that Grow's church in Connecticut disintegrated after his departure—"under another pastorate [it] was by a majority of the members wrecked and destroyed . . . , through the application of the early conception of what constituted true church fellowship and responsibility." About Grow, the family genealogist suggests that "he was more sinned against than sinning seems a justified inference. The puritanical concepts of right and wrong, and of church discipline of those days, are not the accepted canons of today" (Davis 1913, 38). Elisha Ransom had also been involved in doctrinal controver-

sy back in Sutton, Massachusetts, where he had been a church elder before departing for Vermont. He appears to have been defending the orthodox Calvinist position against the Arminian views of the minister of the Sutton Baptist Church, which subsequently split over the issue with Ransom emerging as preacher to "his own faction" (Backus 1979, 3:1354 n. 2).

31. Whereby, as Harry Stout says, "revolution, republican ideology, pure churches, and future millennium all blended in New England preaching, supplying continuity in the midst of change and imparting to the transforming events of 1776 a familiar, atavistic quality" (1986, 310). Stout, however, also points out that most sermons of the New England Congregational clergy were, unless special circumstances intervened, really quite mundane.

32. An American edition of this work was printed in 1796 by a printer whom Elias Smith would use for some of his own publications—Henry Ranlet of Exeter, New Hampshire. First printed in 1720, twenty thousand copies Boston's *Fourfold State* had been, by the account of the author's grandson, exported from Scotland to America by 1784. Boston (1677–1732) himself was a Scots Calvinist minister remembered for his "deeply religious life and exemplary parochial labours." The author of his biographical sketch in *The Dictionary of National Biography* states that at the time of writing, Boston's *Fourfold State* was still "a popular classic of the Calvinistic theology" (A.G. 1963).

33. According to Morgan, "Some narratives were written down. . . . A number of these have survived, and they demonstrate clearly the familiarity of the narrators with the morphology of conversion, a familiarity produced, no doubt, by a great many sermons on the subject. The pattern is so plain as to give the experiences the appearance of a stereotype: first comes a feeble and false awakening to God's commands and a pride in keeping them pretty well, so also must backsliding. Disappointments and disasters lead to other fitful hearkenings to the word. Sooner or later true legal fear or conviction enables the individual to see his hopeless and helpless condition and to know that his own righteousness cannot save him, that Christ is his only hope. Thereafter comes the infusion of saving grace, sometimes but not always so precisely felt that the believer can state exactly when and where it came to him. A struggle between faith and doubt ensues, with the candidate careful to indicate that his assurance has never been complete and that his sanctification has been much hampered by his own sinful heart" (1963, 69, 91). For further details on these narratives themselves, and in what way they differed between England and America, see Caldwell 1983, a work also drawing on Morgan's ideas concerning the morphology of conversion.

34. "The Lord God makes the creature a new creature, as the goldsmith melts down the vessel of dishonour, and makes it a vessel of honour. It is a su-

pernatural change; he that is born again, is born of the Spirit. In regeneration nature itself is changed, and we become partakers of the divine nature; and this must needs be a supernatural change. How can we that are dead in trespasses and sins, renew ourselves, more than a dead man can raise himself out of his grave? Who but the sanctifying Spirit of *Christ,* can form *Christ* in a soul, changing it into the same image? Who but the Spirit of sanctification can give the new heart?" (Boston 1796, 98, 148–49).

35. "It has been a general and true observation, that with the reformation of these realms, *ignorance* has gradually vanished at the increase of *learning* amongst us who take the word of God for a lanthorn [*sic*] to our feet, and a light to our paths. Thus, they who grop'd their way to virtue and knowledge in the days of darkness and implicit zeal, were taught little more than to mumble over a few prayers by heart, and never called upon to read, much less permitted to inquire into the truth of what they professed. Since the sun-shine of the *gospel of Jesus Christ* has risen amongst us; since we are loosed from the bonds of ignorance and superstition; since every *protestant* believes it to be his duty to promote *christian knowledge;* certain it will be confessed that all improvements in learning ought to be encouraged; and consequently that they deserve our particular regard, who study to make the first steps thereof firm and easy. For human prudence teacheth, *That* a good beginning is the most reasonable prospect of a good *ending*" (Dilworth 1789, i).

36. As Smith remembered, "[When] I first saw a dictionary, [I] did not know at first what it was designed for. The occasion of my seeing it was this: two men had been at meeting, and heared the minister use the word *canticles.* One asked the other the meaning of the word; 'get the dictionary, said the other, that will tell you.' He took Entick's dictionary and soon found the word with its meaning. It appeared strange to me that the word used by the minister should be in that little book. This led me to inquire into the nature of it; and how a word could be found; and was surprised when told that almost all words we used, with their meaning could readily be found there. Some may think strange that a person fourteen or fifteen years old should be so ignorant of a book now so common. Such books were not then in common use as now; and further, every person is ignorant of that he never heard of. About all the books I had ever known to that time, were the Primer, Dilworth's *Spelling Book,* Watts's *Psalms and Hymns,* the New Testament and Bible. These were about all the books my father owned, and these commonly were the library of a baptist minister in those days" (42).

37. Watts also staked out the common position of antiauthoritarian dissent in his claim that "when we have arrived at manly age, there is no person on earth, no set or society of men whatsoever, that have power and authority

given them by God, the creator and governor of the world, absolutely to dictate to others their opinions and practices in moral and religious life" (1821, 240).

38. Smith's own experience wherein he saw the Lamb on Mount Zion and saw the world at large in a new light thereafter mirrors Edwards's empiricist psychology of conversion. Following Locke, Edwards stressed the relation between thought and sensory perception; if there is a radical restructuring perception itself, as in required in conversion, then this must be due not to a change in the world but to a reconstruction of the soul that perceives it.

39. Edwards continued, "There are two ways wherein the scriptures give account of the events by which the work of redemption is carried on: one is by *history,* and another is by *prophecy*: and in one or the other of these ways we have in scripture an account of how the work of redemption is carried on from the beginning to the end. Although the scriptures do not contain a proper *history* of the whole, yet the whole chain of great events, by which this affair has both been carried on from the commencement to the finishing of it, is found either in *history* or *prophecy*. And it is to be observed, that where the scripture is wanting in one of these ways, it is made up in the other" (1968, 97).

40. This transformation in the attitudes of the American clergy toward the French Revolution is documented in Nash 1965. By 1795, "the French Revolution, so widely celebrated for five years and more, had become the object of scorn and hatred among the American clergy. The timing of the clergy's change in its view of the French Revolution makes it clear that the change was the product not so much of the drift of events in France as of movements—ideological, political, and social—at home. Of chief importance were the rise of militant deism, the threat of social disorder, and the growing intensity of national political issues. It was perhaps the first of these, the threat to religious orthodoxy, that figured most prominently" (Nash 1965, 399).

41. Smith had in mind certain specific signs: "View the nations of the earth; see their distress, by reason of the present wars, famines, pestilences, earthquakes, and other troubles; see the perplexities of many, on account of the present situation of the seas, fearing their property will fall into the hands of others, by reason of the commotion among the European powers" (1808a, 86).

2. THE FIRE NEXT TIME: RELIGION AND REPUBLICANISM

1. Smith subsequently learned that one of the young men died blaspheming God, and the other backslid from the faith for a time, only in later life to be reunited in Christ. In the 1840 edition the dream vision would have

appeared in the text just after passages concerning his doubts concerning salvation, which conclude as follows: "One thing dwelt much on my mind, which was, that my experience was not so great to me as others was to them, and was often led to say, 'If I had as great an evidence as such ones, my doubts would all be gone forever'" (68).

2. A commentator on the newspapers of the time states that "most publishers appeared to feel they had an obligation to elevate their readers culturally or morally, as well as to present them with helpful facts and to recount recent occurrences. Thus the owner of the *Vermont Journal* announced that he was printing serially the life of Baron Frederick Tronck at the request of some subscribers but that no important news would be omitted, since he "was fond of making his paper *useful as well as entertaining*" (Stewart 1969, 20).

The Ransom-Spooner family connection may extend back to Connecticut, where Alden Spooner's father was a carpenter and builder in New London (which is immediately adjacent to East Lyme), and Spooner himself served as printer's apprentice. In addition to his newspaper venture Spooner was made official state printer of Vermont in 1783. He published the *Journal* until 1817, and a historian of Vermont newspapers characterized it as "until 1808 a newspaper fairly representative of the politics of the Jeffersonian Republicans without being violently partisan" (Wardner 1931, 20). After 1808 Spooner apparently switched to moderate Federalist sentiments. In the less partisan times of 1783, issues of the paper that ended up in Smith's school windows were of a more high-minded character, mixing reports from Vermont and from the nation. Elias Smith and Alden Spooner were certainly in contact with one another, since Spooner is shown as one of Smith's distributors for the latter's *Sermons, Containing an Illustration of the Prophecies* (1808a).

3. As seen in Chapter 1 above, he ended his material involvement with it in 1811, when he sold off his portion of his patrimony from Stephen Smith.

4. The problem arose over where in town a new church building should be constructed: "opinions being divided according to the residence of the members, as *they* were located north or south; and so vehement were those at the south part of the town in their desire to have the house located there, that they held *ex parte* meetings, declared themselves *the* church, cited the Rev. J. Peak to appear before them and resign his office of solicitor of funds, and on his neglecting their citation, proceeded to the extremity of *excommunicating* him for the Christian privileges of the church; all of which proceedings were disallowed and disapproved by a council subsequently called to settle the difficulties which had arisen, and assist in healing the lamentable divisions in the church" (Mrs. E. V. Smith 1854, 312–13).

5. "Besides his labours in this ministry, he has continued more or less

through life, to exercise the function of his medical profession. . . . The calls of his profession, and the extensiveness of his flock made it necessary for him almost incessantly to lead an itinerant life" (Benedict 1813, 1:320–21). See Plumer 1857, 25.

6. Schisms would also result because Jeremiah Condy, Stillman's predecessor as pastor of the First Church, was suspected of Arminian tendencies.

7. Mary's father, Josiah, lived from 1728 to 1808; her mother, Judith Tuttle Burleigh, died in 1801. Mary was the youngest of six children, five girls and a boy (Burleigh 1880). The Josiah Burleigh home, in which Mary was born, still stands outside of Newmarket (Philip B. Mitchell, personal communication; also see Getchell 1984, 168).

8. This was quite a typical type of schism, a pattern often followed when unitary New England communities, in which the church and the town were originally coterminous, subdivided into parishes according to the geographic distribution of the population.

9. Salisbury Baptist Society's Book of Records, in possession of Salisbury Historical Society. I was shown this book and the old Baptist church through the kindness of Mr. Dana Parks, a genealogist and member of the society.

10. Daniel was named in honor of Daniel Drown of Portsmouth, who later was involved in Elias's conversion to Thomsonianism (358).

11. Elias himself reported on the causes of disaffection with the Congregational pastor, who was, Smith says, "as poor a speaker as ever ascended the pulpit stairs. They had for several years labored hard to get rid of him, but he still remained among them. I was told, that when the people complained to him of the badness of his voice, he said the *sounding board* was too high, and that if the sounding board was lowered, he could speak better. The moderator introduced the subject of altering the sounding board. One shrewed [*sic*] old man, rose up instantly, and said, "Mr. Moderator, I move, that the sound *under* the board be altered first." This prevented any further proceedings as to the sounding board, and after that, the great study was how to get rid of the sound under the board" (244).

12. In the 1780s Green had been much involved in cases pertaining to the rights of dissenters to claim exemption from sustaining the establishment and so was already well acquainted with the legal issues involved (McLoughlin 1971, 1:642–46).

13. The Woburn Baptist Society apparently had rather a grandiose idea of what proper worship should be like, as expressed in the way they renovated their first crude church building: "which they did by ceiling and plastering it, and putting in pews, which were square and pannelled, with the seats made to turn up in prayer time; there were two blocks of these, making in all thirty-five

pews, and an aisle running up the middle, and another round the walls. They also put up a gallery, which was reached from a porch in the west end, where also was the main entrance. The pulpit was very high, with a sounding-board over it, as was the fashion in those days; and was reached by two short flights of stairs. In front of the pulpit was the Deacon's Seat, where these elders in the church sat facing the congregation, and apparently supporting the minister, and overlooking the flock."

14. This process began around 1786, when Jones came to a conviction, while out working with his hoe, that he was utterly lost: "it appeared to me that my soul was eternally undone. It came upon me with such force, that I firmly believed it, and now for the first time, I was entirely deprived of *hope*. I really thought that I had begun my eternal, endless, despairing misery" (1842, 18–19).

15. "The first thing that struck me, was the name of our denomination, viz.: BAPTIST. When I had searched the New Testament through, to my great astonishment, I could not find the denomination of baptist mentioned in the whole of it. I only found John the baptist, or baptiser; he is the only one called a baptist in all the New Testament. Christ did not call his disciples baptists; the christian churches in the apostles' time were not called baptists. Christ called his disciples brethren and friends. In the time of the apostles, the disciples were first called CHRISTIANS at Antioch. After this examination, I denied the name of baptist, and so I have continued to do unto this day. I was then willing to own the names disciple, friend, and Christian, unto which I still hold" (Jones 1842, 27–28).

16. A later memorialist also made the same claim at the Rhode Island and Massachusetts Christian Conference in 1861: "Abner Jones . . . gathered the first church of the Christian Denomination in New England" (Hathaway 1861, 5).

17. Clearly the two men already knew each other, for Smith reports that he and Jones had met as early as 1794, while Elias was still preaching as a Baptist in Salisbury (233).

18. See Taylor 1990 for more on Stinchfield's activities in Maine; Taylor, however, associates Stinchfield with the Free-Will Baptists, though in fact he was by then a Christian.

19. As the Free-Will confession of faith says under the heading of Atonement, "As sin cannot be pardoned without a sacrifice, and the blood of beasts could never actually wash away sin, Christ gave his life a sacrifice for the sins of the world, and thus made salvation possible for all men" (General Conference 1848, 48–49). Randall's theology and the social roots of the Free-Will movement are systematically discussed in Marini 1982.

20. As Donald Meyer put it: "The God who had divided mankind arbi-

trarily into the saved and the damned was now superseded by a God whose attribute was less power than love. The governmental theory of the atonement . . . supposed that the sacrifice of Jesus was required to satisfy God and win God to men. But it evolved painlessly in the early nineteenth century into the 'moral influence' theory whereby the sacrifice of Jesus became the means, not of winning God to men, but of winning men to God; all who could learn to love through the example of Jesus were saved" (1963, 76). The western Christians under Barton Stone trod the same path. Stone's memoirs show that his internal wranglings over the atonement were decisive in shifting his theological emphasis away from the Presbyterianism of his upbringing toward Arminianism and the doctrine of free grace (Rogers 1847, 56–60).

21. As a later more formal statement of Christian belief put it: "Whenever the Father and Son are said to be *one*, and also in that passage that says the Father, the Son and the Holy Ghost are one, the connection shows clearly that it does not mean one person, or one being; but union; union in testimony, union in nature, union in action, and perfect oneness, without the least possibility of the contrary. The oneness of the Father and Son may be illustrated by the union of a man and his wife; and by the union of all christians; and indeed Christ prayed to the Father that his disciples might be *one*, even as he and the Father are *one*" (Shaw 1847, 13).

22. Just so with Abner Jones, who explicitly "rejected the Hopkinsian views of *future* punishment, viz.:—and endless punishment for finite sins" (1842, 35).

23. Conforti (1977) has pointed out the complex social gospel actually advanced by Hopkins, and its emphasis on communitarian values as opposed to individual spiritual enlightenment. He points out that earlier scholars have maintained that the abstruse quality of Hopkins's theology served in the end mainly to alienate the laity and missed the great popularity of this 'New Divinity' particularly in rural areas keen on maintaining what was taken to be the values of the old New England Way. That may be so among those who remained orthodox Congregationalists. Radicals such as Smith, however, who in the end dismissed *all* philosophical theology, saw reasonings such as Hopkins's as totally inimical to true scriptural understanding. See also Meyer 1963, 77–78. As documented in McLoughlin 1965, Hopkinsian theology and Federalist politics were seen by Republicans as going hand in glove during the affair over the state assumption of the charter of Dartmouth College.

24. The southern Christians and their northern compatriots exchanged letters about their shared beliefs in the *Herald of Gospel Liberty*. See issues of May 12, June 23, and July 21, 1809. See also MacClenny 1910, 156–57. Some of the defectors from the Methodist connection came to be known as Republican

Methodists because of their antiepiscopal views on the nature of church organization.

25. Hughes and Allen characterize the Christians of the West as "a people so drunk on the wine of freedom that they spurned history with all its inherent constraints and limitations. They supposed instead that they might live their lives in those majestic temples that bracketed human time—the primordial age of the gods and the millennial dawn. Organizationally and theologically vacuous, they vigorously rejected the claims of tradition as 'inventions of men,' resisted structure of all kinds, and lived in simple faith that the approaching new world would both consummate and vindicate their radical insistence on a free church of God" (1988, 115).

26. For the general climate of the times in relation to the anxieties bred by republican thought, see Howe 1967.

27. The issue that animated Elias Smith most personally in these early years, and bedeviled the politics of New Hampshire for years thereafter, was that of state-sanctioned religious taxation. William McLoughlin (1965) notes the frequency with which cases came to the courts over just who should be exempt from such taxation on the grounds that they supported a dissenting church, and the degree to which partisan politics came to be mixed up with such matters. See also L. W. Turner 1962, 75.

28. This conclusion is particularly evident in Smith's explicitly political discourses (1805e; 1809b; 1810).

3. FREE RADICALS: FEDERALISTS, REPUBLICANS, AND THE SECOND AWAKENING

1. "One has the sense of a genuine folk movement rather than a sudden enthusiasm whipped up by the clergy, the function of the clergy being rather to guide and consolidate that which already existed in rather amorphous form" (Birdsall 1970, 355; see also Shiels 1980, 412).

2. "Possessing one of the most beautiful localities, of intermingled land and water, its advantages of harbor and fishing-ground presented an alluring prospect to persons wishing to gain fortunes and to enjoy life. A well-authenticated anecdote shows that the inhabitants themselves would not hypocritically appropriate to themselves the praise of being a religious society. A reverend divine, preaching to them against the depravity of the times said, 'You have forsaken the pious habits of your forefathers, who left the ease and comfort the possessed in their native land, and came to this howling wilderness, to

enjoy the exercise of their religion and a pure worship.' One of the congregation rose and said, 'Sir, you entirely mistake the matter: our ancestors did not come here on account of their religion, but to fish and trade'" (Lee 1851, 37).

3. According to Peabody 1857, Sandeman's "leading dogma was, that justifying faith is a mere intellectual belief of the truth, and that this belief is to him who cherishes it a sufficient ground of hope, without any work wrought upon the soul by the Divine Spirit, and without any of the fruits of an active piety. He went so far as to cast reproach upon all emotions of love for God and for Christ, as but another form of self-love, called forth solely by the sense and the expectation of benefit."

4. Buckminster's successor commented that "he was a firm believer and an able advocate of the great doctrines of the gospel,—doctrines, which were ever maintained by this church" (Putnam 1835). At Yale, Buckminster seems to have been on the side of a conservative old guard increasingly out of touch with student demand (Ellis 1979, 166).

5. These records are in the possession of the Portsmouth Athenaeum (manuscript S.90) and were shown to me through the courtesy of the Athenaeum's director, Richard Candee, with the help of the archivist, Kevin Shupe. The records are somewhat fragmentary. They begin in 1803 and run through April 1804, at which point they jump to 1808 and continue to 1810, whereon they jump again to 1813. A few entries appear in this year, then the records skip on to 1815. The entries become increasingly sketchy as to details of church business around 1809 but fortunately are full of detail in the earlier years. The book ends in 1824.

6. The predominance of women (64 percent of the membership) was not unusual for the churches of the day.

7. Records of the First Church of Christ in Portsmouth, vol. 2, p.501 (New Hampshire State Historical Society Library, Concord).

8. As to the question of mode, Smith—citing Isaac Watts's *Logic*—responded, "It is said by many, that the *mode of baptism* is wholly a matter of indifference; but the person who affects this, must be either ignorant of the nature of *mode*, or mean to deceive others in saying so; for baptism depends wholly on the mode, take that away, and there is nothing left of baptism but the name" (Smith 1807b, 10).

9. "We know that by holiness here, cannot be intended real, positive, internal holiness, for Abraham did not communicate this either to his natural, or to his spiritual seed; nor can any parent, to whatever degree his faith is increased, communicate grace to his children; being born of the flesh, they are flesh; and will be so till they are born of the spirit. But Abraham did commu-

nicate to his posterity a relative and federal holiness, they had a right to the sign of relationship to God, and to the title of a holy nation, and peculiar people. And every believing parent does derive to his children a relative federal holiness, a right to the external privileges of the covenant; to be acknowledged in their relation to God; to be admitted into his family, by the door which he has opened" (Buckminster 1803c, 22–23, 49–50).

10. Kaplanoff has called attention to the political implications of New Hampshire sermonizing in this period, stating that on the Federalist side "the standard form of their campaign was the sermon. . . . Federalists addressed themselves to general principles not specific issues—but the electioneering implications were obvious. Buckminster's sermon on Washington's death was only one element of a body of 'Federal piety,' that had a political as well as a religious import for its audience. The doctrine the Federalists propounded was part of the Calvinist tradition of the first Puritans. Although they did not use theological terms in their electioneering, New Hampshire Federalists addressed themselves to the same issues their forefathers had and reached the same conclusions. The administration supporters had two basic concerns— maintaining the proper relationship between God and society and keeping man in his proper place in the world" (1968, 6).

11. I thank Lisa Compton, the director of the Old Colony Historical Society of Taunton, for providing a copy of this covenant.

12. Here Andros argues against Worcester, who had maintained that the Son could have been with the Father from all eternity and yet not be—as orthodox Trinitarians demanded—a person independent of him at the same time. As in all such cases Andros relied on what he took to be the plain word of Scripture as against the verities of human logic. Though the Trinity is a mystery, it must be accepted on faith. God would not have been constituted in such a way without purpose, and by definition it must be a good one. Andros reasoned that the doctrine of the Trinity "seems to lie at the foundation of the scheme of the redemption of sinners, is introduced into the mode in which God requires christians to worship him, and has a very powerful influence as the exciting cause of all evangelical and truly pious affections."

13. "We did not, like them, consider the existence or property, of political society, of government as infringements on the natural equality and liberty of man. It was not the liberty enjoyed when there was no king in Israel, and every one did that which was right in his own eyes, that we fought. This is not liberty, it is anarchy: it is despotism in its most frightful form" (Andros 1799, 8). Andros is referring to the book of Judges, which describes the anarchy of ancient Israel before the establishment of the kingship (see Judg. 21:25).

14. "This nation turned a deaf ear, declared against being priest-ridden, imposed silence upon their pastors at the peril of being deserted by their flocks and turned out of their livings. When the people of the United States chose this man for their chief ruler, I did at the time and do still, firmly believe that they sinned against Heaven in a grievous and aggravated manner" (Osgood 1810, 20). Calling particular attention to David Osgood, James Banner points out that this type of "jeremiad was so effective in arousing men from the 1790's on because its themes of corruption and potential destruction exactly coincided with major themes of the republican ideology which the clerics and the general public had so thoroughly assimilated. In particular, the jeremiad possessed a close affinity with the cyclical theory of history deeply imbedded within republican thought. The jeremiad assumed a process of decline, a falling off of virtue from some higher state of rectitude and religiosity. The cyclical theory assumed a similar process of decline" (1970, 33). Ruth Bloch's study of millennial themes in this period also calls attention to Osgood and to the use of the jeremiad to deliver both threat and promise in the fevered political climate of the 1790s (1985, 213).

15. For some of these references, see Harris 1811, on Matthew 24:23–25; Porter 1814a, on Jude 4; Burton 1810, on 2 Peter 2:1; and Braman 1810, on Jeremiah 14:14.

16. In any event, Elias was not disputing this point.

17. The historian of Stillman's First Church makes no mention of this controversy.

18. Paul himself left little in the way of a trail; there are no writings under his name in the National Union Catalog or Early American Imprints.

19. McLoughlin observes that in general "the Baptists of New England took conservative stands on the three principal issues concerning Blacks: social discrimination, the slave trade, and the abolition of slavery" (1971, 2:765). It is not possible to decide what actually underlay the decision to establish the African Baptist Church; perhaps the answer falls somewhere between Smith's position and that of the official church history. The creation of specifically *African* branches of established denominations was not uncommon in this period; for example, the African Methodist Episcopal (AME) Church resulted from a decision on the part of black Methodists themselves (see Butler 1990, 149).

20. The founders of what became the First Baptist Church of Boston invoked similar arguments when challenged by the orthodox ministry in 1667 to show justification for their peculiar opinions; among their reasons was a flat rejection of the logic of type and antitype (Hall 1989, 63).

4. A THIEF IN THE NIGHT: PROPHECY AND POLITICS

1. "Cunning people" existed in eighteenth-century America, just as they had in the village England documented by Keith Thomas (Butler 1990, 86–87). Samuel Thomson tapped into a local tradition of root doctoring that he glossed according to Galenic principles. Jon Butler calls specific attention to the mystical experiences of Benjamin Randal, the dreams of Elias Smith, and of course the ecstatic practices of the Shakers (ibid., 222). One could add to these practices what appears to have been the common use of the Bible as a divination device cum projective test (not an uncommon pairing from an anthropologist's point of view); when perplexed one could allow the Bible to fall open to whatever page it would—or it might fall open by accident—then exposing to view a passage resolving the current dilemma.

2. In the latter case the renegade, Jeremiah Ballard, "a very ingenious and flowery preacher," eventually went southward and, according to Randal's biographer later abandoned his extravagances. While preaching in the ironically named Unity, New Hampshire, Ballard's meetings had been characterized by "kissing, loud laughing, and screaming in meetings of worship, &c. &c."

3. The same thing happened in Kentucky after the great Cane Ridge revival of 1801 when "Christians" associated with Barton Stone fell prey to Shaker proselytism. See Conkin 1990.

4. "Many of them got their passions thus wound up, and probably lifted up in their imagination, with an expectation of going immediately into a state of outward perfection. Just at that time, the people called Shakers came along, professing to be the people that had attained to that state; upon which the Elder, and many of the members of the Louden church, joined them, and the rest were left in a scattered situation" (Buzzell 1827, 92). Andrews notes that the Shakers were often able to capitalize on the energy generated by Baptist revivalism and that their unwitting benefactor in this case was the successful preaching of Benjamin Randal (1963, 37).

5. This Smith was unrelated to Elias, nor should he be confused with the Mormon prophet Joseph Smith.

6. See also Smith, *Herald of Life and Immortality* 1, no. 4 (Oct. 1819): 130. Among other things, it was reported that Cochran claimed to be able to interpret the secrets of the Masons.

7. As Stinchfield described them, Cochranite practice resembled that of the Shakers with respect to the use of dance and music. "He has introduced among his followers a feast, which he calls the *passover*, at which they all partake, at one table, provided for the purpose, at which, large quantities of mutton, lamb, bread and wine, &c. are expended. At this feast, he has a method of

marching in a double file, consisting of a male and female, as far as the number of the males will admit, or hold out. But they pretend to have seven women to one man, in the society, alluding, as they told me, to a prophecy in Isaiah—*On that day, shall seven women take hold of one man, &c.*—In these marches, they are instructed to step by the music, as they expect soon to carry a steel sword, and walk over dead bodies. It seems their favorite amusement in this marching exercise, is a military movement, called *whipping the snake.* Cochran, with a favorite Miss, I understand, generally takes the lead in this marching business; and one of his foremost or most favored ministers, with another Miss, brings up the rear."

8. The matter of the Jews is systematically examined in Smith 1808a. "It appears to me from the present situation of things among the Turks, and Jews, that the nation of France and some leader will lead the Jews into the promised land. It is possible that Bonaparte may be the man. He has been engaged in a war against the Turks in Egypt, he has assembled the Jews in Paris, and shewed them such favours as no other king ever has since Titus led them away captive. I think it altogether likely that as a Gentile led them out of their land, (Titus the Roman), so a Gentile will be their head to lead them back. They may think the man who leads them into their land to be the Messiah. The Jews have of late endeavoured to prove that the Emperor of France is a descendant of David" (65–66).

For more on the signs of the times see *CM* 1, no. 4 (1806): 228: "As it respects the Jews, their situation is different now from what it has been for seventeen hundred years past. There are at this time great signs of their being gathered into their own land again, never more to be dispersed."

9. In citing the remarks of Increase Mather on the nature of earthquakes, van de Wetering comments that for the Puritans, "earthquakes, like all other providences, were seen to be divinely ordained as an instructive and balancing agent in the world of human beings" (1982, 434–35).

10. At this time, rather than the Fourth of July being a celebration of national unity, it was often enough given over to partisan demonstrations.

11. Minutes of Berkley Church meetings, August 2, 1816, in possession of the Old Colony Historical Society, Taunton.

12. As early as 1812 Smith reported in the *Herald* an account of the seizure of the property of one Captain Burt in lieu of the taxes he refused to pay for the support of the "town hireling"—Thomas Andros—even though Burt, according to Smith, had been for some time exempted from clerical taxation because he belonged to another denomination. After relating another such case, Elias rhetorically asked: "How contemptible must Mr. ———— [i.e., Andros] appear to all good men, while he is the cause of so much trouble, expense and

contention in the town where he lives! Instead of being a peace maker as all the ministers of Christ are; behold him the cause of strife and contention. Instead of proclaiming liberty to captives, see him the cause of making free men captives" (*HGL* 5, no. 8 [Dec. 11, 1812]: 445–46).

13. Though mainly agricultural, Dartmouth also had ocean access via its rivers.

14. See *HGL* 1, no. 1 (Sept. 1, 1808): 4; no. 3 (Sept. 29, 1808): 11–12; *CM* 1, no. 4 (1806): 241.

15. See also Smith 1840, 310–12; *CM* 1, no. 7 (1807): 295–97.

16. The dateline here must be 1825 because the roll does not identify the specific year in which members joined before this time.

17. In a few cases place of residence at death suggests a permanent affiliation to the towns of New Bedford and Fall River rather than to the agricultural countryside; but perhaps this was an aspect of the life cycle.

18. The information in this section was compiled from Andrews 1880 and 1899 and from the researches of Lisa Compton in the probate records of Bristol County.

19. The church roll and other material pertaining to what became the First Christian Church of Boston was photocopied by the Latter Day Saints and may be found on film reel 0856700; my thanks to the Family Research Centre of Burnaby, British Columbia, for their help in gaining access to this material. The pattern of new admissions is as follows: one was added in 1806, four in 1807, nine in 1808, two in 1809, three in 1811, two in 1814, and one in 1815. A new surge began in 1820, when twelve were added (eleven of these were women), thirty-two in 1821 (all but one were women), eleven in 1822 (nine women), thirteen in 1823 (nine women), and nine in 1824 (six women). The predominance of women in these later years is tantalizing but unexplained.

20. I owe this information to Anne Rose (personal communication).

21. There was a burst of "exclusions" in 1808; two were excluded as early as 1805.

22. The *Advocate* opposed William Plumer in his reelection bid in 1817 because he had appointed Federalist judges to the bench; as Plumer's son recalled, "This factious opposition made, however, little impression on the public mind, beyond the disgust excited by the violence of its abuse, and the manifest falsehood and injustice of its charges" (Plumer 1857, 460).

23. It later resumed its former name.

24. "Those who left the old church in this town joined with others from Hampton, Kensington, and Seabrook, and formed a new society called the Christian Baptist. Mr. William Brown was one of the most active and earnest promoters of the new church, and acted as its clerk for more than thirty years

after its formation, until the society built its new house, when Mr. Brown left and became identified with the Calvin Baptist Society" (Brown 1900, 92). See Lawrence 1856, 80.

25. Austin specifically identified Osgood as a bad example of the uses currently being made of Fast and Thanksgiving sermons, in which "politics, instead of religion, has generally been the theme for contemplation," and in which what should be solemn holy days have been converted "to days of strife . . . by the disgusting conduct and political dogmas of a vindictive bigot" (1803, 58, 76–77).

26. Smith was not alone in these sentiments, which (for example) were echoed by a correspondent writing from Gorham, Maine: "I declare, that I have no fellowship with sending young men to college, with a view of learning them to preach, who serve the devil while they are at college, and then come out into the world with a profession of sanctity, and pretending to be ministers of the gospel, while they are strangers and enemies to the truth, and I solemnly protest against it. Neither have I any fellowship with making a bargain to preach for money, or hiring out to preach by the day, or by the month, or by the year—nor with having a written form to read, and calling it preaching. Moreover I declare, and solemnly affirm, that I heartily believe that many people are deceived & most wickedly imposed upon by such men" (*HGL* 3, no. 63 [Jan. 18, 1811]: 252).

27. "Before this sermon was printed, there was a cry in Boston, which appeared to me to resemble that at Ephesus, with a few exceptions. The cry seemed to be, 'great is the Calvinism of Boston.' Mr. B. publicly opposed me in the vestry, to the joy of the wicked, and the grief of the righteous" (Smith 1805d, 4).

28. See Smith 1840, 308, for another account of this affair, taken nearly verbatim from the *Magazine*.

29. Smith reproduced this decision in the *Herald* on October 1, 1813.

30. Records of the Central Baptist Church, 1826–78, in possession of the Portsmouth Athenaeum (ms. 20).

5. PREPARE YE THE WAY: SMITH AS CHRISTIAN COMMUNICATOR

1. Smith defended Jefferson by reprinting in the *Herald* several letters pertaining to the infidelity issue that had appeared in the *Boston Independent Chronicle* in 1804, including one from the president to the two publishers of a biography of Jesus. As did Jefferson, Smith tried to "purify" Christianity by di-

vesting it of spiritualizing interpretations whenever possible, claiming that these all were later human innovations.

2. The fact that Smith disavowed cathechisms as "the works of men" and yet produced something very like one himself was noted by his most systematic critic: "Though professedly opposed to creeds, he endeavours, indirectly, to introduce his books, among his disciples, to occupy the same place that confessions of faith do, among christian communities. And it will be found, that his votaries pay as much regard to those crudities, as most christians do to the subordinate standards of their respective communities. Of his 'Age of Inquiry,' a scurrilous invective against every thing that bears the image of truth or order, he speaks thus: 'I do not recommend this little book to you as a rule; but as an index pointing to the rule Christ has given.' It is he says, 'calculated for the benefit of the rising generation in leading them into the truth—Let them read it *instead* of the catechisms'" (McMaster 1815, 99).

3. "'The Age of Inquiry' and similar publications of Elias Smith, an illiterate but cunning missionary of Socianism, should have preceded the deistical works of Thomas Paine, in order to give them their full effect" (McMaster 1815, 7).

4. See *HGL* 5, no. 123 (May 14, 1813): 489–91. The passage involved in entitled "Monarchy and Hereditary Succession."

5. For example, "The dependence of salvation upon the ministry, as an appointed means, shows the divinity of the institution" (McMaster 1812, 31).

6. This hymn is also reproduced in the *HGL* 7, no. 174 (June 23, 1815): 701; and in Hatch 1989, 230. Hatch, taking note of the confrontation between Porter and the Christians, presents it as a diacritical episode defining both the ideological character of the Christian movement as well as the tactics it used to confront its opponents.

7. Martin's comment had some truth in it, at least insofar as it correctly identifies the stratum of the population that might find the Christian message most objectionable.

8. John Gilman was a "shipbuilder and sometime merchant, banker, speculator in securities and Maine lands, gentleman farmer. Gilman was a pivotal figure in the so-called 'Exeter Junto,' a little clique of conservative gentlemen, united by temperament, principle, and state patronage" (Fischer 1965, 229). For the New Hampshire political weather in 1800, Kaplanoff points out that in this election the Federalists used the specter of revolutionary France to good effect, but that in the long run it was counterproductive in that it was they, rather than the moderate New Hampshire Republicans, who came to be seen as the fanatics. His conclusion is that "the Federalists finally lost not because

their principles were unpopular; they lost because they would not address themselves to the issues at hand but insisted on making meaningless threats of anarchy and revolution" (1968, 17).

9. See McLoughlin 1971, 2:894–911; Kinney 1955, 97–110; Robinson 1968, 128–50. Smith's old associate Joseph Boodey, a former Free-Willer, gave a speech to that end in opposition to a bill that would have exempted the clergy of all recognized denominations from state taxes; though a long-time minister himself, he concluded that the pastors should be treated the same as other citizens. The bill was defeated, and exemption from civil taxes in fact was explicitly denied to *any* minister.

10. For Wilbour (spelled "Wilbur" by Smith), see "Wilbour, Isaac," 1907, 1971. Isaac Wilbour served in a variety of capacities in the government of Rhode Island in addition to his single term in Congress (1807–9), after which he failed at reelection. He became chief justice of the Rhode Island Supreme Court. His later years seem to have centered on the Friends.

11. Smith may have been right in his claim, at least to the extent that the evangelicals probably tended to be Republican in political sympathy. As William Plumer's son noted in his biography of his father, "The sectaries [i.e., the Baptists, Methodists, and Universalists] were nearly all Republicans; while the Congregationalists, especially the clergy, were generally Federalists" (Plumer 1857, 186).

12. Merritt asked of Smith: "Does the New Testament inform you that there is such a connexion between the church and state that 'a bishop over the church will lead to a king over the whole?' It is the opinion of some of the greatest divines and republicans known, that there is no such connexion and dependence of the church and state as you seem to think; and that such as contend for this supposed connexion, injure both." In the *Herald* Elias later published his parody rendition of the Methodist hierarchy:

1. I. The upper Bishop
2. WE. The under Bishop
3. US. The presiding Elders
4. THESE. The Circuit Preachers
5. THEY. The Local Preachers
6. THEM. The Class-Leaders
7. The people HAVE NO POWER.

Smith then goes on to show that this is exactly the same as the English episcopal hierarchy, with "the oppressed people" at the bottom (*HGL* 4, no. 19 [May 8, 1812]).

13. In 1931 the *Herald* merged with the *Congregationalist* at the time of the

historically ironic union of the two church bodies into the Congregational-Christian Association (Garrison and deGroot 1948, 90). For the publication history of the *Herald,* see Morrill 1911.

14. See *HGL* 2, no. 32 (Nov. 10, 1809); see Butler 1990, 222.

15. Plumer's copies of the *Herald* may be found in the library of the New Hampshire State Historical Society. See Lynn Turner 1962, no. 145, p.187. Plumer "recognized the political advantages of cultivating such Republican preachers as the zealous Elias Smith, to whose *Herald of Gospel Liberty* he subscribed. These moves brought about a final reconciliation between Plumer's religious beliefs and his politics, making him henceforward an unwavering champion of religious liberty" (ibid.).

16. In noting the Republican victory in New Hampshire in 1810, Elias published the following under the heading "SINGULAR": "In *Newhampshire* there are *nine Federal news papers* printed every week, and *two Republican.* Notwithstanding there are *nine* against *two,* the *Republican two,* have obtained a complete victory over the *Federal nine.* How *few* may overcome the *many* in a good cause! *Surely one has chased a thousand, and two put ten thousand to flight*" (*HGL* 2, no. 46 [May 25, 1810]). See E. Smith, in *MSCW* 2, no. 4 (Dec. 1828): 90–91.

17. All told, six agents each were in New Hampshire and Maine, eight in Massachusetts, and one each in Vermont and Rhode Island.

18. The most substantial number of agents outside New England was in Virginia, where Elias had traveled and had many correspondents. The detailed breakdown is as follows: seventeen agents were in Maine, thirteen in New Hampshire, twelve each in Massachusetts and Vermont, three each in Rhode Island and New York, eight in Virginia, four each in Pennsylvania and Kentucky, and one each in Delaware, South Carolina, Ohio, and Indiana Territory. Curiously (or perhaps not, given a long tradition of conservatism), there were no agents in Connecticut.

19. *HGL* 2, no. 38 (Feb. 2, 1810): 149; 3, no. 66 (Mar. 1, 1811): 264; 4, no. 21 (June 5, 1812): 396; 8, no. 7 (Aug. 1817): 252; 8, no. 8 (Oct. 1817).

20. See also *HGL* 3, no. 63 (Jan. 18, 1811): 251.

21. In his sermon "The Whole World Governed by a Jew" (1805e), Elias emphasized that Jesus, according to the New Testament, was a priest of the order of Melchizedek, a king of Salem who conjoined priestly and kingly office; Jesus and Melchizedek are the only two beings who ever have or ever will legitimately combine the two.

22. This report was signed "on behalf of the meeting" by Abner Jones, among others.

23. At least according to two members of the Portland church who

claimed to know about Smith's dealings with Colcord while there and about a dispute between them that the elders were called in to mediate.

24. Elias did not make a habit of placing advertisements in the *Herald*, except for religious publications. On September 29, 1815, he made an exception for his wife, who had "just received from the Manufacturers in Providence, R.I. . . . a handsome assortment of FACTORY GOODS, of an excellent quality— consisting of Shirtings, Sheetings, Diapers, Damask Table Cloths, Bedtick-ings, Ginghams, Chambrays, Checks, cotton Yarn of different numbers, of a superior quality, on reasonable terms, wholesale and retail. Those who wish to purchase for family use will find a good assortment suitable for the season" (*HGL* 7, no. 180, p. 720).

For New England Smith lists eleven preachers in Massachusetts, nine in New Hampshire, six in the District of Maine, fifteen in Vermont, three in Rhode Island, and only one in Connecticut (*HGL* 6, no. 145 [Mar. 4, 1814]: 575).

6. PHYSICIANS OF VALUE: MEDICINE FOR THE PEOPLE

1. See Smith 1822, 15. "This herb stands at the head of all the herbs made for the service of man, and is the king of all diseases, and with its army, has power to overcome all opposed to the health of man while in a curable state. . . . It warms, cleanses, and quickens the circulation of the blood, helps the digestion, removes obstructions, and opens the pores. It does all needful for the sick and distressed; and was in the wisdom of God, as certainly de-signed for the relief of the sick, as, as food and drink was designed for the hungry and thirsty" (Smith 1826, 43, 96).

2. "To illustrate the glory and excellencies of the *Messiah* who was to come, he [Ezekiel] made use of this plant that they might see his superiority above all others when he should appear among them. The plant which I call the *plant of renown*, if not the one mentioned by the Prophet, is superior to any plant in this country, and will with other vegetable medicines, do what no other one will do, and I think well deserves this name" (Smith 1837, 49–50).

3. See *CM* 1, no. 1 (1806): 9; Estes 1979, 115; Smith et al. 1804, 71.

4. In addition to the plague of 1802, Drown also refers to an episode of the fever in 1798, "five years ago."

5. As his son wrote: "It may well be supposed that Elder Jones could give but an exceedingly small share of his time or attention to his ministerial duties. Such was, indeed, the fact. I have known him to be summoned from the pul-pit in the midst of his discourse, and again to be sent after to attend some one

who was seized in church while he was absent" (Jones 1842, 107, 112).

6. See McNeill 1976, 261–65.

7. This address would become the first paragraph of the introduction to Thomson 1822b.

8. According to the testimonial, "In February, 1816, this fever first appeared in the town: Eight persons, heads of families, within one mile of each other, died in about thirty-six hours. In three houses, within one fourth of a mile, ten persons died. In one house was a mother and four children. Six Physicians in this county attended, but to little or no purpose. Upwards of forty had died by the first of May, and but few lived who had the fever. In this month, Dr. Thomson was called on, for assistance. He sold the right of using his Medicine to several individuals, of the town, and gave them liberty to administer the same to the sick. In the course of the month, the men who used the medicine, relieved upwards of thirty who were seized with this violent disease, with the loss of but one. At the same time and place, those who were attended by the regular Physicians, eleven out of twelve died" (*HGL* 8, no. 5 [Apr. 1817]: 10 [Appendix]).

9. As a follower put it: "An empiric is one who is governed in his practice by his own experimental knowledge; and Dr. Thomson can have no reasonable objection to be honored by this title, for there is nothing valuable in the whole range of the medical science, but what has been derived from this source" (Thomson 1835, 10).

10. Rush did note, however, that in the autumn of 1793 "mosquitoes (the usual attendants of a sickly autumn) were uncommonly numerous" (1818, 86).

11. See Kenny 1986, 40–42, which describes the use of Rushian methods on Mary Reynolds, an early case of what would be called multiple personality, who was treated for her curious "mania" by a student of Rush then serving Meadville, Pennsylvania.

12. Letter from Benjamin Waterhouse to W. Beach, July 23, 1836, Countway Library, Harvard Medical School, MS c16.1.

13. Undated Waterhouse document in the Countway Library, MS c16.4. Writing of the spread of the Thomsonian system, Waterhouse wrote that "it excites the attention of the East where it first appeared, and it has so far spread in Boston, that the oldest apothecary establishment in that city has confessed to me that their sale of drugs is not half what it used to be, and all this attributed to the *Thomsonian* innovations in practice" (MS c.16.1). Waterhouse, though he generally approved of Thomson, thought nonetheless that mineral-based remedies also had their usefulness. Had not God created the mineral kingdom also?

14. Elias appended to the 1837 edition of the *American Physician* a copy of

President Andrew Jackson's *Farewell Address* as a tribute to this defender of the people against aristocratic pretension (Smith 1837, 275–303).

15. Notably one Mr. Whitelaw, who, according to Thomson could only have gotten his medical system from Thomson's own writings or from Thomsonian practitioners but claimed he had in fact gotten it from the Indians (Thomson 1835, 169). The major propagator of Thomsonianism in England— Albert Coffin, an American—also claimed native roots for his system and in general appealed to the same antiestablishment biases as powered the Thomsonian movement in its homeland. See Miley 1988, 409; Brown 1982.

16. The council of prominent Universalists that Smith called to investigate the difficulties between Thomson and himself concluded, with whatever justice, that "in the opinion of the council the very circumstance of Thompson's [*sic*] desiring Smith to write his system is full proof that he is not able to do it himself" (*Medical News-Paper*, no. 16 [Sept. 3, 1822]: 62). The work in question was probably the first draft of Thomson's *New Guide to Health*, first published in 1822; Smith followed this with a medical book of his own containing similar material, *The American Physician and Family Assistant*, first published in 1826 and going through four editions, the last in 1837.

17. "The melancholy consequences resulting from the use of *Lobelia inflata*, as lately administered by the adventurous band of a noted *Empiric*, have justly excited considerable interest, and furnished alarming examples of its deleterious properties and fatal effects. The dose in which he is said usually to prescribe it, and frequently with impunity, is a common tea spoon full of the powdered seeds or leaves, and often repeated. If the medicine does not puke or evacuate powerfully, it frequently destroys the patient, and sometimes in five or six hours. Even horses and cattle have been supposed to be killed by eating it accidentally" (Smith 1822, 26).

18. See, for example, Block 1968; Albanese 1990; Fuller 1989. Nissenbaum notes that Sylvester Graham also cultivated a naive image "as a kind of romantic 'natural' who was able to perceive the true nature of things precisely because he had not been corrupted by the artifices of modern civilization— artifices that might include formal book-learning" (1988, 21).

19. In fact his system was in a way the precursor of modern HMOs, in which stress is placed on the prevention of disease, not its cure (Smillie 1951).

20. For documentation relative to Thomsonianism itself, see Forman 1947; Berman 1951; Young 1961, 55. Young rightly states that Thomson's "movement had gotten quite out of hand. It was supposed to be his. He had a patent for it. But 'mongrel Thomsonians' kept stealing the booty. Rascals pirated his medical manual. Agents he had hired went off on their own. Unauthorized manufacturers compounded 'Thomsonian' botanicals. There were even those

who defied the master's motto, 'The Study of Patients, Not Books—Experience, Not Reading,' and sought to make his concepts the basis of medical school education. Even in a democratic age, many Americans, anxious to be treated by Thomsonian principles, wanted a 'doctor' to do it rather than relying on a book." See Thomson 1836, 37–38, which reprints an address delivered to a convention of the Friendly Botanical Societies of the United States in Pittsburgh, which proposed setting up a National Thomsonian Infirmary "for the purpose of preserving Thomsonism in its simplicity."

7. AGE OF MIRACLES: SMITH AND THE UNIVERSALIST MOVEMENT

1. In his 1816 *Life*, Smith quoted Benedict's strictures extensively in order to refute them. The 1840 edition, however, contained none of this.

2. The English divines "say that the scripture positively asserts the doctrine of *destruction;* that the nature of future punishment (which the scripture terms *death*) determines the meaning of the words *everlasting, eternal, for ever,* &c as denoting endless duration; because no law ever did nor can inflict the punishment of death for a limited period; that the punishment cannot be corrective, because no man was ever put to death, either to convince his judgment or to reform his conduct; that if the wicked receive a punishment *apportioned* to their crimes, their deliverance is neither to be attributed to the mercy of God, nor the mediation of Jesus Christ, but is an act of absolute justice; and finally that the mediatorial kingdom of Jesus Christ will never be delivered up, since the scripture asserts that of his kingdom there shall be no end. Those who maintain these sentiments respecting the destruction of the wicked, are accused of espousing the doctrine of *annihilation;* but this accusation they repel, alleging, that philosophically speaking, there can be no annihilation, and that *destruction* is the express phrase used in the New Testament. Of this sentiment there have been many advocates distinguished for their erudition and piety." (Evans 1804, 210–11). That is the totality of Evans's account, but seemingly it was enough for Elias—something he was ready to believe in any event.

3. "That sin is infinite and deserves an infinite punishment; that the law transgressed is infinite and threatens an infinite penalty; that the great Jehovah took on himself a natural body of flesh and blood, and actually suffered death on the cross to appease *his own* wrath, and to satisfy *his own* justice,—and, after all, to leave the one so unappeased, and the other so unsatisfied, as to make it certain that the greater part of mankind would suffer endless punishment,—were dogmas that appeared to [Ballou] to be unfounded in reason, and unsup-

ported by divine revelation" (Whittemore 1854, 1:193–94; see also 208).

4. It could be, given Jones's susceptibility to Smith's influence, that the former's son is here glossing over a period of his father's life that Jones had later come to regret.

5. "The Calvinists cry out against the Universalists, for preaching licentious doctrine; not knowing it is what they all preach. The Universalists have exceeded them, by taking in all instead of part, upon the same plan" (Smith 1805c, 58).

6. Thomas Baldwin responded to this kind of insinuation by asserting that the Calvinist Baptists "do not believe the doctrine . . . because St. Augustine believed it, (and as some say manufactured it,) nor because the first founders of this church believed it; but because we find it established with the utmost clearness in the word of God" (Baldwin 1804).

7. Or, as Smith wrote in response to a Methodist critic, "It is a certain fact that the state of the soul of the wicked is this, *condemned to die the second death;* having no eternal life in them—that the state of the soul of the righteous is this, *justified to live forever;* having eternal life in them, which is given them by the Lord of life, and they shall never perish." (1806b, 7).

8. As proof text Smith cited John 5:28–29, which states that "the hour is coming, in the which all that are in the graves shall hear his voice, and shall come forth; they that have done good, unto the resurrection of life; and they that have done evil, unto the resurrection of damnation. [i.e., death]."

9. In the 1840 edition of his autobiography, at a time when he had again become a Christian, Smith made the curious claim that, in Vermont especially, destructionism had served to bring "many from *universalism* and *deism* to Christ for life" (305).

10. Newman added that "the purity of infants is a deistical as well as socinian sentiment. As to annihilation, or as they (the christians) call it the destruction of the wicked, Elias Smith found it in a book called 'Evans' Sketch!' Elias Smith and thou that believest his creed ought to be called Arisinians, as a badge of merit due to them for their laborious endeavors to promulgate the idea of the Arians and Socinians."

11. Elias, writing of the original cosignatories of the *Articles,* observed that "the design of these men was understood to be this; to leave behind every thing in name, doctrine, or practice, not found in the New Testament. Whither they thought at first this would carry them I cannot tell; though I conclude they did not, for when they saw where it would end, the greater part went back, and apologized for their conduct, and remain with the baptists" (264).

12. This Smith maintained in the face of assertions made by the prominent Baptist David Benedict in his history of the Baptists in America "that I

have advanced the doctrine of the *annihilation* of the wicked. This is [a] false-hood; the word nor doctrine of annihilation is not in any book written by me. Mr. Benedict would by this, have people believe, that I advance, that when the wicked die, that is their end; but my bible does not read so, nor did I ever so preach or write. The wicked are reserved unto the day of judgment to be pun-ished; and all in their graves will hear the voice of the Son of God, and come forth: they that have done evil to the resurrection of damnation. There the wicked will be punished with everlasting destruction; this will be their end. 'Whose end is destruction'" (Smith 1816, 399).

13. Zephaniah Crossman first appears in the *Herald* (3, no. 63 [Jan. 18, 1811]) in the form of a letter from Duxbury, Massachusetts, containing an ac-count of three baptisms that he had performed in Kingston.

14. As we have seen, Jones's son denied that his father ever subscribed to the destructionist thesis.

15. It is difficult to know what effect the use of this particular passage had under the circumstances. Here, Jesus is arguing with the Sadducees about fine points of Jewish law, answering their question about who a widow would be married to in the resurrection, after she had married seven brothers in turn, following the Old Testament levirate. Jesus answered: "In the resurrection they neither marry, nor are given in marriage, but are as the angels of God in heaven" (v. 30). Certainly Elias Smith is (at the very least) here associating Hosea Ballou with Jewish legalists.

16. Writing in 1889, Henry Swan Dana still had access to the memories of those who witnessed the events in question. According to Dana, "Smith in some respects was unsurpassed among the popular preachers of the day. He had labored diligently to make himself familiar with the Scriptures, and had acquired great readiness in quoting from different parts of the Bible, especially from the gospels and epistles. While not so logical in thought as Ballou, and while less weighty and dignified in style, in ease and fluency of speaking and in nimbleness of mind he was perhaps his superior" (Dana 1980, 403–4).

17. Ballou, evidently thinking that the arguments in the case went entirely in his own favor, allowed publication of the letters between himself and the two orthodox ministers (Buckminster 1811).

18. David Osgood provided a particularly odious example in suggesting that the declaration of war "cannot be approved by any but here and there a furious party leader, a few ignorant, deluded fanatics, and a handful of desper-adoes"; as for the authors of this war, he proclaimed that were they not "in character nearly akin to the deists and atheists of France; were they not men of hardened hearts, seared consciences, reprobate minds, and desperate in

wickedness; it seems utterly inconceivable that they should have made the declaration" (Osgood 1812, 14–15, 17).

19 Here Elias appears not to have understood his own text. The *knowledge* to which the verse refers is spurious human knowledge, whereas the angel of Daniel's vision advises him to seal up what has been revealed to him in a book that is not to be opened until the last days. The language of Daniel 12:4 is the language of the book of Job, which tells of a Satan who has been at work, "going to and fro in the earth, and from walking up and down in it" (Job 1:7), who tempts God to test the faithful servant Job to see if he will renounce his Lord after unmerited tribulation.

20. See Jones 1842, 70–71; Burgess 1889, 662; Buzzell 1827, 121, 186.

21. Smith correctly surmised that "Zenas" was Badger and challenged him to come forward under "his real name, like an honest man" (*Herald of Life and Immortality* 1, no. 5 [Jan. 1820]: 169).

22. The new *Herald* was at this time printed in Portsmouth, at the office of the *New Hampshire Gazette*.

23. A satirist suggested in doggerel that such reprobate spirits as Judas and Tom Paine would surely get much comfort from the likes of Smith that hell, the place they now inhabit, is actually unreal (Ireneus 1825). The satirist, who published under the strange pseudonym of Ramboulette Gabrielle Ireneus, associated Smith with Abner Kneeland, a leading Universalist and later radical freethinker who would be one of Samuel Thomson's principal agents. Ireneus went on more specifically about Smith himself: "To the Rev. Elias Smith Esq. I feel a *peculiar* satisfaction in dedicating this work, for that most essential service he has rendered to the cause of human tranquility, by proving that there is no hell; or, rather by proving that the wicked will all be annihilated; and, of course, that there will be no use for such a place, since there will be nobody to put into it."

24. Smith had a way of burning his bridges. In the *Herald of Life* he condemned the Christians at large for following in the Baptist steps toward Babylon, which in his opinion they had done through organizing themselves into a conference that was next to meet in Portsmouth, with costs (including room and board for their horses) to be borne by their congregations. His old friend Frederic Plummer—"a man of much importance among them"—now received the same treatment from Elias as had earlier been meted out to another former comrade, John Peak. The occasion was condemnation of a discourse that Plummer delivered in Boston in 1820. Once more Elias was in the audience. Smith had some bad things to say about Plummer's doctrine, some bad things about his delivery, and also some bad things about the fact that in a circular

letter to the Christian churches Plummer had written of "the *detestable* fall" of Elias Smith into Universalism. From the stilted manner of his old friend's discourse, Elias thought it "not wrong to mention the *fall* of F.P. from that simplicity in which he once stood" (*Herald of Life and Immortality* 1, nos. 3 and 5 [July 1819 and Apr. 1820]: 98–99, 197–200).

25. Elias, evidently still much troubled by gossip originating with Thomson and his friends, reprinted the council's 1822 decision in the *MSCW* 2, no. 1 (1828): 10–21.

26. Smith listed the following as "approved" medicines: Vegetable Elixir, Elixir of Life, Botanic Ointment, Hygenian Compound, Panacea Pills, Cholera Cordial, Health Restorative, Peach Cordial, Acid Cough Syrup, Wine Bitters.

27. In June of the same year, Hazen also announced the death from consumption of twenty-year-old Mary Smith, daughter of Elias's namesake nephew, Elias Smith, son of his brother, Richard Ransom Smith. The previous year, wrote Hazen, another daughter of that same Elias had died of the same cause.

28. See Gannett 1875, 45; Peabody 1881, 475; Lee 1851.

29. Her will, and that of Elias, are to be found in the Essex (Mass.) County Courthouse in Salem (files no. 53474 and 53674).

30. "He believed with all his heart, that if the theology of the Romanist and Protestant—in other words, of the 'Christian' churches could be destroyed, and juster views of God, and of man's relation to God, could be substituted for it, society would feel the change in all its departments, from government affairs to domestic service: every wrong would be righted, every mischief removed, every mistake corrected, every sorrow taken away" (Frothingham 1874, 373).

31. Even at this point Smith was challenging the claim of Abner Jones to have founded the first *free* Christian Church in New England.

32. Badger was even heard to speak approvingly of the Roman Catholics in this regard.

33. See Cross 1965; Numbers 1987; Rowe 1985.

EPILOGUE

1. See Daniel Smith 1837; Ballou 1834; Ballou 1896, 246–50.

2. In 1842 Matthew gave an account of what had happened via a series of lectures entitled *Universalism Examined, Renounced, Exposed.* He said of his former faith that "it was bound up with my earliest associations. Nearly all my

relations and acquaintances were of that faith," and that therefore he had every reason to remain a Universalist if he could in good conscience do so (Smith 1842, 34).

3. According to Universalist critics, Smith renounced Universalism in Hartford, then started for Boston in his chaise, and after having traveled for about thirty miles "all at once discovered that he had been crazy" and had no memory at all of having renounced anything (*Trumpet and Universalist Magazine* 13, no. 52 [Apr. 10, 1841]).

REFERENCES

A.G. 1963. "Boston, Thomas." In *Dictionary of National Biography*, 2:886–88. London: Oxford University Press.

Adams, Nathaniel. 1825. *Annals of Portsmouth*. Portsmouth, N.H.: Nathaniel Adams.

Albanese, Catherine L. 1990. *Nature Religion in America: From the Algonkian Indians to the New Age*. Chicago: University of Chicago Press.

Alden, Timothy. 1808. *An Account of the Several Religious Societies in Portsmouth, New Hampshire*. Boston: Munroe, Francis, & Parker.

Andrews, Edward Deming. 1963. *The People Called Shakers*. New York: Dover Publications.

Andrews, S. M. 1880. *A Sketch of Elder Daniel Hix*. New Bedford, Mass.: E. Anthony & Sons.

Andros, Thomas. 1799. *An Oration delivered at Dighton (Massachusetts), July 4, 1799*. New Bedford, Mass.: John Spooner.

———. 1809a. *The Criminality of Restraining Prayer. A Sermon delivered before the Congregational Society in Berkley, Massachusetts, November 6, 1808*. Providence: Dunham & Hawkins.

———. 1809b. *A Thanksgiving Sermon: Delivered before the Congregational Society in Berkley, December 1, 1808*. Providence: Dunham & Hawkins.

———. 1812. *The Grand Era of Ruin to Nations from Foreign Influence*. Boston: Samuel T. Armstrong.

———. 1813. *Bible News of the Father, Son, and Holy Ghost, as Reported by Rev. Noah Worcester, A.M., not Correct*. Boston: Samuel T. Armstrong.

————. 1814a. *The Place of the Church on the Grand Chart of Scripture Prophecy; or, The Great Battle of Armageddon.* Boston: Samuel T. Armstrong.

————. 1814b. *Seasonable Thoughts on Human Creeds and Articles of Faith by an Orthodox Clergyman, shewn to be very Unreasonable Thoughts in a Letter to a Friend.* Boston: Samuel T. Armstrong.

————. 1815. *Truth in Opinion the Only Foundation of Piety.* Boston: Samuel T. Armstrong.

————. 1816. *The Scriptures Liable to be Wrested to Men's own Destruction, and an Instance of this found in the Writings of Elias Smith.* Taunton, Mass.: A. Danforth.

————. 1817. *Discourses on Several Important Theological Subjects, Adapted to the Present State of Religion.* Boston: Samuel T. Armstrong.

————. 1820. *An Essay in which the Doctrine of a Positive Divine Efficiency Exciting the Will of Men to Sin, as Held by some Modern Writers, is Candidly Discussed.* Boston: Samuel T. Armstrong.

————. 1830. *The Temperance Society Vindicated and Recommended.* Taunton, Mass.: Edmund Anthony.

————. 1833. *The Old Jersey Captive; or, A Narrative of the Captivity of Thomas Andros (now Pastor of the Church in Berkley) on Board the Old Jersey Prison Ship at New York, 1781.* Boston: William Peirce.

Appleby, Joyce. 1977–78. "The Social Origins of American Revolutionary Ideology." *Journal of American History* 64:935–58.

————. 1982. "What Is Still American in the Political Philosophy of Thomas Jefferson?" *William and Mary Quarterly* 39:287–309.

————. 1985. "Republicanism and Ideology." *American Quarterly* 37:461–473.

————. 1986. "Republicanism in Old and New Contexts." *William and Mary Quarterly* 63:20–34.

Austin, Benjamin. 1803. *Constitutional Republicanism in Opposition to Fallacious Federalism.* Boston: Adams & Rhoades.

Backus, Isaac. 1871. *A History of New England, with Particular Reference to the Denomination of Christians called Baptists.* Arno Press Reprint Edition. 2 vols. Newton, Mass.: Backus Historical Society.

————. 1979. *The Diary of Isaac Backus.* 3 vols. Providence: Brown University Press.

Bacon, Henry. 1847. "Dr. Elias Smith, Aged 77." *Ladies Repository,* 77–78.

Bailyn, Bernard. 1967. *The Ideological Origins of the American Revolution.* Cambridge: Harvard University Press.

————. 1973. "The Central Themes of the American Revolution: An Interpretation." In *Essays on the American Revolution,* ed. Stephen G. Jurtz and James H. Hutson. Chapel Hill: University of North Carolina Press.

Baldwin, Thomas. 1804. *The Eternal Purpose of God, the Foundation of Effectual Calling.* Boston: Manning & Loring.

———. 1811. *A Discourse Delivered Jan. 1, 1811, at the Opening of the New Meeting House Belonging to the Second Baptist Church and Society in Boston.* Boston: Lincoln & Edmunds.

———. 1812. *The Supreme Deity of Christ Illustrated.* Boston: Lincoln & Edmunds.

Ballou, Adin. 1896. *Autobiography of Adin Ballou.* Lowell, Mass.: Vox Populi Press.

Ballou, Adin, and Daniel D. Smith. 1834. *Report of a Public Discussion, between the Rev. Adin Ballou, and Daniel D. Smith.* Mendon, Mass.: Independent Messenger.

Ballou, Maturin. 1852. *Biography of Rev. Hosea Ballou.* Boston: Abel Tompkins.

Banner, James. 1970. *To the Hartford Convention: The Federalists and the Origins of Party Politics in Massachusetts, 1789–1815.* New York: Alfred A. Knopf.

Banning, Lance. 1974. "Republican Ideology and the Triumph of the Constitution, 1789 to 1793." *William and Mary Quarterly* 31:167–88.

———. 1978. *The Jeffersonian Persuasion: Evolution of a Party Ideology.* Ithaca: Cornell University Press.

———. 1986. "Jeffersonian Ideology Revisited: Liberal and Classical Ideas in the New American Republic." *William and Mary Quarterly* 63:3–19.

Bell, Charles H. 1888. *History of the Town of Exeter, New Hampshire.* Exeter.

Benedict, David. 1813. *A General History of the Baptist Denomination in America and other parts of the World.* 2 vols. Boston: Manning & Loring.

Bentley, William. 1962. *The Diary of William Bentley, D.D.* 3 vols. Gloucester, Mass.: Peter Smith.

Berman, Alex. 1951. "The Thomsonian Movement and Its Relation to American Pharmacy and Medicine." *Bulletin of the History of Medicine* 25:405–28, 519–38.

———. 1956. "Social Roots of the Nineteenth Century Botanico-Medical Movement in the United States." In *Congrès International d'Histoire des Sciences,* 2:561–65. Florence and Milan: Hermann & Cie. Dépositaire Général.

Bilhartz, Terry D. 1986. *Urban Religion and the Second Great Awakening: Church and Society in Early National Baltimore.* Rutherford, N.J.: Fairleigh Dickinson University Press.

Birdsall, Richard D. 1970. "The Second Great Awakening and the New England Social Order." *Church History* 39:345–64.

Bloch, Ruth. 1985. *Visionary Republic: Millennial Themes in American Thought, 1756–1800.* Cambridge: Harvard University Press.

Boston, Thomas. 1796. *Human Nature in its Fourfold State.* Exeter, N.H.:
H. Ranlet.

Bourne, Edward E. 1875. *The History of Wells and Kennebunk.* Portland, Maine:
B. Thurston.

Braman, Isaac. 1810. *The Spirits that are not of God. Sermon preached in Salisbury
[Ma.], West-Parish, Lord's Day, July 29, 1810.* Haverhill, Mass.: William B.
Allen.

Brown, P. S. 1982. "Herbalists and Medical Botanists in Mid-Nineteenth-
Century Britain, with Special Reference to Bristol." *Medical History*
26:405–20.

Brown, Warren. 1900. *History of the Town of Hampton Falls, N.H.* Manchester,
N.H.: John B. Clarke.

Buckminster, Joseph. 1796a. *The Duty of Republican Citizens in the Choice of
their Rulers.* Portsmouth, N.H.: Charles Peirce at Oracle Press.

———. 1796b. *Remarks Upon Paul's and Barnabas's Dispute and Separation.*
Portsmouth, N.H.: John Melcher.

———. 1798. *A Discourse Delivered in the First Parish in Portsmouth, November
15, 1798, a Day Observed as an Anniversary Thanksgiving.* Portsmouth,
N.H.: John Melcher.

———. 1803a. *A Discourse Delivered in the North Church of Christ in Portsmouth, upon Luke ix:49–50.* Portsmouth, N.H..

———. 1803b. *A Discourse Occasioned by the late Desolating Fire, delivered in the
First Church of Portsmouth, the Lord's Day succeeding that Melancholy Event.*
Portsmouth, N.H.: William & Daniel Treadwell.

———. 1803c. *A Discourse on Baptism.* Portsmouth, N.H.: William & Daniel
Treadwell.

———. 1805. *A Discourse Delivered at the Ordination of the Rev. Joseph S. Buckminster.* Boston: Young & Minns.

———. 1809. *A Sermon Preached at the Installation of the Rev. James Thurston.*
Portsmouth, N.H.: Oracle Press.

Buckminster, Joseph, Joseph Walton, and Hosea Ballou. 1811. *A Series of Letters
between the Rev. Joseph Buckminster, D.D., the Rev. Joseph Walton, A.M.,
and the Rev. Hosea Ballou.* Windsor, Vt.: James G. Watts.

Bumsted, J. M. 1971. *Henry Alline, 1748–1784.* Toronto: University of Toronto
Press.

Burgess, G. A., and J. T. Ward. 1889. *Free Baptist Cyclopaedia.* Chicago:
Woman's Temperance Publication Association.

Burleigh, Charles. 1880. *The Genealogy of the Burley or Burleigh Family of America.* Portland, Maine: B. Thurston.

Burnett, J. F. 1921. *Early Women of the Christian Church: Heroines All.* Dayton, Ohio: Christian Publication Society.

Burton, Asa. 1810. *False Teachers Described: A Sermon, delivered at Thetford, Lord's Day, December 24th, 1809.* Montpelier, Vt.: Samuel Goss.

Bushman, Richard L. 1967. *From Puritan to Yankee.* Cambridge: Harvard University Press.

Butler, Jon. 1990. *Awash in a Sea of Faith.* Cambridge: Harvard University Press.

Buzzell, John. 1822. *A Religious Magazine Containing a Short History of the Church of Christ gathered at New Durham, N.H., in the year 1780.* Portland, Maine:

———. 1827. *The Life of Elder Benjamin Randal.* Limerick, Maine: Hobbs, Woodman.

Caldwell, Patricia. 1983. *The Puritan Conversion Narrative: The Beginnings of American Expression.* Cambridge: Cambridge University Press.

Chessman, Daniel. 1826. *Memoir of Rev. Thomas Baldwin, D.D.* Boston: True & Greene.

Churches, Congregational. 1808. *A Platform of Church Discipline.* Boston: Belcher & Armstrong.

Churches, Synod of the New England. 1812. *The Original Constitution, Order and Faith of the New-England Churches.* Boston.

Clarfield, Gerard H. 1980. *Timothy Pickering and the American Republic.* Pittsburgh: University of Pittsburgh Press.

Cobbett, William. 1815. *An Address to the Clergy of Massachusetts.* Boston: Yankee Office.

Colby, John. 1829. *The Life, Experience, and Travels of John Colby.* Cornish, Maine: S. W. & C. C. Cole.

Cole, Donald B. 1970. *Jacksonian Democracy in New Hampshire, 1800–1851.* Cambridge: Harvard University Press.

Conforti, Joseph A. 1977. "Samuel Hopkins and the New Divinity: Theology, Ethics, and Social Reform in Eighteenth-Century New England." *William and Mary Quarterly* 34:572–89.

Conkin, Paul K. 1990. *Cane Ridge: America's Pentecost.* Madison: University of Wisconsin Press.

Cooper, James F. 1992. "Enthusiasts or Democrats? Separatism, Church Government, and the Great Awakening in Massachusetts." *New England Quarterly* 65:265–83.

Cram, Nancy Gove. 1815. *A Collection of Hymns and Poems. Designed to Instruct the Inquirer, and Furnish the Public with a small variety.* Schenectady, N.Y.

Cross, Whitney R. 1965. *The Burned-over District: The Social and Intellectual History of Enthusiastic Religion in Western New York, 1800–1850.* New York: Harper & Row.

Dana, Henry Swan. 1980. *The History of Woodstock, Vermont.* Taftsville, Vt.: Woodstock Foundation.

Daniels, Bruce C. 1979. *The Connecticut Town: Growth and Development, 1635–1790.* Middletown, Conn.: Wesleyan University Press.

"David Osgood (Class of 1771)." 1975. In *Sibley's Harvard Graduates,* vol. 17: *1768–71,* 570–80. Boston.

Davis [Mr.?]. 1913. "John Grow of Ipswich." Ms. in Connecticut State Library, Hartford.

Day, George T. 1853. *The Life of Rev. Martin Cheney.* Providence: Geo. H. Whitney.

Dearborn, John J. 1890. *The History of Salisbury New Hampshire.* Manchester, N.H.: William Moore.

Denison, John Ledyard. 1900. *Some Items of Baptist History in Connecticut from 1674 to 1900.* Philadelphia: American Baptist Publication Society.

Dexter, Franklin Bowditch. 1903. "Buckminster, Joseph." In *Biographical Sketches of the Graduates of Yale College,* 3:366–74. New York: Henry Holt.

Dilworth, Thomas. 1789. *A New Guide to the English Tongue.* Boston: T. & J. Fleet.

Dowling, John. 1849. "Sketches of New-York Baptists: Rev. Thomas Paul and the Colored Baptist Churches." *Baptist Memorial and Monthly Chronicles* 9:295–301.

Dutton, S. W. S. 1861. "The Safety and Wisdom of Complete Religious Liberty, as Illustrated in Connecticut During the Last One Hundred and Fifty Years." In *Contributions to the Ecclesiastical History of Connecticut,* 118–24. New Haven: William L. Kingsley.

Dwight, Timothy. 1969. *Travels in New England and New York.* 4 vols. Cambridge: Harvard University Press.

Edwards, Jonathan. 1968. *Works of President Edwards.* Vol. 5: *A History of the Works of Redemption.* New York: Burt Franklin.

Ellis, Joseph J. 1979. *After the Revolution: Profiles of Early American Culture.* New York: W. W. Norton.

Emery, Samuel Hopkins. 1853. *The Ministry of Taunton.* Vol. 2. Boston.

Endicott, Frederic, ed. 1896. *The Record of Birth, Marriages and Death and Intentions of Marriage, in the Town of Stoughton.* Canton, Mass.: William Bense.

Ernst, Joseph. 1973. "Ideology and the Political Economy of Revolution." *Canadian Review of American Studies* 4:137–48.

Estes, J. Worth. 1979. *Hall Jackson and the Purple Foxglove: Medical Practice and Research in Revolutionary America, 1760–1820.* Hanover, N.H.: University Press of New England.

Evans, John. 1804. *A Sketch of the Denominations of the Christian World; Accompanied with a Persuasive to Religious Moderation.* Wilmington, Del.: Bonsal & Niles.

Everest, Cornelius B. 1819. *A Defence of the Gospel a Ministerial Duty: A sermon, delivered at Windham, July 28, 1816.* Windham, Conn.: J. Byrne.

Feeley-Harnik, Gillian. 1982. *The Lord's Table: Eucharist and Passover in Early Christianity.* Philadelphia: University of Pennsylvania Press.

Felton, Cornelius C. 1852. *A Memorial of the Rev. John Snelling Popkin, D.D.* Cambridge, Mass.: John Bartlett.

Fenn, William W. 1917. *The Religious History of New England.* Cambridge: Harvard University Press.

Fernald, Mark. 1852. *Life of Elder Mark Fernald.* Newburyport, Mass.: Geo. Moore Payne & D. P. Pike.

Fischer, David H. 1964. "The Myth of the Essex Junto." *William and Mary Quarterly* 21:191–235.

———. 1965. *The Revolution of American Conservatism.* New York: Harper & Row.

Forbes, Charles. 1905. "History of Vermont Newspapers." *Vermonter* 11 (1): 10–12.

Forman, Jonathan. 1947. "The Worthington School and Thomsonianism." *Bulletin of the History of Medicine* 21:772–87.

Freewill Baptist Connection, General Conference. 1859. *Minutes.* Dover, N.H.: Freewill Baptist Printing Establishment.

Frothingham, Octavius Brooks. 1874. *Theodore Parker: A Biography.* Boston: James R. Osgood.

Fulop, Timothy. 1992. "Elias Smith and the Quest for Gospel Liberty." Ph.D. diss., Princeton University.

Gannett, William C. 1875. *Ezra Stiles Gannet. Unitarian Minister in Boston, 1824–1871.* Boston: Roberts Brothers.

Garrison, Winnifred, and Alfred T. deGroot. 1948. *The Disciples of Christ: A History.* St. Louis: Christian Board of Publication.

Gaustad, Edwin Scott. 1965. *The Great Awakening in New England.* Gloucester, Mass.: Peter Smith.

Geertz, Clifford. 1973. "Ideology as a Cultural System." In *The Interpretation of Culture,* 193–233. New York: Basic.

General Conference, Free-Will Baptists. 1848. *A Treatise on the Faith of the Free-Will Baptists.* Dover, N.H.: Free-Will Baptist Printing Establishment.

Getchell, Sylvia Fitts. 1984. *The Tide Turns on the Lamprey: Vignettes in the Life of a River.* Newmarket, N.H.: Newmarket Historical Society.

Goen, C. C. 1962. *Revivalism and Separatism in New England, 1740–1800.* New Haven: Yale University Press.

Graves, Ross Gordon. 1952. *Historical Sketch of the Flanders Baptist and Community Church of East Lyme, Connecticut.* East Lyme: Flanders Baptist and Community Church, Bicentennial Celebration Souvenir.

Hall, David D. 1989. *Worlds of Wonder, Days of Judgment.* New York: Alfred A. Knopf.

Harris, Walter. 1811. *Characteristics of False Teachers: The Substance of Two Discourses, delivered at Dunbarton, New-Hampshire, Lord's Day, August 5, 1811.* Concord, N.H.: George Hough.

Hatch, Nathan O. 1977. *The Sacred Cause of Liberty: Republican Thought and the Millennium in Revolutionary New England.* New Haven: Yale University Press.

———. 1980. "The Christian Movement and the Demand for a Theology of the People." *Journal of American History* 67:545–67.

———. 1982. "Sola Scriptura and Novus Ordo Seclorum." In *The Bible in America,* ed. Nathan O. Hatch and Mark A. Noll, 59–78. New York: Oxford University Press.

———. 1983. "Elias Smith and the Rise of Religious Journalism in the Early Republic." In *Printing and Society in Early America,* ed. William L. Joyce et al., 250–73. Worcester, Mass.: American Antiquarian Society.

———. 1989. *The Democratization of American Christianity.* New Haven: Yale University Press.

Hathaway, Warren. 1861. *A Discourse on Abner Jones, and the Christian Denomination.* Newburyport, Mass: Herald of Gospel Liberty Office.

Hazen, J. 1846. "Elder Elias Smith." *Christian Palladium,* Dec. 2.

Henretta, James A. 1978. "Families and Farms: *Mentalité* in Pre-Industrial America." *William and Mary Quarterly* 35:3–32.

Hill, Christopher. 1971. *Antichrist in Seventeenth-Century England.* London: Oxford University Press.

A History of the Town of Freetown, Massachusetts. 1902. Fall River, Mass.: J. H. Franklin.

Holland, E. G. 1854. *Memoir of Rev. Joseph Badger.* New York: C. S. Francis.

Hopkins, Samuel. 1811. *The System of Doctrines Contained in Divine Revelation Explained and Defended.* 2 vols. Boston: Lincoln & Edmonds.

Howe, John R. 1967. "Republican Thought and the Political Violence of the 1790s." *American Quarterly* 19:147–65.

Hughes, Richard T., and C. Leonard Allen. 1988. *Illusions of Innocence: Protes-*

tant Primitivism in America, 1630–1875. Chicago: University of Chicago Press.

Humphreys, Daniel. 1802. *A Letter to Mr. Elias Smith, Baptist Teacher.* Portsmouth, N.H.: William & Daniel Treadwell.

Hutt, Frank Walcott, ed. 1924. *A History of Bristol County, Massachusetts.* Vol. 2. New York: Lewis Historical Publishing.

Ireneus, Ramboulette Gabrielle. 1825. *The Only Sure and True Key to the Holy Bible.* Providence: Barnum Field.

Jacobus, Donald Lines. 1949. "Smith Number." *American Genealogist* 25:64ff.

James, William. 1958. *The Varieties of Religious Experience.* New York: Mentor.

Jones, A. D. 1842. *Memoir of Elder Abner Jones.* Boston: William Crosby.

Jones, Abner. N.d. *The Vision Made Plain: A Sermon on Election and Reprobation.* Danville, Vt.: Ebenezer Eaton.

———. 1804. *The Melody of the Heart: Original and Selected Hymns for Social Devotion.* Boston: Manning & Loring.

Jones, Henry. 1861. "On the Rise, Growth, and Comparative Relations of Other Evangelical Denominations in Connecticut to Congregationalism." In *Contributions to the Ecclesiastical History of Connecticut.* New Haven: William L. Kingsley.

Kaplanoff, Mark D. 1968. "Religion and Righteousness: A Study of Federalist Rhetoric in the New Hampshire Election of 1800." *Historical New Hampshire* 23:3–20.

Kenny, Michael G. 1986. *The Passion of Ansel Bourne: Multiple Personality in American Culture.* Washington, D.C.: Smithsonian Institution Press.

Kent, Josiah Collman. 1921. *Northborough History.* Garden City, N.Y.: Garden City Press.

Kerber, Linda. 1970. *Federalists in Dissent.* Ithaca: Cornell University Press.

———. 1985. "Republican Ideology of the Revolutionary Generation." *American Quarterly* 37:474–95.

Kinney, Charles B. 1955. *Church and State: The Struggle for Separation in New Hampshire, 1630–1900.* New York: Columbia University Teacher's College.

Kirby, John B. 1970. "Early American Politics—the Search for Ideology: An Historiographical Analysis and Critique of the Concept of Deference." *Journal of Politics* 32:808–38.

Kramnick, Isaac. 1982. "Republican Revisionism Revisited." *American Historical Review* 87:629–44.

Lawrence, Robert F. 1856. *The New Hampshire Churches: Comprising Histories of the Congregational and Presbyterian Churches in the State.* Claremont, N.H.: Published by the author.

Lee, Eliza Buckminster. 1851. *Memoirs of Rev. Joseph Buckminster, D.D., and of his son, Rev. Joseph Stevens Buckminster.* Boston: Ticknor, Reed & Fields.

Lemisch, Jesse. 1968. "The American Revolution Seen from the Bottom Up." In *Towards a New Past: Dissenting Essays in American History,* ed. Barton J. Bernstein, 3–45. New York: Pantheon.

MacClenny, W. E. 1910. *The Life of Rev. James O'Kelly and The Early History of the Christian Church in the South.* Raleigh, N.C.: Edwards & Broughton.

McCoy, Drew R. 1980. *The Elusive Republic: Political Economy in Jeffersonian America.* Chapel Hill: University of North Carolina Press.

McLoughlin, William G. 1965. "The Bench, the Church, and the Republican Party in New Hampshire, 1790 to 1820." *Historical New Hampshire* 20:3–31.

———. 1967. *Isaac Backus and the American Pietistic Tradition.* Boston: Little, Brown.

———. 1971. *New England Dissent, 1630–1833.* 2 vols. Cambridge: Harvard University Press.

———. 1978. *Revivals, Awakenings, and Reform.* Chicago: University of Chicago Press.

McMaster, Gilbert. 1812. *The Embassy of Reconciliation: A Sermon preached at the ordination of the Rev. James Milligan, in the Church of Coldenham.* New York: Whitney & Watson.

———. 1815. *An Essay in Vindication of the Fundamental Doctrines of Christianity against Socinism, including A Review of the Writings of Elias Smith, and the claims of his female preachers.* Schenectady, N.Y.: Riggs & Stevens.

McNeill, William H. 1976. *Plagues and Peoples.* Garden City, N.Y.: Anchor Press.

Main, Jackson Turner. 1977. "The Economic and Social Structure of Early Lyme." In *A Lyme Miscellany, 1776–1976,* ed. George J. Willauer. Middletown, Conn.: Wesleyan University Press.

Marini, Stephen A. 1982. *Radical Sects of Revolutionary New England.* Cambridge: Harvard University Press.

Marsden, George M. 1980. *Fundamentalism in American Culture.* New York: Oxford University Press.

Martin, Christopher William. 1815. *Remarks on "A Discourse in two parts," addressed to the Presbyterian Congregation, in Ballston, on Lord's Day, October 30, 1814, by the Rev. Stephen Porter.* Schenectady, N.Y.: C. W. Martin.

Mathews, Donald G. 1969. "The Second Great Awakening as an Organizing Process, 1780–1830: An Hypothesis." *American Quarterly* 21:23–43.

Merritt, Timothy. 1807. *Animadversions on Mr. Elias Smith's Review of the Doc-*

trines and Discipline of the Methodist Episcopal Church in America. Portland, Maine: J. McKown.

Messerli, Jonathan. 1972. *Horace Mann: A Biography.* New York: Alfred A. Knopf.

Meyer, Donald. 1963. "The Dissolution of Calvinism." In *Paths of American Thought,* ed. Arthur Schlesinger and Morton White, 71-85. New York: Houghton Mifflin.

Miley, Ursula, and John V. Pickstone. 1988. "Medical Botany around 1850: American Medicine in Industrial Britain." In *Studies in the History of Alternative Medicine,* ed. Roger Cooter, 140-54. New York: St. Martin's Press.

Millard, David E. 1874. *Memoir of Rev. David Millard.* Dayton, Ohio: Christian Publishing Association.

Miller, Perry. 1967. "From the Covenant to the Revival." In *Nature's Nation,* 90-120. Cambridge: Harvard University Press.

Miller, Russell E. 1979. *The Larger Hope: The First Century of the Universalist Church in America 1770-1870.* Boston: Unitarian Universalist Association.

Morgan, Edmund S. 1963. *Visible Saints: The History of a Puritan Idea.* New York: New York University Press.

———. 1988. *Inventing the People.* New York: W. W. Norton.

Morrill, Milo True. 1911. *A History of the Christian Denomination in America.* Dayton, Ohio: Christian Publishing Association.

Murrin, John. 1980. "The Great Inversion; or, Court versus Country: A Comparison of the Revolutionary Settlements in England (1688-1721) and America (1776-1816)." In *Three British Revolutions,* ed. J. G. A. Pocock. Princeton: Princeton University Press.

Nash, Gary B. 1965. "The American Clergy and the French Revolution." *William and Mary Quarterly* 22:392-441.

———. 1979. *The Urban Crucible.* Cambridge: Harvard University Press.

Newman, Jonathan. 1818. *A Remonstrance, Bringing to view some errors which the people that call themselves Christians, are advancing in the world.* Hartwick, N.Y.

Nissenbaum, Stephen. 1988. *Sex, Diet, and Debility in Jacksonian America.* Chicago: Dorsey Press.

Numbers, Ronald L, and Jonathan M. Butler, eds. 1987. *The Disappointed: Millerism and Millenarianism in the Nineteenth Century.* Bloomington: Indiana University Press.

The Observance of the One Hundred and Fiftieth Anniversary of the Organization of the Congregational Church in Berkley. 1888. Taunton, Mass.

Olbricht, Thomas H. 1966. "Christian Connexion and Unitarian Relations." *Restoration Quarterly* 9:160–86.

"Orthodox Clergyman." 1814. *Things set in a Proper Light, in Answer to a Letter from T.A. to a Friend.* Boston.

Osgood, David. 1798. *Some facts evincive of the atheistical, anarchical, and in other respects, immoral principles of the French Republicans.* Boston: Samuel Hall.

———. 1804. *The Validity of Baptism by Sprinkling and the Right of Infants to that Ordinance Supported and Defended.* Boston: Munroe & Francis.

———. 1809. *A Discourse delivered before the Lieutenant-Governor, the Council, and the two houses composing the legislature of the Commonwealth of Massachusetts, May 31, 1809, Being the day of General Election.* Boston: Russell & Cutler.

———. 1810. *A Discourse delivered at Cambridge in the hearing of the University April 8, 1810.* Cambridge, Mass.: William Hilliard.

———. 1812. *A Solemn Protest against the Late Declaration of War.* Cambridge, Mass.: Hilliard & Metcalf.

Osterwald, John Frederick. 1788. *A Compendium of Christian Theology.* Hartford, Conn.: Nathaniel Patten.

Our County and its People: A Descriptive and Biographical Record of Bristol County Massachusetts. 1899. Boston: Boston History Company.

Parker, Nathan. 1812. *A Discourse Occasioned by the Death of the Rev. Joseph Buckminster, D.D.* Portsmouth, N.H.: S. Whidden.

Peabody, Andrew. 1857. *A Sermon Delivered at the Closing of the Sunday-School Room at Court Street.* Portsmouth, N.H.: J. F. Shores & J. H. Foster.

———. 1881. "The Unitarians in Boston." In *The Memorial History of Boston,* ed. Justin Winsor, 3:467–82. Boston: James R. Osgood.

Peacock, James L., and Ruel W. Tyson. 1989. *Pilgrims of Paradox: Calvinism and Experience among the Primitive Baptists of the Blue Ridge.* Washington, D.C.: Smithsonian Institution Press.

Peak, John. 1814. *A Sermon on the Subject of Sanctification.* Newburyport, Mass.: W. & J. Gilman.

Pernick, Martin S. 1972. "Politics, Parties, and Pestilence: Epidemic Yellow Fever in Philadelphia and the Rise of the First Party System." *William and Mary Quarterly* 29:559–86.

Plumer, William, Jr. 1857. *Life of William Plumer.* Boston: Phillips, Sampson.

Plummer, Frederick. 1835. "Base Calumny Refuted." *Pennsylvania Inquirer & Daily Courier,* July 3.

Plummer, Frederick, and William M'Calla. 1842. *A Public Discussion on the Doctrine of the Trinity.* Philadelphia: Kay & Brother.

Pocock, J. G. A. 1971. *Politics, Language, and Time*. New York: Atheneum.

———. 1975. *The Machiavellian Moment: Florentine Republican Thought and the Atlantic Republican Tradition*. Princeton: Princeton University Press.

———. 1981. "The Machiavellian Moment Revisited: A Study in History and Ideology." *Journal of Modern History* 53:49–72.

———. 1988. Letter to Editor. *William and Mary Quarterly* 45:817.

Popkin, John Snelling. 1792. Commencement Address. Cambridge: Harvard University Archives.

———. 1806a. *A Sermon, Preached May 4, 1806, the Last Time of Assembling in the Old Meeting House in the First Parish in Newbury*. Newburyport, Mass.: W. & J. Gilman.

———. 1806b. *A Sermon, Preached September 17, 1806, at the Dedication of the New Meeting-House of the First Parish in Newbury*. Newburyport, Mass.: W. & J. Gilman.

———. 1814. *A Sermon Preached in Newbury, First Parish, on the Day of the Annual Thanksgiving in the Commonwealth of Massachusetts, November 25, 1813*. Newburyport: William B. Allen.

Porter, Stephen. 1814. *A Discourse in Two Parts addressed to the Presbyterian Congregation in Ballston, on Lord's Day, Oct. 30th, 1814*. Ballston Spa, N.Y.: James Comstock.

Powell, Sumner Chilton. 1963. *Puritan Village: The Formation of a New England Town*. Middletown, Conn.: Wesleyan University Press.

The Providence Directory. 1841. Providence: H. H. Brown.

Putnam, Israel. 1835. *A Farewell Sermon Preached March 15, 1835, in the North Church, Portsmouth, N.H.* Portsmouth: Miller & Brewster.

Rand, John. 1818. *A Letter to Elder Elias Smith: Containing an Examination of his Thirteen Reasons for Believing the Salvation of All Men*. Danville, Vt.: Ebenezer Eaton.

Rawlyk, George A. 1984. *Ravished by the Spirit*. Kingston: McGill-Queens University Press.

Remich, Daniel. 1911. *History of Kennebunk from Its Earliest Settlement to 1890*. Portland, Maine: Lakeside Press.

Robinson, William A. 1968. *Jeffersonian Democracy in New England*. New York: Greenwood Press.

Rogers, John. 1847. *The Biography of Eld. Barton Warren Stone*. Cincinnati: J. A. & U. P. James.

Rose, Anne C. 1981. *Transcendentalism as a Social Movement, 1830–1850*. New Haven: Yale University Press.

———. 1986. "Social Sources of Denominationalism Reconsidered: Post-Revolutionary Boston as a Case Study." *American Quarterly* 38:243–64.

Rosenberry, Lois K. 1962. *The Expansion of New England.* New York: Russell & Russell.

Roth, Randolph A. 1987. *The Democratic Dilemma: Religion, Reform, and the Social Order in the Connecticut River Valley of Vermont, 1791–1850.* Cambridge: Cambridge University Press.

Rowe, David L. 1985. *Thunder and Trumpets: Millerites and Dissenting Religion in Upstate New York, 1800–1850.* Chico, Calif.: Scholars Press.

Rush, Benjamin. 1818. *Medical Inquiries and Observations.* Vol. 3. Philadelphia: Anthony Finley.

———. 1835. *Medical Inquiries and Observations upon The Diseases of the Mind.* Philadelphia: Grigg & Elliot.

Rutman, Darrett B. 1977. "People in Process: The New Hampshire Towns of the Eighteenth Century." In *Family and Kin in Urban Communities, 1700–1930,* ed. Tamara K. Hareven. New York: New Viewpoints.

Sewall, Samuel. 1868. *The History of Woburn.* Boston: Wiggin & Lunt.

Shalhope, Robert. 1972. "Toward a Republican Synthesis: The Emergence of an Understanding of Republicanism in American Historiography." *William and Mary Quarterly* 29:49–80.

———. 1982. "Republicanism and Early American Historiography." *William and Mary Quarterly* 39:334–56.

Shaw, Elijah. 1847. *Sentiments of the Christians.* Newburyport, Mass.: Christian Herald.

Shepard, Samuel. 1806. *An Examination of the Account lately Published by Mr. E. Smith.* Exeter, N.H.: Ranlet & Norris.

Shiels, Richard D. 1980. "The Second Great Awakening in Connecticut: Critique of the Traditional Interpretation." *Church History* 49:401–15.

———. 1985. "The Scope of the Second Great Awakening: Andover, Massachusetts, as a Case Study." *Journal of the Early Republic* 5:223–46.

Shoemaker, Robert W. 1966. "'Democracy' and 'Republic' as Understood in Late Eighteenth Century America." *American Speech* 41:83–95.

Sibley, John Langdon, ed. 1968. *Samuel Stillman,* pp. 216–27. Boston: Massachusetts Historical Society.

———. N.d. Sibley's Private Journal. Vol. 1. Harvard University Archives, Cambridge.

Smillie, Wilson G. 1951. "An Early Prepayment Plan for Medical Care: The Thomsonian System of Botanical Medicine." *Journal of the History of Medicine* 6:253–57.

Smith, Daniel D. 1837. *Lectures on Domestic Duties.* Portland, Maine: S. H. Colesworthy.

Smith, Elias. 1802. *A Sermon on Baptism.* Exeter, N.H.: N. S. & W. Peirce.

———. 1803a. *The Clergyman's Looking Glass No. 1; or, Ancient and Modern Things Contrasted.* Portsmouth, N.H.: N. S. & W. Peirce.

———. 1803b. *The Clergyman's Looking-Glass No. 2; being a History of the Birth, Life, and Death of Anti-Christ.* Portsmouth, N.H.: N. S. & W. Peirce.

———. 1803c. *A Discourse delivered at Jefferson Hall, Thanksgiving-Day, November 25, 1802.* Boston: Manning & Loring.

———. 1803d. *A Reply to this Congregational Methodistical Question—"Why cannot you commune with us, seeing we are willing to commune with you?"* Portsmouth, N.H.: N. S. & W. Peirce.

———. 1804a. *The Clergyman's Looking-Glass No. 3: The Champion of Reviling, Railing, and Slander, Left Undisputed Master of the Field.* Boston: Manning & Loring.

———. 1804b. *A Collection of Hymns for the use of Christians.* Boston: Manning & Loring.

———. 1804c. *A Letter to Mr. Daniel Humphreys, Sandemanian Teacher.* Portsmouth, N.H.: Gazette Office.

———. 1804d. *A Reply to this Question, How Shall I Know that I am Born Again? or, What are the Evidences of Spiritual Birth?* Boston: Manning & Loring.

———. 1805a. *The Day of Judgment Revealed by the King of Glory and his Servants Collected from the Records of his Kingdom.* Exeter, N.H.: Henry Ranlet.

———. 1805b. *A Discourse Delivered at Hopkinton, N.H., Thursday, Sept. 5, 1804.* Boston.

———. 1805c. *The Doctrine of the Prince of Peace and his Servants, concerning the End of the Wicked.* Boston.

———. 1805d. *A Man in the Smoke, and a Friend Endeavouring to Help him out.* Boston: Elias Smith.

———. 1805e. *The Whole World Governed by a Jew: of the Government of the Second Adam, as King and Priest, Described from the Scriptures.* Exeter, N.H.: Henry Ranlet.

———. 1806a. *A Discourse on the Resurrection.* Windsor, Vt.: Alden Spooner.

———. 1806b. *A Letter to Mr. E. R. Sabin, a Methodist Preacher.* Exeter, N.H.

———. 1807a. *The Age of Enquiry, Christian's Pocket Companion and Daily Assistant.* Exeter, N.H.: Ranlet & Norris.

———. 1807b. *A Sermon on New Testament Baptism in Distinction from All Other.* Exeter, N.H.: Norris and Sawyer.

———. 1808a. *Sermons, Containing an Illustration of the Prophecies.* Exeter, N.H.: Norris & Sawyer.

————. 1808b. *Three Sermons on Election.* Portsmouth, N.H.: Norris & Sawyer.

————. 1809a. *A Golden Sermon: Upon the Candlestick of Gold, with the Bowl, Pipes and Lamps, and two Olive Trees.* Portland, Maine.

————. 1809b. *The Loving Kindness of God Displayed in the Triumph of Republicanism in America.* Taunton, Mass.

————. 1810. *A Discourse on Government and Religion.* Portland, Maine: Elias Smith.

————. 1812a. *Letters to Thomas Baldwin, containing remarks on his Sermon entitled "The Supreme Deity of Christ Illustrated."* Boston: J. Ball for Elias Smith.

————. 1812b. *A New Testament Dictionary.* Philadelphia: Elias Smith.

————. 1816. *The Life, Conversion, Preaching, Travels, and Sufferings of Elias Smith.* Portsmouth, N.H.: Beck & Foster. Reprint. Baptist History Series. New York: Arno Press, 1983.

————. 1822. *The Medical Pocket-Book, Family Physician and Sick Man's Guide to Health.* Boston: Henry Bowen.

————. 1826. *The American Physician and Family Assistant.* 1st ed. Boston: E. Bellamy.

————. 1830. *Medical Tract and Singular Miscellany.* Boston: Elias Smith.

————. 1832. *The American Physician and Family Assistant.* 3d ed. Boston: H. Bowen.

————. 1836. *An Address to the Citizens of Boston and the People of the United States on Poison, Health, Disease, Vegetable Medicine and Manner of Curing the Sick.* Boston: Benjamin True.

————. 1837. *The American Physician and Family Assistant.* 4th ed. Boston: B. True.

————. 1840. *The Life, Conversion, Preaching, Travels, and Sufferings of Elias Smith.* Boston: Elias Smith.

Smith, Elias, and Abner Jones. 1805. *Hymns, Original and Selected, for the use of Christians.* Boston: Manning & Loring.

Smith, Elias, et al. 1802. *Articles of Faith and Church Building.* Portsmouth, N.H.: N. S. & W. Peirce.

————. 1804. *Five Letters, with Remarks.* Boston: J. Ball.

Smith, Matthew Hale. 1841. *A Reply to the Personal Attack of Mr. O. A. Skinner and Others.* Boston: M. H. Smith.

————. 1842. *Universalism Examined, Renounced, Exposed.* Boston: Tappan & Dennet.

————. 1844. *The Blessings Yet Left Us.* Boston: S. N. Dickinson.

————. 1845a. *Impiety in High Places, and Sympathy with Crime, a Curse to any People.* Boston: S. N. Dickinson.

————. 1845b. *Textbook of Universalism*. Salem, Mass.: John P. Jewett.

————. 1847. *The Bible, the Rod, and Religion in Common Schools*. Boston: Redding.

————. 1858. *Why Men Hate the Ministers of Christ*. New York: Rudd & Carleton.

————. [1873] 1972. *Bulls and Bears of New York*. Freeport, N.Y.: Books for Libraries Press.

Smith, Mrs. E. Vale. 1854. *History of Newburyport*. Newburyport, Mass.

Starr, Paul. 1982. *The Social Transformation of American Medicine*. New York: Basic Books.

Stewart, Donald H. 1969. *The Opposition Press of the Federalist Period*. Albany: State University of New York Press.

Stinchfield, Ephraim. 1819a. *Cochranism Delineated; or, A Description of, and Specific for a religious hydrophobia*. Boston: N. Coverly.

Stinchfield, Ephraim. 1819b. *Some Memoirs of the Life, Experience, and Travels of Elder Ephraim Stinchfield*. Portland, Maine: Ephraim Stinchfield at the Argus Office.

Stout, Harry S. 1986. *The New England Soul: Preaching and Religious Culture in Colonial New England*. New York: Oxford University Press.

Taylor, Alan. 1990. *Liberty Men and Great Proprietors*. Chapel Hill: University of North Carolina Press, Institute of Early American History and Culture.

Taylor, Richard H. 1981. "The Congregational Christian Union at Fifty Years: An Assessment." *Bulletin of the Congregational Library* 32:4–13.

Thomas, George M. 1989. *Revivalism and Cultural Change*. Chicago: University of Chicago Press.

Thomson, Samuel. 1822a. *A Narrative of the Life and Medical Discoveries of Samuel Thomson*. Boston: E. G. House.

————. 1822b. *New Guide to Health; or, Botanic Family Physician*. Columbus, Ohio: Horton Howard.

————. 1835. *New Guide to Health; or, Botanic Family Physician. To which is prefixed, A Narrative of the Life and Medical Discoveries of the Author*. Boston: J. Q. Adams.

————. 1836. *Learned Quackery Exposed*. Boston: J. Q. Adams.

"Thomsonian." 1832. *A Portrait of the Conduct of Elias Smith towards Dr. Samuel Thomson, from 1817 up to the Present Time, 1832*. Boston: Boston Investigator.

Towle, Donald T. 1990. "New Hampshire: Birthplace of the Spiritual?" *Historical New Hampshire* 45:296–316.

Turner, Frederick Jackson. 1962. *The Frontier in American History*. New York: Holt, Rinehart & Winston.

Turner, Lynn W. 1962. *William Plumer of New Hampshire: 1759–1850.* Chapel Hill: University of North Carolina Press, Institute of Early American History and Culture.

van de Wetering, Maxine. 1982. "Moralizing in Puritan Natural Science: Mysteriousness in Earthquake Sermons." *Journal of the History of Ideas* 43:417–38.

Wardner, H. S. 1931. "Alden Spooner, Vermont State Printer." *Vermonter,* pp. 15–22.

Warren, Charles. 1931. *Jacobin and Junto.* Cambridge: Harvard University Press.

Watts, Isaac. 1821. *The Improvement of the Mind; or, A Supplement to the Art of Logic.* London: Edwards and Knibb.

Watts, Steven. 1987. *The Republic Reborn: War and the Making of Liberal America, 1790–1820.* Baltimore: Johns Hopkins University Press.

Weinstock, Joanna Smith. 1988. "Samuel Thomson's Botanic System: Alternative Medicine in Early Nineteenth Century Vermont." *Vermont History* 56:5–22.

Whittemore, Thomas. 1854. *Life of Rev. Hosea Ballou.* 4 vols. Boston: James M. Usher.

"Wilbour, Isaac." 1907. In *National Cyclopaedia of American Biography,* 9:393–94. N.p.: James T. White. Reprint. Ann Arbor, Mich.: University Microfilms, 1967.

———. 1971. In *Biographical Directory of the American Congress, 1774–1971.* Washington, D.C.: Government Printing Office.

Williams, Edward H. N.d. "A History of the Christian Church, Woodstock, Vermont." Typescript in possession of Vermont Historical Society, Montpelier.

Willis, Lemuel. 1874. "Recollections Pertaining to the Universalist Church during the First Half of this Century." *Universalist* 56, no. 5 (May 30).

Willis, William. 1865. *The History of Portland, from 1632 to 1864.* Portland, Maine: Bailey & Noyes.

Wills, Gary. 1987. *Reagan's America: Innocents at Home.* Garden City, N.Y.: Doubleday.

Wood, Gordon S. 1982. "Conspiracy and the Paranoid Style: Causality and Deceit in the Eighteenth Century." *William and Mary Quarterly* 39:401–41.

———. 1992. *The Radicalism of the American Revolution.* New York: Alfred Knopf.

Wood, Nathan E. 1899. *The History of the First Baptist Church of Boston*

(1665–1899). Philadelphia: American Baptist Publication Society.

Young, James Harvey. 1961. *The Toadstool Millionaires: A Social History of Patent Medicines in America before Federal Regulation.* Princeton: Princeton University Press.

"Zenas" [Joseph Badger]. 1819. *An Affectionate Address of a Son to his Father, on the doctrine of Universalism: Connected with extracts from the writings of Elias Smith against that doctrine.* New York.

INDEX